SERIAL THRILLERS: THE ADVENTURE SERIAL ON BRITISH RADIO

SERIAL THRILLERS:
THE ADVENTURE SERIAL ON BRITISH RADIO

CHARLES NORTON

First published in the UK in 2012 by
Kaleidoscope Publishing

This revised edition 2025 by
Telos Publishing Ltd
www.telos.co.uk

Telos Publishing Ltd values feedback. Please e-mail us with any comments you may have about this book to: feedback@telos.co.uk

ISBN: 978-1-84583-248-3 (paperback)

Serial Thrillers: The Adventure Serial on British Radio © 2012, 2025 Charles Norton

The moral right of the author has been asserted.

British Library Cataloguing in Publication Data.
A catalogue record for this book is available from the British Library.

This book is sold subject to the condition that it shall not by way of trade or otherwise, be lent, resold, hired out or otherwise circulated without the publisher's prior written consent in any form of binding or cover other than that in which it is published and without a similar condition including this condition being imposed on the subsequent purchaser.

ACKNOWLEDGEMENTS

The following text draws on a number of different sources – interviews, scripts, recordings and other texts. You will find most of these referenced both in the footnotes and in the bibliography.

Special thanks must also go to certain individuals and institutions. Without their help, the compiling of this book would have been impossible and their kindness and co-operation has been invaluable.

In particular, I'd like to single out the remarkable Roger Bickerton, whose knowledge and dedication to the history of British radio drama is unparalleled. Without Roger's patient assistance and general good will, I doubt that there would ever have been a book at all.

I'd also like to thank Charles and Peggy Chilton, for inviting me into their home, cooking me a very nice meal and allowing me to listen to their recollections of life at the BBC.

Much of the physical research has drawn heavily on the collections of the British Library and the BBC Written Archives Centre and I have made extensive use of a number of online newspaper archives (all of which you will find referenced).

I am also grateful to those who gave me so much of their time to be interviewed, including David Jacobs, Ted Kendall, David Chilton, Desmond Carrington and Michael Kilgarriff.

A number of those I originally interviewed for this book in 2010 have died in the intervening years between the publication of the first edition in 2012 and the publication of this second edition in 2025. Charles Chilton and David Jacobs both died in 2013 and Desmond Carrington in 2017. It was a privilege to speak to them all.

In addition, I wish to extend my thanks to: Stephen James Walker, Ian Pritchard for the Index, Patrick Rayner, Fiona Mackenzie-Williams, Stephen Durbridge, Graeme Stevenson, Trish Hayes, Jock Gallagher, Bert Coules, Katie Saarikko, Matthew Davies, Howard Corn, Tony Cowley, Philip Jordan, Christine Graham, Michael Stevens, Philip Harbottle, Rod Barzilay, Retha Buys, Ken Puley, Jeff Walden, Fallon Lee, various members of the Radio Circle, the staff of the Victoria and Albert Museum and my Mum.

I apologise if I've missed anyone.

AUTHOR'S NOTE

This is a corrected, revised and moderately expanded edition of the book that was originally published in 2012. I've taken the opportunity to fix a number of mostly minor errors that slipped past the first time.

The sections on both *Paul Temple* and *Dan Dare* have received the most extensive updates, with much fuller story details for *Dan Dare* and information on numerous further *Paul Temple* productions in the Netherlands and Italy that were not included in the original edition. The 2013 production of *Paul Temple and the Gregory Affair* has also now been added to the episode guide. Thanks to Jeffrey Richards for his help with the *Paul Temple* side of things and to Philip Harbottle for significant further story information on the Radio Luxembourg *Dan Dare* series.

Additions to the *Dick Barton* section have been more modest in scope, but I am pleased to have been able to add additional cast and crew information. The 2013 production of *Dick Barton and the Trail of the Rocket* is now included in the *Dick Barton* guide.

CONTENTS

Acknowledgements	5
Author's Note	6
Contents	7
Foreword: Nicholas Parsons	9
Paul Temple	13
Paul Temple Episode Guide	50
Dick Barton - Special Agent	83
Dick Barton - Special Agent Episode Guide	137
The Adventures of Dan Dare - Pilot of the Future	181
Dan Dare Plot Summaries	204
Dan Dare Production Information	213
Journey into Space	214
Journey into Space Episode Guide	242
Appendix A: *Paul Temple* Archive Holdings	248
Appendix B: *Paul Temple* Serials Issued for International Syndication	252
Appendix C: *Dick Barton* Archive Holdings	255
Appendix D: *Dick Barton*: The ARP Recordings	259
Appendix E: *Dan Dare* Episode List	262
Appendix F: *Dan Dare* Repeat Broadcasts	279
Appendix G: *Riders of the Range* Episode Guide	286
Appendix H: BBC Drama Repertory Company	292
Bibliography	295
Index	299
About the Author	311

FOREWORD
NICHOLAS PARSONS

Drama has always been an integral part of BBC radio output and has survived with great distinction thanks to dedicated producers and performers, in spite of economic cutbacks and the competition from television. After the War, radio, or wireless as it was called then, was the premiere service on our airwaves.

Television only really began to make an impact in the early 50s, and even then there was only a modest amount of programmes transmitted over limited hours during the day, starting in the afternoon and finishing punctually around 10pm in the evening, with a regular short and rather pompous little feature titled, *The Epilogue*. BBC Television then could be described as rather staid and laid back, and though there were some excellent programmes, it was in many ways typically British. It was not for nothing that the organisation was referred to as Auntie BBC.

The turning point, or catalyst, that brought about the dramatic change in the thinking and attitude of BBC Television was the advent of what was then called 'commercial television' in the Autumn of 1955. Suddenly BBC Television had a rival and the competition forced them to rethink their entire output and the quality of the programmes they made. This had a huge impact on BBC Radio.

More money had to be found from the licence fee to fund an increasing output of shows on television over many more hours, and the challenge in some areas of being more professional in the quality of that output. The money allocated to radio from the licence fee was drastically cut, forcing them to rethink their budgets for different shows and still maintain the high standard they had achieved. Some people even thought that with the increase of the popularity of television, and the competition between the BBC and the independent television companies as they fought to increase their respective viewing figures, that radio would decline in popularity and even fade away. It was not to be.

There was too much talent and experience in BBC Radio to allow this to happen. They cut their cloth accordingly and continued to make excellent programmes, so that today with the predictability of a lot of television with the emphasis on reality shows and people shows, forced on the programme makers by increased cuts, the public are returning to their wireless sets.

The standard on BBC Radio has not dropped and ways of being creative within a restricted budget and persuading actors to work for less than they might have received in the old days. I believe most actors enjoy working in radio in preference to other mediums of entertainment. I certainly do. There is not the pressure of learning the dialogue, or co-ordinating this with moves as in a play. There is the challenge of playing to an unseen audience and the demands this makes on your talent as you create images in the minds of the listener, whom you are asking to bring more to the event than in a visual medium. This can be very exciting and certainly rewarding if successful. If we all work for less money comparatively than in other mediums of entertainment, it is because BBC Radio has cleverly established a benchmark of payments that we actors accept and the time involved is less than working elsewhere.

The pleasures of working in radio stems from the very high standards achieved in the past by the actors and producers in the heyday of steam radio during and just after the last War. I had the privilege of working a lot in radio in the late 40s and 50s, so I experienced this at first hand. Some of the actors who starred in dramas, both plays and series, became household names. Unseen by the public, recognised from their distinctive voices, and greatly admired for the versatility and talent they exercised entirely from the use of their voice.

The standard of entertainment on BBC Radio during this period was incredibly high. Light entertainment reached new peaks and was always inventive. The Features Department, now alas gone, created amazingly innovative programmes calling on the talents of some of the finest writers and poets of the time, such as Louis MacNeice and Dylan Thomas.

In drama this was a golden period. Under the creative skills of the Head of the Department, Val Gielgud (John Gielgud's brother) the quality of the output was amazing. It made stars of some of the shining lights in the BBC Drama Repertory Company, such as James McKechnie, Marjorie Westbury, Norman Shelley, Carlton Hobbs, Grizelda Hervey, Belle Crystal and Denise Bryer. Also Deryck Guyler and Patricia Hayes who both went on to achieve great distinction on television.

There were some highly talented producers who created amazing productions, both modern and classical, including new plays and the occasional Shakespeare, such as Raymond Raikes, with whom I had the pleasure of working on more than one occasion, Peter Watts, Howard Rose, Archie Campbell and others too numerous to mention.

This truly was the golden period of radio, and while the standard of performance and production is still as high today, the fierce competition from television and elsewhere means the status of radio is somewhat diminished but still greatly enjoyed and appreciated by a huge listening public. It has certainly not been swamped or overwhelmed by the increasing popularity of television as some predicted, thanks to the skills of those

FOREWORD

running radio and the talents of those who perform in it, and the loyalty of the many listeners who have remained faithful to this medium of entertainment.

Alongside the individual plays BBC Radio produced, they also created some incredibly successful series. One of the early ones was *Mrs Dale's Diary,* transmitted in the morning around 11am. The dramatic incidents in each episode were introduced by Mrs Dale, and she often referred to her Doctor husband, and frequently said, 'I'm very worried about Jim'. This became an iconic phrase from the show, and was frequently quoted by listeners. Mrs Dale was latterly played for a number of years by a former star of the musical theatre, Jessie Matthews. The show was cosy and very popular but very much of its period. It slowly faded away as standards in writing increased and the drama became more positive and reflected real life.

In contrast, the other popular serial that began a little later, *The Archers*, had adapted to changing times and attitudes and kept pace with life as we recognised it today. When it started it was subtitled, 'An everyday story of country folk', but with shrewd production, quality writing and excellent performances it has moved forward into the twenty-first century, kept pace with changing social attitudes, and is still as popular as when it first began, if not more so.

Unlike some of the television series, or soaps as they are called, who have indulged in incredibly dramatic and over-the-top storylines as they seem to try and outshine their rivals, *The Archers* has maintained an incredibly high standard by reflecting life in an interesting country setting with characters we can all recognise.

This is how you achieve longevity in any programme, by continually being aware of changing social attitudes and subtly polishing, or adapting your product so it keeps pace and in tune with those changes while still retaining the freshness and spontaneity that originally made it popular. BBC drama, in fact BBC radio, has a great history and has maintained an incredibly high standard of entertainment since it began very modestly in the early part of the 20 Century.

PAUL TEMPLE

SENDING FOR PAUL TEMPLE

Between 1938 and 1968, the BBC's longest-running and most popular detective series was *Paul Temple*. Over thirty years, the character would explore a decadent world of elegance and violent crime that made him one of the most loved of all the BBC's many radio sleuths.

There were other similar radio shows around the same time and some drew in much bigger ratings. However, *Paul Temple* always had greater staying power. Over multiple adventures, he sat, without challenge, as the most universally accepted of radio crime-fighters. In 1938, Temple was among the first of his kind, and in 1968, he was also one of the last.

Despite the series' cosmopolitan blend of exotic locales around Europe and the Mediterranean, *Paul Temple* always seemed to be firmly based in London. However, that was not where it had started. It began in Birmingham.

At eight o'clock on the evening of the 8 April 1938, the BBC's Midland Service broadcast the first episode of *Send for Paul Temple* – an eight part thriller serial from producer Martyn C Webster. The script was the work of Birmingham-based writer Francis Durbridge.

Durbridge had been born in Hull on 25 November 1912. His interest in professional writing had been sparked after winning an essay competition when he was twelve years old. His particular fascination was in crime fiction. 'I always wanted to write thrillers,' he later recalled. 'From a very early age, when I first started writing, it was always my ambition to write mystery stories – detective stories. I was a great admirer of the people who wrote them at that particular period.'[1]

Durbridge went to school in Bradford, before moving to the West Midlands to read English at Birmingham University. It was around this time that he submitted his first play to BBC radio, which drew on his father's experiences of working in a large department store. Durbridge described this first script as: 'a very serious play, dealing with life in a departmental store. It was called *Promotion* ... Fortunately for me, it was extremely popular. It was repeated several times.'[2]

Promotion was produced in Birmingham for the Midland Regional

---

[1] From *Dick Barton and All That* (31/10/82).
[2] From *Dick Barton and All That* (31/10/82).

Service by respected BBC producer, Martyn C Webster.

Webster had started his career in 1920 as an actor and producer with the Scottish National Players, later joining the BBC in 1926, in its Glasgow variety department. In 1933 he had moved to Birmingham, to produce *Worker's Playtime*, before later moving into the drama department, where Durbridge would encounter him. The BBC's Head of Drama, Val Gielgud would later describe Webster as one of the 'impenitent believers in the present and future of Sound Drama.'[3]

The *Paul Temple* radio serials, for which both Webster and Durbridge would become famous, began when Durbridge made a visit to Webster at his office in Birmingham: 'One day, I went in to see Martyn,' recalled Durbridge, 'and told him I had an idea for a detective serial.'[4]

Webster recalled the meeting. 'He [Durbridge] said to me, "If only I could be half as good as Edgar Wallace." I was surprised as I thought Wallace rather dated. Durbridge would not agree; he considered him the best craftsman in his class. (A million copies of his books were re-issued shortly afterwards!) "So that's what you have been hankering after; you want to write detective stories?" I asked. "I'm afraid I do," he replied. "Well, I have a hankering in the same direction: I've always wanted to produce a serial with an original radio detective. I'm tired of adaptations of Sherlock Holmes and so on. So why not have a shot at creating an original radio sleuth?" He just smiled. But next morning he rang me. "I've been thinking it over and I'd like to have a shot. In fact I've already thought of a name – Paul Temple – how does it sound to you?"'[5]

Durbridge continued: 'I wrote the first episode. He liked it very much and, of course, from that moment on we started what was a very long and very successful partnership with *Temple*.'[6]

Durbridge's new eight-part detective serial (*Send for Paul Temple*) opened with a police investigation. There has been a spate of violent diamond robberies across the north of England. Following a campaign in the newspapers, novelist Paul Temple is called in to help find the perpetrators. Along the way, Temple encounters journalist Louise Harvey (or Steve, to her friends) and Sir Graham Forbes of Scotland Yard. The criminals go by a number of mysterious codenames such as 'The Green Finger' and 'The Knave of Diamonds'. At one point, Steve's life is endangered with a booby-trapped gramophone. Eventually all the suspects are brought together and the true mastermind is revealed.

---

[3] From *British Radio Drama: 1952-1956* by Val Gielgud – George G Harrap and Co. Ltd. (1957)
[4] From *Dick Barton and All That* (31/10/82).
[5] From *Radio Times* (20 – 27 April 1968)
[6] From *Dick Barton and All That* (31/10/82).

This unlikely set-up would be a template Durbridge would scarcely deviate from in any of the many *Paul Temple* adventures that were to follow.

The actor chosen for the part of Paul Temple was Hugh Morton. Born in Devon in June 1903, he was the son of a naval officer and the first cousin of future Prime Minister Sir Anthony Eden. In the 1920s he had appeared in a run of musicals, cabarets and comedies. He then came into contact with the early British Broadcasting *Company* and its 2LO service and had been a regular fixture on BBC radio ever since.

Across eight evening slots (with a Saturday afternoon repeat), Webster and Durbridge's serial was a comparatively modest production, but was a massive (and somewhat unexpected success) with the public.

'After the broadcast of *Send for Paul Temple*,' said Durbridge, 'Webster telephoned me and said: "I think you've created two interesting characters in Paul Temple and Steve, and it's my bet they'll become established favourites." Many years later, when the *Paul Temple* adventures were being broadcast and published in numerous languages and in over twenty countries, I recalled Webster's words. At the time I felt sure he was just trying to encourage a young and very ambitious writer. But he was right!'[7]

'On the morning after the broadcast of our first episode,' said Webster, 'we had over seven thousand letters asking for more.'[8]

THE FRONT PAGE MEN

By the time the final instalment of *Send for Paul Temple* had concluded on 27 May, a sequel was almost guaranteed, with Webster already pushing his superiors for one.

In a letter to London, from the BBC's Midland Regional Director on 10 June 1938, it was even proposed that this next serial should be broadcast nationwide, rather than just within the BBC Midland region. However, it seems, that suggestion was not taken up.

Durbridge's second *Paul Temple* serial was to be called *Paul Temple and the Front Page Men*. Again running to eight episodes, Durbridge would submit his first five scripts to Webster on 7 October, with the last three following shortly afterwards.

Actor Hugh Morton was retained from the cast of the first serial, to play Paul Temple with Bernadette Hodgson returning to play Steve. Lester Mudditt was also back as Sir Graham Forbes. This time, recording took place away from Birmingham at the BBC's Evesham studios in late 1938.

The new story centred on the publication of a best-selling novel called *The Front-Page Men*, written by the enigmatic Andrea Fortune. When the

---

[7] From *Radio Times* (10 - 17 April 1965)
[8] From *Radio Times* (20 – 27 April 1968)

words 'Front Page Men' start to appear at the scenes of a number of recent robberies, Paul Temple is called in to investigate.

The serial was broadcast between 2 November and 21 December 1938 on Wednesday evenings at 6.35 PM. As with *Send for Paul Temple*, it was repeated on Saturday afternoons at 12.20 PM and was an even greater success than the original. It seemed that *Temple*'s place in the public affections was now assured.

Following the broadcast of the serial's final episode, Webster himself took to the microphone to thank listeners for their support, saying: 'Good evening everyone. Well, I do sincerely hope that you've enjoyed the show, and that our efforts during the last eight weeks have met with your approval. May I take this opportunity of thanking all those listeners who so kindly wrote in after the last *Paul Temple* serial. There were well over seven thousand of you and this is the first chance I've had to thank you all personally.'[9]

NEWS OF PAUL TEMPLE

Another *Paul Temple* sequel wasn't pursued quite as quickly as before. However by May 1939, discussion had turned to the idea.

Yet again, the Midland Regional staff pushed for a national broadcast. This time, London were open to the suggestion. However, the BBC's Head of Drama, Val Gielgud, was reticent to commit to the production straightaway. In a BBC memo dated 1 June 1939, he explained his position to Birmingham, stating that although he accepted Durbridge's popularity, he felt unwilling to grant the production a slot at the present time.

Autumn 1939 was to see only one more full drama serial from the BBC and the schedules were already clogged with new productions. There was a long run of J B Priestley readings, a Sax Rohmer story and the possibility of a P G Wodehouse dramatisation. Added to this was a more general reluctance on Gielgud's part to broadcast populist drama.

By the time the new *Paul Temple* serial did materialise, the wider national audiences were already prepared for it, following the publication of two *Paul Temple* novels, which were selling well at the time. The first of these books had been co-written by Durbridge with John Thewes, based on *Send for Paul Temple*. The second, co-written with Charles Hatton was based on *Paul Temple and the Front Page Men*.

Paul Temple had also begun to find a market overseas. Dutch radio network AVRO had already purchased the rights from the BBC to produce their own version. Their translation of *Send for Paul Temple* (*Spreek met Vlaanderen en het Komt in Orde*) would be broadcast from 12 February to 2 April 1939. A translation of *Paul Temple and the Front Page Men* (*Paul Vlaanderen en de Mannen*

---

[9] *Paul Temple and the Front Page Men* – Episode 8: *The Front Page Men* (21/12/38)

van de Frontpagina) would follow between 28 May and 16 July. In fact, *Paul Temple* proved so popular in Holland that a series would run until 1969, produced first by Kommer Kleijn and later by Dick Van Putten. Paul Temple was played by Theo Frenkel and later Jan Van Ees and Johan Schmitz.

A version of *Paul Temple* also found its way to Australia in April 1939, when the Australian Broadcasting Commission (ABC) produced their own dramatisation of *Send for Paul Temple*, courtesy of the BBC's Overseas Services Executive. It starred Donnell Downey as Paul, with Margerie Crosbie as Steve and was produced by Laurie Lange. It was clearly judged to be a success, as the same serial would be recorded twice more for ABC for productions in 1942 and 1945, with different casts each time. Australia would produce remakes of numerous subsequent BBC *Paul Temple* serials (including *Paul Temple and the Front Page Men*) in the years that followed. A recording of *Send for Paul Temple* would later also emerge from the CBC in Canada starring Bernard Braden as Temple in Spring/Summer 1940.

Back in the UK, *News of Paul Temple* (as the BBC's third serial was called) would be a shorter offering than before, only running to six episodes, which would eventually enter production in November. Webster would this time use the BBC's Bristol studios. The recording schedule was tight and as the first few episodes were broadcast in the second half of November 1939, rehearsals continued for later instalments that were still yet to be recorded.

Surviving paperwork records that these rehearsals continued through from 26 November, with an evening session from 7 to 9.30 PM; then a morning session the following day from 10 AM to 1 PM. Rehearsals finally concluded on the same day between 4.45 PM and 6 PM. The final episode itself was broadcast on 18 December.

As before, Hugh Morton, Bernadette Hodgson and Lester Mudditt all returned to the fold, but were joined by a largely new supporting cast, including Norman Shelley, Dick Francis and Maurice Denham (seven years before he found fame with *Much Binding in the Marsh*).

Durbridge's novelisation of the serial (co-written with Charles Hatton) would emerge in 1940.

Paul Temple did tolerably well in his new slot, early on Friday evenings as part of the BBC's (national) Home Service and the new serial's exciting story of international espionage generally seemed to justify the show's higher profile. However, it was very much the end of an era. Not just for the radio series.

On 3 September 1939, Neville Chamberlain announced that Britain was 'at war with Germany'.

WAR SERVICE:

Paul Temple's war career was a chequered one. There were to be no further entirely new episodes until 1942 and after that, not until 1945. However, with the outbreak of war, everything had changed.

'On September 3 ... just about Noon,' remembered Val Gielgud, 'I was called to the telephone ... and instructed that the BBC 'emergency period' had begun.'[10]

The BBC's television operations were closed down shortly after 'for the duration'. BBC Regional Services (including the Midland region) were suspended and a number of other emergency measures were put into effect across the corporation.

'The BBC was by no means unprepared for war,' Gielgud continued. 'Far-reaching plans had been laid accordingly. [However] it was not altogether surprising that for the most part such plans were designed for a war quite different from that which fell upon us.'[11]

With London an obvious Nazi bombing target, most of the capital's BBC departments evacuated the city, with an initially chaotic effect on production. The variety department was moved to Bristol. The Gramophone department was sent to Bedford and the Drama department wound up in Evesham (codenamed Hogsnorton).

BBC Drama would not return to Broadcasting House until 1943. By this time, however, the building was not what it once was. 'The suite of dramatic studios,' recalled Gielgud, 'had been demolished in a raid when one of the two direct hits received by the building wrecked the sixth and seventh floors inside the studio tower beyond the possibility of temporary repair.'[12]

Charles Chilton, who was working in the still to be evacuated Gramophone department remembers: 'I was on the roof when the bomb hit and people I was working with were among the people who were up there putting fires out. Seven of them were killed.'

The war threw the BBC as a whole into a predictable chaos that would take some time to subside.

Gielgud again: 'Scripts went easily and frequently astray. Actors found themselves playing leading parts in two plays on the same night. Plays went from first read-through to microphone in a single day. One of my colleagues found himself quartered on a bird-farm, with wallabies at large in the garden. Another – his luck had always been proverbial – was quartered on an epicure with a French cook. We tried to maintain our morale by reminding ourselves that as we had been 'reserved' our work must be of some importance to the national war-effort. We were not very succesful.'[13]

---

[10] From *British Radio Drama: 1952-1956* by Val Gielgud – George G Harrap and Co. Ltd. (1957)
[11] From *British Radio Drama: 1952-1956* by Val Gielgud – George G Harrap and Co. Ltd. (1957)
[12] From *British Radio Drama: 1952-1956* by Val Gielgud – George G Harrap and Co. Ltd. (1957)
[13] From *British Radio Drama: 1952-1956* by Val Gielgud – George G Harrap and Co.

Webster remained in his department throughout the duration, with an intention to continue his pre-war work with *Temple* as far as was possible, not that it would be easy. The first of Webster's wartime *Paul Temple*s would arrive in 1941, although it was not a wholly original work.

With little time to write anything new, Durbridge was instead commissioned to take the scripts from the original 1938 *Send for Paul Temple* serial and condense them. The end product was a special hour-long play and feature length abridgement of the original serial. The script for this boiled down version was delivered to Webster on 30 July 1941. The broadcast itself came from the Home Service at 9.20 PM on the evening of 13 October.

Carl Bernard played Paul with Thea Holme as Steve. Later a noted essayist, Holme would gain greater fame as a novelist in the 1960s. In 1941, she was also part of a new initiative.

The war had had a devastating effect on the acting talent available to the BBC. With mass call-ups, the pool of able-bodied actors had shrunk almost overnight. Something had to be done quickly.

The result was one of the great innovations of the war-years, that had a lasting impact on the way *Paul Temple* was produced at the BBC – the formation of the BBC Drama Repertory Company. This was a group of actors, who were effectively contracted to be on the staff of the BBC and would service the BBC's many drama productions as needed. Gielgud saw 'the overall result ... [as] a return to simplicity.'[14] Thea Holme was a member.

Michael Kilgarriff, who was in 'the Rep' in the 1960s says: 'It was just like being in a marketplace really. There was a big chart in the Rep' office and your name was logged along down the side, with the dates across the top and so you went in with your diary and checked on your bookings and if you didn't have enough bookings to justify your salary, you didn't get your contract renewed. People always used to panic if they didn't have enough bookings. The contract was for six months ... So, every six months, you'd be summoned to the office and be told whether your contract would be renewed or not. That was always slightly worrying.'

There had, to some extent, been something of a repertory company before the war (in 1925) and certain producers (including Webster) often used the same actors again and again. Nevertheless, the new company certainly brought about a drastic change to the way radio producers would operate at the BBC and it would stay in place for many decades to come.

Most of the dramatic leading parts would still go to freelancers, or Outside Artists (OAs) as the BBC referred to them. However, much of the

---

Ltd. (1957)
[14] From *British Radio Drama: 1952-1956* by Val Gielgud – George G Harrap and Co. Ltd. (1957)

supporting cast would be drawn from the new pool.

Kilgarriff again: 'If you were on the Rep', they didn't like you being in long parts in the soaps and the serials, because you weren't available for other work. The whole point of you was that you were a pool that could be assigned to all sorts of other bits and pieces wherever you were needed. So they didn't like you being tied up in a long serial. So, you never had a running part ... You might get a couple of episodes now and then, but you wouldn't get a running part because you wouldn't be available.'

By 1942, attention had once again turned to another (all new) *Temple* serial from Webster and Durbridge. The result would be *Paul Temple Intervenes*, and like most of its predecessors it was another eight episodes of cryptic clues, violent murder and cocktails, with a reluctant Temple assisting Scotland Yard with their investigations. However there was one very significant change to the formula.

Hugh Morton had now played Paul Temple for the last time and had already moved on to other things.

He would later become a regular on the BBC's flagship comedy show *ITMA* (*It's That Man Again*). In the late 1940s, he'd even star in *ITMA* as a spoof detective called Paul Tremble. However, although it had ended, he was clearly happy about his association with Paul Temple. In 1947 he commented with pride that, 'The name of Paul Temple has become as familiar as those of Holmes, Lupin or Thorndike.'[15]

Morton's (short-lived) replacement was Carl Bernard. He had previously appeared in the previous year's one-off *Send for Paul Temple* play. Like many in the new cast, he was a member of the BBC Drama Repertory Company. 'Carl Bernard played one,' remembered co-star Marjorie Westbury. 'Very very funny man. He had us in hysterics. Very difficult to play with, Carl.'[16] Alongside him, both Bernadette Hodgson (for the final time) and Lester Muddit were back in their familiar rôles. Vincent Curran (OA) also returned from the cast of the very first *Paul Temple* serial (here playing Sergeant O'Brien).

Seen as good material for the troops, *Paul Temple Intervenes* was broadcast on the BBC Programme for the Forces on Fridays at 6.40 PM between 30 October and 18 December. Durbridge's novelisation was published in1944.

There would not be another *Paul Temple* radio serial for some time. However, fans in the Birmingham area were able to see him in the flesh as part of a *Send for Paul Temple* stage play, which began its short run at the Alexandra Theatre on 25 October 1943.

Back at the BBC, Temple's war career was largely brought to an end in

---

[15] From *The World Radio and Television Annual* ed. Gale Pedrick - Sampson Low (1947)
[16] *Dick Barton and All That* (31/10/82)

July 1944 when the scripts for *News of Paul Temple* were abridged for a one-hour Wednesday afternoon play on the Home Service. This time Richard Williams would play Temple and Australian Lucille Lisle was Steve (Lisle and Williams were both 'on the Rep' at the time).

Paul Temple wouldn't make a full return to BBC Radio until 1945 – a little less than a month after VJ Day.

AFTER THE WAR:

On 29 July 1945, the BBC introduced a new service. It was called the BBC Light Programme and it was here that *Paul Temple* found a new home, with the transmission of the first post-war *Temple* serial, *Send for Paul Temple Again* beginning on 13 September 1945. It had a new slot at 4 PM on a Friday.

As ever, Webster stayed at the helm, with an all-new script in eight episodes from Durbridge. However, by now most of the original cast had departed. Only Lester Mudditt remained (as Sir Graham Forbes) from the earliest days of the Midland Service.

The most significant challenge now facing Webster was finding a permanent replacement for Bernadette Hodgson, to play the new Steve Temple. He eventually found her in the form of versatile Birmingham actress, Marjorie Westbury.

Westbury had been born in June 1905. In 1927 she had trained as a singer with the Royal College of Music, before turning to acting. A regular on the BBC Midland Programme from the early 1930s, she entered the BBC Drama Repertory Company in 1942 and was very soon after cast by Webster in his production of *Paul Temple Intervenes* in the part of Dolly Fraser. Webster had worked with her before on various Midland programmes in the mid-thirties. 'Marjorie was a very well known voice on radio,' remembers Desmond Carrington (who worked with her in 1949). 'She was there for many years.' In 1945 she was cast as the new Steve Temple.

The new Paul Temple was to be Barry Morse. Morse was not a member of the Repertory Company, but an outside artist brought in by Webster as a more permanent replacement for the now long departed Hugh Morton. 'One of the very best was Barry Morse,'[17] remembered Westbury.

The plot of *Send for Paul Temple Again* would become something of a favourite with Durbridge. It was later loosely reworked into another *Paul Temple* serial in 1969. He novelised it with co-writer Charles Hatton in 1948 and it was even adapted for the cinema as the film *Calling Paul Temple*, later that year. The story concerned itself with a set of apparent serial killings linked by an enigmatic mastermind named 'Rex'. Temple is once again

---

[17] *Dick Barton and All That* (31/10/82)

called in to investigate when the body of a famous actress is discovered on a train.

Only a few months after the broadcast of the final episode of the new serial, Paul would return to the air again in *A Case For Paul Temple*, in February 1946. However, it wasn't with Barry Morse.

Morse wasn't available. In fact, he would soon leave the UK altogether. 'Barry became very ill. He had a tubercular lung and he had to get out of this country,' Westbury recalled. 'He went to Canada, which not only cured him but he went on to become a very big star.'[18] Today, Morse is probably best known for his television work, co-starring in *The Fugitive* (1963-1967) and *Space 1999* (1975-1976).

Webster cast outside artist Howard Marion Crawford as Morse's replacement. However it was only a stopgap and like Williams and Morse before him, Crawford would only ever play Temple once. Only Westbury and Mudditt saw their characters carried over from the earlier production.

A Case for Paul Temple aired in a Thursday evening slot at 8 PM on the Light Programme. Repeats followed at 4 PM on Fridays and Tuesdays. It was another success for Webster and his team and in a BBC memo dated 4 April, Webster was asked how soon Durbridge could write another. A query was also raised over the possibility of other writers being brought in to increase the number of episodes being produced per year.

A NEW PAUL:

A new serial followed quickly, and in extravagant style, in October 1946. Perhaps in order to cater for the BBC's increased appetite for the sleuth, *Paul Temple and the Gregory Affair* would be the longest *Temple* serial ever commissioned. Running to ten episodes, it was a tale of epic proportions.

As with previous serials, there was yet another new actor playing the part of Paul Temple. However, in this case, he would prove to be rather more long lasting.

Outside artist Kim Peacock was to be the latest Paul. Born in 1901, Peacock had become an actor in 1924, leaving behind a position in his family's printing business. A prolific radio and stage actor with a number of small film rôles to his credit, *Paul Temple* was his first major job after being discharged from the navy the previous year.

Distinguished by his languid slow-talking style (which would later become a problem), he made a slightly bumbling addition to the *Temple* cast and would remain in the part until 1953, making him the longest running actor to play Temple up until that point.

The new serial retained the services of both Lester Mudditt as Sir Graham

---

[18] *Dick Barton and All That* (31/10/82)

PAUL TEMPLE

Forbes and Marjorie Westbury as Steve. However, it also introduced a new character in the form of Charlie, the Temples' latest manservant. Charlie would be played here by Frank Partington, a member of the Repertory Company, who had previously had a small rôle in *A Case for Paul Temple*, earlier in the year.

The character of Charlie was always considered a minor part and was rarely given to anyone outside the Repertory Company – as such there would be many Charlies in the years to come – with only a few playing him more than once or twice.

Paul Temple and the Gregory Affair also marked something of a change in the way *Paul Temple* would be appreciated abroad. Although Durbridge's scripts for the *Temple* serials would still be made available to foreign broadcasters to record their own versions, a second option was now also available. *Paul Temple and the Gregory Affair* seems to have been the first *Temple* serial to be specially recorded and offered for international distribution directly. The operation was co-ordinated by the BBC Transcription Service (Originally, London Transcription Services) – part of BBC External Services. This serial, along with many other programmes would have been cut to 33 RPM coarse-groove discs and then made available to overseas customers via an internationally distributed catalogue of BBC titles. Among the countries on Transcription Services' list of clients were: New Zealand, Venezuela, Australia, Northern and Southern Rhodesia, Kenya, Malta and Ceylon. By 1958, the service would see 658 programmes a year distributed in this way, including many *Paul Temple* serials.

1946 was also the year that *Paul Temple* would make the transition to the silver screen in the first of a series of cinema features based on the BBC's radio serials.

The movie version of *Send for Paul Temple* would be produced by Butcher's Film Services – an old London-based production company that had originally been formed by a Blackheath chemist during the Boer war. Filmed at Nettleford Studios in Walton-on-Thames, the film would stick fairly closely to the story of the very first *Temple* serial from 1938, with a number of only small changes (eg Miss Parchment was changed to Miss Marchmont). The movie's director, John Argyle adapted the BBC's original scripts, with Durbridge also receiving a credit. Anthony Hulme played Temple with Joy Shelton (better known for the BBC's *PC 49* series) as Steve. However, the eighty-three minute picture was not a massive success and it would be over a year before Butcher's took up the BBC's option for a follow-up.

Back on the Light Programme, despite its unprecedented duration, *Paul Temple and the Gregory Affair* generally seemed to have justified the faith the BBC had had in it and it was another moderate success in a Thursday night slot at 8 PM, with repeats early on a Saturday evening. It was followed up with another new serial in the Spring of 1947.

The simply titled *Paul Temple and Steve* would be Durbridge and Webster's eighth full *Paul Temple* serial together. The ten-part structure of *Paul Temple and the Gregory Affair* was dropped in favour of the more traditionally established eight-part set-up of most of the previous serials and work began on the recording in early 1947.

In the new story, Paul and company were heard taking part in an international manhunt for 'the notorious Dr Belasco', across eight Sunday night slots at 9.30 PM on the Light Programme between 30 March and 18 May 1947.

The new broadcasts were not entirely without incident, with some criticism levelled at the volume of incidental music and sound effects in the serial. This was later raised by Aidan Thomson of the BBC's Overseas Presentation department in an internal memo on 11 June 1947 – which particularly singled out moments in the first episode, where sound-effects and music reportedly drowned out sections of key dialogue.

Regardless of technical issues, *Paul Temple and Steve* would soon find itself being issued for international sale by BBC Transcriptions in a printed catalogue of six BBC serials that also included a ten-part adaptation of *Beau Geste* from Webster and featuring former Paul Temple Barry Morse. The catalogue advertised *Paul Temple and Steve* as featuring 'Kim Peacock and Marjorie Westbury, as Paul and Steve, repeating the successful partnership they began in *Paul Temple and the Gregory Affair*.'[19]

Another full *Paul Temple* serial would soon be lined up on BBC radio for Christmas 1947. However, before that, listeners were treated to just one more *Paul Temple* adventure in the November of that year, in the form of the 45 minute 'afternoon play' *Mr And Mrs Paul Temple*. It was a new story from Durbridge and Webster (unlike some of the earlier *Paul Temple* shorts) and entered the studio for a single day's recording on 14 November 1947. Kim Peacock and Marjorie Westbury both starred alongside a supporting cast made up of the usual mix of outside artists and Repertory Company members – although neither Charlie nor Sir Graham took part. The play was broadcast on the Light Programme on 23 November. Unlike the *Temple* serials, it was never issued by Transcription Services.

A little over a week later the *Paul Temple* series would resume proper with another eight-part serial beginning transmission on 1 December 1947 and running through to the 19 January 1948. The new serial was called *Paul Temple and the Sullivan Mystery*.

Once again, Peacock, Westbury and Mudditt returned to the microphone, with Webster as producer and a script from Durbridge. With a slightly

---

[19] From *Six Serial Plays* – A Catalogue issued by the BBC Transcription Service (Circa: 1947-1949)

uncharacteristic hint of the exotic, the action included a holiday to Egypt, taking in a variety of sophisticated hotels and bars in and around Cairo.

However, there was something else a little different about this new *Paul Temple* serial – the music.

From the show's inception in 1938, each episode of *Paul Temple* had been introduced with a section of music from the second movement of *Scheherazade* by Rimsky-Korsakov. The recording came off a BBC stock disc from the Boosey and Hawkes label. By 1947, the BBC was paying a royalty fee of two pounds per episode to the MCPS for the use of this piece of music.

However, for *Paul Temple and the Sullivan Mystery* there was to be a new signature tune for the programme. The piece of music that was chosen was *Coronation Scot* by Vivian Ellis. The sweeping crescendos of Ellis' music had been heard in *Paul Temple* before in a number of episodes (including *Paul Temple and Steve*). However, it had never been anything more than incidental music. Now it was taking centre stage as the programme's new anthem. The recording came from the Chappell music collection, with the BBC paying the higher fee of two pounds and five shillings for its use in the programme.

The new opening theme was an instant hit with audiences and the BBC have continued to use it to begin every new *Paul Temple* recording to date. Perhaps more than anything else, it has become the most memorable aspect of the *Paul Temple* brand – a much loved classic among radio themes.

'Whenever it's played now, I get nervous, because it started it off every programme,' actor Peter Coke (who played Paul Temple from 1954) later recalled. 'I still get shivers down my back when I hear it.'[20]

Butcher's Film Services would also reinvent Temple's on-screen image in 1948, with a sequel to their 1946 film *Send for Paul Temple*. Gone was director John Argyle and actors Anthony Hulme and Joy Shelton from the first film. The new feature would be directed by Maclean Rogers, with two of Butcher's favourite actors John Bentley (Paul) and Dinah Sheridan (Steve) as the two leads. Loosely based on the BBC's *Send for Paul Temple Again* from 1945, the new 92 minute supporting feature was entitled *Calling Paul Temple*. And this time the new format was enough of a success to spawn a further two sequels over the next four years – all with Rogers and Bentley.

'FROM LONDON ... ':

It would be another full year before *Paul Temple* returned to the BBC's airwaves, in December 1948's *Paul Temple and the Curzon Case*.

Peacock, Westbury and Mudditt were this time joined by Billy Thatcher (OA) as the latest incarnation of Charlie, the manservant, alongside a now familiar line-up of guest artistes that included Grizelda Hervey, Hugh

---

[20] *The Radio Detectives* (20/05/98)

Manning and Duncan McIntyre. Hervey in particular would become a regular on the programme. She had memorably played Irene in the Home Services adaptation of *The Forsyte Saga* (1945-1947) directed by Val Gielgud and was a highly respected name in radio at that time.

The plot of *The Curzon Case* centred on a group of missing schoolchildren and a mysterious message inscribed on a cricket bat. The serial saw *Temple* back on the Light Programme for eight nights at 9.30 PM on a Tuesday (7 December 1948 to 25 January 1949). Repeats followed on Thursday at 5.45 PM.

In what was increasingly becoming an annual fixture, the next *Paul Temple* adventure, *Paul Temple and the Madison Mystery,* arrived in late Autumn 1949.

Among the returning cast of Peacock, Westbury and Mudditt, there were a number of new additions drawn from the Repertory Company and farther afield. The latest Company member to play Charlie the manservant was Desmond Carrington, who had joined the Rep' earlier in the year.

'I wouldn't have been out of the army terribly long before that – 1948, I should think ... I started broadcasting in Forces radio in Ceylon,' says Carrington. '[I] came back and knocked on the door of the BBC, who, frankly didn't want to know ... I think that Martyn C Webster probably was a help in that, though I can't be quite sure now, but he certainly put in a good word for me with somebody that was involved with the Drama Repertory Company ... I probably said to him, "Ooh, I would like to join the BBC Drama Repertory Company." I did quite a lot of other things for the BBC around about that time.'

Carrying on the theme of foreign travel, established the previous year, the new serial opened with Paul and Steve on board ship, returning from New York. They befriend the millionaire Sam Portland (played by Macdonald Parke), who is travelling on the same trip – only for Portland later to be found murdered.

'There were people like Grizelda Hervey [playing Eileen Greene],' continues Carrington. 'I don't think that he [Charlie] had very much to do in each episode. I don't think he did. I don't remember if I said more than "Cup of tea, sir?" But, after all, Charlie was his manservant. He wouldn't have been in the main plot of the drama. He's just there as set-dressing ... You got four guineas for a broadcast you were very grateful for that, because four guineas was worth quite a lot.'

By the late 1940s, the *Temple* series was now firmly rooted in London, leaving most of its early BBC Midland roots behind it. Paul Temple himself was increasingly absent from his country home in Evesham (Bramley Lodge) spending most of his time at a smart new apartment in Montpelier Square with a fast sports car and a generally metropolitan lifestyle. Much of the studio production was now largely London-based as well.

The BBC had a number of radio studios available to it in post-war

London. Broadcasting House was, of course, the most regularly used. By 1949, much of the wartime damage had been repaired and Webster was able to make use of state of the art facilities in all new purpose-built drama studios.

Val Gielgud explained that: 'Almost complete reconstruction of the sixth and seventh floors of the building was one of the results of the notorious bomb.' The new set-up 'favoured bigger studios capable of subdivision by means of screens or curtains with Control Panels directly adjoining the studios.'[21] The new facilities were modelled on a similar studio suite then used by the Scandinavian broadcasting organisation, that made life easier for producers like Webster and grams operators (such as Patience Sheffield, who worked on many of the *Temple* serials).

The two principally used drama studios at Broadcasting House, were studios 6A and 8A. The two studios differed only slightly, in the positioning of the control room (6A had an upstairs control room, while 8A's was downstairs). *Paul Temple and the Madison Mystery* would use 8A (although other serials would also sometimes record away from Broadcasting House).

'I don't know if we rehearsed in there all the time, but Studio 8 was the main drama studio at that time,' recalls Carrington. 'Of course, Broadcasting House has been taken to pieces and put together again a hundred times since then, but it was up on the eighth floor ... You would all be there together ... just walking up and going and sitting down, when you weren't doing anything. That's the way drama was done in those days. It's probably very different now, because of course you're concerned with stereo, as well, but you certainly weren't in 1949 ... You worked hard for perhaps two days on those episodes and then everybody went away.'

1949 also saw *Paul Temple* reach something of a zenith in its popularity abroad. The year saw West Germany begin their own *Temple* series on WDR. Produced by Eduard Hermann and starring René Deltgen as Paul, the series began with a translation of *Paul Temple and the Gregory Affair* (*Paul Temple und die Affäre Gregory*) and continued with further selected *Temple* stories until 1968. The series was very popular, with Germany later co-financing the BBC's television series of *Paul Temple* in the early 1970s. Italian radio would later produce similar translations of the *Temple* radio shows.

The year also saw *Temple* appear in a special Christmas programme from BBC radio on December 27.

THE NIGHT OF THE TWENTY-SEVENTH:

The Night of the Twenty-Seventh was something of an idiosyncratic one-off. To

---

[21] From *British Radio Drama: 1952-1956* by Val Gielgud – George G Harrap and Co. Ltd. (1957)

celebrate Christmas 1949, the Light Programme elected to make a special hour-long drama to show off all of its most popular radio characters and stars. Accordingly, the characters of Dick Barton, PC 49, Mrs and Dr Dale (from *Mrs Dale's Diary*), Valentine Dyall (from *The Man in Black*) and Paul and Steve Temple were teamed up in a special collaboration between the production teams of *Dick Barton – Special Agent* and *Paul Temple*.

Edward J Mason (writer of the then hugely popular *Dick Barton* series) wrote the script, with *Paul Temple*'s Martyn C Webster acting as producer. All of the actors from their respective series also took part, including Brian Reece as PC 49 and Duncan Carse as Dick Barton.

The resultant programme was an unusual blend of styles. The episode opened in the home of Dr and Mrs Dale, at Parkwood Hill in London. The Dales are invited to a party held on the night of 27 December at Hallows Court, the home of the recently deceased Silas Ephraim. The party is to have many invited guests, and each are to be paid £500 for attending, with the Dales receiving £750 for acting as hosts. Paul and Steve enter the story, as guests at the party. The true purpose of the party is only finally explained when a mysterious voice makes its presence felt via a loudspeaker. It says: 'I am Silas Ephraim and I am not dead, but very much alive. I propose to kill you all, but first there will be some fun and games. I am going to enjoy this. I am talking through a hidden loudspeaker and I can hear every word you say; YOU are now the slaves to the loudspeakers, just as I have been for years ... For years I have been chained to my radio, craving to know what would happen next, but I always had to wait until next week!'[22]

After much (largely *Dick Barton* centric) excitement, the evil Mr Ephraim is finally defeated following a gigantic explosion that destroys the house.

Although little more than a pantomime for BBC radio, it nonetheless demonstrated how central to the British radio landscape *Paul Temple* had become. It was broadcast at 8.30 PM on the Light Programme, later being repeated as part of the *Curtain Up* series at the same time on 22 March 1950.

A NEW DECADE:

The *Paul Temple* series proper would resume with a new eight-part serial between October and December 1950. *Paul Temple and the Vandyke Affair* was another missing persons storyline. This time, Temple is called in to help investigate the disappearance of the eighteen-month old Sarah Desmond and her babysitter Ms Millicent. It was a violent tale linked by the menacing presence of the mysterious Mr Vandyke. Locations this time took in Paris, London and the Thames Valley.

It was broadcast on Mondays at 8.45 PM on the Light Programme from 30

---

[22] *The Night of the Twenty-Seventh* (27/12/49)

October to 18 December, repeated Fridays at 5 PM.

The serial was later to be found as one of four serial plays being offered to a thriving foreign market in a 1951 BBC Transcriptions Services brochure, alongside dramatisations of *Pride and Prejudice* and *Bligh of the Bounty*.

There was also another *Paul Temple* film from Butcher's Film Services in 1950. The eighty-minute *Paul Temple's Triumph* (their third *Temple* picture) was (very loosely) based on the scripts of 1939's serial *News of Paul Temple*. John Bentley and Dinah Sheridan were back as Paul and Steve alongside director Maclean Rogers. However, box-office receipts were not as high as hoped, resulting in a rethink for Butcher's soon afterwards.

Another *Temple* serial followed from Webster and Durbridge in Spring 1951 (a little sooner than usual). *Paul Temple and the Jonathan Mystery* was the usual mix of violence and glamour, with the Temples returning from another trip to New York (see *Paul Temple and the Madison Mystery*) only to be called in to investigate the murder of an Oxford undergraduate. The series ran from 10 May to 28 June in a Thursday slot at 8 PM on the Light Programme. Peacock, Westbury and Mudditt, were this time reunited with Frank Partington, back in the rôle of Charlie. Although, it was to be a short-lived reunion.

Paul Temple and the Jonathan Mystery would mark something of a (temporary) end-point in the *Temple* saga for the time being. There would be no *Temple* serial running that Christmas and in 1952, there was no *Temple* of any description from the BBC at all. Things were only slightly more promising for *Temple's* cinematic career.

Butcher's Film Services hadn't been entirely happy with their previous *Paul Temple* movie, *Paul Temple's Triumph* (1950) and by 1952 had also started looking into other projects to take its place. One of the results of this was a series of pictures based on the character of 'The Toff' from a series of books by John Creasey. Both John Bentley and Maclean Rogers were retained from the *Temple* series for this new project. However, the concept ground to a halt after just two films with disappointing box-office returns.

In 1952, the company made a reluctant return to *Temple* for one last time, to make *Paul Temple Returns* – a seventy-one minute adaptation of the BBC's 1942 *Paul Temple Intervenes*. It was again produced at Nettleford Studios by Ernest G Roy. The director was still Maclean Rogers and Temple was still John Bentley, but the rest of the cast were new – with Patricia Dainton taking over as Steve. Other cast members included the still little known Christopher Lee and *'The Man in Black'* Valentine Dyall. Reviews were a little better than before, with the *British Monthly Film Bulletin*, calling it a, 'slickly made, American style thriller … Competent acting ensures this inoffensive thriller some measure of success.'[23] Despite this, it would be the final *Paul Temple* film.

---

[23] From *Famous Movie Detectives – Volume III* by Michael R Pitts – Scarecrow Press (2004)

EXIT PEACOCK, ENTER COKE:

Temple wouldn't be heard of on BBC radio again until 8 April 1953. However, the BBC wouldn't commit to another full serial. Instead, Webster and Durbridge made the single hour-long play *Paul Temple and Steve Again*.
It was to be a coda to an era that had already drawn to a close. After seven years in the part, this would be the last time that Kim Peacock would play Paul Temple.

Peacock didn't depart entirely willingly, but with concerns over his languid delivery (which played havoc with the timing of programmes), he was told that his services would no longer be required. 'He was very very slow and we never got through rehearsals because of that,'[24] recalled a co-star.

In early 1954, Webster found himself looking for yet another leading man. With scripts for Durbridge's latest serial already set, the job of playing the new Paul would fall to veteran actor, Peter Coke (pronounced Cook). Warmly erudite and debonair, for many, he would become the definitive Paul Temple.

Peter John Coke was born in Southsea on April 3 1913, but spent much of his childhood in Kenya, returning to the UK for schooling at Stowe. He graduated from RADA at the age of 24, and was singled out by the *Daily Mail* as one of their Stars of the Future. The *Daily Mail* quoted that although he'd been offered a seven-year Hollywood contract, Coke had declined on the basis that he 'will be a better actor in a few years, and Hollywood will still want him.'[25]

Coke continued a successful stage career with occasional work on the silver screen. However, with the outbreak of war, Coke joined the Royal Artillery and his acting was put on hold for the duration. He later rose to the rank of Major. Following his discharge (with a painful spinal injury), his career would not be properly resumed until he returned to the theatre in 1947, both as actor and budding writer.

By 1954, Coke was doing well (barring an incident in January 1952, when he was accidentally stabbed, during a staging of *King Lear*) and he had recently been involved in a number of projects for the BBC both on radio and television – most recently as the lead in Ivor Novello's *King Monmouth* in 1953.

'I'm extremely lucky, in that I have a voice, or had a voice, that the microphone liked. This is rather comparable to a film star having the camera fall in love with her. And I had a lucky voice,'[26] Coke later explained.

---

[24] *Peter Coke and the Paul Temple Affair* (13/12/05)
[25] From *The Daily Telegraph* (31/07/08)
[26] *Peter Coke and the Paul Temple Affair* (13/12/05)

PAUL TEMPLE

He came to the attention of Webster when he appeared as Terry Palmer in the 1950 production of *Paul Temple and the Vandyke Affair*.

'I had been in *Paul Temple* before I actually took over, because I had once been the villain. So they knew my voice – the *Paul Temple* people. Francis Durbridge said, "I want you to come out to lunch with me." I thought that was rather odd because, he was the writer and I was only the actor. And I didn't play big parts in *Paul Temple*. So, he came and he said, "We want you to take over Paul Temple." So, I said, 'That would be absolutely marvellous.'[27]

And yet, possibly wary after their experiences with Peacock, Webster and Durbridge had one stipulation.

'Francis said, "Before we have any agreement, you should come out to lunch with me tomorrow." So, I got awfully worried. I thought "what the hell can he have found out, that I can't do." So, we had lunch and we talked about a lot of subjects and eventually, he came to why. He said, "Now, I want to get this absolutely clear. I am the writer of *Paul Temple*. I know you're a playwright (I had two plays on in the West End at the time, actually.) and I don't want any of your ideas or words put into *Paul Temple*."[28]

'He said … "You are not to alter one single sentence or word of what I write, although you're a writer." So I said, "Of course I wouldn't." And I only once ever did.'[29]

Coke knew Kim Peacock and had hoped for his blessing, but it was not to be. 'He never forgave me,' Coke recalled. 'He thought I had engineered it, which I had no more idea of doing than flying … but he never forgave me and I've always felt guilty. But, it was nothing to do with me.'[30]

Peter Coke's first serial playing Paul would be *Paul Temple and the Gilbert Case*, airing on Monday nights on the Light Programme, with two repeat runs on Friday and Sunday afternoons. The new story was a great success – a piece of solid story telling with a genuinely surprising conclusion (clearly 'borrowed' from Agatha Christie). It is still among the very best of the *Paul Temple* serials. It is a race-against-time storyline, where Temple must clear the name of a man charged with murder.

The production was recorded at the BBC's Grafton Studios, described by Coke as, 'a very strange studio on Tottenham Court Road. It was really very too small and awful. I remember well, playing a love-scene with Marjorie over in a tiny lavatory … The sound acoustics were supposed to be

---

[27] *The Radio Detectives* (20/05/98)
[28] *Peter Coke and the Paul Temple Affair* (13/12/05)
[29] *Peter Coke and the Paul Temple Affair* (13/12/05)
[30] *Peter Coke and the Paul Temple Affair* (13/12/05)

absolutely right.'³¹ It was here, where all the locations for the latest serial were created – including a new flat for the Temples at 127A Eaton Square.

Co-starring with Coke, were regulars Westbury and Mudditt and James Beattie as the latest incarnation of Charlie (who had joined with 1953's *Paul Temple and Steve Again*.) They were also joined by Richard Williams (playing Lance Reynolds). Williams had appeared as Paul Temple himself back in the 1944 abridged version of *News of Paul Temple* and had since become a member of the BBC Drama Repertory Company, from which he was recruited for this latest serial.

Another interesting cast member was Peggy Hassard (playing Lyn Ferguson). The actress had spent many years before the war acting in radio drama in Canada. It was in Canada that she had appeared in CBC Radio's 1940 production of *Send for Paul Temple*. She had played Steve. Evidently, at some point between 1940 and 1954, she had emigrated (or returned?) to the UK, where she found herself in the cast of *Paul Temple* yet again. She is the only actress to appear in *Paul Temple* for two separate broadcasters across two continents. She would become a regular guest artiste in the *Temple* series in the years that followed.

The new *Temple* prompted a good deal of press coverage and the first episode of *Paul Temple and the Gilbert Case* (*The Unlucky One*) was reviewed by theatre critic J C Trewin in *The Listener* on 8 April: 'I was not surprised when Peter Coke's Temple observed to Marjorie Westbury, "Steve, would you be terribly disappointed if we postponed our holiday?" Steve was not disappointed; like us, she had come to expect these postponements in the first, and expository, eighth of a serial that will grow.'³²

In August 1954, *Paul Temple and the Gilbert Case* would also make it to commercial radio in New Zealand (via the BBC Transcription Services). It ran on Sundays at 8 PM. from 29 August on the 2ZA service, before being circulated to other New Zealand stations (4ZB, 3ZB, 2ZB and 1ZB) from September through to November. The serial had already reached the country over 2XA radio's Wanganui station on Sunday evenings the previous month.

An edition of the *New Zealand Listener*, published on 20 August, alerted its readers to the, 'adventures of this civilised sleuth as he unravels ... what turns out to be one of his most successful cases.'³³

The article continued with a short description of the life of Temple, describing how: 'Paul Temple was born in Ontario, son of the late Lt General Ian Temple, and went to England at an early age. He was educated at Rugby and Magdalen College, Oxford, and from age of 22 earned his living as a

---

³¹ *Peter Coke and the Paul Temple Affair* (13/12/05)
³² From *The Listener* (08/04/54)
³³ From *New Zealand Listener* (20/08/54)

writer of detective novels. While on holiday in Cornwall he became accidentally involved in the notorious Tenworthy case ... Temple has been in the detection business ever since. Outside his work, Temple is alleged to like fishing and collecting first editions; the music of Beethoven, Debussy and Jerome Kern, the plays of Noel Coward; the lyrics of Cole Porter; and, of course, dry martinis. He dislikes people who always have "ideas" for plots, women who ask him if he writes under his own name, "hot" music, and oysters.'[34]

Riding high on the success of the reinvigorated *Temple* series, Webster would reassemble the team of Coke, Westbury, Muddit and Beattie for another recording for June the following year. However, this time, there would be no new script from Durbridge. The decision was instead taken to exhume the scripts from an earlier *Temple* production and re-record it with the (mostly) new cast. Accordingly, 1949's *Paul Temple and the Madison Mystery* was revisited for a new production.

The new recording would retain only a few of the original cast in their original parts, with the rest being recast afresh. Marjorie Westbury and Lester Muddit of course remained from 1949 as Steve and Sir Graham and Grizelda Hervey also returned to the part of Eileen Greene. Ian Sadler again played Don Alfaro. Those who had since left the BBC's Repertory Company were recast. Such was the case with Desmond Carrington, who had played Charlie in 1949. Carrington had left the Company in the early 1950s and was now working for Radio Luxembourg. His part was now taken James Beattie. Other actors like Arthur Ridley were still in the company but were replaced for other reasons.

The serial would occupy eight Monday night slots at 8 PM on the Light Programme. Unlike the original, it was not repeated.

Coke's second (entirely original) serial would *Paul Temple and the Lawrence Affair*, broadcast in the April of 1956. Westbury, Muddit and Beattie were all back alongside Coke, in the new eight-part serial, which was set around a largely fictional stretch of the British coastline, where the Temples were holidaying.

Among the now familiar names of regular guest actors (Simon Lack, Brewster Mason and Arthur Ridley), Richard Williams was also back (here playing Sir Carlton Ross).

The latest mystery would air over eight weeks on the Light Programme in its traditional 8 PM timeslot (on a Wednesday) between 11 April and 30 May 1956. The repeats were also back, at 4.30 PM on the following Sundays.

1957 would also be the year of the first entirely original *Paul Temple* novel – *The Tyler Mystery*. Co-written by Durbridge with Douglas Rutherford, it was actually printed as being 'written by Paul Temple'. Hodder &

---

[34] From *New Zealand Listener* (20/08/54)

Stoughton were the publishers.

Coke, Westbury, Mudditt and Beattie returned in November 1957 for *Paul Temple and the Spencer Affair*. A tale of a murdered drama student (Mary Dreisler), the serial was broadcast on the Light Programme between 13 November 1957 and New Year's Day. It occupied another 8 PM slot (except on Christmas Day, when it went out at 6.30 PM).

A BEQUEST:

By now, many of the series' co-stars were seasoned *Paul Temple* veterans, with something of a family atmosphere created through their annual studio get-togethers.

'I just loved it,' remembered Coke. 'We were really a family by that time. Both Marjorie and myself had a lot of acting friends and slowly we got them in and they came over and over again. They played different parts. One day they'd be the housemaid and the other day they'd be a countess.'[35]

The public clearly shared in the evident affection. 'We had a mass of letters. They said, "You must be married,"' Coke continued, 'because there's this atmosphere between you and I suppose there was ... Neither of us was married actually[36], but it did come over that we loved each other.'[37]

It was in August 1957, that this adoration from *Paul Temple*'s fans, brought Marjorie Westbury into the spotlight, with a tragic incident that would make headline news. The story began some years previously in the mid-1950s. Westbury was sent a fan letter from an Essex woman called Olive Louisa Parker.

The letter was an unusually impassioned one, in which Miss Parker told Westbury that she had fallen in love with the actress' voice.

Further letters continued for some years, until one day in 1956, Westbury received a letter from Parker, in which she made a promise to leave Westbury a large bequest in her will.

Coke: 'The woman said, "I'm going to leave you all my possessions." So Marjorie said, "Don't be absurd ..." She wrote back to the woman and said, "I'm not what I sound and you're not to leave me [anything], because it's quite absurd. You don't know me. I'm not the character I appear."'[38]

'As she did not know me, she could not possibly leave money,' said Westbury. 'I then went to see her, had lunch with her, and that was our only meeting.'[39]

---

[35] *Peter Coke and the Paul Temple Affair* (13/12/05)
[36] Coke would never marry, but would spend his final years living with his partner Fred Webb.
[37] *Peter Coke and the Paul Temple Affair* (13/12/05)
[38] *The Radio Detectives* (20/05/98)
[39] From *The Times* (17/08/57)

'She met the woman,' said Coke, 'and the woman said, "I haven't changed my mind. I think you're wonderful. You've got the sort of voice that I admire more than anything."'[40]

On March 9 1957, Olive Parker was found dead in a gas-filled room at her home in Creekview Avenue in Hullbridge, Essex. A coroner's inquest returned a verdict of suicide. In her will, she had left Westbury an inheritance of £18,699.

'I was very much surprised when I found that the amount she had left me was so much,'[41] said Westbury.

The case made most of the major national newspapers and left Westbury shaken.

A NEW SIR GRAHAM:

There was little *Paul Temple* activity in 1958. *Paul Temple and the Spencer Affair* would be repeated in the Summer (from 11 July to 5 September) in a Friday evening slot on the Light Programme at 10 PM. However, there were no new recordings.

The series resumed in 1959 – an exceptionally busy year for the show. It started with a remake of *Paul Temple and the Vandyke Affair,* which began its run on 1st January in a Thursday 9.30 PM slot on the Light Programme (with Home Service repeats). It was Coke's second remake of a Kim Peacock serial. However, more significantly, it was also the first *Paul Temple* serial not to feature Lester Mudditt.

The character of Sir Graham Forbes had been an established part of the programme's central cast from day one and Lester Mudditt had always been the voice behind it. However, Mudditt had already appeared in his last *Paul Temple* the previous year, with *Paul Temple and the Spencer Affair*. He was the last core cast member to have had any link with the very first *Paul Temple* serial. With the remake of *Paul Temple and the Vandyke Affair* a new actor would be introduced as Sir Graham Forbes. The actor chosen to take over was Richard Williams.

Williams had originally joined the BBC Drama Repertory Company in 1942, later appearing as Paul Temple in the 1944 remake of *News of Paul Temple*. He remained with the Repertory Company for ten years, resigning in 1952 to pursue freelance work. However, in 1954, he rejoined the Repertory Company and very soon found himself back appearing as a regular guest actor in *Paul Temple*. In 1954, he won a national award as the best radio actor of the year.

Williams was not a well man when the remake of *Paul Temple and the*

---

[40] *The Radio Detectives* (20/05/98)
[41] From *The Times* (17/08/57)

SERIAL THRILLERS

Vandyke Affair entered the studio. Although he was only fifty-eight years old, he had already been enrolled in a London nursing home. However, he was a highly respected actor and the BBC were happy to keep him on their books, despite his infirmity. Webster also liked the actor and Williams would continue to play Sir Graham Forbes for the rest of his life.

The transmission of the remake of *Paul Temple and the Vandyke Affair* ended on Thursday, 19 February and within weeks a new *Paul Temple* serial was already in the studio.

Paul Temple and the Conrad Case was an entirely original serial beginning on the Light Programme on 2 March. It was another missing-persons story, this time centring on the disappearance of Betty Conrad from her Bavarian finishing school.

The new serial ran in a Wednesday 7.30 PM slot on the Light Programme with repeats following on Fridays at 10 PM.

1959 concluded with one last *Paul Temple* serial beginning in November – a remake of Coke's first story, the celebrated *Paul Temple and the Gilbert Case*. There were fewer cast changes than usual, with the only major change among the leads being from Mudditt to Williams. The repeat serial ran from 22 November 1959 to 10 January 1960 on the Light Programme.

One of the busiest ever years for *Paul Temple*, 1959 also saw the publication of another *Temple* novel – *East of Algiers* (again credited as being written by Paul Temple). It was another product of the Francis Durbridge and Douglas Rutherford writing partnership. However despite its original title, it was actually a loose novelisation of the 1947 serial, *Paul Temple and the Sullivan Mystery*. It would be the last *Temple* novel for over ten years.

Of course, it wasn't quite the end of *Temple* in print. On 19 November 1951 the *London Evening News* had begun to carry a *Paul Temple* cartoon strip drawn by John McNamara, Alfred Sindall and Bill Bailey, which would continue to run until May 1 1971.

THE SIXTIES:

With the arrival of the 1960s, *Paul Temple* found itself in a rapidly changing radio landscape. Many of the perennial certainties of radio's 'Golden Age' had gone and by the end of the decade, *Paul Temple* was to join them.
1960 was not a great year for the series' 'family'. There were no new *Temple* productions on the air and in January, the family was to lose another of its members.

On Wednesday 6 January, Richard Williams died at his nursing home in London. He had only just finished recording the remake of *Paul Temple and the Gilbert Case*. He died mere days before the broadcast of the final episode. He was the only man to play both Sir Graham Forbes and Paul Temple. He was just sixty years old.

PAUL TEMPLE

When Coke, Westbury and Beattie finally reformed for the recording of a new *Paul Temple* serial around Christmastime 1960, it was with a new actor, (James Thomason) as Sir Graham Forbes.

Paul Temple and the Margo Mystery arrived in 1961 – broadcast from New Year's Day to 19 February, on Sundays at 7.05 PM on the Light Programme (with repeats on succeeding Thursdays at 8 PM). The plot revolved around a drug-smuggling operation (as it had many times before).

Frederick Laws reviewed the new serial in the 2 February edition of *The Listener*, commenting that: 'I cannot recommend the serial thrills of *Paul Temple and the Margo Mystery* (Sundays Light) with … much enthusiasm, but Temple has served us well and retained his capacity for getting into bad company and perpetually awkward situations. It is the mixture very much as before, and, as they say in the radio theatre, "that's all right on the Light."'[42]

Paul Temple and the Margo Mystery would be the last (original) *Paul Temple* serial for over three years. By the mid-sixties, radio had already lost the battle against television and the attention of the listening (and viewing) public was now firmly elsewhere.

Durbridge had been among the first to see the shifting trend and had already started to carve out a prolific career on television.

It was Durbridge who had written the script for one of television's first ever thriller serials – *The Broken Horseshoe* (directed by Webster). A live studio-bound production from the BBC's Alexandra Palace, it ran for six episodes from 15 March to 19 April 1952. A great hit with audiences, Durbridge followed it up with *Operation Diplomat*, another six-part thriller in October/November of the same year. *The Teckman Biography* followed around Christmas 1953 and his *Portrait of Alison* (1955) cemented his reputation among television's foremost dramatists (even rivalling the legendary Nigel Kneale).

Further serials included: *My Friend Charles* (1956), *The Other Man* (1956), *A Time of Day* (1957) and *The Scarf* (1959).

The television scene was changing rapidly in the 1960s, but Durbridge was still very near the top of the tree.

However, the frenetic pace of his (higher paid) television work was to have a negative effect on the *Temple* serials. With his work in much demand, other commitments meant that *Temple* was away from the radio for much of the decade. Webster himself would later comment that 'in recent years, with Durbridge so busy on his television and film work, it has been almost impossible to get a new *Temple* serial.'[43]

Durbridge's TV work would peak in 1960/1961, with *The World of Tim*

---

[42] From *The Listener* (02/02/61)
[43] From *Radio Times* (20 – 27 April 1968)

Frazer – at the time, the longest serial ever produced for British television. An 18 part serial co-written with Clive Exton, Charles Hatton (with whom Durbridge had written some of his *Temple* novels) and Barry Thomas it would be Durbridge's only biggest hit away from *Temple*.

By 1963, Webster (who had also had a brief secondment to television drama) was keen for another *Temple* serial and had waited over two years for a new script from Durbridge. However, with Durbridge busy at work on his latest TV serial, *The Desperate People* (24 February – 31 March), it didn't look like there would be anything new any time soon. Accordingly the decision was taken to remake another old Kim Peacock serial, with a new cast. This time it would be 1951's *Paul Temple and the Jonathan Mystery*.

Coke, Westbury, Thomason and Beattie (for the last time) were all re-recruited for the new recording, which aired on the Light Programme on Mondays at 8 PM from 14 October to 2 December. The production also featured original Charlie, Frank Partington, back after a few years absence (here playing a Porter).

The remake was popular enough to be repeated on the Home Service in December 1964 (and later in 1967), but with Durbridge's TV commitments persisting, it would be 1965, before there was another all new *Paul Temple* serial on the BBC.

A few months after work finished on his highly successful *Melissa* for BBC television, Durbridge would return to *Paul Temple* in early 1965 for *Paul Temple and the Geneva Mystery*.

The new serial was only six episodes long, rather than the traditional eight, but this reflected both the direction radio dramas was taking in the 1960s and Durbridge's recent six-part serials for television. In another break with tradition, the serial also failed to feature a prominent rôle for Sir Graham Forbes. However, Peter Coke and Marjorie Westbury were both back alongside a recently recast Charlie, in the form of actor John Baddeley.

It's arguable that the new story worked even better in the new six-part format, which removed much of the obvious padding and cyclical plotting that had become the norm in *Temple*. However, it was also, in all but name, the final original *Paul Temple* serial to come from Durbridge.

It was transmitted on the Light Programme from 11 April to 16 May on Sundays at 7 PM. (It was also later repeated on the Home Service in October/November). The broadcasts overlapped with the transmission of Durbridge's latest television serial, *A Man Called Harry Brent*. And from this point on, Durbridge would essentially concentrate on his television work. Even Paul Temple himself, would eventually migrate to the small-screen.

THE END:

In October 1967, Webster reached the BBC's then compulsory staff retirement age (60 years old) and was required to leave his job in the BBC drama department. 'I ... was sad at the thought that I would never produce another *Temple*,' he recalled. However, before he left, there was still one last script awaiting his attention. 'The week before I actually did retire,' he continued 'Durbridge came into my office carrying a parcel. "A little present for you," he said. I opened it and found the scripts.'[44]

The parcel contained (what appeared to be) the scripts of an all new eight-part *Paul Temple* serial, called *Paul Temple and the Alex Affair*. It was a very special retirement present for Webster and a final farewell to a series that had served BBC radio for thirty-years. The new serial was trailed with the usual fanfare and *Temple* fans waited for the latest adventure ... However, *Paul Temple and the Alex Affair* wasn't entirely what it seemed.

In reality, *Paul Temple and the Alex Affair* wasn't a completely new serial at all. It was actually a very slightly tweaked re-packaging of the 1945 serial *Send for Paul Temple Again*. The individual episode titles had been changed or swapped over (Episode seven of *Paul Temple and the Alex Affair* was called *The Girl in Brown*, which had originally been the title of episode five of *Send for Paul Temple Again*). However, in most respects, it was the same set of scripts, with most of the same characters. The only major change was the altering of the villain's name from Rex, to Alex. One of the original cast members from 1945 even reprised his original part, with Basil Jones returning as Wilfred (originally Wilfrid) Davies (originally Davis). Whatever else it was, *Paul Temple and the Alex Affair* wasn't an original script.

However, all things considered, the deception seemed to work and listeners welcomed *Paul Temple and the Alex Affair* as the final *Paul Temple* serial, when it was broadcast between 26 February and 21 March 1968. Both the Light Programme and the Home Service had been shut down by the BBC in 1967 (the *Temple* series had seen them arrive and depart), to be replaced by a new streamlined radio network, consisting of Radio 1, Radio 2, Radio 3 and Radio 4. It was on Radio 2 that the final *Paul Temple* was to be broadcast on Mondays and Thursdays at 7.45 PM, with repeats on Radio 4 in Spring 1969.

Paul Temple had meant a regular stream of work for what had become a close-knit group of actors. Although, for Peter Coke in particular, it had a downside too. As he explained in 2005: 'Once I played Paul Temple, all my other work died ... All the producers suddenly dropped me and said, "Oh yes, of course you play Paul Temple, so you couldn't possibly do anything else."'[45]

Paul Temple would not reappear on BBC radio until the 1980s, when a string of Peter Coke repeats were broadcast. However, although the radio

---

[44] From *Radio Times* (20 – 27 April 1968)
[45] *Peter Coke and the Paul Temple Affair* (13/12/05)

series was over, it wasn't entirely the end for *Paul Temple*.

TELEVISION:

As early as 1960, Durbridge had contemplated a *Paul Temple* TV series and by the time *Paul Temple and the Alex Affair* had aired, the decision had already been taken that *Paul Temple* should transfer from radio to television before the arrival of the new decade.

'Eventually they decided they'd put it on TV,' remembered Coke with little enthusiasm. 'Marjorie wasn't the right shape and I was a bit old. So they got two other people to do it.'[46]

The *Paul Temple* television series was a radically different creation to the radio original.

The serialised format of the radio show was almost completely abandoned, in favour of a series of largely standalone episodes, with a self-contained story each week. The series was in colour (one of the BBC's first) and mixed studio recording with exotic foreign location shoots. The old Vivian Ellis theme tune was also discarded – in its place was a piece of almost melancholic soft jazz from celebrated TV theme writer Ron Grainer (*Doctor Who* and *The Prisoner*). Altogether it was a much more contemporary drama – locked into the present day as firmly as the radio show had been locked into the past. There was no Sir Graham Forbes or Charlie either. The two leads were Francis Matthews (Paul) and Ros Drinkwater (Steve).

Francis Matthews had worked on Durbridge serials before, appearing in 1955's *My Friend Charles* and 1960/1961's *The World of Tim Frazer*. It was during the production of the latter that he had gotten to know Durbridge.

'I had lunch with Francis one day,' recalled Matthews. 'He said, "I'm thinking about trying to get *Paul Temple* done on television and you're the man I'd like to play him." Now this was years before *Paul Temple* was actually done. So when it came to the point and the producer was casting around for someone to play it, I think Francis must have put in a word for me ... I went to meet them – Francis and the producer and the head of drama at the BBC and they offered me the part then and there.'[47]

Perhaps the most significant break from the radio series came with the scripts themselves. Francis Durbridge didn't write them. 'He couldn't write one off thrillers,' explained Matthews. 'He depended for his skills on the cliffhanger.'[48] A number of writers would eventually work on the TV series, under the direction of a central script-editor. Although Durbridge

---

[46] *Peter Coke and the Paul Temple Affair* (13/12/05)
[47] From *Being Paul Temple*, produced by Acorn Media in 2009
[48] From *Being Paul Temple*, produced by Acorn Media in 2009

did pitch some stories for the television show early on, none were ever taken up.

The first series was produced by Alan Bromley, who'd worked with Durbridge on a number of his earlier television serials. However, from series two there were two new producers, Peter Bryant and Derrick Sherwin, who came straight from recently producing *Doctor Who*..

The series ran for four thirteen-part series from 1969 to 1971 and drew solid and appreciative audiences, particularly in Germany who co-financed the series from series two onwards. However, despite an excellent star-making performance from Matthews, the series wouldn't prove as durable as its more fondly remembered radio predecessor.

'For reasons they will never explain to me,' recalled Matthews, 'they stopped the show. It was something to do with the financial involvement of the German company, which was publicising it.'[49]

Partly as a tie-in with the television series, Durbridge would write four further *Paul Temple* novels during the 1970s. Two were new works of fiction (*Paul Temple and the Kelby Affair* and *Paul Temple and the Harkdale Robbery*), seemingly based on Durbridge's rejected storylines for the TV show. A further two novels were adapted from radio originals (*The Geneva Mystery* and *The Curzon Case*). Hodder and Stoughton published the first three, with the fourth from Coronet Books.

Following the publication of the fourth book in 1972, there would be no further *Paul Temple* activity in the UK for quite some time. Although, the series continued to be popular on Italian radio through the RAI broadcaster until 1977.

REBIRTH:

The seeds of *Paul Temple*'s unlikely renaissance seem to have been planted when BBC Radio 4 repeated all six episodes of 1965's *Paul Temple and the Geneva Mystery* in December 1985. The episodes were stripped daily across a single week from Monday to Saturday (23 to 28 December). The repeats went down well enough with listeners for another serial to be repeated the following Christmas. 1959's *Paul Temple and the Conrad Case* filled eight weekly Thursday evening slots on Radio 4, running from Christmas Day 1986 through to New Year's Day 1987.

By the late eighties, there was a renewed interest in the *Paul Temple* series. Durbridge would even write two more *Paul Temple* novels, both based on radio originals – *Paul Temple and the Margo Mystery* (1986) and *Paul Temple and the Madison Mystery* (1988) (again through Hodder).

---

[49] From a 1995 interview with Francis Matthews from *The Paul Temple File* website (www.oocities.com/gregorym101/Temple1.html)

SERIAL THRILLERS

Then, in 1989, BBC Audio (the arm of the BBC responsible for the commercial release of BBC radio on audiotape and CD) released a double tape cassette edited compilation of *Paul Temple and the Conrad Case*. The new release sold well and before long other *Paul Temple* serials were being lined up for release on cassette (and later CD).

These commercial reissues of Peter Coke episodes continued to sell well from BBC Audio, with BBC 7 later starting a regular set of repeat broadcasts. However a problem had already begun to present itself.

The simple fact was that very few of the *Temple* radio serials still existed in the BBC's archives. Some tapes and discs were lost after transmission. Many had never been archived to begin with.

'It was probably never recorded,' says Desmond Carrington of the *Paul Temple* he appeared in). 'They didn't do that in those days. Recordings were still on seventeen inch black discs and some of them were glass discs, which revolved at thirty-three and a third. It was quite a palaver to record something off the air. So, they didn't do it very often ... Obviously, the BBC could and did record some things on acetate and 78 records, but that's why their archives from those days are, to some extent, thin. They had to be fairly choosy about what they did record and keep. And, they've got rid of a lot of stuff, as I think everybody knows, since then – to their detriment, really.'

Even the vast majority of the *Temple*s that did still exist, rarely survived in the BBC's main sound archive. For many years, in the fifties and beyond, recordings had been marketed for international syndication by the BBC Transcription Services (now known as BBC Radio International) and it was in the Transcription archives where most of the surviving material was held.

'There were a slew of Peter Coke *Paul Temple*s issued in the fifties,' explains former BBC Transcription Services engineer Ted Kendall. 'They were reissued by Transcriptions for commercial slots – twenty-seven minutes – in the 1960s. Now, most of the audiobook issues derive from the reissues. So, there's some material missing ... The reissues for commercial slots started in about 1963 ... when they were pushing very hard for the American market.'

Sadly, many of the *Paul Temple*s that we know were sold through Transcription Services before 1954, are no longer in the Radio International archive with the rest of the surviving transcriptions. Once the commercial usefulness of a particular recording was judged to have come to an end, it is most likely that any material from that recording would have been destroyed. The BBC Transcription Service had no mandate to act as an archive for historically important material and so the view was generally taken that material was better thrown out than left to clutter up valuable shelf-space. We don't know exactly how many *Paul Temple* stories were distributed through the Transcriptions Service, but surviving records indicate that the following are among the serials Transcription Services once held, that have since been lost or destroyed:

> *Paul Temple and the Gregory Affair* (1946)
> *Paul Temple and Steve* (1947)
> *Paul Temple and the Sullivan Mystery* (1947)
> *Paul Temple and the Curzon Case* (1948)
> *Paul Temple and the Madison Mystery* (1949)
> *Paul Temple and the Vandyke Affair* (1950)
> *Paul Temple and the Jonathan Mystery* (1951)

Happily a recording of *Paul Temple and the Vandyke Affair* (1950) has since been returned to the National Sound Archives at the British Library in London and has been released on BBC Audio CD. However, there is little trace of any other lost serials. Although a short extract (2 minutes, 11 seconds) from the final episode of *Paul Temple and the Jonathan Mystery* (1951) does survive in the hands of a private collector. These two recordings are all that is currently known to survive from Kim Peacock's lengthy service in the series.

As Kendall points out, it is also worth taking into account that even the surviving Transcription tapes are not always entirely unedited recordings, with certain trims having been made for commercial radio. In one unknown Peter Coke serial, one character was even re-voiced for the Transcription Services re-issue, as she'd since gone on to become rather famous and the BBC could no longer afford her repeat fee.

Of the earlier pre-war and wartime serials even less survives in the archives. The BBC retained recordings of the sixth episode of the very first *Paul Temple* serial *Send for Paul Temple* (1938) and also retained a recording of the final episode of *Paul Temple and the Front Page Men* (1938), but little else survives of those early BBC Midland years.

Similarly, nothing survives of the April 1939 Australian production of *Send for Paul Temple*. Nor does very much survive from the 1940s either.

However, in 2009, one further recording did come to light in Canada. Following investigations by this author, on behalf of BBC Audio, it was discovered that the National Archives in Canada still had copies of all eight episodes of CBC's 1940 production of *Send for Paul Temple*, starring Bernard Braden and Peggy Hassard. The recordings survive on both tape and disc and stand as the only complete recording of *Temple*'s very first serial.

Paul Temple was a great international success story and at some point recordings of many *Paul Temple* serials did find their way to countries like Australia and New Zealand (See Appendix B). In 2002, the BBC bore this in mind, when they launched a special public campaign. The BBC Treasure Hunt Appeal was an international appeal for recordings of BBC programmes that were otherwise not known to exist anymore. Among the many programmes that the BBC were on the lookout for, were episodes of *Paul Temple*.

The chances of finding any lost material from a series like *Paul Temple*, after such a long time, were staggeringly remote, but against the odds, something did turn up – a recording of the long-lost 1942 serial *Paul Temple Intervenes*.

The exciting find was soon lined up for a special commercial CD release by BBC Audio, with Ted Kendall assigned the task of restoring the aged recording for the digital age.

'*Paul Temple Intervenes* ... was found on the Treasure Hunt in Australia. It was sent over as a complete transfer,' says Kendall, 'badly processed and really not up to scratch. And all I had to work on unfortunately was the bad transfer. The major problem with it was that it was an absolute thicket of clicks and bangs – all of which had been rounded off by previous processing, so I couldn't get at them with CEDAR [an audio restoration system]. I had to go through and take the damn things out by hand. Very laborious process, but I think that actually the results were worth it. It's of its time, but at least it's now well-tolerable to listen to.'

The *Paul Temple* releases had been a highly successful and profitable run of releases for BBC Audio and they were pleased to release the resultant CD of *Paul Temple Intervenes* in 2005. However, by now, almost all hope of finding recordings of any other lost *Temple* material had all but evaporated and BBC Audio had simply run out of surviving recordings left to issue on CD.

It was at this point that thoughts turned to the obvious possibility of simply re-recording the serials again. It had been a regular activity during *Temple*'s original run and with many of the scripts still surviving in the archives, the question of a new *Paul Temple* radio series was once again under active consideration.

PAUL TEMPLE RETURNS:

The first outside proposal to resurrect *Paul Temple* as a radio series came from writer Bert Coules in February 2005. The radio dramatist had a long-standing track record with detective drama at the BBC, with a repertoire that included *Cadfael* and *Sherlock Holmes*. Coules' suggestion was that he would adapt one or more of Durbridge's *Paul Temple* novels for the radio – either based on one of the original novels or one of the novelisations.

However, the suggestion was never taken up, as simultaneously, another project had been suggested by BBC Audio. It is here where radio producer Patrick Rayner entered the story.

Patrick Rayner was a prolific radio producer, then working at BBC Scotland. Rayner was asked by BBC Audio to help them create some remakes of lost *Temple* serials – specifically for the commercial audiobooks market.

'In 2005,' Rayner remembers. 'They had a look in the archive and realised there were several which had been lost or never been recorded or, for one reason or another, weren't in the archives. So, they approached me saying, "Would you like to think about making one of the lost ones, purely for commercial distribution and not for transmission?" And I said, "Yes. It sounds interesting." But, when I budgeted it for them, it was clearly too expensive for them to make just for going out on CD. Their sales wouldn't recover their costs.'

With BBC Audio's blessing, Rayner then took the project to BBC Radio 4. Rayner's proposal was to track down the original scripts for one of the *Paul Temple* serials that was no longer known to exist. He would then re-record it, as a period recreation, with an all-new cast. The suggestion went down well during one of BBC Scotland's 2005 commissioning rounds and an all new adaptation of 1947's *Paul Temple and the Sullivan Mystery* was promptly commissioned for the following year.

'I can't remember quite why we picked *The Sullivan Mystery*,' says Rayner. 'It seemed like a good place to start.'

Rayner was very keen that the new serial would be an accurate and faithful recreation of the original 1947 version and as such set to work on assembling as much contemporary material as possible.

The first step was to obtain copies of as many of the original recordings as possible, for reference. 'I listened to all the existing stuff again and again,' says Rayner, 'to immerse myself not just in the acting style, but also in the production style, which is very different from today's.'

Microfiche copies of the original 1947 scripts had been kept at the BBC's Written Archives Centre in Caversham Park and were called up by Rayner. These would form the basis of the new production.

'Although we stuck scrupulously to the text,' Rayner continues, 'we usually tried to observe all the cuts they'd made at the time, although sometimes I had to put material back in, to make ours last as it should … We certainly never invented any of it.'

Also of great use were the BBC's Programme As Broadcast documents (PASBs). It was these that enabled Rayner to track down many of the original music and sound effects recordings.

'Those were invaluable,' remembers Rayner. 'They give you the complete list, not just of all the music used, but also the sound effects used and things like that – the Queen's Light Orchestra and all of that stuff. Some of that was in the BBC library. Other stuff had to come from the British Sound Archives, because it was no longer in the library. Some of it had been bombed out during the war. Some of it was lost and some of it was still on 78s and had to be transcribed. So, gathering all of the original music together was great fun, but it was quite a treasure hunt.'

In something of a return to the regional roots of the *Paul Temple* series, the new production was to be recorded away from London at the BBC's Scotland studios. 'I work and live in Scotland,' says Rayner. 'I wanted to make it up here.'

'There was a fanciful idea that we should ask Peter Coke to take part, as he was still alive when we started, but I think we decided that ... would be perhaps too backward looking ... looking back on the others too much.'

The task of recreating Paul Temple himself would eventually fall to Scottish actor Crawford Logan.

Logan was a predominantly radio-based actor who Rayner had worked with before. Alongside a lot of talking-books, his career has also taken in *The Archers*, *Doctor Who* and *EastEnders*.

Gerda Stevenson would play the new Steve – an actress who Rayner had also worked with before. The new Sir Graham Forbes was *Blake's Seven*'s Gareth Thomas.

'I wanted to work with people I knew,' says Rayner, 'but I also wanted to work with people who I knew were vocally very clever, because I knew that we had to somehow get back inside that acting style, without sending it up ... We wanted to do it straight, but in terms of acting style, if you suddenly start pronouncing flat as "flet" and shortening all those vowels, play it in that almost 1950s' film style, the danger of course is that you slip over into parody.'

The serial was recorded using largely modern recording techniques and equipment, except with period microphones.

'We recorded it digitally, so all the recordings were done into a computer,' Rayner explains, 'but the microphones were old microphones. We dug out mics that had been left in cupboards. You'd recognise them from old black and white photographs you'd see of the BBC newsreaders – these great lozenge-shaped things. We used those. Sometimes we had to augment them with the modern microphones, because we simply didn't have enough, but those were then switched into having the same technical characteristics as the old microphones – that slightly rounder more Bakelite sound.'

The new production was broadcast on BBC Radio 4 between 7 August and 2 October 2006. It was a tremendous success with listeners. Many soon wrote in asking for more.

In due course, a second remake was put into production. This time it was 1949's *Paul Temple and the Madison Mystery* that was remade. Crawford Logan, Gerda Stevenson and Gareth Thomas all returned for the new production, along with many of the supporting cast from the first remake, including Greg Powrie as Charlie and guest actor Nick Underwood.

'I've used the same body of actors in all three so far. I've brought new people in, but there's still that same core there, which again, is trying to recreate that sense of the company that they'd had at the time.'

This second re-staging ran on Radio 4 from 16th May to 4 July 2008.

A further *Temple* remake then followed from Rayner's team, with a production of the early (pre-*Coronation Scot*) *Paul Temple and Steve* from 1947. This again used much of the same cast and was broadcast between 11 June and 30 July 2010.

Patrick Rayner left the BBC's staff in 2010, but continued with freelance work for the corporation. And in 2011, Paul's adventures picked up again with a remake of *A Case for Paul Temple* (1946). Recorded between 3 and 10 July 2011, this again saw the return of Rayner's regular cast of Logan, Stevenson and Thomas. It was broadcast between 24th August and 12th October that year.

The remakes concluded in 2013, with the broadcast of a re-recording of *Paul Temple and the Gregory Affair* – a ten part epic first produced with Kim Peacock in 1946. 'It's great fun. I just enjoy being involved with it,' Rayner explained in 2012.

'When I was making it, I took the plot of *The Sullivan Mystery* to pieces and there's one murder that's totally inexplicable. The only person that could have done it was Steve. She has the motive and the means, so I think she probably killed him. I don't know. I have this theory that Steve is actually a serial murderer, because there's another one in *The Madison Affair* (sic), where the only person who could have killed him would be Steve.'

WITHOUT A TRACE:

Sadly, even with the later remakes, there still remain thirty-nine episodes that do not exist in any recorded form in the archives. It was thought for many years that the only record of these missing adventures existed in the BBC's Written Archives Centre at Caversham Park near Reading. Unfortunately, even this is not entirely true, as research reveals there to be forty episodes for which even the Written Archives Centre has no record. As of 2012, the following scripts for otherwise lost episodes, are all missing[50] from the Written Archives' collection of microfiche copies:

---

[50] The scripts for the first three *Temple* serials, together with episodes 1 and 2 of *Paul Temple and the Gregory Affair* and episode 1 of *Paul Temple and the Curzon Case* aren't listed as ever having been in the archive to begin with. Episode 6 of *Paul Temple and the Gregory Affair* and episode 3 of *Paul Temple and the Curzon Case* are logged as 'missing', on existing records and may have been lost or damaged, at some point after being sent to the archive. Ultimately, the true reason why the scripts aren't where we'd expect them to be isn't known.

Send for Paul Temple (1938) – All eight episodes
Paul Temple and the Front Page Men (1938) – All eight episodes
News of Paul Temple (1939) – All six episodes
Paul Temple and the Gregory Affair (1946) – Episodes 1, 2 and 6
Paul Temple and the Curzon Case (1948) – Episodes 1 and 3

Happily the 1940 Canadian recording of *Send for Paul Temple* gives us something for the very first serial (alongside the BBC's surviving recording of episode 6) and we also have a recording for the eighth episode of *Paul Temple and the Front Page Men*. A complete bound set of scripts for *Paul Temple and the Gregory Affair* have since been rediscovered by Patrick Rayner in the archives of a foreign radio station. However, that still leaves the scripts for episodes 1 to 7 of *Paul Temple and the Front Page Men*, all of *News of Paul Temple* and episodes 1 and 3 of *Paul Temple and the Curzon Case* that remain entirely unaccounted for.

The archives of Francis Durbridge's family are sadly of little help here either. Many of Durbridge's own scripts and papers were destroyed in a fire at a private depository, over thirty years ago. Durbridge's son (Stephen) has recently turned his attention to the archives of foreign broadcasters (eg Germany) to look for the remaining lost scripts.

LEGACY:

The likelihood of any further lost *Paul Temple* material coming to light is sadly not great. However, the fact that so much of what does survive is so celebrated so long after it was first broadcast, still stands as a testament to the magic of the original series.

'Some of the plotting,' says Rayner 'doesn't quite hang together, but people don't care. They're not sitting there, trying to work it out as a logical mystery, because they know that's not what the game is. It's interesting. I gave up trying to work out who did what in the last one we did, because it's just not clear who killed someone and why. It's a terribly winning formula … It takes people off into a different kind of world … Although it's hugely violent – the body count is enormous – nevertheless, it seems to come from a more innocent age.'

'I was very surprised to hear *Paul Temple* on Radio 7,' says Desmond Carrington. 'I could not believe it – what it sounded like after all those years. It sounded so naïve and so incredible.'

Certainly, in terms of sheer longevity, *Temple* is without equal among any of the radio thriller serials produced by the BBC. It survived against the odds, through a combination of charm, solid plotting and simple good luck. It straddles the 'golden age' of the radio serial from before its inception until after its decline.

However, in the late 1940s it was overshadowed by another very different radio serial. And although *Paul Temple* would outlast its rival, it would never wholly succeed in outshining a serial that, in its day, was by far the most sensationally popular piece of drama in Britain. That other serial was *Dick Barton – Special Agent*.

PAUL TEMPLE EPISODE GUIDE

1: *Send for Paul Temple* **(1938)**
1 x 25 minute episode and 7 x 20 minute episodes (approx.)
1938 Production – BBC Radio
1939 Production – ABC Radio (Australia)
1940 Production – CBC Radio (Canada)
1941 Production – BBC Radio
1942 Production – ABC Radio (Australia)
1945 Production – ABC Radio (Australia)
Written by Francis Durbridge
Producer: Martyn C Webster *(1938 and 1941 Productions)*
             Laurie Lang *(1939 Production)*
             Andrew Allen *(1940 Production)*
             Unknown *(1942 Production)*
             Charles Wheeler *(1945 Production)*

CAST:
Paul Temple	Hugh Morton *(1938 Production)*
	Donnell Downey *(1939 Production)*
	Bernard Braden *(1940 Production)*
	Carl Bernard *(1941 Production)*
	Peter Bathurst *(1942 Production)*
	George Randall *(1945 Production)*
Steve	Bernadette Hodgson *(1938 Production)*
	Margarie Crosbie *(1939 Production)*
	Peggy Hassard *(1940 Production)*
	Thea Holme *(1941 Production)*
	Neva Carr-Glyn *(1942 Production)*
	Bettie Dickson *(1945 Production)*
Dr Milton	E Stuart Vinden *(1938 Production)*
	Lister Sinclair *(1940 Production)*
	Ivan Samson *(1941 Production)*
Diana Thornley	Cecily Gay *(1938 Production)*
	Grace Matthews *(1940 Production)*
	Grizelda Hervey *(1941 Production*
Ms Parchment	Courtney Hope *(1938 Production)*

PAUL TEMPLE: EPISODE GUIDE

	Alice Mather *(1940 Production)*
	Amy Veness *(1941 Production)*
	Marie Rosenfeld *(1945 Production)*
Sir Graham Forbes	Lester Mudditt *(1938 Production)*
	Ray Walsh *(1939 Production)*
	Earle Grey *(1940 Production)*
	Cecil Trouncer *(1941 Production)*
	George Wilouby *(1945 Production)*
Superintendent Harvey	Duncan Blythe *(1938 Production)*
	Alan King *(1940 Production)*
	Cyril Gardiner *(1941 Production)*
Chief Inspector Dale	Vincent Curran *(1938 Production)*
	Hedley Rainie *(1940 Production)*
	Ivor Barnard *(1941 Production)*
	Rupert Chance *(1945 Production)*
Inspector Merritt	Cedric Johnson *(1938 Production)*
	Tommy Tweed *(1940 Production)*
	William Trent *(1941 Production)*
	Jim Pembleton *(1945 Production)*
Pryce	William Hughes *(1938 Production)*
	James Glennon *(1939 Production)*
	Laurence Burford *(1940 Production)*
	Edgar Norfolk *(1941 Production)*
	Alfred Bristowe *(1945 Production)*
Alec Rice	John Morley *(1938 Production)*
'Skid' Tyler	Hal Bryant *(1938 Production)*
	Anthony Holles *(1941 Production)*
	Eddie Finn *(1945 Production)*
Horace Daley	Dennis Folwell *(1938 Production)*
	Arthur Young *(1941 Production)*
	Bert Barton *(1945 Production)*
'Snow' Williams	Wortley Allen *(1938 Production)*
Dixie	Butts Marchant *(1938 Production)*
	Allan Jeayes *(1941 Production)*
Mrs Neddy	Mabel France *(1938 Production)*
	Elise Bernard *(1940 Production)*
Sergeant Leopold	John Bryning *(1941 Production)*
	Leo Stark *(1945 Production)*
'Other Actors'	Arundel Nixon *(1939 Production)*
	Yvonne Banard *(1939 Production)*
	Howard Smith *(1939 Production)*
	John Darcy *(1939 Production)*
	Frank Preddie *(1940 Production)*

SERIAL THRILLERS

Rex Devlin *(1940 Production)*
Alan Pearce *(1940 Production)*
Edwin Ross *(1940 Production)*

STORY:
A series of linked murders coincide with a number of unsolved diamond robberies in the north of England. A baffled police are forced to, 'send for Paul Temple'.

FIRST BROADCAST:

Broadcast Station:	BBC	ABC	CBC	3AR
EPISODE 1 *The Green Finger*	08/04/38	25/04/39	31/05/40	19/02/45
EPISODE 2 *Room Seven*	14/04/38	26/04/39	07/06/40	26/02/45
EPISODE 3 *Murder at Scotland Yard*	22/04/38	02/05/39	14/06/40	05/03/45
EPISODE 4 *Reply to a Murder*	29/05/38	03/05/39	21/06/40	12/03/45
EPISODE 5 *Action at the Inn*	06/05/38	09/05/39	28/06/40	19/03/45
EPISODE 6 *The First Penguin*	13/05/38	10/05/39	05/07/40	26/03/45
EPISODE 7 *The Knave of Diamonds*	20/05/38	17/05/39	12/07/40	02/04/45
EPISODE 8 *Exit the Knave*	27/05/38	24/05/39	19/07/40	09/04/45

SPECIAL
One Hour Abridgement   13/10/41   19/04/42

NOTES:
Australian listeners tuning into the 3LO network got to listen to the serial a few days earlier. They got episode one on 12th April 1939. Australian radio was not broadcast nationally, but regionally. So you got to listen to a drama on a different day depending on where in the country you lived. The above dates are the only complete set of transmission dates I've been able to pin down and refer to broadcasts on the 2BL network.

Also translated into Dutch by J C Van Der Horst for AVRO radio, as *Spreek Met Paul Vlaanderen en het Komt In Orde*. Broadcast in February 1939 and produced by Kommer Kleijn.

Novelised as *Send for Paul Temple* by Francis Durbridge (and John Thewes). Published by LONG in 1938.

PAUL TEMPLE: EPISODE GUIDE

Adapted for the stage as the play, *Send for Paul Temple* (1943) by Francis Durbridge.

Adapted for the cinema as the film, *Send for Paul Temple* (1946) directed by John Argyle.

2: *Paul Temple and the Front Page Men* (1938)
8 x 25 minute episodes (approx.)
1938 Production – BBC Radio
1939 Production – ABC Radio (Australia)
Written by Francis Durbridge
Producer: Martyn C Webster *(1938 Production)*
               Paul O'Loughlin *(1939 Production)*

CAST:

Paul Temple	Hugh Morton *(1938 Production)*
	Donnel Downey *(1939 Production)*
Steve	Bernadette Hodgson *(1938 Production)*
	Margerie Crosbie *(1939 Production)*
Sir Graham Forbes	Lester Mudditt *(1938 Production)*
	Ray Walsh *(1939 Production)*
Pryce	James Glennon *(1939 Production)*
'Other Actors'	Agnes Dobson *(1939 Production)*
	Edgar Wise *(1939 Production)*
	Kenneth Robertson *(1939 Production)*
	Frank Part *(1939 Production)*
	Edwin Aldridge *(1939 Production)*
	Dulcie Davenport *(1939 Production)*
	Cedric Trigg *(1939 Production)*
	Don Nicholson *(1939 Production)*
	Sydney Grandfeldt *(1939 Production)*

STORY:
Nobody knows the true identity of mysterious author, Andrea Fortune. However, her new book 'The Front Page Men', has taken the country by storm. The suspicions of the police are aroused when the words 'Front Page Men' start appearing at the scenes of several recent robberies. Then someone is murdered …

BROADCAST:

Broadcast Station:		BBC	ABC
EPISODE 1	Title Unknown	02/11/38	xx/09/39
EPISODE 2	*The Glass Bowl*	09/11/38	13/09/39

SERIAL THRILLERS

EPISODE 3	Title Unknown	16/11/38	19/09/39
EPISODE 4	*Paul Temple receives a warning*	23/11/38	26/09/39
EPISODE 5	Title Unknown	30/11/38	xx/10/39
EPISODE 6	Title Unknown	07/12/38	10/10/39
EPISODE 7	Title Unknown	14/12/38	xx/10/39
EPISODE 8	*The Front Page Men*	21/12/38	21/10/39
SPECIAL	One Hour Abridgement	xx/xx/42	

NOTES:
Also translated into Dutch by J C Van Der Horst for AVRO radio, as *Paul Vlaanderen En De Mannen Van De Frontpagina*. Broadcast in May 1939 and produced by Kommer Kleijn. The character of Mr Goldie was changed to Mr Ludo for this production.

Novelised as *Paul Temple and the Front Page Men* by Francis Durbridge (and Charles Hatton). Published by Long in 1939.

3: *News of Paul Temple* (1939)
6 x 25 minute episodes (approx.)
BBC Radio
Written by Francis Durbridge
Producer: Martyn C Webster

CAST:
Paul Temple	Hugh Morton *(1939 Production)* (Final appearance)
	Richard Williams *(1944 Production)*
Steve	Bernadette Hodgson *(1939 Production)*
	Lucille Lisle *(1944 Production)*
Sir Graham Forbes	Lester Mudditt *(1939 Production)*
	Laidman Browne *(1944 Production)*
Rex Bryant	Ivan Sampson (1939 Production) (Episode 1 only)
	Maurice Denham (1939 Production) (Episode 3 onwards)
	Lewis Stringer *(1944 Production)*
Editor	Dick Francis *(1939 Production)*
	Arthur Ridley *(1944 Production)*
Dr Ludwig Steiner	Maurice Denham *(1939 Production)* (Episode 1 only)
	Leo De Pokorny *(1939 Production)* (Episode 2 onwards)
Pryce	Clifford Bean *(1939 Production)*
Iris Archer	Diana Morrison *(1939 Production)*
	Grizelda Hervey *(1944 Production)*
Mrs Moffat	Mary O' Farrell *(1939 Production)* (Episode 1 only)
	Mona Harrison *(1939 Production)* (Episode 2 onwards)

PAUL TEMPLE: EPISODE GUIDE

	Molly Rankin *(1944 Production)*
David Lindsay	Geoffrey Wincott *(1939 Production)* (Episode 1 only)
	Ben Wright *(1939 Production)* (Episode 2 onwards)
	Basil Jones *(1944 Production)*
Laurence Van Draper	Norman Shelley *(1939 Production)* (Episode 1 only)
	Bruce Winston *(1939 Production)* (Episode 2 onwards)
	Alexander Sarner *(1944 Production)*
Major Guest	Cyril Nash *(1939 Production)*
	Cyril Gardiner *(1944 Production)*
Mrs Weston	Audrey Cameron *(1939 Production)* (Episode 1 only)
	Gwen Lewis *(1939 Production)* (Episode 2 onwards)
	Gladys Young *(1944 Production)*
Alec	Duncan McIntyre *(1944 Production)*
Ernie Weston	Dick Francis *(1939 Production)*
	Preston Lockwood *(1944 Production)*
Ben Collins	Ewart Scott *(1939 Production)*
	Frank Cochrane *(1944 Production)*
Inspector Fuller	Alan Howland *(1939 Production)*

STORY:
Temple is drawn into the shady world of espionage, when he is called in to help discover the true identity of mysterious secret agent, Z4.

BROADCAST:

Broadcast Station: BBC

EPISODE 1	*The Stage is Set*	13/11/39
EPISODE 2	*Concerning Z4*	20/11/39
EPISODE 3	*Instructions For Murder*	27/11/39
EPISODE 4	*Appointment with Danger*	04/12/39
EPISODE 5	*Mrs Moffat Receives a Visitor*	11/12/39
EPISODE 6	Title Unknown	18/12/39
SPECIAL	One Hour Abridgement	05/07/44

NOTES:
Also translated into Dutch by W Vogt for AVRO radio, as *Paul Vlaanderen En Het Z-4 Mysterie*. Broadcast from April 1940 and produced by Kommer Kleijn, only the first four episodes of this Dutch version were originally transmitted. Before episode five could be broadcast, the Netherlands was invaded by the Nazis and in the ensuing 'Battle of the Netherlands', AVRO radio was taken off the air (until 20 May). A second production was broadcast (as a standalone play) in December 1946 and a third in February 2009.

SERIAL THRILLERS

Novelised as *News of Paul Temple* by Francis Durbridge (and Charles Hatton). Published by Long in 1940.

Adapted for the cinema as the film, *Paul Temple's Triumph* (1950) directed by Maclean Rogers.

4: *Paul Temple Intervenes* (1942)
8 x 20 minute episodes (approx.)
1942 Production – BBC Radio
1944 Production – 3AR Radio (Australia)
1949 Production – 5CL Radio (Australia)
Written by Francis Durbridge
Producer: Martyn C Webster *(1942 Production)*
  Charles Wheeler *(1944 Production)*

CAST:
Paul Temple	Carl Bernard *(1942 Production)* (First appearance)
	Phillip Colledge *(1949 Production)*
Steve	Bernadette Hodgson *(1942 Production)* (Final appearance)
Sir Graham Forbes	Lester Mudditt *(1942 Production)*
	George Willouby *(1944 Production)*
Inspector Ross	Edgar Norfolk *(1942 Production)*
Superintendent Bradley	Godfrey Baseley *(1942 Production)*
Announcer	Alan Howland *(1942 Production)*
Sergeant Leopold	David Compton *(1942 Production)*
Dolly Fraser	Marjorie Westbury *(1942 Production)*
Sammy Wren	Hal Bryant *(1942 Production)*
Roger Storey	Sydney Tafler *(1942 Production)*
Ted Wilson	Chris Gittins *(1942 Production)*
Sergeant O'Brien	Vincent Curran *(1942 Production)*
Mrs Clarence	Mabel France *(1942 Production)*
Sir Felix Reybourn	Ronald Simpson *(1942 Production)*
Derek Slater	Philip Garston-Jones *(1942 Production)*
Rex Carlton	Geoffrey Wincott *(1942 Production)*
Maisie	Bessie Love *(1942 Production)*
'Other Actors'	Lyndall Barbour *(1944 Production)*
	Alfred Bristowe *(1944 Production)*
	George Hewlett *(1944 Production)*
	Ron Randell *(1944 Production)*

STORY:
A girl is found dead on the banks of the Thames – attached to her dress, a small square of card, bearing the name of 'The Marquis'. The girl's murder is

PAUL TEMPLE: EPISODE GUIDE

just one of many and with the police at a loss, the Home Secretary requests that Paul Temple intervenes.

BROADCAST:

Broadcast Station:	BBC	3AR	5CL
EPISODE 1 *The Marquis*	30/10/42	07/02/44	xx/07/49
EPISODE 2 *Considering Sir Felix Reybourn*	06/11/42	14/02/44	xx/xx/49
EPISODE 3 *Kellaway Manor*	13/11/42	21/02/44	xx/xx/49
EPISODE 4 *A Warning From the Marquis*	20/11/42	28/02/44	xx/xx/49
EPISODE 5 *Temple Keeps An Appointment*	27/11/42	06/03/44	xx/xx/49
EPISODE 6 *Above Suspicion*	04/12/42	13/03/44	xx/xx/49
EPISODE 7 *The October Hotel*	11/12/42	20/03/44	xx/xx/49
EPISODE 8 *Introducing ... The Marquis*	18/12/42	7/03/44	xx/xx/49

NOTES:
Also translated into Dutch by J C Van Der Horst for AVRO radio, as *Paul Vlaanderen Contra De Markies*. Broadcast in April 1947 and produced by Kommer Kleijn, it was the first *Temple* drama to broadcast in the Netherlands for a number of years. The previous one had been aborted partway through its run, following the Nazi invasion of the country in 1941.

Novelised as *Paul Temple Intervenes* by Francis Durbridge. Published by LONG in 1944.

Adapted for the cinema as the film, *Paul Temple Returns* (1952) directed by Maclean Rogers.

5: *Send for Paul Temple Again* (1945)
8 x 30 minute episodes (approx.)
BBC Radio
Written by Francis Durbridge
Producer: Martyn C Webster

CAST:
Paul Temple	Barry Morse
Steve	Marjorie Westbury

SERIAL THRILLERS

Sir Graham Forbes	Lester Mudditt
Sir Ernest Cranbury	Bryan Powley
Inspector Crane	Laidman Browne
Carl Latham	Ralph Truman
Mrs Trevelyan	Grizelda Hervey
Wilfrid Davis	Basil Jones
Spider Williams	Frank Tickle
Webb	Eric Lugg
Don Shaw	Alan Howland
Lord Flexdale	William Trent
Walter Day	George Owen
Maid	Hilda Davies

STORY:
The body of a famous actress is discovered on a train. Her death is part of the Rex murders – a spate of killings, which Temple is called in to investigate.

BROADCAST:
EPISODE 1	*Paul Temple Takes Over*	13/09/45
EPISODE 2	*Rex Strikes Again*	20/09/45
EPISODE 3	*Concerning Dr Kohima*	27/09/45
EPISODE 4	*Mr Carl Lathom is Perturbed*	04/10/45
EPISODE 5	*The Girl In Brown*	11/10/45
EPISODE 6	*Who Is Rex?*	18/10/45
EPISODE 7	*Temple Makes a Decision*	25/10/45
EPISODE 8	*Rex*	01/11/45

NOTES:
Also translated into Dutch for AVRO radio, as *Paul Vlaanderen En Het Rex Mysterie*. Broadcast in February 1946 and produced by Kommer Kleijn.

Novelised as *Send for Paul Temple Again* by Francis Durbridge (and Charles Hatton). Published by Long in 1948.

Adapted for the cinema as the film, *Calling Paul Temple* (1948) directed by Maclean Rogers.

6: *A Case For Paul Temple* (1946)
8 x 30 minute episodes (approx.)
BBC Radio
Written by Francis Durbridge
Producer: Martyn C Webster *(1946 Production)*
Patrick Rayner *(2011 Production)*

PAUL TEMPLE: EPISODE GUIDE

CAST:

Paul Temple	Howard Marion Crawford *(1946 Production)*
	Crawford Logan *(2011 Production)*
Steve	Marjorie Westbury *(1946 Production)*
	Gerda Stevenson *(2011 Production)*
Sir Graham Forbes	Lester Mudditt *(1946 Production)*
	Gareth Thomas *(2011 Production)*
Sir Gilbert Dryden	Alexander Sarner *(1946 Production)*
	Michael Mackenzie *(2011 Production)*
Captain O'Hara	Tommy Duggan *(1946 Production)*
	Robin Laing *(2011 Production)*
Superintendent Wetherby	Gilbert Davis *(1946 Production)*
	Richard Greenwood *(2011 Production)*
Major Peters	Cyril Gardiner *(1946 Production)*
	Greg Powrie *(2011 Production)*
Riley	Frank Partington *(1946 Production)*
Charles Kelvin	Olaf Olsen *(1946 Production)*
	Nick Underwood *(2011 Production)*
Sheila Baxter	Rita Vale *(1946 Production)*
Mary	Dorothy Smith *(1946 Production)*
	Eliza Langland *(2011 Production)*
Daisy	Vivienne Chatterton *(1946 Production)*
Melody	Sheila Baxter *(2011 Production)*
Snooker	Jimmy Chisolm *(2011 Production)*
Joy	Lucy Paterson *(2011 Production)*

STORY:

Temple is once again called in by Sir Graham Forbes to look into his latest case and help discover the identity of an enigmatic drug-dealer known only as 'Valentine'.

BROADCAST:

EPISODE 1	*Valentine*	07/02/46	24/08/11
EPISODE 2	*Steve Meets Captain O'Hara*	14/02/46	31/08/11
EPISODE 3	*Sir Gilbert Explains*	21/02/46	07/09/11
EPISODE 4	*Sir Gilbert is Surprised*	28/02/46	14/09/11
EPISODE 5	*Mr Layland Tells the Truth*	07/03/46	21/09/11
EPISODE 6	*Valentine Strikes*	14/03/46	28/09/11
EPISODE 7	*The Net Tightens*	21/03/46	05/10/11
EPISODE 8	*Paul Temple Meets Valentine*	28/03/46	12/10/11

NOTES:

Also translated into Dutch by J C Van Der Horst for AVRO radio, as *Paul*

SERIAL THRILLERS

Vlaanderen Grijpt in. Broadcast in October 1946 and produced by Kommer Kleijn.

Also translated into German for WDR radio, as *Ein Fall Fur Paul Temple.* Broadcast in February 1951 and produced by Eduard Hermann.

Also translated into Italian for RAI radio as *Paul Temple, il Roman Cers Poliziotto.* Broadcast in January 1953 and produced by Umberto Benedetto. For this version, the character of Steve Temple had her first name changed to Betty.

7: *Paul Temple and the Gregory Affair* (1946)
10 x 30 minute episodes (approx.)
BBC Radio
Written by Francis Durbridge
Producer: Martyn C Webster *(1946 Production)*
            Patrick Rayner *(2013 Production)*

CAST:
Paul Temple	Kim Peacock *(1946 Production)* (First appearance)
	Crawford Logan *(2013 Production)*
Steve	Marjorie Westbury *(1946 Production)*
	Gerda Stevenson *(2013 Production)*
Sir Graham Forbes	Lester Mudditt *(1946 Production)*
	Gareth Thomas *(2013 Production)*
Peter Davos	Olaf Olsen *(1946 Production)*
	Richard Greenwood *(2013 Production)*
Inspector Vosper	Arthur Ridley *(1946 Production)*
	Michael Mackenzie *(2013 Production)*
Coral Davis	Olive Gregg *(1946 Production)*
	Francesca Dymond *(2013 Production)*
Sir Donald Murdo	Duncan McIntyre *(1946 Production)*
	Simon Donaldson *(2013 Production)*
Charlie	Frank Partington *(1946 Production)*
	Greg Powrie *(2013 Production)*
Vic	Charles Leno *(1946 Production)*
Edward Day	Geoffrey Wincott *(1946 Production)*
	Nick Underwood *(2013 Production)*
Pat	Charles Maunsell *(1946 Production)*
Charles Zola	Alexander Sarner *(1946 Production)*
	Greg Powrie *(2013 Production)*
Kay Wiseman	Meg Fraser *(2013 Production)*
Miss Marcia	Eliza Langland *(2013 Production)*
Madison	Robin Laing *(2013 Production)*

PAUL TEMPLE: EPISODE GUIDE

STORY:
Paul and Steve join the search for the elusive criminal mastermind, known only as Mr Gregory.

BROADCAST:
EPISODE 1	*With the Compliments of Mr Gregory*	17/10/46	03/07/13
EPISODE 2	*Introducing Sir Donald Murdo*	24/10/46	10/07/13
EPISODE 3	*The Madrid*	31/10/46	17/07/13
EPISODE 4	*Mr Davos has an Alibi*	07/11/46	24/07/13
EPISODE 5	*Virginia Van Cleeve*	14/11/46	31/07/13
EPISODE 6	*Concerning Mr Zola*	21/11/46	07/08/13
EPISODE 7	*A Woman's Intuition*	28/11/46	14/08/13
EPISODE 8	*News of Mr Gregory*	05/12/46	21/08/13
EPISODE 9	*Millgate Steps*	12/12/46	04/09/13
EPISODE 10	*Presenting Mr Gregory*	19/12/46	11/09/13

NOTES:
Also translated into Dutch by J C Van Der Horst for AVRO radio, as *Paul Vlaanderen En Het Gregory Mysterie*. Broadcast in November 1947 and produced by Kommer Kleijn.

Also translated into German by Marianne de Barde for WDR radio, as *Paul Temple und die Affäre Gregory*. Broadcast in November 1949 and produced by Eduard Hermann and Fritz Schroder-Jahn.

Also translated into Italian by Ippolito Pizzetti for RAI radio as *Paul Temple e il Caso Gregory*. Broadcast in March 1960 and produced by Giacomo Colli.

8: *Paul Temple and Steve* (1947)
8 x 30 minute episodes (approx.)
BBC Radio
Written by Francis Durbridge
Producer: Martyn C Webster *(1947 Production)*
            Patrick Rayner *(2010 Production)*

CAST:
Paul Temple	Kim Peacock *(1947 Production)*
	Crawford Logan *(2010 Production)*
Steve	Marjorie Westbury *(1947 Production)*
	Gerda Stevenson *(2010 Production)*
Sir Graham Forbes	Lester Mudditt *(1947 Production)*
	Gareth Thomas *(2010 Production)*
David Nelson	Martin Lewis *(1947 Production)*

SERIAL THRILLERS

	Jimmy Chisholm *(2010 Production)*
Mary Hamilton	Joan Clement Ross *(1947 Production)*
	Eliza Langland *(2010 Production)*
Philip Kaufman	Richard Williams *(1947 Production)*
	Nick Underwood *(2010 Production)*
Charlie	Kenneth Morgan *(1947 Production)*
	Greg Powrie *(2010 Production)*
Henry Worth	Olaf Olsen *(1947 Production)*
	Greg Powrie *(2010 Production)*
Ross Morgan	Alan Pearce *(1947 Production)*
Braddock	Neville Mapp *(1947 Production)*
Inspector Perry	Andrew Crawford *(1947 Production)*
	Michael Mackenzie *(2010 Production)*
Billie Chandler	Vivienne Chatterton *(1947 Production)*
	Emma Currie *(2010 Production)*
Mrs Forester	Elizabeth Maude *(1947 Production)*
	Candida Benson *(2010 Production)*
Joseph	Alexander Sarner *(1947 Production)*
	Richard Greenwood *(2010 Production)*
Ed Bellamy	Tommy Duggan *(1947 Production)*
	Robin Laing *(2010 Production)*
Sergeant O'Day	Lionel Stevens *(1947 Production)*
	John Paul Hurley *(2010 Production)*
Waiter	Frank Atkinson *(1947 Production)*
Waitress	Lucy Paterson *(2010 Production)*

STORY:
Paul is called in by Scotland Yard to help hunt down the notorious Doctor Belasco – the great criminal mastermind.

BROADCAST:

EPISODE 1	*The Notorious Dr Belasco*	30/03/47	11/06/10
EPISODE 2	*27a Berkeley House Place*	06/04/47	18/06/10
EPISODE 3	*Presenting Ed Bellamy*	13/04/47	25/06/10
EPISODE 4	*Mrs Forester is Surprised*	20/04/47	02/07/10
EPISODE 5	*David Nelson Explains*	27/04/47	09/07/10
EPISODE 6	*Steve's Intuition*	04/05/47	16/07/10
EPISODE 7	*The Suspects*	11/05/47	23/07/10
EPISODE 8	*The Final Curtain*	18/05/47	30/07/10

NOTES:
Also translated into Dutch by J C Van Der Horst for AVRO radio, as *Paul Vlaanderen En Ina*. Broadcast in October 1948 and produced by Kommer Kleijn.

PAUL TEMPLE: EPISODE GUIDE

9: *Mr and Mrs Paul Temple* (1947)
45 minute episode (approx.)
BBC Radio
Written by Francis Durbridge
Producer: Martyn C Webster

CAST:

Paul Temple	Kim Peacock
Steve	Marjorie Westbury
Harry McRoy	Tommy Duggan
Kurt Wagner	Olaf Olsen
Alfred Wintermann	Alexander Sarner
Diana Long	Diana King
Clerk	Lionel Stevens

STORY:
While on holiday, Paul and Steve become lost in a dense fog and stumble across a strange and mysterious mansion.

BROADCAST:
SPECIAL 45- Minute Episode   23/11/47

NOTES:
Also translated into Dutch for AVRO radio, as *De Hear en Merow Paul Vlaanderen*. Broadcast in April 1948 and produced by Kommer Kleijn.

10: *Paul Temple and the Sullivan Mystery* (1947)
8 x 30 minute episodes (approx.)
BBC Radio
Written by Francis Durbridge
Producer: Martyn C Webster *(1947 Production)*
              Patrick Rayner *(2006 Production)*

CAST:

Paul Temple	Kim Peacock *(1947 Production)*
	Crawford Logan *(2006 Production)*
Steve	Marjorie Westbury *(1947 Production)*
	Gerda Stevenson *(2006 Production)*
Sir Graham Forbes	Lester Mudditt *(1947 Production)*
	Gareth Thomas *(2006 Production)*
Miss Fraser	Vivienne Chatterson *(1947 Production)*
	Eliza Langland *(2006 Production)*

SERIAL THRILLERS

Joyce Raymond	Margaret Inglis *(1947 Production)*
	Lucy Paterson *(2006 Production)*
Victor Armstrong	Laidman Browne *(1947 Production)*
	Michael Mackenzie *(2006 Production)*
Inspector Fowler	Stanley Groome *(1947 Production)*
Constantine	Sid James *(1947 Production)*
Rossetti	Ian Sadler *(1947 Production)*
	Greg Powrie *(2006 Production)*
Harold Darwin	Cyril Gardiner *(1947 Production)*
	Richard Greenwood *(2006 Production)*
Olaf Schreider	Olaf Olsen *(1947 Production)*
	Nick Underwood *(2006 Production)*
Charlie	Kenneth Morgan *(1947 Production)*
	Greg Powrie *(2006 Production)*
Hakim	Leo Dr Pokorny *(1947 Production)*
Zoltan Bahri	Leslie Perrins *(1947 Production)*
	Angus MacInnes *(2006 Production)*
Gustav Valkerie	Fritz Kremm *(1947 Production)*
Colonel Marquand	Tommy Duggan *(1947 Production)*
	Angus MacInnes *(2006 Production)*
Sidney Jeans	Tucker McGuire *(1947 Production)*
	Wendy Seager *(2006 Production)*
Tom Durant	Richard Williams *(1947 Production)*
	John Paul Hurley *(2006 Production)*
'Other Actors'	Frank Partington *(1947 Production)*
	Basil Jones *(1947 Production)*
	Beryl Calder *(1947 Production)*
	Joan Clement Scott *(1947 Production)*
	Charles Leno *(1947 Production)*
	Andrew Chruchman *(1947 Production)*
	Alec Ross *(1947 Production)*
	Arthur Ridley *(1947 Production)*
	Betty Baskomb *(1947 Production)*
	Peter Claughton *(1947 Production)*
	Harry Hutchinson *(1947 Production)*
	Edddy Read *(1947 Production)*
	Norman Webb *(1947 Production)*
	George Owen *(1947 Production)*
	David Kossoff *(1947 Production)*

STORY:
Paul and Steve are on holiday in Egypt, when a mysterious pair of spectacles draws them into another adventure.

PAUL TEMPLE: EPISODE GUIDE

BROADCAST:
EPISODE 1	*Having a Wonderful Time*	01/12/47	07/08/06
EPISODE 2	*Interlude at Augusta*	08/12/47	14/08/06
EPISODE 3	*Introducing Colonel Marquand*	15/12/47	21/08/06
EPISODE 4	*Cairo*	22/12/47	04/09/06
EPISODE 5	*The House of Bahri*	29/12/47	11/09/06
EPISODE 6	*A Message from Sir Graham*	05/01/48	18/09/06
EPISODE 7	*Mr Darwin Entertains*	12/01/48	25/09/06
EPISODE 8	*Still Having a Wonderful Time*	19/01/48	02/10/06

NOTES:
Also translated into Dutch by J C Van Der Horst for AVRO radio, as *Paul Vlaanderen En Het Sullivan Mysterie*. Broadcast in November 1949 and produced by Kommer Kleijn.

Novelised as *East of Algiers* by Francis Durbridge (and Douglas Rutherford). Published by Hodder & Stoughton in 1959.

11: *Paul Temple and the Curzon Case* **(1948)**
8 x 30 minute episodes (approx.)
BBC Radio
Written by Francis Durbridge
Producer: Martyn C Webster

CAST:
Paul Temple	Kim Peacock
Steve	Marjorie Westbury
Sir Graham Forbes	Lester Mudditt
Lord Westerby	Leslie Perrins
Peter Malo	Kenneth Morgan
Doctor Stuart	Duncan McIntyre
Inspector Morgan	Philip Cunningham
Diana Maxwell	Grizelda Hervey
Tom Doyle	Hugh Manning
Charlie	Billy Thatcher

STORY:
When the children of a wealthy stockbroker go missing on their way home from school, the only clue is a cricket bat.

BROADCAST:
EPISODE 1	*Title Unknown*	07/12/48
EPISODE 2	*Welcome to Dulworth Bay*	14/12/48

SERIAL THRILLERS

EPISODE 3	*Title Unknown*	21/12/48
EPISODE 4	*Miss Maxwell keeps an Appointment*	28/12/48
EPISODE 5	*Presenting Carl Walters*	04/01/49
EPISODE 6	*A Message for Charlie*	11/01/49
EPISODE 7	*The Deciding Factor*	18/01/49
EPISODE 8	*Curzon*	25/01/49

NOTES:
Also translated into Dutch by J C Van Der Horst for AVRO radio, as *Paul Vlaanderen En Het Curzon Mysterie*. Broadcast in October 1950 and produced by Kommer Kleijn.

Also translated into German for WDR radio, as *Paul Temple und der Fall Curzon*. Broadcast in 1951 and produced by Eduard Hermann.

Novelised as *The Curzon Case* by Francis Durbridge. Published by Coronet in 1972.

12: *Paul Temple and the Madison Mystery* (1949)
8 x 30 minute episodes (approx.)
BBC Radio
Written by Francis Durbridge
Producer: Martyn C Webster *(1949 and 1955 Productions)*
              Patrick Rayner *(2008 Production)*

CAST:
Paul Temple	Kim Peacock *(1949 Production)*
	Peter Coke *(1955 Production)*
	Crawford Logan *(2008 Production)*
Steve	Marjorie Westbury *(1949 and 1955 Productions)*
	Gerda Stevenson *(2008 Production)*
Sir Graham Forbes	Lester Mudditt *(1949 and 1955 Productions)*
	Gareth Thomas *(2008 Production)*
Charlie	Desmond Carrington *(1949 Production)*
	James Beattie *(1955 Production)*
	Greg Powrie *(2008 Production)*
Sam Portland	Macdonald Parke *(1949 Production)*
	John Gabriel *(1955 Production)*
	Angus MacInnes *(2008 Production)*
Stella Portland	Catherine Campbell *(1949 Production)*
	Marjorie Mars *(1955 Production)*
	Emma Currie *(2008 Production)*
George Kelly	John McLaren *(1949 Production)*
	Stan Thomason *(1955 Production)*

PAUL TEMPLE: EPISODE GUIDE

	Robin Laing *(2008 Production)*
Percy	Stanley Groome *(1949 Production)*
	Brian Haines *(1955 Production)*
Hubert Greene	Ivan Samson *(1949 Production)*
	Richard Williams *(1955 Production)*
	Richard Greenwood *(2008 Production)*
Mark Kendell	Andrew Faulds *(1949 Production)*
	Michael Turner *(1955 Production)*
	Nick Underwood *(2008 Production)*
Moira Portland	Wendy Gibb *(1949 Production)*
	Peggy Hassard *(1955 Production)*
	Lucy Paterson *(2008 Production)*
Purser	Hugh Manning *(1949 Production)*
	Richard Waring *(1955 Production)*
Chris Boyer	Donald Gray *(1949 Production)*
	Simon Lack *(1955 Production)*
	Nick Underwood *(2008 Production)*
George Denson	Raf de la Torre *(1949 Production)*
	Richard Waring *(1955 Production)*
Archie Brooks	John Dodsworth *(1949 Production)*
	Derek Hart *(1955 Production)*
	Greg Powrie *(2008 Production)*
Maitland	David Enders *(1949 Production)*
Sergeant Carver	Ellis Chesney *(1949 Production)*
	Geoffrey Matthews *(1955 Production)*
Inspector Vosper	Arthur Ridley *(1949 Production)*
	T St John Barry *(1955 Production)*
	Michael Mackenzie *(2008 Production)*
Doctor Elzec	Olaf Olsen *(1949 Production)*
	John Carson *(1955 Production)*
	Greg Powrie *(2008 Production)*
Eileen Greene	Grizelda Hervey *(1949 and 1955 Productions)*
	Eliza Langland *(2008 Production)*
Inspector James	Alan A Aldridge *(1949 Production)*
	Manning Wilson *(1955 Production)*
Owen Scaley	Malcolm Farquhar *(1949 Production)*
	Hugh David *(1955 Production)*
Telephone Operator	Gladys Spencer *(1949 Production)*
	Michael Turner *(1955 Production)*
Harry	Geoffrey Bond *(1949 Production)*
	Richard Waring *(1955 Production)*
Don Alfaro	Ian Sadler *(1949 and 1955 Productions)*
	Jimmy Chisholm *(2008 Production)*

SERIAL THRILLERS

Bennett	Brian Haines *(1955 Production)*
Sergeant Finley	Geoffrey Matthews *(1955 Production)*
Sergeant Baker	Hugh David *(1955 Production)*
Sergeant	Michael Mackenzie *(2008 Production)*
'Other Actors'	Denis Lehrer *(1949 Production)*
	Frank Coburn *(1949 Production)*
	Belle Chrystal *(1955 Production)*
	Edward Jewesbury *(1955 Production)*
	Peter Claughton *(1955 Production)*
	Rolf Lefebvre *(1955 Production)*
	Mairhi Russell *(1955 Production)*

STORY:
Paul and Steve are returning from New York aboard a luxury liner, when millionaire Sam Portland is found dead, floating in the ship's swimming pool.

BROADCAST:

EPISODE 1	*Penny For Your Thoughts*	12/10/49	20/06/55	16/05/08
EPISODE 2	*The Manilla*	19/10/49	27/06/55	23/05/08
EPISODE 3	*Eileen*	26/10/49	04/07/55	30/05/08
EPISODE 4	*Hubert Greene Entertains*	02/11/49	11/07/55	06/06/08
EPISODE 5	*Steve Takes Over*	09/11/49	18/07/55	13/06/08
EPISODE 6	*Just a Red Herring*	16/11/49	25/07/55	20/06/08
EPISODE 7	*The Four Suspects*	23/11/49	01/08/55	27/06/08
EPISODE 8	*Introducing Madison*	30/11/49	08/08/55	04/07/08

NOTES:
Also translated into Dutch by J C Van Der Horst for AVRO radio, as *Paul Vlaanderen En Het Madison Mysterie*. Broadcast in January 1951 and produced by Kommer Kleijn.

Also translated into German for WDR radio, as *Paul Temple und der Fall Madison*. Broadcast in 1955 and produced by Eduard Hermann.

Novelised as *Paul Temple and the Madison Case* by Francis Durbridge. Published by Hodder & Stoughton in 1988.

13: *The Night of the Twenty-Seventh* (1949)
60 minutes (approx.)
BBC Radio
Written by Edward J Mason
Producer: Martyn C Webster

PAUL TEMPLE: EPISODE GUIDE

CAST:

Paul Temple	Kim Peacock
Steve	Marjorie Westbury
Dick Barton	Duncan Carse
PC 49	Brian Reece
Philip Odell	Robert Beatty
Mrs Dale	Ellis Powell
Dr Dale	Douglas Burbridge
The Man In Black	Valentine Dyall
Silas Ephraim	Leon Quartermane
Walter Leesham	Max Adrian
Servant	Malcolm Hayes

STORY:
A bizarre Christmas special from the BBC, in which all of Britain's most famous radio characters (from various different programmes) team up to foil the machinations of the insane Mr Silas Ephraim.

BROADCAST:
SPECIAL 27/12/49

14: *Paul Temple and the Vandyke Affair* **(1950)**
8 x 30 minute episodes (approx.)
1950 and 1959 Productions – BBC Radio
1952 Production – 5CL Radio (Australia)
Written by Francis Durbridge
Producer: Martyn C Webster *(1950 and 1959 Productions)*

CAST:

Paul Temple	Kim Peacock *(1950 Production)*
	George Randall *(1952 Production)*
	Peter Coke *(1959 Production)*
Steve	Marjorie Westbury
Sir Graham Forbes	Lester Mudditt *(1950 Production)*
	Richard Williams *(1959 Production)*
Mary Desmond	Joan Hart *(1950 Production)*
	June Tobin *(1959 Production)*
Terry Palmer	Peter Coke *(1950 Production)*
	Peter Wilde *(1959 Production)*
Philip Droste	Roger Delgado *(1950 Production)*
	Simon Lack *(1959 Production)*
Roger Shelly	Richard Hurndall

SERIAL THRILLERS

Louis France	Olaf Olsen *(1950 Production)*
	Rolf Lefebvre *(1959 Production)*
Marian Faber	Susan Burette *(1950 Production)*
	Betty Hardy *(1959 Production)*
Bill McCall	Tommy Duggan *(1950 Production)*
	John Scott *(1959 Production)*
Vanessa Droste	Grizelda Hervey
Charlie	Michael Harding *(1950 Production)*
	James Beattie *(1959 Production)*
Inspector Eden	Donald Gray *(1950 Production)*
	Frederick Treves *(1959 Production)*
'Other Actors'	John Morgan *(1952 Production)*
	Betty Randall *(1952 Production)*
	Shirley Davis *(1952 Production)*
	Anne Mitchell *(1952 Production)*
	Roy Laywood *(1952 Production)*
	John Gray *(1952 Production)*
	Syd Conabere *(1952 Production)*
	Bettine Kaufmann *(1952 Production)*
	Joyce Swadesir *(1952 Production)*

STORY:
Paul is contacted by Scotland Yard, following the disappearance of 18-month old, Sarah Desmond and her babysitter, Ms Millicent. The only clue – an enigmatic telephone call from the mysterious Mr Vandyke.

BROADCAST:

Broadcast Station:	BBC	5CL	BBC
EPISODE 1 *The Sitter-In*	30/10/50	20/10/52	01/01/59
EPISODE 2 *The Marlow Incident*	06/11/50	2?/10/52	08/01/59
EPISODE 3 *Introducing Mr Droste*	13/11/50	xx/xx/52	15/01/59
EPISODE 4 *Boulevard Seminaire*	20/11/50	xx/xx/52	22/01/59
EPISODE 5 *Roger Shelley Makes a Suggestion*	27/11/50	xx/xx/52	29/01/59
EPISODE 6 *Suspect No 1*	04/12/50	xx/xx/52	05/02/59
EPISODE 7 *Steve Entertains*	11/12/50	xx/xx/52	12/02/59
EPISODE 8			

Presenting Mr Vandyke 18/12/50   xx/xx/52   19/02/59
NOTES:
Also translated into Dutch by J C Van Der Horst for AVRO radio, as *Paul Vlaanderen En Het Van Dyke Mysterie*. Broadcast in September 1951 and produced by Kommer Kleijn.

Also translated into German for WDR radio, as *Paul Temple und der Fall Vandyke*. Broadcast in 1953 and produced by Eduard Hermann.

15: *Paul Temple and the Jonathan Mystery* (1951)
8 x 30 minute episodes (approx.)
BBC Radio
Written by Francis Durbridge
Producer: Martyn C Webster

CAST:
Paul Temple	Kim Peacock *(1951 Production)*
	Peter Coke *(1963 Production)*
Steve	Marjorie Westbury
Charlie	Frank Partington *(1951 Production)*
	James Beattie *(1963 Production)*
Sir Graham Forbes	Lester Mudditt *(1951 Production)*
	James Thomason *(1963 Production)*
Reggie Mackintosh	Duncan McIntyre *(1951 Production)*
	Simon Lack *(1963 Production)*
Red Harris	John Baddely *(1963 Production)*
Mavis Russell	Rita Veil *(1951 Production)*
	Isabel Rennie *(1963 Production)*
Mark Elliott	Martin Lewis *(1951 Production)*
	William Fox *(1963 Production)*
Rudolf Charles	Olaf Olsen *(1951 Production)*
	Anthony Hall *(1963 Production)*
Dinah Nelson	Belle Chrystal *(1951 Production)*
	Valerie Kirkbright *(1963 Production)*
Max Wyman	Frederick Treves *(1963 Production)*
Inspector Gerrard	Stanley Gould *(1951 Production)*
	Rolf Lefebvre *(1963 Production)*
Mrs Gulliver	Vivienne Chatterton *(1963 Production)*
Helen Ferguson	Grizelda Hervey
Richard Ferguson	David Peel *(1951 Production)*
	Gabriel Woolf *(1963 Production)*
Robert Ferguson	George Margo *(1951 Production)*
	John Glen *(1963 Production)*

SERIAL THRILLERS

Mrs Parsons	Eva Stuart *(1963 Production)*
Simo	Lee Fox *(1963 Production)*
Dobby	David Spenser *(1963 Production)*
Peggy	Jo Manning Wilson *(1963 Production)*
Messenger	Peter Bartlett *(1963 Production)*
Porter	Frank Partington *(1963 Production)*
'Other Actors'	Gabrielle Blunt *(1951 Production)*
	Roger Delgado *(1951 Production)*
	Charles Lefeaux *(1951 Production)*
	Harry Hutchinson *(1951 Production)*
	Brian Poley *(1951 Production)*
	Glyn Dearman *(1963 Production)*
	Alan Haines *(1963 Production)*
	Lewis Stringer *(1963 Production)*

STORY:
Returning from a trip to New York, the Temples are called in to investigate the murder of Richard Ferguson, found shot dead in his rooms at Oxford University.

BROADCAST:
EPISODE 1	*The Fergusons*	10/05/51	14/10/63
EPISODE 2	*That Good Old Intuition*	17/05/51	21/10/63
EPISODE 3	*The Ring*	24/05/51	28/10/63
EPISODE 4	*The Encounter*	31/05/51	04/11/63
EPISODE 5	*Concerning Richard Ferguson*	07/06/51	11/11/63
EPISODE 6	*A Surprise For Mavis Russell*	14/06/51	18/11/63
EPISODE 7	*An Invitation for Mr Elliot*	21/06/51	25/11/63
EPISODE 8	*Jonathan*	28/06/51	02/12/63

NOTES:
Also translated into Dutch by J C Van Der Horst for AVRO radio, as *Paul Vlaanderen En Het Jonathan Mysterie*. Broadcast in January 1953 and produced by Kommer Kleijn.

Also translated into German for WDR radio, as *Paul Temple und der Fall Jonathan*. Broadcast in 1954 and produced by Eduard Hermann.

Also translated into Italian by Franca Cancogni for RAI radio, as *Chi e Jonathan?* broadcast in April 1971 and produced by Umberto Benedetto.

PAUL TEMPLE: EPISODE GUIDE

16: *Paul Temple and Steve Again* **(1953)**
60 minute episode (approx.)
BBC Radio
Written by Francis Durbridge
Producer: Martyn C Webster

CAST:

Paul Temple	Kim Peacock (Final appearance)
Steve	Marjorie Westbury
Sir Graham Forbes	Lester Mudditt
Mr Reagan	Ralf Lefebvre
Inspector Marlow	Ivan Samson
Dr Schumann	Anthony Jacobs
Katherine Davis	Mary Williams
Inspector Kendal	Norman Claridge
Dan White	Gerald Green
Papa Bendix	Cyril Shaps
Miss Wilton	Susan Richmond
Daisy	Daphne Maddox
Mavis	Lisa Sibley
Charlie	James Beattie
Sergeant Colfrod	Lee Fox
'Other Actors'	John Cazabon
	Stanley Groome
	Douglas Hayes
	Arthur Lawrence
	Susan Neil
	Aubrey Richards
	Margaret Ward

STORY:
Temple joins the police in their investigation of the great Westfield robbery, in which a large amount of valuable jewels have been stolen. The perpetrator is believed to be the mysterious Harry King, but when King's body is found on a stretch of the Cornish coast, it seems that the case will remain unsolved.

BROADCAST:
SPECIAL   60- Minute Episode   08/04/53

NOTES:
Also translated into Dutch by Jan Van Ees for AVRO radio, as *Het Mysterie van de Westfield Juwelen*. Broadcast in January 1954 and produced by Kommer Kleijn.

SERIAL THRILLERS

17: *Paul Temple and the Gilbert Case* (1954)
8 x 30 minute episodes (approx.)
BBC Radio
Written by Francis Durbridge
Producer: Martyn C Webster

CAST:

Paul Temple	Peter Coke
Steve	Marjorie Westbury
Sir Graham Forbes	Lester Mudditt *(1954 Production)*
	Richards Williams *(1959 Production)*
Inspector Kingston	Duncan McIntyre
Charlie	James Beattie
Wilfred Stirling	Charles Leno *(1954 Production)*
	Douglas Storm *(1959 Production)*
Betty Wayne	Grizelda Hervey *(1954 Production)*
	Eva Stuart *(1959 Production)*
Lance Reynolds	Richards Williams *(1954 Production)*
	Simon Lack *(1959 Production)*
Lyn Ferguson	Peggy Hassard *(1954 Production)*
	June Tobin *(1959 Production)*
Louis Fabian	Olaf Olsen *(1954 Production)*
	John Hollis *(1959 Production)*
Johnson	Alec Ross *(1954 Production)*
	George Hagan *(1959 Production)*

STORY:
When Brenda Stirling is found dead on a London bombsite, her boyfriend Howard Gilbert is arrested for her murder. It is up to Paul Temple to save an innocent man from the gallows and find the real perpetrator, before it is too late.

BROADCAST:

EPISODE 1	*The Unlucky One*	29/03/54	22/11/59
EPISODE 2	*The Third Shoe*	05/04/54	29/11/59
EPISODE 3	*Peter Galina*	12/04/54	06/12/59
EPISODE 4	*La Martella*	19/04/54	13/12/59
EPISODE 5	*That Good Old Intuition*	26/04/54	20/12/59
EPISODE 6	*A Warning From Ms Wayne*	03/05/54	27/12/59
EPISODE 7	*The Note*	10/05/54	03/01/60
EPISODE 8	*The Guilty Party / Mr Hamilton*	17/05/54	10/01/60

PAUL TEMPLE: EPISODE GUIDE

NOTES:
Episode 8 of the 1954 Production was called 'The Guilty Party'. The 1959 production retitled the episode, 'Mr Hamilton'.

Also translated into Dutch by Jan Van Ees for AVRO radio, as *Paul Vlaanderen En Het Gilbert Mysterie*. Broadcast in October 1954 and produced by Kommer Kleijn.

Also translated into German by Marianne de Barde for WDR radio, as *Paul Temple und der Fall Gilbert*. Broadcast in 1956 and produced by Eduard Hermann.

18: *Paul Temple and the Lawrence Affair* **(1956)**
8 x 30 minute episodes (approx.)
BBC Radio
Written by Francis Durbridge
Producer: Martyn C Webster

CAST:

Paul Temple	Peter Coke
Steve	Marjorie Westbury
Sir Graham Forbes	Lester Mudditt
Inspector Vosper	Arthur Ridley
Inspector Ivor	Manning Wilson
Charlie	James Beattie
Salty West	Brewster Mason
Brian Dexter	Simon Lack
Johnny Teako	Brian Haines
Linda Teako	Belle Chrystal
Ernest de Silva	John Gabriel
Julie de Silva	Marjorie Mars
Mary Gardner	Dorothy Holmes-Gore
Burford	Allan McClelland
Barker	Hamilton Dyce
Sgt Thomas	Gordon Davies
Mrs Purdie	Molly Rankin
Bob Gardner	Leonard Trolley
Sir Carlton Ross	Richard Williams
Sylvia Ross	Cecile Chevreau
Stan Walters	Denis Goacher
Foster	Geoffrey Hodson
'Other Actors'	Greta Gouriet
	Annette Kelly
	George Merritt

SERIAL THRILLERS

Jeffrey Segal
James Thomason
Michael Turner

STORY:
A pleasant coastal holiday is derailed, when the Temples' boat is opened fire upon by an unknown gunman.

BROADCAST:
EPISODE 1	*The Little Things*	11/04/56
EPISODE 2	*Salty West*	18/04/56
EPISODE 3	*The Handbag*	25/04/56
EPISODE 4	*Return to Downburgh*	02/05/56
EPISODE 5	*A Present for Steve*	09/05/56
EPISODE 6	*News from Sir Graham*	16/05/56
EPISODE 7	*Another Suspect*	23/05/56
EPISODE 8	*Return to London*	30/05/56

NOTES:
Also translated into Dutch by Jan Van Ees for AVRO radio, as *Paul Vlaanderen En Het Lawrence Mysterie*. Broadcast in September 1956 and produced by Kommer Kleijn.

Also translated into German for WDR radio, as *Paul Temple und der Fall Lawrence*. Broadcast in 1958 and produced by Eduard Hermann.

19: *Paul Temple and the Spencer Affair* (1957)
8 x 30 minute episodes (approx.)
BBC Radio
Written by Francis Durbridge
Producer: Martyn C Webster

CAST:
Paul Temple	Peter Coke
Steve	Marjorie Westbury
Sir Graham Forbes	Lester Mudditt (Last appearance)
Charlie	James Beattie
Rupert Dreisler	Brewster Mason
Clutch Brompton	Lockwood West
Peter Wallace	Frank Partington
Adrian Frost	Simon Lack
Judy Milton	June Tobin
Inspector Vosper	Hugh Manning

PAUL TEMPLE: EPISODE GUIDE

Terry Gibson
Pete Roberts
Eric Lansdale
Ritchie
Warren
Andre Reynaud

Isabel Dean
Thomas Heathcote
John Graham
Hamilton Dyce
James Thomason
Denis Goacher

STORY:
Drama student Mary Dreisler is found dead in her flat – murdered. Called in by the girl's father, Paul must investigate a crime for which there is no evident motive or reason.

BROADCAST:
EPISODE 1 *My Heart and Harry*   13/11/57
EPISODE 2 *Concerning Judy Milton*   20/11/57
EPISODE 3 *Introducing Pete Roberts*   27/11/57
EPISODE 4 *That Old Intuition*   04/12/57
EPISODE 5 *A Surprise for Pete Roberts* 11/12/57
EPISODE 6 *Home Again*   18/12/57
EPISODE 7 *Dinner at the Stardust*   25/12/57
EPISODE 8 *A Party of Four*   01/01/58

NOTES:
Also translated into Dutch by Jan Van Ees for AVRO radio, as *Paul Vlaanderen En Het Spencer Mysterie*. Broadcast in January 1958 and produced by Kommer Kleijn.

Also translated into German for WDR radio, as *Paul Temple und der Fall Spencer*. Broadcast in 1959 and produced by Eduard Hermann.

Also translated into Italian by Franca Cancogni for RAI radio, as *Cabaret*. Broadcast in March 1977 and produced by Umberto Benedetto.

20: *Paul Temple and the Conrad Case* (1959)
8 x 30 minute episodes (approx.)
BBC Radio
Written by Francis Durbridge
Producer: Martyn C Webster

CAST:
Paul Temple
Steve
Sir Graham Forbes
Herr Breckshaft

Peter Coke
Marjorie Westbury
Richard Williams
Jeffrey Segal

SERIAL THRILLERS

Mrs Weldon	Virginia Winter
June	June Tobin
Elliot France	James Thomason
Gerda	Hilda Schroder
Madame Klein	Dorothy Holmes-Gore
Denis Harper	John Bryning
Elsa Countess Dekker	Joan Matheson
Doctor Conrad	Rolf Lefebvre
Joyce Gunter	Dorothy Smith
Fritz Gunter	George Hagan
Captain Williams	John Bennett
Inspector Vosper	Hugh Manning
Inspector Digby	Peter Wilde
Paddy	John Hollis
Betty Conrad	Jane Jordan Rogers

STORY:
Betty Conrad has vanished from her finishing school in Bavaria. Paul and Steve join the case, but the only clue is a small cocktail stick.

BROADCAST:
EPISODE 1	*The Man from Munich*	02/03/59
EPISODE 2	*Concerning Elliot France*	09/03/59
EPISODE 3	*Hotel Reumer*	16/03/59
EPISODE 4	*A Visit to Innsbruck*	23/03/59
EPISODE 5	*A Dry Martini*	30/03/59
EPISODE 6	*Concerning Captain Smith*	06/04/59
EPISODE 7	*Coffee for Miss Conrad*	13/04/59
EPISODE 8	*Person Unknown*	20/04/59

NOTES:
Also translated into Dutch by Jan Van Ees for AVRO radio, as *Paul Vlaanderen En Het Conrad Mysterie*. Broadcast in September 1959 and produced by Dick Van Putten.

Also translated into German by Marianne de Barde for WDR radio, as *Paul Temple und der Fall Conrad*. Broadcast in 1959 and produced by Eduard Hermann.

Also translated into Italian by Franca Cancogni for RAI radio, as *La Ragazza Scomparsa*. Broadcast in February 1975 and produced by Umberto Benedetto.

PAUL TEMPLE: EPISODE GUIDE

21: *Paul Temple and the Margo Mystery* **(1961)**
8 x 30 minute episodes (approx.)
BBC Radio
Written by Francis Durbridge
Producer: Martyn C Webster

CAST:
Paul Temple	Peter Coke
Steve	Marjorie Westbury
Sir Graham Forbes	James Thomason
Mrs Fletcher	Joan Matheson
George Kelburn	Julian Summers
Superintendent Rain	Simon Lack
Tony Wyman	John Rollason
Linda Kelburn	June Tobin
Doctor Benkhari	Mary Wimbush
Mike Langdon	Tommy Duggan
Larry Cross	Hugh Manning
Charlie	James Beattie

STORY:
Sir Graham Forbes sends for Paul Temple yet again, to help investigate a drug-running operation.

BROADCAST:
EPISODE 1	*The Coat*	01/01/61
EPISODE 2	*Concerning Ted Angus*	08/01/61
EPISODE 3	*A Change of Mind*	15/01/61
EPISODE 4	*Bill Fletcher's Story*	22/01/61
EPISODE 5	*Breakwater House*	29/01/61
EPISODE 6	*Mainly About Wyman*	05/02/61
EPISODE 7	*A Time to Worry*	12/02/61
EPISODE 8	*The Visitor*	19/02/61

NOTES:
Also translated into German by Marianne de Barde for WDR radio, as *Paul Temple und der Fall Margo*. Broadcast in 1961 and produced by Eduard Hermann.

Also translated into Dutch by Jan Van Ees for AVRO radio, as *Paul Vlaanderen En Het Margo Mysterie*. Broadcast in September 1962 and produced by Dick Van Putten.

Also translated into Italian by Franca Cancogni for RAI radio as *Margo*. Broadcastin June 1967 and produced by Guglielmo Morandi.

SERIAL THRILLERS

Novelised as *Paul Temple and the Margo Mystery* by Francis Durbridge. Published by Hodder & Stoughton in 1986.

22: *Paul Temple and the Geneva Mystery* (1965)
6 x 30 minute episodes (approx.)
BBC Radio
Written by Francis Durbridge
Producer: Martyn C Webster

CAST:

Paul Temple	Peter Coke
Steve	Marjorie Westbury
Maurice Lonsdale	Patrick Barr
Margaret Milbourne	Isabel Dean
Charlie	John Baddeley
Julia Carrington	Polly Murch
Danny Clayton	Nigel Graham
Vince Langham	Simon Lack
Insp Lloyd	Wilfrid Carter
Lucas	Pat Connell
Den Roberts	Alan Haines
Dolly Brazer	Isabel Rennie
Stone	Frederick Treves
Green	Anthony Hall
Doctor	James Thomason

STORY:
Carl Milbourne seemingly died in a car accident in Geneva. However, Paul believes that he may still be alive and well.

BROADCAST:

EPISODE 1	*Too Young to Die*	11/04/65
EPISODE 2	*Concerning Mrs Milbourne*	18/04/65
EPISODE 3	*A Note for Danny*	25/04/65
EPISODE 4	*A Change of Mind*	02/05/65
EPISODE 5	*A Surprise for Mrs Milbourne*	09/05/65
EPISODE 6	*See You in London*	16/05/65

NOTES:
Also translated into German by Marianne de Barde for WDR radio, as *Paul Temple und der Fall Genf*. Broadcast in 1966 and produced by Eduard Hermann.
Also translated into Dutch by Jan Van Ees for AVRO radio, as *Paul*

PAUL TEMPLE: EPISODE GUIDE

Vlaanderen En Het Milbourne Mysterie. Broadcast in January 1966 and produced by Dick Van Putten.
Novelised as *The Geneva Mystery* by Francis Durbridge. Published by Hodder & Stoughton in 1971.

23: *Paul Temple and the Alex Affair* (1968)
Based on *Send for Paul Temple Again* (1945).
8 x 30 minute episodes (approx.)
BBC Radio
Written by Francis Durbridge
Producer: Martyn C Webster

CAST:
Paul Temple	Peter Coke
Steve	Marjorie Westbury
Sir Graham Forbes	James Thomason
Mrs Trevelyan	Barbara Mitchell
Dr Kohima	Rolf Lefebvre
Carl Lathom	Simon Lack
Wilfred Davies	Basil Jones
Leo Brent	Denys Hawthorne
Inspector Crane	Haydn Jones
Ricky	Frank Henderson

STORY:
Three deaths: A man is shot dead in his car. A woman is poisoned and left on a train. A man dies in the studio, during a live radio show. The only connection is a name – ALEX.

BROADCAST:
EPISODE 1	*Mrs Trevelyan*	26/02/68
EPISODE 2	*Dr Kohima*	29/02/68
EPISODE 3	*Mr Karl Lathom*	04/03/68
EPISODE 4	*Mr Spider Williams*	07/03/68
EPISODE 5	*Mr Wilfred Davis*	11/03/68
EPISODE 6	*Mr Leo Brent*	14/03/68
EPISODE 7	*The Girl in Brown*	18/03/68
EPISODE 8	*Introducing Alex*	21/03/68

NOTES:
Also translated into German by Marianne de Barde for WDR radio, as *Paul Temple und der Fall Alex*. Broadcast in 1968 and produced by Eduard

Hermann.

Also translated into Dutch by Alfred Gerin for AVRO radio, as *Paul Vlaanderen En Het Alex Mysterie*. Broadcast in January 1969 and produced by Dick Van Putten.

24: *Paul Temple and Light Fingers* (1995)
20 minute episode (approx.)
BBC Radio Scotland
Written by Francis Durbridge

READ BY:
Sandy Nelson

STORY:
A special short story reading from BBC Radio Scotland, based on a 1946 tale from Francis Durbridge.

BROADCAST:
SPECIAL   15/03/95

NOTES:
Based on 'Light Fingers', a short story originally published in *The Daily Mail Annual for Boys and Girls*, published in 1946.

DICK BARTON – SPECIAL AGENT

LIGHT RELIEF:

When the BBC launched its new Light Programme in July 1945[51], it was intended to provide a different sort of radio for the masses – populist pleasures of entertainment, music and fun. Such things were all firmly denied them in the pre-war era of Lord Reith and his hardened religious principles.

The Light Programme's new approach had grown out of the BBC's wartime Force's Programme, which although meant to boost *army* morale, had also found a healthy *civilian* listenership as well.

The new network's first permanent head of programming was Norman Collins[52] – then a well known novelist, whose most recent book *London Belongs to Me*, would become his best known work. Charged with the task of creating a very different kind of BBC radio service, it was Collins who first mooted the idea of a daily radio adventure serial on the BBC – something light, but compelling – a serial that would appeal very broadly to the public at large. Something classless that united a healthy proportion of the listening public over a sustained period.

There was something of a precedent for such a series. The BBC had already enjoyed some degree of success with *The Robinsons* (AKA *The Robinson Family*) – a sedate family serial that had much in common with *Mrs Dale's Diary*.

However, Collins had in mind a quite different type of serial. Something which would go some way to replicate the thrills and excitement he had found in the *Sexton Blake* books of his youth.

The first recorded mention of this new serial in the BBC's files, is to be found in an internal memo sent to *Paul Temple* producer Martyn C Webster

---

[51] The Light Programme began broadcasting on 29 July 1945. On the same day, the BBC Regional Services, which had been suspended during wartime, also returned to the air.

[52] Collins only formally assumed his position on 1 January 1946, nearly six months after the establishment of the new service. The service's first (interim) head was Maurice Gorham, who left the Programme, after only a few months, in November 1945 (to work in television). Collins had previously worked with the BBC Overseas Service (alongside George Orwell).

on 4 April 1946. In the memo, T W Chalmers from the Light Programme, inquires about the feasibility of the character of Paul Temple being used as the central figure in a new daily serial. The memo asks whether Temple's creator Francis Durbridge would be willing to allow the character to be used by an entirely new pool of writers, who would work on the programme.

Durbridge and Webster's reply is not recorded, but clearly no agreement was ever reached over the idea. Paul Temple remained as the hero of his own occasional series until 1968 and Collins was forced to consider the development of an entirely new character for his 'cloak-and-dagger soap-opera.'[53]

BILL BARTON – SPECIAL AGENT:

Collins assigned the task of pursuing the daily serial further to one of his assistants – programme planner, John McMillan. McMillan was a sensible choice. He had a very rare background in commercial radio and had worked for Radio Luxembourg from 1934 to 1939, producing hundreds of sponsored serial dramas. The most popular of McMillan's shows was probably *Vic Samson: Special Investigator*. This had been a daily thriller serial which ran very much along the lines that Collins wished to explore. Radio Luxembourg had been taken over by the Nazis and their propaganda machine during the war and McMillan came to the BBC to work on radio programmes with the British Forces Overseas Service, eventually winding up working as one of the first programme planners in the fledgling Light Programme.

By July 1946, Collins and McMillan's plans for their new serial had begun to mature and attention turned to the premise of the programme itself.

The show's hero would be a charismatic adventurer. A list of possible names for the character included: Peter Grant, Peter Fenton, Peter Drake, Michael Drake, Rex Drake, Rex Barton, Pat Barton, Bill Barton and Peter Barton. The name that was originally chosen was Bill Barton.

A set of frighteningly detailed character notes introduced us to Bill Barton, as having being born in High Wycombe at 5 PM on 10 December 1912. It was a Tuesday. The weather that day had been warm, with a temperature of between 43 and 52 degrees Fahrenheit. By early evening it had begun to rain. Bill's father was (Sheffield born) Robert Barton and his mother was (Ealing born) Mary Barton (nee Smith). Bill's parents had been married on 25 July 1911 (a respectable 18 months before the arrival of their son). Bill would be their only child.

Bill was a strong-willed boy with an innate sense of honour. He attended King Edward Grammar School, where he became an active sportsman. He

---

[53] From *The Wireless Stars* by George Nobbs – Wensum Books (1972)

later studied Engineering at Glasgow University, leaving with a good degree in 1933.

Following university, Bill soon resigned his steady but uneventful job as a draftsman and walked into a new position with a British aeronautical company in Peru. By 1936, he was overseeing the construction of an oil-pipe in Persia, later taking up a post with the (wholly fictional) International Construction Company Ltd.

He joined the forces on 10 October 1939 with the Royal Engineers – later being evacuated from Dunkirk and earning the Military Cross.

July 1940 saw him working as a member of Number 20 Commando Unit with Combined Operations in the Middle East, South-East Asia and Central Europe.

Captain Bill Barton was finally demobbed on 5 November 1945, left at a loose end, itching for more adventure.

McMillan's attention to detail also saw him check Barton's astrological charts, before contacting the Air Ministry and the Town Clerk of High Wycombe, to verify the weather forecast for the character's fictional birthday.

A number of possibilities were under consideration for the job of producing the new serial. One early suggestion was Martyn C Webster, who was still engrossed in production of the *Paul Temple* serials (among many other programmes). Webster was attached to the new programme for some of its earliest days of pre-production and development, before moving on at a later stage. It would be Webster who would first speak of the programme with the man who would become its star, Noel Johnson.

Noel Johnson was born in Birmingham on 28 December 1916. He went to Bromsgrove School in Worcestershire, before moving straight into professional acting. During the war, he'd fought with the Royal Army Service Corps at Dunkirk, where he had been wounded in action. Invalided out of the forces following his injuries, he was free to resume his acting career, which he did very successfully in 1941. Much stage work with regional rep followed.

The BBC were keen to acquire Johnson's services and offered him a place in their (still relatively new) BBC Drama Repertory Company in 1944. Johnson turned down the offer, only to accept it when it was offered again in 1945.

Johnson eventually only stayed with the Repertory Company for three months, but nevertheless continued to pursue a healthy career with the corporation. By 1946, he was already one of their most prolific actors, working with them on a number of radio productions during the dying days of the war.

In 1946, he had just finished working with Webster on a six-part serial for the Light Programme, when he first heard about Webster's involvement with the new *Bill Barton* show.

'After we had recorded the last episode, we all went to a pub (The Feathers in Wand Street) for a drink,' Johnson later recalled. 'I remember asking Martyn ... what his immediate plans were. It was just a general question, but he answered with something about "being busy with a big new radio serial" and as he said it, he put his finger to his lips, as if to say that nobody was supposed to know about it. And that was my first inkling that something was afoot.'[54]

Johnson was ideal material for Barton. Of a similar age, with a similar background and with the ideal clipped heroic voice, he was later informally approached by Webster, to join the cast.

'I never knew whether Martyn had accidentally let out the information about the serial or whether he did it so that I could be in on it,'[55] remembered Johnson.

'Martyn said to me ... "I've just got this daily serial to set up, before I go on leave". I said, "Daily serial?" He put down his whiskey and I can see it quite clearly in my mind, he looked at me and said, "Why? Would you like to be associated with it?" And those were his exact words.'[56]

'I replied, "What do you think? Work every day!"'[57]

Despite his enthusiasm, Johnson didn't sign straightaway. He was still committed to his work as presenter on the BBC's *Music by Melachrino* (a live Saturday night music programme). However, he was already the BBC's clear favourite to play the new character.

Webster soon moved on from the programme to return to *Paul Temple* and the other programmes that fell under his jurisdiction at the BBC's recently re-launched Midland Service. Accordingly, another member of staff was brought in to become the *Bill Barton* show's first producer. The man chosen to take on this job was BBC staff producer, Neil Tuson.

'I was invited by Martyn to come to his office,' Tuson later explained. 'He said, "We're doing a new serial. Would you be interested?" And I said, "Yes. Do you want me to write it?" And he said, "No. I want you to produce it." Well, I hadn't produced a thing in my life, before that.'

It was around this time that Norman Collins returned from holiday, with one further change to the new series. He was unhappy with the name Bill Barton and had a suggestion. His suggestion was to change Bill to Dick.

'He was called originally, Bill Barton,' continued Tuson, 'but you see, when you think about names, Dick Barton has a much stronger impact. "Dick

---

[54] From *The Wireless Stars* by George Nobbs – Wensum Books (1972)
[55] From *Dick Barton – A Very Special Agent* – BBC Radio 4 (15/07/10)
[56] From *Dick Barton – A Very Special Agent* – BBC Radio 4 (15/07/10)
[57] From *The Wireless Stars* by George Nobbs – Wensum Books (1972)

Barton" – it's got that punch to it.'[58]

From this point on, the BBC's new daily thriller series would become known as *Dick Barton – Special Agent*.

BIRMINGHAM BEGINNINGS:

Two writers were chosen to share the script-writing duties for the new programme: Edward J Mason and Geoffrey Webb.

Mason, who would launch the series, was another Birmingham-based radio man. He had been born in Birmingham, where he had returned after the war to work for BBC radio. His first script was for a revue produced by Webster and it may well have been Webster who put forward the writer's name to work on the new programme.

Norman Painting, who first worked with Webb and Mason in the 1950s, remembered that Mason, 'was a very sociable man: easy going, friendly and apparently relaxed … His parents were ill and incapacitated and this was enough to make him decide to stay in Birmingham within reach of them … Among his peers Ted was much loved and very highly regarded: a professional among professionals.'[59]

Mason's striking facial-hair would also cause his later collaborator Denis Norden, to describe the writer as, a 'King Edward VII lookalike.'[60]

Geoffrey Webb was the more experienced of the two new writers (at least in radio production). And like John McMillan, had previously worked in commercial radio. Webb was from Gloucestershire, but commuted to Birmingham on a regular basis.

Norman Painting recalled that, 'Although he [Webb] had both written and produced radio serials … he was never, I felt, at his best with actors. He was a countryman and had little time for actors' shoptalk. His earthy common-sense, his slow speech … and his enormous frame made him at times daunting.'[61]

Webb and Mason would work exceptionally well together and formed a lasting professional partnership and personal friendship that would continue until Webb's premature death in 1962.

Around August 1946, with the BBC anxious over the planned programme, it was decided that the newly formed production team would make a number of short test-recordings, to be circulated around the BBC for assessment. Unfortunately, this plan wasn't without its obstacles.

At the time, all the studios in Broadcasting House were fully booked, as

---

[58] From *Forever Ambridge* by Norman Painting – Michael Joseph Ltd. (1975)
[59] From *Forever Ambridge* by Norman Painting – Michael Joseph Ltd. (1975)
[60] From *Clips From a Life* by Denis Norden – Harper Collins (2008)
[61] From *Forever Ambridge* by Norman Painting – Michael Joseph Ltd. (1975)

were all the other studios in London. Birmingham also had problems. There were studios available in Bristol, but there were no secretaries nor programme engineers on hand to make the recording. 'This gets worse and worse,'[62] commented one BBC memo at the time. In the end, the team returned to the studios in Birmingham, where an agreement was reached for a studio session to be set up.

It was at this stage that (short-term) contracts began to be issued to the cast. Top of the list was, of course, Noel Johnson. Johnson had heard little further about the production since his conversation in the pub with Webster.

He only heard of the BBC's latest plans by accident. It was over a Saturday evening meal, following the latest transmission of *Music by Melachrino*.

'We'd just finished dinner and were having a drink,' said Johnson 'when somebody – a stranger to me – came over and said, "I hear you're going to be our new hero." I asked him what he meant and he said, "I believe that you're going to play Dick Barton."'[63] The stranger was John McMillan, who had assumed Johnson was already signed for the production.

'At that time, I hadn't made up my mind about it,' continued Johnson. 'So I said, "Well, there's one or two things that will need to be ironed out before I take it. For a start, I'm not going to just play Barton. I want to do other work – stage work and radio. They haven't got an exclusive ... And to hell with what the programme planner thinks."'[64]

Needless to say, Johnson was unaware that it was the programme planner to whom he was then speaking.

The initial contract, which was offered to Johnson, was not a particularly generous one. However, at such an early stage in the programme's development, this was not greatly surprising and the BBC made an agreement to potentially re-negotiate his fee, if the series was a success. He would also be free to take on other work.

'Once I had made sure I could still do other work, I eagerly accepted,' he explained. 'Even though the money was poor, it was still regular work.'[65]

Alongside Johnson, was (outside artist) John Mann, who'd been cast as Dick Barton's best friend Snowey White. 'Somebody phoned me up on the Friday evening,' said Mann 'way back in '46. Would I be interested in playing the part of a cockney in some serial or other. So, I said, "Of course. Thank you very much."'[66] With a cast set, the pilot test programmes soon entered the studios in Birmingham.

---

[62] From *The Wireless Stars* by George Nobbs – Wensum Books (1972)
[63] From *The Wireless Stars* by George Nobbs – Wensum Books (1972)
[64] From *The Wireless Stars* by George Nobbs – Wensum Books (1972)
[65] From an interview with Noel Johnson in *The Independent* (19/12/98)
[66] From *Dick Barton – A Very Special Agent* – BBC Radio 4 (15/07/10)

'Strangely enough ... there's only one piece of dialogue that has stuck in my mind [from the pilot recordings],' remembered Johnson. 'It was the "curtain line" in one of the pilot programmes and I was with Colonel Gardiner I believe. We all had to rush for the lift and as the door opened, Gardiner said, "Great Heavens! There's no floor in the lift!"'[67]

Copies of the pilot recordings[68] were circulated to the various heads of department in September. The series was never popular with head of drama Val Gielgud, who showed little interest in the new serial. 'I was aware that Val Gielgud always hated the show for being so downmarket,'[69] Johnson later remarked.

However, others in the drama department were more supportive. Norman Collins was particularly protective of his new baby, commenting in a BBC memo to Gielgud, on 14 September: 'I know that you'll hate hearing this, but the first instalment of the *Dick Barton* series ... is really awfully good of its kind and is just what we wanted: on this showing the thing will run for years!'[70] Despite his reservations, Gielgud's reply was encouraging, saying, 'If you are pleased, so am I.'[71]

Similar praise came from Denis Morris, programme director for the Midland Region, commenting that, 'Several of us have pencilled in our diaries 7 October 1967 for the twenty-first birthday party.'[72]

With the test programmes established as a success, work then began in earnest on the show's first full series.

THE FIRST SERIAL:

There were still some final negotiations over Johnson's contract before recording on the series proper could finally begin. The result of this would see the actor engaged for three days per week, to both rehearse and record five episodes during those three days. A letter from the BBC dated 19 September read: 'We should like to offer you an engagement to take part in our serial, *Dick Barton*. The salary will be eighteen pounds a week.'[73] Although, subject to the pre-arranged terms, this would be re-negotiated dependant on the success of the series.

---

[67] From *The Wireless Stars* by George Nobbs – Wensum Books (1972)
[68] There are conflicting reports over exactly how many pilot recordings were made. Some documents indicate that six test episodes were initially recorded. However, Neil Tuson later remembered only recording two episodes. It is unlikely that the truth will ever be entirely clear.
[69] From an interview with Noel Johnson in *The Independent* (19/12/98)
[70] From *The Wireless Stars* by George Nobbs – Wensum Books (1972)
[71] From *The Wireless Stars* by George Nobbs – Wensum Books (1972)
[72] From *The Wireless Stars* by George Nobbs – Wensum Books (1972)
[73] From *Dick Barton – A Very Special Agent* – BBC Radio 4 (15/07/10)

SERIAL THRILLERS

The series' first serial was set for broadcast in early October. Written by Edward J Mason, it was twenty episodes long (expanded from the scripts of the pilot recordings) and included much of the set up material for the new series – introducing Dick and Snowey and following them as they become involved in the insane machinations of the evil Wilhelm Kramer. The story (often referred to as *Dick Barton and Kramer* in BBC paperwork) began with the recently demobbed Dick Barton and Snowey White having returned home restless and hungry for adventure after their wartime exploits in the Commandos. The pair soon get what they desire when they are hired by Colonel Gardiner of military intelligence to help track down a stolen super-weapon.

During the serial, we are also introduced to the other regular members of the programme's family of characters. Chief amongst these characters was Jock Anderson. Not introduced until episode 17, Jock would go on to form a core trio alongside Dick and Snowey, which would stay with the programme for the rest of its run. Jock was already working with Colonel Gardiner, when Dick and Snowey arrive. A young no-nonsense army type from Scotland, Jock was played by Alex McCrindle.

McCrindle, like Jock, was Scottish. He was born on 3 August 1911 in Glasgow. After starting work at the age of 10, on a milk round, his acting career began in plays put on by the local Boys Brigade. He later joined the Glasgow Clarion Players – the famous Scottish theatre group with strong links to the British Communist Party. Following a time lecturing on drama with the Workers' Education Authority at Glasgow University, he eventually moved to London. It was in London that he became an indentured apprentice at the Queen Theatre, near the north end of Kew Bridge. This would lead to further stage work. His first major part, had been in *The 39 Steps*, for Alfred Hitchcock in 1935 and between 1937 and 1939, he also appeared in twelve plays on the BBC's fledgling television service. During the war, McCrindle had served with the Royal Navy and (like Jock) had himself only recently been discharged back to civilian life.

McCrindle was also known as a passionate and committed Marxist and life-long member of the Communist party – something that would make life difficult for him later on. His second wife was the Communist children's author and *Daily Worker* film critic, Honor Arundel and their home was a frequent hub for left-wing intellectuals. Doris Lessing later noted in her autobiography: 'In a garden on the canal known as Little Venice, now very smart, then dingy and run down, there were held ceilidhs ... The house belonged to Honor Tracy [Arundel], an upper-class young woman whose education had destined her for a very different life, and her husband Alex McCrindle ... who was in a radio series of immense popularity. There were people from the worlds of radio, music, and nascent television, and of course, women with children. Most of them were communists, but none of them were communists ten years later, except for Alex.'[74]

'I think it was all a great lark,' remembered McCrindle of his time with *Dick Barton*. 'What child could resist the kind of antics that we got up to? You know, we were there one week, on top of a building: "Right Mr Barton, you ready? Right, take a jump now. Off we go. Right, away. Snowey, come on."'[75]

The last among the new regular cast was Lorna Dermott playing Jean Hunter – one of the only female members of Colonel Gardiner's staff and something of a potential love-interest for Dick. Much of the remaining cast came from the BBC Drama Repertory Company.

Another important ingredient for the show would be its music, to which Neil Tuson turned his attention at a very early stage of pre-production. There was never any intention for the programme to make use of especially composed music. It would instead rely on stock-music drawn from the BBC's own extensive record library at Broadcasting House.

'I went down to the bowels of the BBC,' said Tuson. 'I went through old classics, modern classics; you name it, I went through them. But I couldn't find an "in" and an "out", if you know what I mean – something to start the programme and something to finish it with. Anyway, I went through this, including some mood music and at long last, I put this thing on and I got a "Bbbbrrrrrruuuummmm brrrrruuuumm brrrruuummm." I thought, "that's it."'[76]

The piece of music Tuson had chosen was *The Devil's Galop* by prolific composer Charles Williams. A frenetic orchestral piece, it perfectly suited the pacy serial cliff-hangers of the show. It has since become almost wholly synonymous with the programme.

'I decided that it was going to be the fastest thing on radio,' continued Tuson. 'That's why *The Devil's Galop* fitted it. You think of a tune that goes faster than *The Devil's Galop*.'[77]

Episode 1 of *Dick Barton – Special Agent* was broadcast on the Light Programme at 6.45 PM on Monday 7 October 1946. The broadcast opened with an announcement from BBC Announcer Derek Birch, saying: 'Tonight we present the first instalment of a new adventure serial. Each evening at this time – Saturdays and Sundays excepted – we invite you to follow the exploits of Dick Barton!'[78]

With a series of specially commissioned illustrations for each episode appearing in the *Radio Times*, the first (originally untitled[79]) serial aired with

---

[74] From *Walking in the Shade* by Doris Lessing – Flamingo Books (1998)
[75] From *Walking in the Shade* by Doris Lessing – Flamingo Books (1998)
[76] From *Walking in the Shade* by Doris Lessing – Flamingo Books (1998)
[77] From *Walking in the Shade* by Doris Lessing – Flamingo Books (1998)
[78] *Dick Barton and the Secret Weapon* – Episode 1 (07/10/46)
[79] None of the *Dick Barton* serials broadcast their story titles on air. Each episode was merely introduced as another episode in the series. However, this doesn't

appropriate fanfare. It was largely judged to have been a solid success within the BBC and after about a fortnight, the first reviews began to trickle in. They were however, decidedly mixed.

On Saturday 19 October (just after episode 10 had gone out), the *Daily Worker* (for which Alex McCrindle's second wife worked) reported that: '*Dick Barton, Special Agent* ... is so bad as to be almost beyond criticism.'[80] *Picture Post* joined in, calling Dick a lower middle class spiv, while *Illustrated* criticised the programme's depiction of 'characters leading abnormal lives.'[81]

However, despite the evident snobbery from some quarters, the show had certainly become enough of a hit for Collins to fairly quickly confirm an extended run for the series.

Dick Barton's first full serial concluded on 1 November 1946, but by then there was little question that more was to follow and a second serial picked up almost right away on the following Monday, with many more to come.

SERIES ONE:

Series one continued with another twenty-part serial from Mason running through much of November (*Dick Barton and the Paris Adventure*). Then Geoffrey Webb contributed his first script with serial three – *Dick Barton and the Cabatolin Diamonds*. The serials would then largely alternate between the two, with a Webb serial followed by a Mason serial and so on.

By this stage, the *Dick Barton* template had now been comfortably established. The plots were far-fetched and frenetic, but never quite beyond the realms of the theoretically possibly. It was in fact 'straightforward crook stuff'[82], as Webb and Mason would later explain. The pace was fast and urgent. Both Webb and Mason would build four dramatic 'developments' into each instalment that would act as to build tension. The suspense would then be released across three dramatic 'peaks'. Webb and Mason classified each 'development' from A to D (eg Development C) and each 'peak' from A

---

mean that the serials were always untitled. Most (if not all) of the *Barton* serials had specific story titles. These titles were normally written on the first page of the production's script. Sometimes another title would be given to serial for the purposes of BBC paperwork. The very first *Barton* serial seems to have originally been referred to as *Dick Barton and Kramer*. However, since the 1970s the serial has been more commonly referred to as *Dick Barton and the Secret Weapon*. In Australia the story was later known as *Dick Barton and the Weapon of Hate*. None of these titles were read out by the announcers. Although a very few of them did appear in the *Radio Times*.

[80] From the *Daily Worker* (19/10/46)
[81] From *Boys Will Be Boys* by E S Turner – Hollen Street Press (1975)
[82] From *The Inside Story of Dick Barton* by Geoffrey Webb and Edward J Mason – Contact Books (1950)

to C. This meticulous formula would alter little across the series run and was used to brief other contributing writers, as they joined the programme.

Webb and Mason would continue as the show's sole writers until the arrival of freelance contributors in 1947.

As 1946 drew to a close, the programme's popularity spread. However, things were not developing entirely as predicted.

The *Dick Barton* adventures had always been light-hearted and generally frothy pieces of escapism for their listeners. However, what they had never been designed for was a specifically child-based audience. However, by the close of 1946, more and more children were beginning to follow the show and it was increasingly being seen, in the eyes of the public at least, as a children's programme. This was not without its problems.

On 17 December, a letter about homework was (now infamously) sent into the letters' page of *The Times*. It very much demonstrated the public image of *Barton* as a show for children. The letter from Mrs Wright-Newsome ran: 'Will the BBC please have mercy on the children? For the sake of their future the children ought to give their minds to their prep. The BBC seems bent on turning the children into a new kind of drug addict. For most of the prep-time the programmes consist of serial thrillers, so that the poor children grow more concerned from day to day about what Dick Barton and others may do next, than about their own futures or the future of England.'[83]

Quite possibly to the producer's delight, the hysterics elicited an immediate response, with further letters appearing for the rest of the year and beyond. On 19 December Sheelagh Hardie from Northumberland countered that, 'Our children, having wrestled with compound fractions or Latin verbs on top of a long day's schooling are entitled to their 15 minutes' reward.' She then concluded: 'Heaven postpone the day when our priggish offspring forsake such unsophisticated thrills for the sober contemplation of their own importance.'[84]

Other responses were somewhat less liberal, with Hylda Nelson from Kensington, having given up listening to the BBC altogether and finding herself able to, 'heartily endorse the opinion of Mrs Wright-Newsome.'[85]

Nevertheless, the general sway of opinion seemed to be very much on *Barton*'s side. A F Osborne, criticised the overburdening of homework altogether, saying: 'that our children would benefit from an increase of *Dick Barton* ... and a decrease in "prep".'[86]

Whether it was a response to these letters or whether the letters simply

---

[83] From *The Times* (17/12/46)
[84] From *The Times* (19/12/46)
[85] From *The Times* (19/12/46)
[86] From *The Times* (19/12/46)

provided a good platform to announce a change to the scheduling, action was soon taken by the BBC themselves, and the decision was taken to introduce a new slot for *Barton*.

There would now be a weekend *Barton* omnibus.

Possibly wishing to mollify his critics, or maybe just seeing a good opportunity to boost the programme's profile, Norman Collins himself made an announcement in another letter to *The Times*. It was published on 21 December. In it, he wrote that: 'Parents who are concerned about the rival claims of "prep" and *Dick Barton* will be relieved to hear that from the first Saturday in the New Year there will be a special omnibus weekly edition at 11 o'clock … on Saturday mornings.'[87]

Even Noel Johnson waded in, writing to *The Times* on 19 December (published 23 December): 'It does seem to me that in this austere age there is a danger of all work and no play certainly making Jack a dull boy … Let us see that children of to-day enjoy themselves as much as possible.'[88] There were, other letters too, all commenting with varying degrees of support and condemnation.

Of course, the introduction of the new omnibus may partly have been a simple response to the increasing popularity of the programme. However, the cynicism can't be too over-egged. The BBC's strength of concern over the children in its audience was real and it would go on to have deeper consequences in the New Year.

Whatever, the reasons, the Light Programme's new slot seems to have gone down well. Even Mrs Wright Newsome herself seems to have been (comparatively) happy, when she appeared in the letter's columns again on New Year's Day. She wrote: 'May I thank Mr Norman Collins, head of the BBC's Light Programme, for so promptly trying to help by arranging an omnibus *Dick Barton* … Although Mr Osborne's advocacy of the abolition of "prep" accords with the trend of the time towards less and less work. If Dick Barton had not done his "prep" he would now be a listening fan and somebody else would now be Dick Barton.'[89]

Backhanded compliments aside, the flurry of publicity seemed to have done Barton no harm at all, as the programme marched through the Christmas period[90], as one of the BBC's most listened to programmes. *The Times* editorial summarised the situation in its 3 January edition, stating that,

---

[87] From *The Times* (21/12/46)
[88] From *The Times* (23/12/46)
[89] From *The Times* (01/01/47)
[90] For the programme's first series, *Barton* would continue throughout the Christmas period. The programme's weekly schedule continued unabated. There were episodes on Christmas Eve, Christmas Day and Boxing Day. This would change in future years, when the programme would traditionally take a few days break over the festive period.

'Barton ... may not be everyone's perfect hero, but he must be gratified by the number of voices raised on his behalf.'[91]

1947 continued very much as before, with Mason's *Dick Barton in South America* being the first serial to be broadcast after the Christmas holidays. The cast of Johnson, Mann, McCrindle and Dermott remained, as did producer Neil Tuson.

It was to prove an eventful year for the programme. There was some talk from Collins' colleague Bill MacLurg that *Dick Barton* should be dropped altogether, but support from the programme in other quarters was still fairly strong. Only head of drama Val Gielgud seemed to have any serious reservations and even that went rarely beyond tacit resistance.

On 13 January, the BBC published details of its top three rated radio programmes. *Radio Forfeits* was at number one. However, *Dick Barton* wasn't far behind and sat comfortably in second place. The comparatively new *Woman's Hour* took the number three spot.

The next serial along (Webb's *Dick Barton and the Smugglers*) received even greater publicity, when *Dick Barton* made the front-cover of the *Radio Times* (February 2 – February 8 edition). The cover featured a staged photograph of Johnson, Mann and McCrindle with actor Alan Tilvern (Limpy) during the studio recording of the previous year's *Dick Barton and the Cabatolin Diamonds*.

The new serial itself revolved around the unlikely location of an artificial iceberg, used by the villains as a secret base. 'It was based on an idea that Churchill had during the war,'[92] recalled Johnson.

The serial also received some coverage in *The Listener*[93]. Philip Hope-Wallace wrote for their 13 February edition: 'No doubt one day it will be Aristophanes and Milton who are quoted in the pubs and offices, but for the moment it is still *Dick Barton*. Surely never since the days of the evangelical revival has there been such an awareness of a common background of myth and story ... They are the new mythology. Men whose lives, homes and accents have nothing at all in common are here on common ground.'[94]

Even the *Daily Telegraph* praised Dick for his 'initiative, quick decision and private enterprise.' It added: 'Can anyone see Barton referring any matter to a committee?' The series was riding high. However, as *Barton* passed its 100 episode (21 February 1947), there were to be lasting changes

---

[91] From *The Times* (03/01/47)
[92] From *The Wireless Stars* by George Nobbs – Wensum Books (1972)
[93] Despite the programme's massive popularity (or possibly because of it) the notoriously highbrow *Listener* would not mention *Dick Barton* again in any issue until 1990. There would never be another review of another episode ever again. Surprisingly, for the whole of the programme's original run, this is the only coverage *Barton* ever got from the publication.
[94] From *The Listener* (13/02/47)

to the programme.

On 20 February 1947, Norman Collins sent a detailed memo to John McMillan, concerning the programme's future. Collins noted that *Dick Barton – Special Agent* had never been intended for 'an exclusively juvenile audience.'[95] However, he continued, 'that is what we have got and we must act accordingly.' The memo emphasised, 'the really considerable responsibilities that lie upon us as teenage entertainers. Perhaps the easiest way of saying all this is that we should accept the same general standards of *The Boy's Own Paper.*'[96]

The upswing in concern over the younger end of the programme's audience may have been brought to the fore by the letters in *The Times* over Christmas. However, even without such prompting, it was already very clear that the core audience for *Barton* was something a little different from what had originally been envisioned.

From the programme's earliest days, Tuson, McMillan and Collins had kept a watchful eye on the show's more adult content. One memo to the production team said: 'I have put a pencil through an exchange between Barton and Gardiner on page three in which Barton poses the question about Miss Hunter's morals.' Another commented that, 'we should draw the line about using the word "bitch" if applied to a woman.'[97] Such self-censorship was a sensible part of radio production routine and helped ensure that no programme ever over-stepped the bounds of good-taste.

However, with a children's audience now part of the new demographic, the BBC were proposing a much more radical rethink of the show's approach.

It wouldn't be until the programme's second series that many of these changes would swing into place. However, other changes were more immediate.

The most noticeable alteration was the removal of a core character from the show's line-up. The character was Jean Hunter, played by Lorna Dermott. She had been part of the central team from the earliest days of the first serial, but now found herself quickly phased out. She did not appear in the next serial (*Dick Barton and the Smash and Grab Raiders*). It was felt that the character was no longer a figure in which the juvenile listenership took much interest.

Jean had essentially been introduced as a potential love-interest for Dick. This was, of course, a fairly standard ingredient for an adventure story of the time. However, the device was arguably only ever going to be of interest to a very thin slice of the audience. It would (in theory) appeal

---

[95] From *Sound & Vision* by Asa Briggs – Oxford University Press (1979)
[96] From *The Wireless Stars* by George Nobbs – Wensum Books (1972)
[97] From *The Wireless Stars* by George Nobbs – Wensum Books (1972)

to both the more adult listeners and also (again in theory) offer an identification point for female listeners. However, it had become clear that most of *Dick Barton*'s fans failed to fall into either camp. A massive chunk of the listenership were schoolboys who seemed to demonstrate very little enthusiasm for the character at all.

Added to this was the more general problem that many of the writers (Geoffrey Webb in particular) seemed almost totally incapable of giving any of their female characters a remotely believable personality.

Jean was simply no longer serving the purpose for which she had been designed and was thus discarded. It may have been a little narrow-minded (and sexist) to have looked at it in such terms, but the decision was not an overly surprising one.

There would still be a female presence in the show in the form of Barton's faithful housekeeper, Betsy Horrock, played by Courtney Hope. However, the character was little more than an occasional cast-member, similar to *Paul Temple*'s 'Charlie'. *The Daily Worker* would describe her as 'a Tory working woman with a heart of gold,'[98] and they were probably right.

Ultimately, the pruning of the cast did the programme little damage, and, if anything helped to cement the dynamic between Dick, Snowey and Jock. However, it was only part of larger more sweeping changes that were slowly being introduced.

Johnson was not entirely in favour, commenting: 'I never went along with this idea that it was harmful to children ... Dick Barton was quite normal when the programme started; he smoked, enjoyed a drink and had a girlfriend, Jean, but gradually that all disappeared.'[99] He later added that, 'as soon as the producers cottoned on to the fact we had a youth audience, they felt they had to become moral guardians.'[100]

Another change introduced with *Dick Barton and the Smash and Grab Raiders* was the introduction of other writers, to help with the pace of turnaround on the programme. In this case freelance writers Ronnie and Arthur Colley were brought in with their tale of criminal mastermind Paragon (Morris Sweden) and his gang of violent smash and grab robbers. It was to be their only *Dick Barton* serial, with Geoffrey Webb writing all of the other serials for the remainder of the series.

Possibly taking something of a page or three out of Herge's books, Webb's remaining serials, would take in a variety of global destinations such as Tibet, Canada and the entirely fictional Pacific outcrop of Black Panther Island.

---

[98] From *The Wireless Stars* by George Nobbs – Wensum Books (1972)
[99] From *The Wireless Stars* by George Nobbs – Wensum Books (1972)
[100] From an interview with Noel Johnson in *The Independent* (19/12/98)

There was one further tweak to the scheduling, with the series now being broadcast six days a week, with one episode per day Monday to Saturday. *Dick Barton and the Canadian Adventure* was the first to go out on Saturdays and was also notable for a guest appearance from the still comparatively little known Michael Hordern.

Possibly due to the increased turnaround, Neil Tuson would temporarily leave the programme as producer from *Dick Barton and the Tibetan Adventure* and for the rest of the programme's first season (episode 121 onwards). It is not clear if this was ever intended to be a permanent departure, as Tuson would return for the next series.

Tuson's (temporary) replacement was Raymond Raikes. Raikes had only just joined the drama department that year (1947) and *Barton* was one of his first responsibilities. A former actor, he would go on to be an unusual (even maverick) figure in the department. Reports were that the chain-smoking Raikes insisted on never looking at any of the actors during recordings in the studio, in case the sight of a pretty (female) member of the cast distracted him. However, despite his singular lack of interaction with his artistes, he was a great technical innovator, gaining international recognition for his later experiments in stereo recording. He would stay with the series for the rest of the season, also returning in later years.

The first series finally concluded its run on Saturday 31 May 1947.

Only one major hiccup had taken place, when two episodes were broadcast in the wrong order in April 1947 (episodes 3 and 4 of *Dick Barton and the Canadian Adventure*). However, it was otherwise a highly successful first year, with more to come – both on radio and even the silver screen.

Raikes would later recall one particular memory of his time on the show that clearly showed the growing popularity of the programme with children. 'A young friend of mine aged 10,' said Raikes, 'was at his Sunday School class. The teacher said: "Who made you?" "God, sir," "And who looks after you all the day?" "God, sir" "And who would you turn to if you were in trouble?" "Dick Barton, sir."'[101]

RULES OF CONDUCT:

Before the second series of *Dick Barton* could take to the air in September 1947, the changes to programme policy, introduced for series one, were first to be reinforced and codified.

On 27 August 1947, Collins began to circulate '*Dick Barton* – Rules of Conduct' – a twelve point document that spelt out in the clearest of terms

---

[101] From *Popular Radio Drama* by David Wade (Published in Radio Drama ed. Peter Lewis) – Longman (1981)

what would and would not be acceptable in the new child-friendly order. The document (which was later slightly amended) ran as follows:

1. Barton is intelligent as well as hard-hitting. He relies as much on brains as upon brawn.
2. He only uses force when normal, peaceful means of reaching a legitimate goal have failed.
3. Barton never commits an offence in the criminal code, no matter how desirable the means may be argued to justify the end.
4. In reasonable circumstances, he may deceive but he never lies.
5. Barton's violence is restricted to clean socks on the jaw. The refinements of unarmed combat, taught to British Commandos, cannot be practised by him or his colleagues. When involved in a brawl, which ends in victory for the Barton side, he must be equally matched or outnumbered.
6. Barton's enemies have more latitude in their behaviour, but may not indulge in giving any injury or punishment, which is basically sadistic.
7. Barton and his friends do not wittingly involve innocent members of the public in situations, which would cause them to be distressed. For example, a motor car cannot be requisitioned for the purpose of chasing bandits, without the owner's permission.
8. Barton has now given up drink altogether. No reference should be made to its existence in the Barton circle. The villains may drink but never to excess. Drunken scenes are barred.
9. Sex, in the active sense, plays no part in Barton's adventures. In other words, Dick has no flirtations or affairs and his enemies have no molls or mistresses (as opposed to partners). This provision does not of course rule out the possibility of a decent marriage (not involving Dick personally) taking place.
10. Horrific effects in general must be closely watched. Supernatural or pseudo-supernatural sequences are to be avoided – ghosts, night-prowling, gorillas, vampires.
11. Swearing and bad language generally may not be used by any character. This ban ranges from 'bloody' through 'God', 'Damn' and 'hell' to ugly expressions currently heard in certain conversations but not considered admissible for child usage in middle-class homes.
12. Political themes are unpopular as well as being occasionally embarrassing. The-man-who-wants-to-control-the-Earth creates little impact and is best left out of the Barton world.

SERIAL THRILLERS

That last point seems to have been cheerfully ignored by most of the Barton writers, but the others were much more firmly enforced.

The effect that this new childproofing had on the show itself has been perhaps overstated. In some ways the new list of protocols merely codified things which Mason, Webb and Tuson had established from the start. For instance, rules 1 and 10 were more to do with the deliberate style of the programme than they were censorship. However, nevertheless, the new rules did have some effect.

The rules affected Johnson more than anyone. 'He was whiter than white,'[102] said Johnson. 'He became a sort of pure character – not that he was ever anything but good, but he really became almost unplayable.'[103]

Scripts were changed and stories reshaped under the new regime. Perhaps the most bizarre story from the period is how the word 'twerp' was apparently cut from one script, as it was judged to be unseemly for 'middle-class homes'. Oddly, this was simply down to the fact that the BBC were unable to trace the origin of the word in any dictionary and so made the slightly illogical assumption that it was probably vulgar. 'I remember one script which called for the villain to go into a bar for a drink,' recalled Johnson. 'It had to be altered to a *milk* bar and a glass of milk.'[104]

The 'Rules of Conduct' themselves were published for the consumption of the general public on January 16 1948, later finding themselves the subject of parody in a spoof episode of 'child-friendly' *Dick Barton*, made with the cast of the BBC's *Take it From Here*.

In spite of the new restrictions however, the team of Tuson, Webb and Mason still somehow managed to produce a show that continued to enthral much of its target audience. In fact *Barton* was about to reach something of a zenith, both in terms of outreach and national awareness.

SERIES TWO:

On 14 September 1947, Noel Johnson's contract was renewed for another series as the maverick special agent. True to the BBC's earlier promise, he was now paid at a higher rate. The new contract was signed for £24 per week. This was six pounds more than the original 1946 contract and was a generous (although not vast) salary for the time. To place it in context, the average BBC staff producer (such as Tuson) would have brought in around ten to fifteen pounds per week, with writers (such as Mason and Webb) also averaging around the same. If nothing else, it certainly illustrated the esteem in which the BBC held its newest radio star.

---

[102] From *The Radio Companion* by Paul Donovan – Grafton Books (1992)
[103] From *Dick Barton – A Very Special Agent* – BBC Radio 4 (15/07/10)
[104] From *The Wireless Stars* by George Nobbs – Wensum Books (1972)

There had been attempts to replace *Barton* altogether with a new daily serial, but these had now been pushed to one side. A failed replacement series called *The Daring Dexters* had begun in June 1947. Featuring Granville Eves as Dan Dexter, a circus high-wire man, the series had been written by Webb with Raymond Raikes as producer. Dan's son Bill was played by James Viccars, and Sherry (his daughter) was Olive Kirby. The series was not judged to have been anywhere near as big a hit as Barton and it ended on 3 October, with *Barton* granted a lengthy second run.

Many listeners looked forward to the new series, with ex-Paul Temple actor Hugh Morton commenting that, 'I have heard listeners of four and eighty-four talking about *Dick Barton – Special Agent*.'[105]

The first serial of the new season was *Dick Barton and the Vulture* by Edward J Mason – his first script following a lengthy time away at the end of the first series.

Returning to five days a week (Monday to Friday,) both Mann and McCrindle were back alongside Johnson in a tale of stolen bullion and a kidnapped girl. Despite the newly imposed restrictions, there was little outward sign of a change in the *Barton* style. However, as it had been Mason who had helped shape the new rule-book, this is not surprising.

The new guidelines were really designed for incoming freelance writers, rather than the semi-resident Webb and Mason. The first new freelancer to join the show during the second season was Basil Dawson.

Dawson was a logical choice – a writer with a strong interest in mystery and adventure stories, he later co-wrote the comic mystery plays: *Alibi for a Judge* (1964), *According to the Evidence* (1967) and *Whose Baby?* (1968) and also did a considerable amount of work for ITV on series such as *The Adventures of Robin Hood* and *Ghost Squad*.

Dawson would become a semi-regular member of the *Barton* writing pool – writing a total of three serials for the programme and would return later with 1948's *Dick Barton and the Case of the Conrad Ruda* (in which Dawson would also act.)

Dawson's first serial – the oddly titled *Dick Barton and the Production Report* would see a return from Colonel Gardiner's character (played by George Bishop) and would also feature former Paul Temple Richard Williams as an RAF officer. The serial would take *Barton* comfortably up to its 200th episode and then beyond.

There would be a number of subtle additions to the formula as the second series progressed. Most obvious among these was the introduction of Inspector Burke (Colin Douglas) in episode 219. It's also worth noting the appearance of (future Mrs Tuson) Anne Cullen in the cast lists.

---

[105] From an interview with Hugh Morton in *The World Radio and Television Annual* ed. Gale Pedrick – Sampson Low (1947)

The plots were subtly different too, with (slightly) less world domination and a few more domestic threats. In *Dick Barton and the Case of the Conrad Ruda* a Hollywood actress is the central character. While *Dick Barton and the Firefly Adventure* sees Dick take on a London-based protection racket. The series clearly hadn't lost any sparkle for its still dedicated followers, but there were signs (if you knew where to look) of a gradual softening of some of the broader aspects of the show.

However, whatever the policy decisions, it was clear that the programme was something the BBC had confidence in and on 7 November 1947, Norman Collins underlined this confidence in a letter to the BBC's Director General. In the letter he explained that, although it had only been his intention to bring *Barton* back for a stint of four months (running two other serials during the course of the year) *Barton* was now doing so well that he proposed an extended run of six months for the series, taking the show through much of 1948.

This proposed extension was accepted and a lengthened second series concluded with the final episode of *Dick Barton and the Firefly Adventure* on 2 April 1948.

The period between late 1947 and early 1948 had seen interest in the show grow and for the first time it wasn't only radio listeners who would have a stake in events. While the second series was being broadcast, external parties were beginning to present themselves to the BBC with plans for *Dick Barton* of their own. The programme was set to expand like never before and the first stop was the picture house.

HAMMER FILMS:

Originally founded in November 1934 by William (Hammer) Hinds and Enrique Carreras, Hammer Film Productions was among Britain's smallest independent film companies. After the war, the running of the business fell to Anthony (Tony) Hinds and James Carreras (sons of the company's founders) and in January 1947 they began making a modest living working on small-scale 'quota-quickie' features at London's Marylebone Studios[106].

Success on films like *Death in High Heels* and *The Dark Road* had been limited and one Hammer feature (*There is No Escape*) was even banned on legal grounds. By the tail end of 1947, the company was not doing well and was on the lookout for a project that could buck the trend in their fortunes. They turned to *Dick Barton*.

Having successfully bid for the rights to *Dick Barton* from the BBC,

---

[106] Hammer didn't own its own film studios (yet). They simply rented studio space from others, when needed. Hammer's main office at this time was on Wardour Street in London.

Hammer went about making their first *Barton* picture in late 1947. However, the film was not to feature Noel Johnson.

'They thought I didn't look tall enough or tough enough,' said Johnson. 'Although I wasn't approached at first, they did ring me up some months later and said that they had had great difficulty in casting it – "Would you consider playing the lead?" By this time I'd had a chance to think it over and I politely declined.'[107]

The part would eventually go to Don Stannard (born Donald Gordon Stannard). The actor had worked with Hammer before on their *Death in High Heels* feature, earlier in the year and was an oft-used supporting actor for small British quota pictures. Only Colin Douglas returned from the radio cast.

Directed by Alfred Goulding, Hammer's 69-minute *Barton* film (obviously named: *Dick Barton – Special Agent*) was produced quickly at Marylebone Studios for a meagre budget of £12,000. The plot concerned itself with Barton's attempts to stop a plague of cholera.

Released in early 1948, the movie never came close to replicating the popularity of the BBC's original. However, it was enough of a success to help revive the fortunes of Hammer and by 16 June the film had secured 1,400 bookings in British cinemas.

The critics were mixed in their reactions – generally spotting it for the cynical cash-in that it was. *To-Day's Cinema* called it a 'cast-iron title attraction for the masses and juveniles ... The actual story is confused, the action crude, and the general presentation hardly up to slick modern standards. Yet the magic of *Barton* nullifies all this.'[108]

Johnson considered that, 'I think I was wise to refuse because the picture really was a big hoot – even little children in remote villages laughed all the way through it.'[109]

It was obvious that Hammer would take up its option for another *Barton* picture. In fact there would be a further two. The next one to be released was *Dick Barton Strikes Back*. With an increased budget, the new picture would be Hammer's biggest *Barton* picture.

B-movie regular Mario Zampi was hired to produce the film and much of Zampi's crew was duly attached to the Hammer payroll. However, all did not go as planned and Zampi left the project quite suddenly without explanation before shooting began – leaving Hammer without its producer.

Zampi's third assistant director was Jimmy Sangster who recalled that; 'Zampi ... absconded a couple of weeks before it was due to start. Whether he took any of the money with him, I have no idea, but suddenly the movie

---

[107] From *The Wireless Stars* by George Nobbs – Wensum Books (1972)
[108] From *To-Day's Cinema* (05/03/48)
[109] From *The Wireless Stars* by George Nobbs – Wensum Books (1972)

was left rudderless.'[110]

Anthony Hinds stepped into the breach as producer, with Godfrey Grayson as director. Studio work took place at Viking Studios – 'A tiny place off Kensington High Street in London,'[111] remembered Sangster. There was a greater amount of location material than before, culminating in an ambitious shoot at the top of the Blackpool Tower. Cinematography on the production was handled by Cedric Williams, who later recalled the dangerous Blackpool shoot: 'I remember we were shooting ... at the top of the tower ... Our production team at that time included Prudence Sykes, our continuity girl, and she would sit on the outermost girder with this horrendous 600 ft drop below her, as cool as a cucumber while all around her were having kittens. Some of the sequences filmed in the tower had Don Stannard as Dick Barton running up and down the stairs. These shots had to be filmed from the elevator ... While Godfrey Grayson and myself were filming one such scene from the elevator, it suddenly plunged at an enormous speed 600 ft, to the bottom of the tower, stopping with a bounce just short of the ground. We climbed out with and, with ashen faces and a desperate need of a change of trousers, we asked the engineer what would have happened if we had hit the bottom. He relied in a deep Northern accent, "You wouldn't have wanted to come in't lift again."'[112]

The film was released in 1949 and was better received than the first. *To-Day's Cinema* described the Blackpool footage as, 'the final sensation, with the incessant screaming of the atomic apparatus, [it] may well prove too much for all but the stoutest of nerves. It is punched over with stern resolution by Don Stannard as the implacable Barton.'[113]

There was to be one other Hammer *Barton* movie: *Dick Barton at Bay* (working title – *Dick Barton Vs the Death Plague*), shot at Marylebone and also from Grayson and Stannard. Shot back in 1948, the film would get a delayed release in 1950. However, it would be *Barton's* last brush with the cinema.

In July 1949, Stannard was among members of Hammer's *Barton* crew who were attending a garden party at Dial Close, a mansion overlooking the Thames at Cookham Dean near Maidenhead. The party had been organised by Hammer and their sister company Exclusive. While driving back from the party, there was a car accident in which a number of guests were hurt. Stannard was killed.

'I was in the car behind Don's and watched as it went out of control, off the road and down a steep hill,' said Jimmy Sangster. 'I was the only person around a couple of days later when the police called and asked if I'd identify

---

[110] From *Inside Hammer* by Jimmy Sangster – Reynolds and Hearn Ltd. (2001)
[111] From *Inside Hammer* by Jimmy Sangster – Reynolds and Hearn Ltd. (2001)
[112] From *The House of Hammer* by Allen Eyles – Lorrimer (1973)
[113] From *To-Day's Cinema* (11/03/49)

the body.'[114]

Music supervisor Frank Spencer also had a narrow escape from the same vehicle. 'He nearly lost his life with poor Don Stannard,'[115] recalled continuity girl Renée Glynne.

With Stannard dead, there would be no more *Barton* films from Hammer and no other companies would ever succeed in taking the character back to the cinema. His big screen adventures ended here.

DOWN UNDER:

Of course, during the whole time that Hammer had pursued *Barton*'s career in the cinema, the radio series had continued at the BBC without hindrance.

However, by 1948 the BBC were no longer purely thinking in national terms with their *Dick Barton* franchise, and as Tuson geared up for a third series on the Light Programme, work had already begun on bringing Dick's radio adventures to an even broader audience beyond the UK.

As early as 1947, a number of broadcasting companies and networks from overseas, had started to approach the BBC about broadcasting the *Dick Barton* series in territories outside Britain.

Some of the most vocal interest in the series came from Australia and New Zealand. In early 1948, an outfit called Frank Mason and Co. Ltd. from Melbourne contacted the BBC concerning the international rights to *Barton*.

Foreign distribution of programmes like *Paul Temple* on recorded disc would soon become common through the BBC Transcription Services. However, by 1948, the simple distribution of pre-existing *Dick Barton* recordings was sadly no longer an option for the BBC.

By now, the series had been running for over a year, but most of the actual episodes themselves no longer existed as recordings. *Barton* recordings (in common with most radio serials of the time) had been routinely disposed of soon after broadcast. A *Barton* episode would be recorded, broadcast and then discarded. Nobody had given much thought to what should happen to a programme's recordings *after* it had been broadcast. No doubt some would have been kept on the shelf for possible repeats, but after nearly two years on the air, much had gone. In fact the BBC, recognising little historical importance in *Barton* had only officially archived one *Dick Barton* episode – episode 100 (the final episode of *Dick Barton and the Smugglers*). This single episode had been kept in the BBC Recorded Programmes Library at Broadcasting House, as a representative sample of the series, for the reference of future generations. The idea of

---

[114] From *Inside Hammer* by Jimmy Sangster – Reynolds and Hearn Ltd. (2001)
[115] From *Hammer Films: The Unsung Heroes* by Wayne Kinsey – Tomahawk Press (2010)

supplying an Australian network with an even semi-complete set of episodes, was totally out of the question.

However, Frank Mason and Co. Ltd. were keen to start broadcasting the series from the very first episode onwards.

After much negotiation, it was decided that the series earlier episodes would simply be re-recorded from scratch. This would create a new set of international transcriptions that could be distributed to any country that wished to pick up the series – starting with Australia.

The general manager for Frank Mason and Co. Ltd.'s London operations was a man called Noel Dickson. It would be Dickson who would handle most of the negotiations with the BBC. This was done through W L Streeton, the BBC's Head of Overseas Programme Services, and Cyril Conner, the BBC's Director of Overseas Programme Services.

It was decided that Frank Mason and Co. Ltd. would be sent the original scripts and a list of all the music and sound effects. The company's production arm, Australasian Radio Ltd. would then recreate the episodes in an Australian studio. The resultant recordings would then be used as the new masters for any overseas broadcasts of *Dick Barton – Special Agent*. These international re-recordings would first be broadcast in Australia and then New Zealand.

To help Australasian Radio more accurately understand the *Dick Barton* style of production, it was arranged for four sample episodes to be sent over to Frank Mason and Co. Ltd.'s offices at 352 Collins Street in Melbourne. It is not clear which four episodes were sent. However, an existing docket from the BBC Transcription Service shows that the four 15 minute *Dick Barton* programmes (Serial No. 1964) were dispatched from their Oxford Street office on 15 October 1947.

On 18 May 1948, an initial sales agreement was reached over the scripts. This was confirmed in a letter to W L Streeton on 19 July. The agreement granted Frank Mason and Co. Ltd. the exclusive broadcasting rights to *Dick Barton* within Australia. This initially only applied to the first fifty-two episodes (*Dick Barton and the Secret Weapon, Dick Barton and the Paris Adventure* and the first twelve episodes of *Dick Barton and the Cabatolin Diamonds*), with an option to include later episodes. The BBC would be paid five Australian Guineas per episode under the arrangement. Frank Mason and Co. Ltd. would also be left with an option to the exclusive broadcasting rights in New Zealand, for which they would have to pay an additional three Australian Guineas per episode.

A letter from Noel Dickson to Cyril Connor (dated 11 August 1948) confirmed the deal and sent an initial bank draft for 105 Australian Guineas (the equivalent of eighty-three pounds, eighteen shillings and three pence). Payment to cover the first sixty episodes were later to paid in instalments until the end of January 1949.

Dickson spoke in his letter of his concerns over getting a good timeslot for the programme in Australia and there was also talk of how to publicise the show. However, his attitude was generally upbeat with hopes riding high on the venture. Dickson predicted that the Australian transmissions alone would clock up over two hundred episodes per year.

The series would, as agreed, begin first in Australia. However, Dickson also confirmed his plans to complete negotiations for New Zealand broadcasts, once the Australian run had been confirmed.

The producer for the transcriptions would be the novelist and prolific Australian radio man, Morris L West, working with Australasian Radio.

For obvious reasons, it was never going to be practical to use the BBC's original cast of Johnson, Mann and McCrindle for the new recreations and so new actors were to be brought in by West to replicate the original characters. This new cast included Moira Carleton (Mrs Dale in the Australian version of *Mrs Dale's Diary*), Clifford Cowley, Richard Davies, William Lloyd, John Morgan, Robert Peach and Patricia Kennedy. Surviving paperwork doesn't make it clear who played what.

Prolific Australian radio actor Douglas Kelly would play Dick Barton. Kelly had also played Little John in an Australian radio production of *The Story of Robin Hood* and would later play Inspector West in a long-running Australian radio thriller based on the book series by John Creasey.

The series' Australian broadcasts were to be sponsored by Cadburys and began on 7 February 1949. The February 5 edition of *The ABC Weekly* trailed the broadcasts with a full-page advert saying that, 'Dick Barton Invites You to Breathless Adventure!' It continued to say that, 'by special arrangement with the BBC, you will be able to thrill to the first breath-taking episode of this splendid Secret Service series.'[116]

Due to its vast geographical size, Australia was not able to simultaneously broadcast all of its programmes nationwide. A radio signal broadcasting from a transmitter in Sydney simply wouldn't stretch all the way to other side of the continent in Perth. Consequently, programmes would routinely be circulated around the country via a series of regional substations (some of them independent, others not). These regional stations had names like 2WL and 4BH. The new *Dick Barton* series began Mondays to Thursdays at 7.45 PM through the Macquarie stations, before then moving to Southern Australia and the 2GB, 2HR, 3AW, 3CV, 4BH and 5DN-RM stations for a 7.15 PM slot. The discs would then finally wind up on Mondays and Wednesdays at 7.45 PM on 7HO, 2WL and 2CA.

The show soon caught on in both Australia and later New Zealand and at least two comic-book adaptations followed from Land Newspapers in Australia.

---

[116] From *The ABC Weekly* (05/02/49)

Then in Autumn 1950, the J Walter Thompson advertising agency helped negotiate the rights from the BBC to broadcast *Barton* in South Africa. The Australasian recordings were again used for these broadcasts.

However, in October 1950, Frank Mason and Co. Ltd. were informed that Cadburys no longer wished to sponsor the series in Australia. In a letter to Cyril Conner from 10 October 1950, Noel Dickson indicated his hopes that another sponsor might have been about to join the show. However, there is no evidence to suggest that this ever happened and the re-recordings essentially stopped here. By this point a total of 360 episodes (the first 18 serials) had been re-recorded for international syndication by Australasian Radio and continued to be repeated in both South Africa and Australia for many years to come. The repeats seemed to eventually ground to a stop in the 1960s.

In the early 1950s, Morris West sold his Australasian Radio business. Under its new owners, it became Austalasian Radio and Television Productions (ART) and their reliance on radio drama tailed off through the decade.

SERIES THREE (DEPARTURES):

Things such as the Hammer cinema features and the international syndications had all contributed to establishing Barton as one of the BBC's biggest radio brands. However, its home was still on the Light Programme and away from the many outside distractions of the growing franchise, Tuson and his team were still firmly focussed, when the time rolled round for a third radio series in September 1948.

Things were largely as before and Noel Johnson and John Mann were both still in place; as was Colin Douglas as Inspector Burke. And Alex McCrindle returned as Jock, after (voluntarily) sitting out a number of serials in the latter half of series two.

The first serial of the new season was *Dick Barton and the J B Case* (the only story ever to have its title credited in the *Radio Times*). Written by Edward J Mason, it saw Barton and his friends acting as personal bodyguards to an imperilled millionaire.

The production of the serials had now been refined to a precise formula, which would allow the *Barton* team to work quickly and energetically without too much evident repetition.

Something approaching a family atmosphere had been arrived at through the frequent use of a small pool of actors including John Calthrop, Denis McCarthy, Basil Jones, James Raglan, Jack Shaw, Arthur Bush and others. The regular announcer was usually either Hamilton Humphreys or John Fitchen.

However, there was one very important voice that was about to leave the series – Noel Johnson.

Johnson was finding life with *Barton* very difficult. Due to a deluge of fan-mail, he had asked the BBC to help with his correspondence to listeners, but this ended in confusion. In principle, Johnson was free to pursue other work outside of *Dick Barton*, but internally many BBC producers had effectively black-balled him due to their basic snobbery. Some in the drama department were even vocally annoyed with Johnson for having anything to do with the programme. To make life even harder, head of BBC Drama Val Gielgud had also made it plain that he disliked *Dick Barton* and frowned upon the previously respected Johnson for lowering his standards in taking part. When Gielgud published his 1957 survey of British Radio, he made his feelings plain, by saying, 'nothing – or little – of *Dick Barton*.'[117]

The pressure of fame was also great. 'We used to travel a lot in the summer on the paddle steamers going up and down the Bristol channel,' recalled Johnson's son, Gareth. 'We were always invited to the bridge. Now, that was the power of *Dick Barton*. It's extraordinary. Dad was being asked to open fetes – to do things left, right and centre, which were all to do with *Dick Barton*. And, in a kind of a way, it coloured his career for better and for worse.'[118]

Noel Johnson explained: 'I could not get the BBC to realise that I was in the position, if you like, of a film star, so far as fan mail and popularity and everything else, with something like a fraction of a film star's earnings.'[119]

With work hard to come by within the BBC and typecasting outside of it, Johnson's plight was familiar to many of the BBC's radio stars.

In 1949, after much thought he made the inevitable decision to leave.

'I'd been taking part in a radio play with Brenda Bruce,' he said. 'As she lived in a flat just round the corner from Broadcasting House, she asked me back for a drink during a Sunday lunchtime break in rehearsals. As we sat talking ... I told her that I'd made up my mind to leave. Her late husband Roy Rich was at that time working on the *Daily Express* and ... he came in and said "Does anybody else know? If not, can I have an exclusive?"'[120]

Naturally, it wasn't long before the story broke. The BBC certainly made some attempts to change Johnson's mind, but they did not succeed. Johnson indicated that an increased salary could sway him, but none was forthcoming. 'They asked me to name my price. I said: "one hundred pounds per week." They said: "It sounds like you want danger money."

---

[117] From *British Radio Drama: 1922-1956* by Val Gielgud – George G Harrap Ltd (1957)
[118] From *Dick Barton – A Very Special Agent* – BBC Radio 4 (15/07/10)
[119] From *Dick Barton – A Very Special Agent* – BBC Radio 4 (15/07/10)
[120] From *The Wireless Stars* by George Nobbs – Wensum Books (1972)

SERIAL THRILLERS

"That's precisely what I want," I replied. And that was the end of it.'[121]

There had been numerous things Johnson had been required to turn down during his time with *Barton* (such as advertising work for Kelloggs' Cornflakes). However, once he left the show, he found the offers also seemed to taper off. 'I went straight into a West End play,' he said. 'Needless to say it flopped.'[122]

Johnson would eventually make a triumphant return to radio adventuring, alongside many of his *Barton* colleagues. However, that would be a few years off and for the moment Johnson quietly dropped from the public radar.

With the public departure of the programme's star, the BBC were inundated with casting suggestions. Some were serious, many were not.

'I want to be Dick Barton. I have a gruff voice and I can shout,'[123] read one postcard sent in by a seven-year-old boy.

There was never any intention of ending the programme entirely (they were part way through production of *Barton*'s third season) and the BBC were keen to find a replacement. They eventually found their man in the form of part-time actor and part-time explorer, Duncan Carse.

Carse was born Verner Duncan Carse-Wilen in Fulham in 1913. An only child, he was left in the care of his aunt and grandmother when his parents moved to America while he was still young. He joined a boarding school at age nine, but was unhappy there. He later wrote: 'I was afraid of just about everything, but chiefly of pain, danger and people – especially people, because it was they who inflicted most of the miseries.'[124]

The troubled Carse later found a purpose in his life through learning of the exploits of Arctic explorers like Shackleton and Scot. He duly became an apprentice seaman with the Royal Research Ship *Discovery II* in 1933 on an Antarctic survey expedition. His ambitions were to follow in the footsteps of Shackleton and complete what he had not. Of course, the war saw such plans put on hold, when he joined Royal Navy.

On paper, he was the ideal candidate for Barton – If anything, even tougher and more adventurous than Dick himself. The situation was possibly similar to the recasting of James Bond in the late sixties, when Polar explorer Ranulph Fiennes was under consideration for the part.

Despite Carse's chequered career, there was no denying that there was a certain logic in his casting. Perhaps the only truly odd aspect was that he was interested in auditioning in the first place. However, the restless Carse would always be difficult to predict.

---

[121] From an interview with Noel Johnson in *The Independent* (19/12/98)
[122] From an interview with Noel Johnson in *The Independent* (19/12/98)
[123] From *Dick Barton – A Very Special Agent* – BBC Radio 4 (15/07/10)
[124] From *The Guardian* (30/06/07)

He later glossed over the decision, commenting that: 'I went through the usual vetting process. I had a run-through with Alex McCrindle and Johnny Mann – Jock and Snowey. And there it was. Bob's your uncle.'[125]

Noel Johnson would quietly bow out of the Barton rôle part way through series three. His last serial was *Dick Barton and Jordan's Folly* and his last episode went out on 4 February 1949. Carse took over the following week, with as little fuss made about the transition as possible. However, it's clear that the dynamic of the programme had been massively altered.

Behind the scenes, continuity remained as Mason and Webb continued to serve as resident writers and wrote all bar one of the serials for the third season.

The one serial not to come from either Webb or Mason was *Dick Barton and the Secret Formula*. The idea for this storyline appears to have come from programme planner John McMillan. In a BBC memo, McMillan suggested a storyline for the show where, 'a psychotic dwarf arranges the murder of his cousin in baffling and bizarre circumstances. His motive? Jealousy of the cousin, whose good looks and personal charm earn the dwarf's enmity in childhood days.'[126]

The story didn't quite materialise as McMillan proposed, but the idea was clearly adapted to make up the plot of *Dick Barton and the Secret Formula*. The serial, written by John Sharp and George Court, involved an unlikely pair of criminals called Ventrio and Blitzer. Outwardly, Ventrio and Blitzer were a stage-act. Ventrio (Charles Lloyd Pack) was a ventriloquist and Blitzer (John Blythe) was simply a wooden puppet used in the act. However, Ventrio was secretly behind the theft of the missing formula and was simply using the ventriloquism as a cover for his activities. Blitzer wasn't a vent's doll at all. He was actually a dwarf working as Ventrio's accomplice. (A deranged dwarf had also appeared in *Dick Barton and the Paris Adventure*.) The story was clearly a return to some of the more bizarre storylines of earlier serials. It was a trend that was followed in stories like *Dick Barton and the Voice*, in which a consignment of radium has gone missing. However, the fantasy truly peaked with the season's finale *Dick Barton and the Betts Plan*.

The Betts Plan (by Mason) revolved around a powerful new weed-killer being used to hold the world to ransom.

The chief foe was the titular Betts – a Nazi war criminal with plans of world domination (which clearly contravened the series' 'Rules of Conduct'). The character was played by well-known BBC man Felix Felton. He was best known for playing the Mayor in Toy Town during wartime editions of *Children's Hour*. However, he was also a senior radio producer on programmes like *From the London Theatre*, as well as working as a freelance

---

[125] From *Dick Barton – A Very Special Agent* – BBC Radio 4 (15/07/10)
[126] From *Dick Barton – A Very Special Agent* – BBC Radio 4 (15/07/10)

composer of light music. He may have seemed like an unusually illustrious figure to play villain of the week in *Dick Barton*. However, his casting helps illustrate both the esteem in which the BBC held *Barton* and the very close-knit working nature of BBC radio drama at the time. In fact, Felton wasn't the only BBC producer to return to acting in the series.

Dick Barton and the Betts Plan was the last serial that Neil Tuson would produce for *Dick Barton*.

Tuson had already had a co-producer working with him during some of series three (Frank Hauser). Now Tuson would leave the series altogether. He had been with the programme from day one and had shaped its identity along the way. He left the BBC Drama Department to work for the Light Programme's chief commercial rival – Radio Luxembourg (of which more later). Tuson had, by this point, married occasional *Dick Barton* actress Anne Cullen, who would continue to work for him over on Radio Luxembourg.

To mark Tuson's departure and the end of another successful series, a special scene was tacked onto the end of the final episode of *Dick Barton and the Betts Plan* (Episode 444). It was recorded at the Grafton Studios on Tottenham Court Road on the afternoon of Wednesday, 9 March 1949.

With the villainous Betts now dispatched to a fiery death in the wreckage of a burning plane, Barton and company return home, only to be greeted by Neil Tuson. Tuson says: 'Well now chaps, as this is the end of the present series, I thought it might be an idea to introduce our two main authors to you and also to the listeners.' At this point Webb and then Mason are brought to the microphone. Then the cast of Colin Douglas, Alex McCrindle, John Mann and Duncan Carse are introduced in turn. Tuson then thanks those listening in Britain's hospitals before asking, 'Could I have a spot of music please?' In crashes the famous *Devil's Galop* theme tune and Tuson concludes with a word to the announcer John Fitchen: 'Will that do John?'[127] An era had passed.

SERIES FOUR:

In spite of changes to cast and crew, the third series of *Dick Barton –Special Agent* maintained its popularity. And even with the original Dick now gone, the fans continued to stick with it. And there were lots of fans, hailing from all quarters (even including a young Michael Bentine).

One of the show's most surprisingly ardent admirers was Labour party stalwart and Cabinet minister Herbert Morrison.

Future Minister for Food Maurice Webb visited Morrison in Hammersmith around March 1947, on party business. However, partway through Webb's report, Morrison stopped his colleague and went to the

---

[127] *Dick Barton and the Betts Plan* – Episode 15 (25/03/49)

radio. 'Just shut up for a quarter of an hour,'[128] he was reported to say, before settling down with his fellow politician to listen to the latest *Dick Barton* episode – afterwards explaining to Webb the background to that week's story. Morrison was also reported to have told Lady Allen of Hurtwood to cut short one of her visits, so as he would not miss that night's episode. It is sadly unlikely that news of either incident did his already dwindling political standing much good. However, he later defended his unrepentant enjoyment of the series in a speech, saying: 'I like *Dick Barton* and listen to him when I get a chance. I listen because I like it, which seems a good reason for doing a thing provided you don't get yourself into trouble.'[129]

Other Westminster colleagues shared Morrison's instantly loveable justification. 'Utterly fantastic,' was how one civil servant described the programme, 'very absorbing. Like ivy, it grows on one.'[130] It was an interesting sign that the programme still had a broad fanbase, as it embarked upon its fourth season.

John McMillan[131] doesn't seem to have had any ill feeling toward Neil Tuson over his defection to the commercial sector earlier in the year. He had himself worked for independent radio before the war. However, Tuson's departure had left him with an empty space at the top of one of his most highly rated programmes[132].

The BBC wouldn't appoint an entirely full-time replacement for Tuson. Instead the job of *Barton*'s producer would be filled by a changing roster of names drawn from the BBC's tenured workforce in the BBC Drama Department. There would no longer be a resident producer on the programme from this point on. However, the most regularly used members of staff on the programme were Charles LeFeaux and David H Godfrey and it would be these two men who would be the nearest thing to permanent editors for the show over the next few years.

Godfrey had worked on the programme before, filling in for Tuson on the 1948 production of *Dick Barton and the Case of Conrad Ruda* during series two.

LeFeaux hadn't been a producer long. However, he had been a member of the Drama Repertory Company, through which he acted in a number of

---

[128] From *Herbert Morrison: Portrait of a Politician* by Bernard Donoughue and G W Jones – Weidenfeld and Nicolson (1973)
[129] From *Boys Will Be Boys* by E S Turner – Hollen Street Press (1975)
[130] From *Popular Radio Drama* by David Wade (Published in Radio Drama ed. Peter Lewis) – Longman (1981)
[131] McMillan was now Chief Assistant Controller of the Light Programme. Norman Collins had left the Light Programme by this point and had moved on (briefly) to become Controller of BBC Television.
[132] *Barton* had now begun to pull in ratings of an estimated 16 million.

earlier *Barton* serials, including *Dick Barton and the Bonazio Gang* (1947). He'd also been in numerous stage productions both in the West End and provincial theatre.

The first serial of the latest batch would be *Dick Barton and the Vallonian Adventure*, with Godfrey as producer. Carse was back for his first season-opener with the ever-reliable Mann and McCrindle also offering support. Colonel Gardiner returned as well, here played by the appropriately named Cyril Gardiner. Inspector Burke was also recast, with Colin Douglas replaced by James Raglan.

Webb and Mason continued to provide the lion's share of the scripts alongside another serial from Basil Dawson (*Dick Barton and the Black Rock*) There was also the arrival of new writer, Bertie (B D) Chapman with his script for *Dick Barton and the House of Windows*. Mason was also responsible for the script of the Christmas special, *The Night of the Twenty-Seventh* (see *Paul Temple* chapter).

Series four continued after a short break for Easter[133] until finally drawing to a close with episode 13 of Mason's *Dick Barton and the Lucky Gordon Affair* (co-starring a young Donald Pleasence) on 14 April 1950.

THE CENSORS STRIKE BACK:

Following the transmission of *Barton*'s fourth series, the BBC once again gave a rethink to the possibly corrupting influence that the programme may have been casting over the country's youth.

Since the introduction of the 'Rules of Conduct' some years before, much of the more adult content of the show had been firmly removed and many of the programme's more vocal critics had been, at the very least, subdued.

However, with neither Neil Tuson nor Norman Collins any longer around at the BBC to defend it, the show's more conservative detractors were once again circling. Even in the pre-Mary Whitehouse days of 1950, there were plenty of vocal criticisms of the rash fripperies of Barton and his friends and it was early in the year that the BBC sought to assuage some of these concerns.

One of the earliest actions was the BBC's distribution of a special audience research questionnaire in early 1950. These questionnaires were circulated to more than seventy child-guidance clinics across the country, in a bid to accurately gauge the impact *Barton* was having on the nation's children. The replies to this survey are interesting, possibly telling us as

---

[133] In a break in the normal schedule, the BBC didn't broadcast any *Barton* episodes on either Good Friday (07/04/50) or Bank Holiday Monday (10/04/50). A break over Christmas was now routine for the programme, but this was the first instance of a break over Easter.

much about the attitudes of the supervising adults, as they do about the actual children themselves.

The Portman Children's Clinic in London wrote back to say that, 'Nightmares and undue mental tension are produced in some children ... The educational value seems poor ... Many of them look on Barton as a fool who gets away with too much and miss the moral issues raised.'[134]

'It fills a vacuum, but is not constructive,' reported the department of psychological medicine at Great Ormond Street Children's Hospital, with yet more patrician overtones. It concluded: 'There is no indication that years of strenuous preparation precede heroic exploits. The characters are shadowy. The heroes are complimentary to "spivs", rather than their opposites.'[135]

Perhaps the strangest condemnation however came from a child guidance clinic in Chatham, who said: 'The fact that the child listens to *Dick Barton* is frequently mentioned by mothers of over-anxious children.'[136]

Meanwhile, up at the Royal Hospital for Sick Children in Edinburgh, a more generous view was that 'it is a useful medium for the projection of phantasy (sic).'[137]

The final verdict of the report was actually two to one in favour of the programme, however the criticisms had hit home back at the BBC and the corporation's concerns once again made headlines.

In Australia (where the programme was increasingly popular), *The Hobart Mercury* reported on 2 May, how the show had 'been suitably cleaned up for young audiences.' It also commented on the 'large dossier at Broadcasting House, which not only gives data about his [Barton's] personal background and adventures so far, but lists certain things he must not do or say.'[138]

A BBC Listener Research Paper appeared called *Dick Barton and Juvenile Delinquency* on 15 May. Then a BBC Memo issued on 29 June introduced yet another set of new rules, adopted to ensure that *Barton* remained child-friendly.

Soon after, the BBC made the decision to appoint an official censor (editor) to keep an eye on *Barton*. The man initially chosen for the job was Australian John Burke. He was a probation officer to a London court and also had done some work for Twentieth Century Fox. He accepted the job. However, he'd ultimately only remain in the position for half a day. It was later claimed that Burke had disliked the publicity surrounding his

---

[134] From *Austerity Britain: 1945-51* by David Kynaston – Bloomsbury Publishing (2007)
[135] From *Austerity Britain: 1945-51* by David Kynaston – Bloomsbury Publishing (2007)
[136] From *Austerity Britain: 1945-51* by David Kynaston – Bloomsbury Publishing (2007)
[137] From *Austerity Britain: 1945-51* by David Kynaston – Bloomsbury Publishing (2007)
[138] From *The Hobart Mercury* (02/05/50)

appointment and made the decision not to go any further with it.

Around July, the BBC convened something akin to a court of inquiry over the entire *Dick Barton* series, with the continued future of the programme on the line. Evidence was provided by Cecily Monchaux (another Australian) who worked as a lecturer in psychology.

The *Sydney Morning Herald* picked up the story in its 20 July edition, commenting on the affect the programme could be having on young Australian listeners.

'Officials of Station 2GB said last night,' it reported, 'that all their serials conformed with the standards of practice of the Federation of Commercial Broadcasting Stations. They said serials were approved from the point of view of public interest, the standard of production and entertainment value. No serious complaints had been received about *Dick Barton, Special Agent*.'[139]

Of course, why the BBC so fervently sought to undermine one of its top-rated programmes, is an obvious question. Although a combination of paternal snobbery and Reith-like austerity had always dogged *Barton*, there wasn't really any massive groundswell of opinion against the programme in 1950 – at least, not until the BBC itself stirred it up. To the outsider, the entire storm-in-a-teacup could almost have looked like deliberate sabotage from within the BBC. Of course, that is exactly what it was.

The brooding presence of former Director General and BBC founder Lord Reith still cast a heavy shadow over the older-guard at the BBC. It may seem strange, but the simple fact is that many of the more conservative elements within the BBC just didn't like *Dick Barton* and they didn't think that it was the kind of thing the BBC should be doing. It was a silly fantasy. It may have entertained, but it didn't inform and it didn't educate. It just made a lot of people very happy and if there was one thing that Reith's BBC had never stood for, it was that.

It was, by now, very well known that among the country's most ardent critics of the show was head of BBC Drama himself, Val Gielgud (a devoted advocate of Reith's austere BBC vision). Gielgud was politic enough not to shout about it too much, but it was plain that he disliked the series intensely and would have much rather spent the time and money on more culturally significant pieces of work.

Ex-producer Neil Tuson (now firmly established at Radio Luxembourg), later explained that 'Val Gielgud decided that it wasn't the right thing to be broadcast. I think he thought that it was a bad influence on the youth of Britain.'[140]

Of course, you can't just axe such a massively popular show as *Dick Barton*. Instead you have to do your best to stop it being a massively popular

---

[139] From The *Sydney Morning Herald* (20/07/50)
[140] From *Dick Barton – A Very Special Agent* – BBC Radio 4 (15/07/10)

show. You wind it down, and do your best to kill off the listeners. And then, when the programme is spiralling, you take it into the woods with a shotgun and put it out of its misery. The idea is that nobody will miss it, because nobody is any longer listening. It sounds deeply cynical, but it's a well-worn technique for network executives to get rid of otherwise popular shows with the minimum of public outcry. Almost exactly the same thing happened with television's *Doctor Who* in the late 1980s (and arguably even *Top of the Pops* in 2006).

It's impossible to be definitive on people's motivations so long after the event. However it is, at least highly likely, that the BBC and Gielgud's actions were as much motivated by personal feeling as they were genuine concern for the direction of the programme. Certainly, Gielgud was an acolyte of Lord Reith's original vision of the BBC[141] as a 'healthy agent of repression'[142], believing that you gave the people what was good for them, not necessarily what they wanted.

By 1950, there was also another BBC radio series that Gielgud was keen to push forward – something altogether worthier than *Barton* – more educational – more informative. It was a simple programme – an everyday story of country folk.

DICK BARTON – EXPLORER:

The fifth and (as it turned out) final season of *Dick Barton – Special Agent* would start in October 1950. It was even more toned-down than before and would be a slightly shorter run than previously. There were more cast changes too. Duncan Carse would not be coming back for another series.

Always an unpredictable and restless man, in 1950, Carse left the acting world, in order to throw himself back into some real-life adventuring. He was still seeking to be the modern-day Shakleton he had dreamt of as a boy.

Now 46, he was twice divorced, bankrupt and an alcoholic. He only appeared in a BBC studio once more. In 1953, he stirred up a small commotion when Roy Plomley interviewed him for *Desert Island Discs*. Asked what luxury he would take with him to a desert island, he replied that he'd have an inflatable rubber woman.[143]

Leaving the BBC behind, Carse headed back to Antarctica in 1951, on the first of four cartographical survey expeditions. It was a surprising success, but Carse's luck wouldn't last.

---

[141] Gielgud dedicated his 1957 radio memoirs to Lord Reith and also had a full-page photograph of the man printed on the inside as a frontispiece.
[142] From Cambridge University: *Varsity* (02/03/10)
[143] In 1972, Oliver Reed was a guest on *Desert Island Discs*. He repeated Carse's request and also asked for an inflatable woman.

In 1961, just days after he proposed to his fiancée Venetia Kemp, he set out on an experiment in isolation. His plan was to travel to Undine South Harbour, a desolate cove near South Georgia. He'd build a small wooden hut and live there in total solitude for 18 months. It was to have been an experiment in how isolation could strengthen the human soul.

Speaking to a press conference just before he left, he said: 'I am disillusioned with my fellow men ... Since I was a boy, I have yearned to live an existence away from it all, and with middle age the feeling is irresistible ... I hope to find something. I think I'll become a stronger character.'[144]

He never did find that something he was looking for. The expedition was an utter disaster. On 20 May 1961, a huge wave smashed his makeshift hut into fragments. He was in bed at the time, only semi-dressed, with many of his possessions already slipping away beneath the tide. Scientific equipment, medical supplies, his gramophone player, Harry Belafonte records and a pair of stuffed toys were all washed away. With no radio or means of outside help, Carse had a total mental breakdown – all alone in the freezing Antarctic wastes.

He drank heavily and contemplated suicide, writing in his diary: 'Carse stiff looks like a better bet for posterity than Carse animate!'[145] However, it is likely that his drinking actually saved him, as he was invariably too intoxicated to carry through with the act.

Astonishingly, against all odds, Carse survived the ordeal. His skills and knowledge of the region kept him alive and after 116 days, he was spotted by a ship and finally rescued on September 12 1961.

Physically broken, he was later described as looking like a returning prisoner of war. His drinking continued and the failure of the expedition had left him with an insurmountable financial debt.

The story had a happy ending, however. Fiancée Venetia Kemp had waited for him. She married Carse in December 1962. Carse spent the rest of his life with Venetia in a quiet country cottage in Sussex. He died in 2004, aged 91.

ANOTHER DICK BARTON (SERIES FIVE):

When the BBC had first announced Carse's departure from the cast in 1950, they had been inundated with the same volume of rabid applicants as before (around 750), but this time settled on a quieter replacement.

Gordon Davies would be the new Dick Barton for series five. The 28-year-old Davies was about as unlike his predecessors as it was possible to

---

[144] From *The Guardian* (30/06/07)
[145] From *The Guardian* (30/06/07)

get. A little-known radio and theatre actor, he had no aspirations to explore the globe or do anything other than act. 'I am not a very glamorous person,'[146] he would say.

Controversially, he hadn't fought in the war at all and had actually been a registered conscientious objector. 'I was medically unfit, but I'm not sheltering behind doctors' certificates,' he explained to the press. 'I was exempted from national service as a conscientious objector.'[147] Both Johnson and Carse of course, had had illustrious war records.

Following on from the raw and moody Carse, the BBC had perhaps finally decided that you didn't really need to *be* Dick Barton in real-life in order to play the part in a drama serial. With memories of the war still very fresh, the actor's avoidance of conscription did cause some comment. However, a BBC spokesman said, 'We cannot penalise the most suitable actor for the part on these grounds.'[148] The new actor certainly seemed a safer pair of hands than the starry Johnson or the erratic Carse.

Dick Barton and the SS Golden Main Story would be Davies' first serial and the first of the new series – starting on 2 October 1950. Charles LeFeaux was back as producer, although David H Godfrey, Archie Campbell and Ayton Whitaker also produced later serials. James Raglan returned as Burke for most of the season, but was replaced for the very last serial (*Dick Barton and the Trail of the Rocket*) by Arnold Diamond. Mann and McCrindle were also back as usual.

COUNTRY FOLK:

Edward J Mason and Geoffrey Webb continued to contribute to the new run. However, they wrote less for the new series than ever before (both only wrote two serials each) and Bertie Chapman was brought back to write for a good deal of the remainder (with newcomer Anthony Garwood also contributing).

Interestingly a script was also submitted in July 1950 by a man called Desmond Briscoe. The script was rejected, but Briscoe would go onto work with the BBC much later, forming the famous BBC Radiophonic Workshop, as a studio manager in 1958.

Mason and Webb's reduced involvement in the new series shouldn't simply be put down to a lack of interest in the new order. There is still every sign they were actively engaged in the show and had only recently written a book on it – *The Inside Story of Dick Barton* (1950). Their reduced commitment to *Barton* was actually down to their involvement in another BBC radio

---

[146] From *The Sunday Herald* (27/08/50)
[147] From *The Guardian* (30/06/07)
[148] From *The Sunday Herald* (27/08/50)

programme, which was then in development – *The Archers*.

The Archers is incorrectly assumed by many to have been *Barton*'s replacement at the BBC. This isn't exactly true, as in fact, both programmes briefly overlapped – being in production at the same time.

BBC Midland staff producer Godfrey Basely, was at the time mainly concerned with the BBC's rural affairs output, when in 1950, he was left with a problem: 'I couldn't find any listeners to listen to the standard BBC type of farming programme' he recalled. 'There was this conference in Birmingham to see what country-folk wanted in the way of programmes about farming and gardening and country life and there was nothing came out of that, until this farmer [Henry Burt from Lincolnshire] stood up at the back and said, "Well, what we farmers want, is a farming *Dick Barton*." Well, of course, everybody burst out laughing and that was the end of the conference.'[149]

The suggestion would end up being taken very seriously. The concept was developed and eventually the obvious idea of bringing in personnel from *Dick Barton* itself was suggested. 'When it was learnt that Edward J Mason was on board,' remembered *Archers*' actor Norman Painting, 'the idea suddenly seemed more viable. Edward J Mason (Ted) brought with him his fellow scriptwriter from *Dick Barton*, Geoffrey Webb, who luckily was a countryman ... Ted and Geoff soon produced draft scripts.'[150]

The Archers first took to the air on Whit-Monday, 29 May 1950[151] on the Midlands Regional Home Service. Four episodes followed over that week, as part of a short pilot series.

Webb and Mason weren't the only *Barton* personnel on the new project. *Dick Barton*'s regular studio manager and sound engineer Tony Shryane also joined the new programme. Shryane had worked with the BBC since the mid-1930s and had been carried over to *Barton* from the earlier *Robinson Family*. By 1950, he was one of BBC Birmingham's most senior broadcast engineers and joined *The Archers* almost by default.

Desmond Carrington recalls running into Mason and Webb in Birmingham's BBC club at the time. 'I remember,' he says, 'after I'd done a *Children's Hour* written by Edward J Mason – he and Geoffrey were in the club and they said they'd just done a pilot of *The Archers* or something. They thought it would run for three months and they were quite pleased with themselves.'

---

[149] From *Dick Barton – A Very Special Agent* – BBC Radio 4 (15/07/10)
[150] From *Forever Ambridge* by Norman Painting – Michael Joseph Ltd. (1975)
[151] For some peculiar reason, the BBC themselves have almost always failed to recognise this date as the first broadcast of *The Archers*. They instead credit 1 January 1951 as the start date for the series. This was actually the date when the main-programme run began. As such, January 2011 was credited as the 60 anniversary of the show, even though the programme itself was closer to 61 years old, by that time.

DICK BARTON – SPECIAL AGENT

For the moment, *The Archers* was little more than another prospective serial proposal – feeling its way every bit as much as the fledgling *Barton* had done in 1946. However, in a very short time, it would become of much greater significance.

SWAN SONG:

The fifth series of *Dick Barton* was shorter, but no less eventful, than its predecessors. Guest star Roger Snowdon who returned from series four for *Dick Barton and the Green Triangle Gang*, later recalled the series fondly, saying: 'I shall always remember ... an extremely pretty effects girl[152] [Junior Programme Engineer] on her knees by a box of sand, doing horses galloping across the desert with a pair of coconut shells ... She held a bunch of keys in her teeth, shaking her head from time to time and managing simultaneously to make horse-blowing noises.'[153]

The final serial of the fifth series would be the 13-part *Dick Barton and the Trail of the Rocket*. It was written by neither Mason nor Webb, but instead came from the pen of Bertie Chapman. Long before the serial entered the studio, the production team knew that it was to be the last *Dick Barton* serial.

After five eventful series, which still showed little sign of growing stale, *Barton* was finally to be retired. The decision was (at least in part) Gielgud's, who had won through with his argument that the action-orientated froth of *Barton* really wasn't what the BBC had been set up to broadcast. It was also robbing his higher-brow *Wednesday Matinee* of its listeners. It simply did not (as Gielgud phrased it) encourage listeners to 'better examples of dramatic listening.'[154]

The final episode (the 711th [155]) was recorded at the BBC's famous Maida Vale studios in London and was transmitted on 30 March 1951. It was all over.

'That was the end,' remembered Gordon Davies. 'My option wasn't taken up. They were closing the programme. We had a lovely party that night, I recall – a super party, actually. And that was it.'[156]

The final episode itself ended with Barton closing his freelance adventuring days altogether with the following speech from Davies (as Barton): 'In October 1946, we started something beyond our wildest dreams. We started our own, almost private, war. It's been a war against crime. The

---

[152] This was probably either Antonia Madden or Sheila Blower. Both were still teenagers when they started as Junior Programme Engineers on *Dick Barton*.
[153] From *Dick Barton and All That* – BBC Radio 4 (31/10/82)
[154] From *Radio Drama at the Crossroads* by R Wood – De Montfort University Press (2008)
[155] It's really 712 episodes, if you include *The Night of the Twenty-Seventh* Christmas special from 1949.
[156] From *Dick Barton – A Very Special Agent* – BBC Radio 4 (15/07/10)

pace has quickened up right through the past six years and we think we need a rest ... We've made a lot of friends and a few enemies, but we've tried to stick to the rules.'[157]

Many fans were, of course, distraught. Perhaps the show's most devoted fan Pat Hetherington remembered: 'I thought it was a tragedy. I was heartbroken. I did have a weep over it – definitely. It takes a lot to make me weep. I don't do it easily, but I'm afraid that I did weep that night.'[158]

Meanwhile, the cast and crew of *The Archers* took the news in a more understandably upbeat frame of mind – for obvious reasons.

'The programme had been running for some seven weeks or so,' said Norman Painting, 'when the good news was broken to us that, not only were our contracts to be renewed for three months, but *Dick Barton – Special Agent* was being taken off, and we were to take its place at the peak time of 6.45 PM.'[159]

The less controversial and more conservative tales of everyday rural life had won through against the salacious Barton. And *The Archers* (at the time of writing) is still roughly in the same timeslot even today.

A critic for *Radio Review* magazine considered *Barton*'s unlikely usurper in an issue from 25 May 1951. 'When the new family serial took over the 6.45 PM daily spot from *Dick Barton*, many people though it would prove a flop,' wrote the reviewer. 'To follow an all action serial with a story about everyday life and people on a farm seems a little like anti-climax. Well, the doubters have been proved wrong.'[160]

The Archers finally succeeded in breaking past 9.5 million listeners in early 1953. However, it would be a very long time before the series ever managed to soar past the 16 million mark set by *Barton* at his height.

Some *Barton* fans would never forgive the series for its perceived part in Dick's downfall. Terry Wogan was later quoted as saying: 'As a young boy I never missed an episode. I've never been able to listen to *The Archers* with any degree of affection because they replaced *Dick Barton* and I've never really forgiven Ambridge for it.'[161]

In one final twist, many years later, Noel Johnson's son, Gareth would join the cast of *The Archers*, playing a character called Roger Travers Macy. 'Dad was always rather silly,' said Gareth Johnson, 'about the fact that he'd done *Dick Barton* and then his son was sort of in the thing that took over from it.'[162]

---

[157] *Dick Barton and the Trail of the Rocket* – Episode 13 (03/03/51)
[158] From *Dick Barton and All That* – BBC Radio 4 (31/10/82)
[159] From *Forever Ambridge* by Norman Painting – Michael Joseph Ltd. (1975)
[160] From *Radio Review* (25/05/51)
[161] From *The Radio Companion* by Paul Donovan – Grafton Books (1992)
[162] From *Dick Barton – A Very Special Agent* – BBC Radio 4 (15/07/10)

DICK BARTON – SPECIAL AGENT

AFTER BARTON:

Following the end of *Dick Barton*, both Geoffrey Webb and Edward J Mason would continue to work together as the chief scriptwriters for *The Archers* – a job that would last the rest of their lives. Their final brush with *Dick Barton* came in 1953, when they were behind the script of a *Dick Barton* comic strip that ran until 1954 in the *Comet* comic from Amalgamated Press. The strip featured only Dick and Snowey (no Jock) and began in issue 247 of the comic on April 11 1953. Webb and Mason's story of *Dick Barton and the Flying Saucer Mystery* didn't catch on, but later some of its plot points were reworked in a new radio project, again with Noel Johnson, for Radio Luxembourg (of which, more later).

Gordon Davies would continue to work as a radio actor and became a member of the BBC Drama Repertory Company in 1955. That same year he appeared in an episode of *Appointment with Fear* and later acted in 1960's *Saturday Night Theatre* production of *Dr Jekyll and Mr Hyde*.

Alex McCrindle's post-*Barton* career was more interesting. While still working on *Barton*, he had branched out as a BBC producer and scriptwriter and produced the first series of *Larry the Lamb* for television. He continued as a producer after *Barton*'s cancellation. However, his career began to falter in the early fifties. He was a publicly avowed Marxist and member of the Communist party and during the fifties and sixties he found himself the victim of a general paranoia and prevailing ignorance that left him effectively blacklisted, due to his political convictions. He would continue to act in a series of low-budget features, but rarely appeared under his own name (to avoid the blacklisting). With work in McCarthyist America completely out of the question, he threw himself into work with Equity, particularly helping to build up the union's strength in Scotland.

He returned to television in the mid-1960s, with parts in *The Saint* and later *All Creatures Great and Small* and *Taggart*. Then, in 1977 he had an unlikely brush with Hollywood, playing a General in the first *Star Wars* film.

His politics followed him to *Star Wars*. And in a minor dispute, with director George Lucas over pay and the nature of percentile royalties, it was McCrindle who campaigned, through Equity, for bonuses for all of the *Star Wars* cast.

McCrindle's later career was dominated by big parts in TV and film dramas like, *Reilly: Ace of Spies* and the film *Eye of the Needle*. He died on 20 April 1990.

And what of Val Gielgud – the executioner himself? Around 1949, he attempted to concentrate his efforts on working in television. His superiors had hoped that he would make a lasting impact on the infant medium. However, his time behind the camera was not a great success and his brand of management failed to lend itself to the format. A new head of drama (purely for television) was appointed in 1952 and Gielgud was moved back to a radio-only position.

Gielgud remained respected by a number of his colleagues at the corporation and further afield. However, many others considered him to be an elitist snob, who disdained all but the most highbrow of dramas and stifled the creativity of those around him. Many felt forced to leave the corporation, later setting up in commercial competition to the BBC. He was highly opinionated, proud of his achievements (and there were many), but also all too willing to brush under the carpet his many misjudgements.

It is not unfair to see Gielgud as the principal reason for *Barton*'s sidelining and eventual cancellation. And for all his valuable work in the early days of the BBC, Gielgud did as much harm to the corporation in the long-term as he ever did good in the short term.

He relented only slightly in his views on *Barton*. He would later write: 'Though originally opposed to the idea of *Dick Barton*, I am inclined to believe that he can be justified as the modern equivalent of the Penny Blood which all nice boys used to read under the bedclothes.'[163]

Gielgud died in 1981.

REUNION:

In 1972, the BBC celebrated its fiftieth anniversary. A number of special programmes were recorded as a part of the Golden Jubilee, which was marked across the BBC's network on both radio and television.

Many of the BBC's former glories were to be revisited in documentaries, retrospectives and dramas and an obvious candidate, for inclusion in the festivities, was *Dick Barton – Special Agent*.

In September, the controller of Radio 1 and 2, Douglas Muggeridge, announced that after over twenty years *Dick Barton* would be returning to BBC radio, in a special 10-part serial on Radio 2.

It wouldn't be an entirely original serial, but rather a new (abridged) re-recording of Edward J Mason's original scripts of the very first *Dick Barton* adventure from 1946 – *Dick Barton and the Secret Weapon*.

Very much intended as a recreation of the original series, a number of old faces were to be brought back from the show's original line-up. John Mann was back as Snowey White; Alex McCrindle returned as Jock Anderson and, most importantly of all, Noel Johnson was back as the original Dick Barton. The team were all finally reunited in an adventure they'd originally recorded over a quarter of a century before.

Of course, Neil Tuson was no longer on the BBC's staff and neither was

---

[163] From *Radio Drama at the Crossroads* by R Wood – De Montfort University Press (2008)

Barton's last producer Charles LeFeaux. However, Raymond Raikes, who'd produced the final three serials of series one, was still with the BBC and he returned to the show as producer of the new remake.

The new production was to be (in the words of Muggeridge) an 'unashamed, nostalgic wallow'[164]. However, there was also a less romantic reason for the show's unexpected revival. The BBC had once again begun to turn its attention to the idea of another daily radio serial (after years of life in Ambridge). The new *Barton* serial would serve to test the water for such a project, with careful attention paid to the audience reaction.

The new recording attracted its share of publicity and it was clear that little of the public's ardour for *Barton* had cooled.

'Although twenty-five years have passed,' explained Raikes, 'people have remembered it and the fact that we are going to revive it with the original actors … seems to have caught the imagination in some extraordinary way. Their voices haven't changed a lot. They've gotten a little older, but they can still act.'[165]

The new serial was recorded in Studio 6A at Broadcasting House in Autumn 1972. Much of the cast were made up from members of the BBC Drama Repertory Company. Many had worked on *Dick Barton* before, such as Heron Carvic and Derek Birch. Others were new additions. One such new cast-member was Michael Kilgarriff.

Kilgarriff was a regular on the Rep' and had rejoined it in 1971, following an earlier stint in the mid-sixties. In *Dick Barton*, he played the part of Blom (a henchman).

'I don't think that he had many lines,' says Kilgarriff. 'He grunted and made noises. I played some sort of heavy … That would have been around three days for me.'

Other notable cast members included Richard Hurndall as Sir Archie Wrangle and Francis de Wolff. De Wolff was another repertory veteran who had worked with Johnson, Mason and Webb for Radio Luxembourg. 'Franky went on and off like me,' remembers Kilgarriff. 'Franky – I worked with quite a lot.'

Despite its backward-looking nature, one of the major innovations on the production was the decision to record the whole serial in stereo. Stereo was still very new to BBC radio at the time (and didn't exist on television at all). The idea might have come from Raikes, who was something of a pioneer in the field. It was Raikes who had produced the BBC's very first stereo recording on 6 July 1958 (a *Sherlock Holmes* play) and it would have been something he would have been keen to push further.

'We used to get paid five percent extra of our fee when we did stereo'

---

[164] From *The Times* (15/09/72)
[165] From *Dick Barton – A Very Special Agent* – BBC Radio 4 (15/07/10)

Kilgarriff recalls. 'Normally ... the recording would be done in one go – as per live ... Because it was very difficult to do when we started and we were still in uncharted territory doing the stereo drama, you did it in bits and pieces. You didn't do it in one go. You did it a scene at a time and you might do them out of order. So, instead of giving one performance, you were giving lots of little performances. So, you got five percent extra.'

The stereo recording may also have accounted for Raikes' use of Studio 6A. It was one of the corporation's top and most up-to-date drama studios and was among the few that could handle stereo productions of this complexity.

'The studio floor used to be marked out in squares and things,' continues Kilgarriff. 'You had to mark on your script where you moved to, which of course one hadn't done before. With the old mics, you just walked in and out. If you were leaving a room, you'd back out, but the angle you were at didn't matter, because you all worked off the one mic – standing either side of the same mic ... That's the way stereo was done, when it first came in. Although, it later got more relaxed and it wasn't so difficult.'

The new production was broadcast daily (Monday to Friday) in traditional 15-minute episodes over the course of a fortnight. It was given a slot on Radio 2 at 12.30 PM as part of *The Tony Brandon Show* with a repeat following at 6.15 PM within *The Teddy Johnson Show*.

It was a fairly unusual experiment in serial drama for the predominantly music-based Radio 2, but although well received, it did not lead to any further daily dramas on the station. For one reason or another, it was not deemed to have been sufficiently successful for any follow-up.

'They didn't continue with it, so obviously it wasn't thought to have been that much of a success,' reasons Kilgarriff. 'It probably seemed rather old-fashioned I suppose by then – that style ... smacking your fist into your palm, saying, "Take that for Jock!" and "That's for Snowey!"'

Nevertheless, the serial clearly went down well in some quarters and many *Barton* fans were glad of the reunion.

Barton fan and singer Tommy Steele wrote to *The Times* letters' page saying: 'Twenty years on, my beloved *Barton* is back. I ... hereby give notice to Auntie Beeb that all is forgiven.'[166]

'You know,' says Kilgarriff. 'I had a notification only this week about various things I still get pennies from, various productions going back to the sixties – including *Dick Barton*.'

There would be little further *Barton* activity on BBC Radio over the next few decades. The only notable further exposure came through a lovingly compiled Radio 4 documentary – *Dick Barton: Still a Special Agent* (14 February 1990). Containing interviews with all the BBC's Dicks (Johnson,

---

[166] From *The Times* (15/09/72)

Carse and Davies), it was produced by Jock Gallagher. Gallagher had recently left the BBC's Birmingham offices as their Network Radio Editor, where, among other things he'd worked on *The Archers*. He'd apparently 'always resented *The Archers* for knocking off his schoolboy hero.'[167] Remembering the cancellation, he recalled, 'I was especially distraught because it was the eve of my thirteenth birthday and I thought I might die before its dawning.'[168] Gallagher's programme was an affectionate tribute to *Dick Barton*. However, it would be virtually the last opportunity that anyone had to hear many of the (now elderly) cast back together on BBC radio.

There would never again be another original *Dick Barton* episode from the BBC[169]. However, a new production of *Dick Barton and the Trail of the Rocket* (the final story of series 5) was re-recorded for BBC Audio CD in 2013. Dick Barton was voiced by Tim Bentinck, with Terry Molloy playing Snowey. The pair were, appropriately enough, both then regular cast members in *The Archers*. The producer was someone called Charles Norton.

THE TELEVISION SERIES:

Away from the BBC, there was only one other serious attempt to bring back *Dick Barton* on any real scale – although, this time, on television rather than radio. To date, it is the only time the character has ever been successfully translated to the small screen. The impetus for the project was small ITV franchisee, Southern Television.

Southern Television had been awarded the sole commercial franchise to produce independent television in the South of England, in 1957[170]. They began broadcasting the following year and at the end of 1969 switched to colour television. They were always among the smallest of the independent networks, never managing to compete with metropolitan rivals like Thames. In 1978, the company decided to boost its profile with a twice-weekly adventure serial and with memories of happy childhood adventures on the Light Programme chief in their minds, the people at Southern decided that their new serial would see the TV debut of a radio legend – *Dick Barton*.

There is much that survived the translation from wireless to television. The stories were still spread across a series of multi-episode serials and each individual episode ran to around 15-minutes. *The Devil's Galop* theme-tune was back as well and the principal cast of characters was largely left intact.

---

[167] From *Forever Ambridge* by Norman Painting – Michael Joseph Ltd. (1975)
[168] From *The Listener* (15/02/90)
[169] However, there would be a comedy spin-off show (essentially a spoof) called *Richard Barton – General Practitioner!* The series was written by Lol Mason (the son of Edward J Mason) and ran on Radio 4 for a short time in the late 1990s.
[170] Commercial television franchises were originally awarded by the ITA (Independent Television Authority).

However, here most of the similarities ended.

There were a total of four individual serials (all of them untitled) told over the course of run of twenty-six episodes. With such a brief series, the individual stories were far shorter than any of the *Barton* radio tales. The longest were eight episodes and the shortest, only four. As such, if nothing else, there was usually a lot less incident in the series than had been the norm at the BBC.

The new Dick was Tony Vogel – an altogether harder, even brutal, character than the urbane Johnson. Jock was James Cosmo and Snowey was Anthony Heaton. Characters like Betsy Horrock, Jean Hunter and Colonel Gardiner were excised for the television and a new character Sir Richard Marley (played by John Gantrel) was introduced. Clive Exton and Julian Bond alternated the writing duties (as Mason and Webb had done) and David Pick and Jon Scoffield directed and produced.

It would be unfair to condemn the series out of hand, but it failed to entirely recapture the magic of the original. Criticisms ranged from accusations of thuggishness to observations of the obviously slender budget. The series was very well marketed by Southern, with a number of tie-in books (some making a lot of reference to the radio series) and plenty of promotion. However, it soon became apparent that something was missing from this new series and it was soon dropped. There would only be this one series and no follow-ups.

Perhaps a little unfairly, it is seen by very few as a valuable (or even valid) part of the *Dick Barton* canon. It's a fate that is essentially shared by the *Barton* movies from Hammer and this is a shame really, because there is one major point where both the movies and TV episodes score well ahead of the radio episodes. They still exist.

Every *Barton* movie and TV serial ever shot, still comfortably exists in the archives[171]. Sadly, the same cannot be said of the original radio series.

THE BBC SOUND ARCHIVES:

The 1947 *World Radio and Television Annual* edited by the BBC's Gale Pedrick, is one of the first publications of its kind to explain in any detail about the BBC's fledgling programme archive (formed in 1936).

It says, somewhat romantically, that 'the BBC Recorded Programmes Library ... houses some 10,000 separate items on disc alone and then there are half-a-dozen copies of each disc as well as the "masters"' copy. Speeches, plays, music, documentaries, outside events – the sounds of Britain and the voices of all its people – all are in and on the record. When future generations seek to know what we were like and how we lived today,

---

[171] Both have also been made available to buy on DVD.

our voices will be there to tell them – just as, in this same library, precious discs preserve for us the voices of other days. For in the Recorded Programmes Library at Broadcasting House you may hear Gladstone speak again.'[172]

It's an enthusiastic and utopian mission-statement for an institution that clearly had an eye on recorded history from its earliest days. Unfortunately, despite the optimism, the book fails to point out that, due to the limitations of both space and technology, it wasn't practical in the forties and fifties to keep copies of anywhere near as much as would have been wished. The archives were extremely selective. Whether a programme found a home in the archive was judged strictly on technical feasibility and on the merit of the programme itself. Many long-running series were logged in some form, but usually only the odd sample episode was kept – rarely any complete serials. After all, the BBC had no intention of ever releasing these in any commercial manner. Such ideas weren't even considered. The archive was there to offer footnotes to the cultural history of a nation, nothing else.

It shouldn't therefore be surprising, that the BBC does not retain a complete archive of the *Dick Barton* saga. In fact, it doesn't even come close.

It isn't made entirely clear (in existing paperwork) exactly how *Barton* was recorded in the studio, but it would have been via one of three radio recording techniques in use by the BBC at the time. One technique was to record a programme on a special kind of film. This was the Phillips-Miller film system. However, it was very expensive and only used on recordings of the most outstanding cultural importance. It's unlikely *Dick Barton* would have qualified for the honour. *Barton* itself would have been more likely to have been recorded to either disc or steel tape. Disc was quite expensive and the steel tape system seems the most likely suggestion.

This was the Marconi-Stille process – a forerunner of the modern tape-recorder that had evolved from a much older Danish wire-recording system. The set-up was basically that of a tape-recorder. However, it used spools of steel tape instead of plastic tape. The steel tape was mounted on 24-inch spools that fed over a recording head. The machinery was massive and cumbersome and used razor-sharp tape that was almost impossible to edit.

The steel tape was also obscenely expensive. However, like all magnetic tape, it did have the advantage that it could be wiped and then re-recorded over with another programme. Of course, this isn't great news for those looking for archive recordings from the forties and fifties. However, as Charles Chilton (who was a BBC producer at the time) explains, the 'tape was as big as a cartwheel. Where do you store hundreds of cartwheels?'

As far as BBC paperwork indicates, every single episode, bar seven, of

---

[172] From *The World Radio and Television Annual* ed. Gale Pedrick – Sampson Low (1947)

Dick Barton was disposed of shortly after it had been broadcast (probably wiped). The BBC's archives were growing, but it was never deemed practical to keep everything and *Dick Barton* was never going to be judged of sufficient cultural value to have been archived in its entirety.

It seems that the BBC only ever made permanent/semi-permanent recordings of seven episodes of *Barton*, in the form of directly transcribed disc recordings. Sadly only two of these seven recordings still exist in the BBC archives (with a copy of a third in a private collection).

The first episode of *Dick Barton* to be formally archived by the BBC was episode 100 (*Dick Barton and the Smugglers* – Episode 20) from 21 February 1947. It is not known exactly why this episode was chosen for archiving, but it seems likely that it was retained as a representative sample – a recorded example of the series to give future interested generations an idea of the programme.

On 15 October 1947, the BBC had a record of four further 15-minute recordings being flown over to Australasian Radio Ltd, courtesy of the BBC Transcription Service. These were 'audition' episodes recorded to allow the BBC's Australian partners to get an accurate feel for the show. These episodes are recorded in both BBC and Australian paperwork. However, neither source mentions which episodes they were.

The BBC also archived a further episode in 1949. This was episode 442 (*Dick Barton and the Betts Plan* – Episode 13) from 23 March 1949. The BBC Sound Archives catalogue reference for this episode refers to it as 'an example of Duncan Carse in the role of Dick Barton.'

Only one additional complete episode was ever officially archived – episode 711 (*Dick Barton and the Trail of the Rocket* – Episode 13). This was, of course, the very last *Dick Barton* episode of all and was possibly retained for this very reason. The BBC's recording is actually taken from the omnibus repeat of the final five episodes, rather than from the original 15-minute edition, but the recording seems to only contain material from the final episode itself and runs to a total of 13 minutes and 37 seconds. The entire serial was also re-recorded for BBC Audio CD in 2013.

A few other isolated fragments from other *Barton* episodes have also survived in the BBC archives (almost by accident).

On 1 June 1948, the BBC Home Service transmitted a special radio programme for schools. The programme was called *Off The Syllabus: Backwards From Dick Barton*. The programme wasn't specifically about *Dick Barton* alone. However, it did make use of a short clip from *Dick Barton and the Bonazio Gang* – Episode 20 (episode 237). This short clip came from a complete transmission recording that no longer survives. However, although the BBC didn't judge *Dick Barton* itself to be worth keeping, they did keep this documentary programme. As such a short extract from *Dick Barton and the Bonazio Gang* still exists in the Sound Archives.

Similar extracts exist for similar reasons from episode 341 and 384 from 1 November 1948 and 31 December 1948 respectively. The extract from 341 runs to 1 minute 35 seconds and the one from 384 is 3 minutes 20 seconds and comes from the end of the episode (including the closing theme).

Finally, a 1 minute 48 second extract from episode 444 (*Dick Barton and the Betts Plan* – Episode 15) was also archived, when it was used as a clip during another BBC programme called *Boys Will Be Boys*.

Sadly, there seems to be little evidence as to what happened to the four Australian episodes from 1947. They have been lost somewhere along the way, leaving only a reference in the catalogue of the National Film and Sound Archive of Australia (NFSA).

As such, the (confirmed) list of material surviving from the BBC's run of *Dick Barton* (stored in the BBC archives when the series ended in 1951), was as follows:

Episode 100 – *Dick Barton and the Smugglers* – Episode 20 (21/02/47)
Episode 237 – *Dick Barton and the Bonazio Gang* – Episode 20 Extract (19/12/47)
Episode 341 – Title Unknown – Episode 11 Extract (01/11/48)
Episode 384 – *Dick Barton and the Voice* – Episode 14 Extract (31/12/48)
Episode 442 – *Dick Barton and the Betts Plan* – Episode 13 (23/03/49)
Episode 444 – *Dick Barton and the Betts Plan* – Episode 15 Extract (25/03/49)
Episode 711 – *Dick Barton and the Trail of the Rocket* – Episode 13 (30/03/51)

There is unfortunately no existing paperwork leading to the suggestion that any other *Dick Barton* episodes were ever permanently archived by the BBC at any time during the programme's original run between 1946 and 1951.

In 2009, as part of some research that I undertook for BBC Audio, it was discovered that the BBC Sound Archive no longer officially held any recordings of episode 100. Nor did they have any separate log for many of the individual programme extracts. This is particularly surprising, as the archive still seemed to have had copies less than ten years before. The fact that an archive recording had managed to survive for nearly sixty years in the BBC's vaults, only to have been 'mislaid' during the past ten, is particularly worrying (even shocking). Happily however, it has since been possible to locate other copies of all of this missing material in the hands of a private collector.

Sadly, after much further searching, no further recordings from the original (1946-1951) BBC series have emerged.[173]

However, that is not entirely the end of the story.

---

[173] However, a (nearly) complete set of the original *Barton* scripts does still exist in the BBC Written Archives Centre, stored on microfiche.

SERIAL THRILLERS

THE DEVOTED PAT HETHERINGTON:

If there is one person who deserves a mention in the research and preservation of the *Dick Barton* legacy, more than any other, that person is Pat Hetherington.

Pat Hetherington was ten years old when *Dick Barton* started broadcasting in 1946. She soon became a dedicated follower of the series. She was a spina bifida sufferer and, following a failed operation, she would spend the rest of her life almost totally wheelchair-bound. It was her disability that saw her confined to her Carlisle home for much of the day. Due to her confinement, Hetherington became a more ardent fan of *Barton* (and other similar programmes).

Domestic tape recorders were very rare in the late 1940s and early 1950s. Consequently, fans like Hetherington had little practical way of recording their favourite programmes for posterity. However Hetherington did her best. She started keeping comprehensive scrapbooks on the *Barton* series – pasting in press-cuttings and articles relating the show. She was a fully-trained shorthand typist and soon began making copious notes on the *Barton* serials – sitting by the wireless, carefully recording the events of each episode as they were broadcast. These notes would then be transferred to the scrapbooks, where they have gone on to form a near comprehensive collation of material on the *Barton* saga.

'It's a thousand page file,' she later explained. 'It's the details of every episode of *Dick Barton* ... I have the date of the recordings; when it was recorded; the date of broadcast and a summary of the programme and who was in it and all the details.'[174]

The Hetherington scrapbooks – lovingly compiled over many years, have become almost legendary within fan circles – and rightly so. Although much of the information is held elsewhere (eg within the BBC's own archives) – it is still a valuable guide to the series and brings together in one place that which would otherwise be difficult to track down.

Hetherington's fascination with the show went far beyond the borders of obsession and shaped her life.

Later, she explained that: 'I wanted to preserve it for posterity and ... when the serial finished, I followed the same people doing other work. So really, the marvellous contribution they gave to the programme was transferred to their own careers and I still follow that and keep a record with dates and cuttings and this sort of thing and it brings back all the magic again. Nothing whatever can drag me away from the radio or the television, if they're on. If they could only know what a tremendous amount of

---

[174] From *Brief Lives* – BBC Radio 5 (30/08/98)

pleasure that they have given me. It's a lifetime of pleasure.'[175]

Among the many stars from the series with whom she got in touch was Alex McCrindle, who recalled in 1982: 'She wrote to me a short while ago, after John Mann died and apparently, she'd been writing to him all those years regularly. And she listed all the things that I'd ever appeared in since 1953 – films, television, radio. She's got every photograph of me that was ever published anywhere, it seems to me. In fact, she lists some things that I don't even remember what they were. Quite astonishing. She's ... completely devoted to the whole concept of *Dick Barton*.'[176]

In the late 1980s, all these years of devotion paid off when she was contacted by the BBC itself. In 1989, following the success of a number of tape cassette releases of *Paul Temple* in the BBC Radio Collection, BBC Audio turned its attention to the possibility of releasing the 1972 *Dick Barton* remake as a commercially available cassette release.

However, there was a problem, when BBC Audio contacted the main BBC Sound Archive, it was discovered that some of the 1972 series was missing. The Sound Archive was highly selective over what material it kept and frequently only kept sample episodes of a series, rather than complete serials. Unfortunately, this is what had happened with the 1972 recording of *Dick Barton*.

The Sound Archive held recordings of around half of the episodes as copies of the original stereo master tapes. However, they did not have a complete set. Of course, Pat Hetherington had been rather more careful with her collection.

Hetherington had recorded all ten episodes at home, back in 1972, and still had a complete set of tapes for the entire serial. Her interest in *Barton* was now widely known and the BBC duly contacted her. Pleased to help, she donated copies of her recordings to the BBC. The Hetherington tapes were only mono recordings whereas the originals had been stereo, but in all other respects, the tapes were of good quality. A new patchwork of the surviving masters and Hetherington's tapes was built up, completing the serial. The whole lot was then released onto the market as a special double-cassette pack in 1989. For the first time ever, the BBC even gave a credit to their unlikely benefactor on the packaging. A note appeared on the printed sleeve thanking Hetherington for a part in the piecing together of the release. It was later reissued on CD and later still repeated on BBC 7.

Pat Hetherington was also active in a number of charities and societies and was awarded the British Empire Medal for services to the Royal National Lifeboat Institution and other charities in 1971.

She died in 1998, aged 62, but her work did not go to waste. Her original

---

[175] From *Dick Barton and All That* – BBC Radio 4 (31/10/82)
[176] From *Dick Barton and All That* – BBC Radio 4 (31/10/82)

scrapbooks still exist and reside in the care of her friend and fellow *Barton* fan Roger Bickerton.

Hetherington's devotion to *Barton* brought her much joy in her lifetime and helped preserve something very special to a lot of people. It's hard to fault the results of her implacable determination to keep the show's spirit alive.

REDISCOVERED:

In 2009, I undertook some research for BBC Audio – investigating how many *Dick Barton* recordings were still known to exist. The BBC and British Library archives were checked and a number of private collectors were contacted. The results were very much as I have already explained. Although a number of odd episodes and extracts did still exist, the only complete serial recording available was of the 1972 remake. Nothing earlier existed in any British archive in anything approaching a complete form.

However, this did not take into account material that might exist outside of the UK altogether.

Back in 1949, many early *Barton*s had been re-recorded for transmission in Australia, New Zealand and South Africa (as we have already seen). For some time, certain collectors had been vaguely aware that at least some of these 'international' transcription recordings probably still existed in an Australian archive (*somewhere*). A number of 'bootleg' recordings of some episodes had been circulating among collectors for a little while. It was clear that a lot more existed from the *Dick Barton* series in Australia than it did in Britain.

I soon discovered that the 'bootleg' recordings originated from New Zealand. A routine search of the catalogue of the National Film and Sound Archive of Australia (NFSA) then revealed the startling extent of the *Dick Barton* archive in Australia.

In all, a total of 360 episodes had been transmitted in Australia. Remarkably, the NFSA had kept a substantially complete archive of them. Out of a total of 360 episodes, 338 were listed as still surviving in the NFSA vaults.

Only twenty-two episodes were missing. The missing episodes were: 51, 52, 73, 74, 75, 76, 77, 78, 79, 80, 81, 82, 145, 146, 155, 156, 217, 218, 357, 358, 359 and 360. All of these twenty-two episodes have gone missing in pairs (eg episodes 145 and 146) because each of the NFSA's discs has two episodes on it (one episode on side A and one on side B).

Happily, two private collectors have since come forward with recordings of episodes 51, 52, 155, 156, 357 and 358. How these collectors came by their recordings is unclear. Although a source in New Zealand has been cited. As a consequence of the generosity of these private collectors, only sixteen episodes are now currently missing from the Australian run.

It was an unlikely find and provides us with a nearly complete archive of the first eighteen *Dick Barton* serials. In some instances, we even have multiple recordings of certain episodes. For instance, episode 100 exists in both British and Australian form.

Over the course of 2009 and 2010, negotiations were conducted with the NFSA, by Fiona Mackenzie-Williams of BBC Audio (later AudioGo Ltd.). The result of these negotiations saw an agreement between the two parties where recordings would be copied and shipped over to Britain. The episodes would then begin to be released on commercially available CD.

The first two of these NFSA releases hit shops in April 2011, with others following between 2011 and 2015. Nine were released in total.

The current state of the *Dick Barton* archives (See Appendix C) is not great. However, things are significantly better than they were. The biggest gaps are in the final two series, for which little recorded material is known to survive in any form.

It is hoped that more material may still come to light and recent rumours of a collection of the first 100 episodes existing in a private collection (having originated with Cadburys in the 1950s) do offer some hope. However, these recordings were, of course, all made a very long time ago and, the chances of further recoveries are remote. There are the four episodes that were sent over to Australia from the BBC Transcription Service in October 1947. Nobody seems to know what happened to these. Then there are the episodes that seem to have gone missing from the NFSA. It is perhaps too much to hope that any of this material will ever again resurface. However, the series was broadcast in both New Zealand and South Africa and some recordings may still survive … somewhere.

Needless to say, I would be very interested to hear from anyone who has material they think may be of interest and I can be contacted either via this publisher or BBC Audio.

LEGACY:

Series like *Paul Temple* and *The Archers* both outlasted *Dick Barton*. They did so, by playing it safe (at least most of the time). They were both essentially conservative and largely inoffensive serials. Through many years of being inoffensive and not really upsetting anybody, they have endured and there's nothing essentially wrong with that. However, *Dick Barton* was never like that. It outraged as many people as it entertained. It was something very different – unlike anything the BBC had ever done before. It fought internal stuffiness and outside pettiness, to triumph as one of Britain's greatest radio legends. This is not to say that *Paul Temple* and *The Archers* are not without their charms. They too were ground breaking, in their own quiet way. However *Dick Barton* was always something that little bit special. Sometimes a little racist, often a little sexist, but never taking itself so seriously that either ever became a problem. It was special because it was a one-off. It burned very brightly indeed and then it was gone. However its legacy would continue to shape the pace and identity of British drama for many years to come.

At the time of writing, it is too early to say whether or not the new series of *Dick Barton* CD releases will re-ignite that same devotion that saw 16 million fall in love with their wirelesses, but the show is still remembered and it is still remembered for a reason.

Edward J Mason and Geoffrey Webb explained it in their 1950 book on the show – *The Inside Story of Dick Barton*. They said: 'He is a holiday – a conscious play fantasy – a folk tale away from the immense problems of conforming to standards. Dreams relieve, but do not satisfy. They express problems, but don't cause them. Barton, in fact, provides a restful and reassuring dream.'[177]

Of course, In 1951, just as *Barton* breathed his last, an expectant post-war audience wouldn't have to wait long for something else to come along and quench their thirst for the fantastic. Over on commercial radio, the very first 'Son of Dick Barton' had just been born and his name was Dan Dare …

---

[177] From *The Inside Story of Dick Barton* by Geoffrey Webb and Edward J Mason – Contact Books (1950)

DICK BARTON – SPECIAL AGENT: EPISODE GUIDE

SERIES ONE

1: *Dick Barton and the Secret Weapon* **(1946)**
AKA *Dick Barton and Kramer*
AKA *Dick Barton and the Weapon of Hate*
1946 and 1949 Productions – 20 x 15 minute episodes (approx.)
1972 Production – 10 x 15 minute episodes (approx.)
1946 Production – BBC Radio
1949 Production – ARP (Australasian Radio Productions)
1972 Production – BBC Radio
Written by Edward J Mason
Producer: Neil Tuson *(1946 Production)*
Morris West *(1949 Production)*
Raymond Raikes *(1972 Production)*

CAST:

Dick Barton	Noel Johnson *(1946 and 1972 Productions)*
	Douglas Kelly *(1949 Production)*
Snowey White	John Mann *(1946 and 1972 Productions)*
	William Lloyd *(1949 Production)*
Sir Archie Wrangle	Gordon Gow *(1949 Production)*
	Richard Hurndall *(1972 Production)*
Jean Hunter	Lorna Dermott *(1946 Production)*
	Patricia Kennedy *(1949 Production)*
	Margaret Robertson *(1972 Production)*
Colonel Gardiner	William Fox *(1972 Production)*
Wilhelm Kramer	Damerton Court *(1946 Production)*
	Francis de Wolff *(1972 Production)*
The Professor	Heron Carvic *(1972 Production)*
Jock Anderson	Alex McCrindle *(1946 and 1972 Productions)*
James Thirgood	Denis McCarthy *(1946 and 1972 Productions)*
	Robert Peach *(1949 Production)*

SERIAL THRILLERS

Blom	Michael Kilgarriff *(1972 Production)*
Jimmy Low	Derek Birch *(1946 and 1972 Productions)*
Announcer	Derek Birch *(1946 Production)*
	Arthur Bush *(1946 Production)*
	Alan Tilvern *(1946 Production)*
	Geoffrey Collins *(1972 Production*
'Other Actors'	John Morgan *(1949 Production)*
	Moira Carleton *(1949 Production)*
	Clifford Cowley *(1949 Production)*
	Richard Davies *(1949 Production)*

STORY:
Dick Barton and his army friend Snowey White join Colonel Gardiner of military intelligence. Their first adventure sees them up against the villainous Wilhelm Kramer. A new super-weapon has been stolen and Kramer plans to use it to hold the world to ransom.

BROADCAST:

Broadcast Station		BBC	ARP	BBC
PART 1	*Episode 1*	07/10/46	07/02/49	06/11/72
PART 2	*Episode 2*	08/10/46	08/02/49	07/11/72
PART 3	*Episode 3*	09/10/46	09/02/49	08/11/72
PART 4	*Episode 4*	10/10/46	10/02/49	09/11/72
PART 5	*Episode 5*	11/10/46	14/02/49	10/11/72
PART 6	*Episode 6*	14/10/46	15/02/49	13/11/72
PART 7	*Episode 7*	15/10/46	16/02/49	14/11/72
PART 8	*Episode 8*	16/10/46	17/02/49	15/11/72
PART 9	*Episode 9*	17/10/46	21/02/49	16/11/72
PART 10	*Episode 10*	18/10/46	22/02/49	17/11/72
PART 11	*Episode 11*	21/10/46	23/02/49	
PART 12	*Episode 12*	22/10/46	24/02/49	
PART 13	*Episode 13*	23/10/46	28/02/49	
PART 14	*Episode 14*	24/10/46	01/03/49	
PART 15	*Episode 15*	25/10/46	02/03/49	
PART 16	*Episode 16*	28/10/46	03/03/49	
PART 17	*Episode 17*	29/10/46	07/03/49	
PART 18	*Episode 18*	30/10/46	08/03/49	
PART 19	*Episode 19*	31/10/46	09/03/49	
PART 20	*Episode 20*	01/11/46	10/03/49	

NOTES:
The third (1972) production of *Dick Barton and the Secret Weapon* was abridged from twenty episodes to ten episodes.

DICK BARTON - SPECIAL AGENT: EPISODE GUIDE

Adapted into the short story, 'Dick Barton and the Secret Weapon' by Elwyn Jones. Printed in *Dick Barton - Special Agent*, published by Arthur Barker in 1977.

Adapted into the comic strip, 'Dick Barton and the Weapon of Hate'. Produced by Frank Mason and Co. Ltd. Released through Land Newspapers Ltd. for Ayres and James Co.

2: *Dick Barton and the Paris Adventure* (1946)
20 x 15 minute episodes (approx.)
1946 Production - BBC Radio
1949 Production - ARP (Australasian Radio Productions)
Written by Edward J Mason
Producer: Neil Tuson *(1946 Production)*
             Morris West *(1949 Production)*

CAST:
Dick Barton	Noel Johnson *(1946 Production)*
	Douglas Kelly *(1949 Production)*
Snowey White	John Mann *(1946 Production)*
	William Lloyd *(1949 Production)*
Jock Anderson	Alex McCrindle *(1946 Production)*
Spider Kennedy	Michael Peake *(1946 Production)*
Jean Hunter	Lorna Dermott *(1946 Production)*
Announcer	Alan Tilvern *(1946 Production)*

STORY:
Barton and his friends join forces with the French police on the trail of an international smuggling operation.

BROADCAST:
Broadcast Station		BBC	ARP
PART 1	*Episode 21*	04/11/46	14/03/49
PART 2	*Episode 22*	05/11/46	15/03/49
PART 3	*Episode 23*	06/11/46	16/03/49
PART 4	*Episode 24*	07/11/46	17/03/49
PART 5	*Episode 25*	08/11/46	21/03/49
PART 6	*Episode 26*	11/11/46	22/03/49
PART 7	*Episode 27*	12/11/46	23/03/49
PART 8	*Episode 28*	13/11/46	24/03/49
PART 9	*Episode 29*	14/11/46	28/03/49
PART 10	*Episode 30*	15/11/46	29/03/49
PART 11	*Episode 31*	18/11/46	30/03/49

PART 12	*Episode 32*	19/11/46	31/03/49
PART 13	*Episode 33*	20/11/46	04/04/49
PART 14	*Episode 34*	21/11/46	05/04/49
PART 15	*Episode 35*	22/11/46	06/04/49
PART 16	*Episode 36*	25/11/46	07/04/49
PART 17	*Episode 37*	26/11/46	11/04/49
PART 18	*Episode 38*	27/11/46	12/04/49
PART 19	*Episode 39*	28/11/46	13/04/49
PART 20	*Episode 40*	29/11/46	14/04/49

NOTES:
Adapted into the comic strip, 'Dick Barton and the Spider's Web'. Produced by Frank Mason and Co. Ltd. Released through Land Newspapers Ltd. for Ayres and James Co.

3: *Dick Barton and the Cabatolin Diamonds* (1946)
AKA *Case of the Synthetic Diamond Smugglers* (Australian Title)
20 x 15 minute episodes (approx.)
1946 Production – BBC Radio
1949 Production – ARP (Australasian Radio Productions)
Written by Geoffrey Webb
Producer: Neil Tuson *(1946 Production)*
             Morris West *(1949 Production)*

CAST:
Dick Barton	Noel Johnson *(1946 Production)*
	Douglas Kelly *(1949 Production)*
Snowey White	John Mann *(1946 Production)*
	William Lloyd *(1949 Production)*
Jock Anderson	Alex McCrindle *(1946 Production)*
Henri De Flambeau	Malcolm Hayes *(1946 Production)*
Jean Hunter	Lorna Dermott *(1946 Production)*
Limpy	Alan Tilvern *(1946 Production)*
Betsy Horrock	Courtney Hope *(1946 Production)*
Announcer	Stuart Ruttledge *(1946 Production)*
	Hamilton Humphreys *(1946 Production)*

STORY:
Dick and Snowey's holiday plans for a Mediterranean cruise are curtailed, when they are asked to help Freddy Belfont from the Home Office break a gang of smugglers. The gang are using a new substance called Cabatolin to create fake diamonds, which they then plan to flood the market with.

DICK BARTON – SPECIAL AGENT: EPISODE GUIDE

BROADCAST:

Broadcast Station		BBC	ARP
PART 1	*Episode 41*	02/12/46	18/04/49
PART 2	*Episode 42*	03/12/46	19/04/49
PART 3	*Episode 43*	04/12/46	20/04/49
PART 4	*Episode 44*	05/12/46	21/04/49
PART 5	*Episode 45*	06/12/46	25/04/49
PART 6	*Episode 46*	09/12/46	26/04/49
PART 7	*Episode 47*	10/12/46	27/04/49
PART 8	*Episode 48*	11/12/46	28/04/49
PART 9	*Episode 49*	12/12/46	02/05/49
PART 10	*Episode 50*	13/12/46	03/05/49
PART 11	*Episode 51*	16/12/46	04/05/49
PART 12	*Episode 52*	17/12/46	05/05/49
PART 13	*Episode 53*	18/12/46	09/05/49
PART 14	*Episode 54*	19/12/46	10/05/49
PART 15	*Episode 55*	20/12/46	11/05/49
PART 16	*Episode 56*	23/12/46	12/05/49
PART 17	*Episode 57*	24/12/46	16/05/49
PART 18	*Episode 58*	25/12/46	17/05/49
PART 19	*Episode 59*	26/12/46	18/05/49
PART 20	*Episode 60*	27/12/46	19/05/49

NOTES:
Adapted into the short story, 'Dick Barton and the Cabatolin Diamonds' by Elwyn Jones. Printed in *Dick Barton – Special Agent*, published by Arthur Barker in 1977.

4: *Dick Barton in South America* **(1946)**
AKA *The Godstone of Maribana* (Australian Title)
AKA *Dick Barton and the Death Stone*
20 x 15 minute episodes (approx.)
1946 Production – BBC Radio
1949 Production – ARP (Australasian Radio Productions)
Written by Edward J Mason
Producer:	Neil Tuson *(1946 Production)*
	Morris West *(1949 Production)*

CAST:
Dick Barton	Noel Johnson *(1946 Production)*
	Douglas Kelly *(1949 Production)*
Snowey White	John Mann *(1946 Production)*

SERIAL THRILLERS

	William Lloyd *(1949 Production)*
Jock Anderson	Alex McCrindle *(1946 Production)*
Zorio	Philip Stainton *(1946 Production)*
Jean Hunter	Lorna Dermott *(1946 Production)*
Announcer	Hamilton Humphreys *(1946 Production)*

STORY:
Before the war, the noted scientist Professor Carey led an expedition deep into the Amazon Basin. He didn't return. Now, Dick and his friends have been tasked with finding the lost expedition.

BROADCAST:

Broadcast Channel		BBC	ARP
PART 1	*Episode 61*	30/12/46	23/05/49
PART 2	*Episode 62*	31/12/46	24/05/49
PART 3	*Episode 63*	01/01/47	25/05/49
PART 4	*Episode 64*	02/01/47	26/05/49
PART 5	*Episode 65*	03/01/47	30/05/49
PART 6	*Episode 66*	06/01/47	31/05/49
PART 7	*Episode 67*	07/01/47	01/06/49
PART 8	*Episode 68*	08/01/47	02/06/49
PART 9	*Episode 69*	09/01/47	06/06/49
PART 10	*Episode 70*	10/01/47	07/06/49
PART 11	*Episode 71*	13/01/47	08/06/49
PART 12	*Episode 72*	14/01/47	09/06/49
PART 13	*Episode 73*	15/01/47	13/06/49
PART 14	*Episode 74*	16/01/47	14/06/49
PART 15	*Episode 75*	17/01/47	15/06/49
PART 16	*Episode 76*	20/01/47	16/06/49
PART 17	*Episode 77*	21/01/47	20/06/49
PART 18	*Episode 78*	22/01/47	21/06/49
PART 19	*Episode 79*	23/01/47	22/06/49
PART 20	*Episode 80*	24/01/47	23/06/49

NOTES:
Adapted into the comic strip, 'Dick Barton and the Death Stone'. Produced by Frank Mason and Co. Ltd. Released through Land Newspapers Ltd. for Ayres and James Co.

DICK BARTON – SPECIAL AGENT: EPISODE GUIDE

5: *Dick Barton and the Smugglers* **(1947)**
20 x 15 minute episodes (approx.)
1947 Production – BBC Radio
1949 Production – ARP (Australasian Radio Productions)
Written by Geoffrey Webb
Producer: Neil Tuson *(1947 Production)*
              Morris West *(1949 Production)*

CAST:

Dick Barton	Noel Johnson *(1947 Production)*
	Douglas Kelly *(1949 Production)*
Snowey White	John Mann *(1947 Production)*
	William Lloyd *(1949 Production)*
Jock Anderson	Alex McCrindle *(1947 Production)*
Aldo Weimar	Arthur Bush *(1947 Production)*
Jean Hunter	Lorna Dermott *(1947 Production)*
Announcer	Hamilton Humphreys *(1947 Production)*

STORY:
Dick smashes a smuggling ring, based in a hideout on a synthetic iceberg.

BROADCAST:

Broadcast Station		BBC	ARP
PART 1	*Episode 81*	27/01/47	27/06/49
PART 2	*Episode 82*	28/01/47	28/06/49
PART 3	*Episode 83*	29/01/47	29/06/49
PART 4	*Episode 84*	30/01/47	30/06/49
PART 5	*Episode 85*	31/01/47	xx/07/49
PART 6	*Episode 86*	03/02/47	xx/07/49
PART 7	*Episode 87*	04/02/47	xx/07/49
PART 8	*Episode 88*	05/02/47	xx/07/49
PART 9	*Episode 89*	06/02/47	xx/07/49
PART 10	*Episode 90*	07/02/47	xx/07/49
PART 11	*Episode 91*	10/02/47	xx/07/49
PART 12	*Episode 92*	11/02/47	xx/07/49
PART 13	*Episode 93*	12/02/47	xx/07/49
PART 14	*Episode 94*	13/02/47	xx/07/49
PART 15	*Episode 95*	14/02/47	xx/07/49
PART 16	*Episode 96*	17/02/47	xx/07/49
PART 17	*Episode 97*	18/02/47	xx/07/49
PART 18	*Episode 98*	19/02/47	xx/07/49
PART 19	*Episode 99*	20/02/47	xx/07/49
PART 20	*Episode 100*	21/02/47	xx/07/49

6: *Dick Barton and the Smash and Grab Raiders* (1947)

20 x 15 minute episodes (approx.)
1947 Production – BBC Radio
1949 Production – ARP (Australasian Radio Productions)
Written by Ronnie and Arthur Colley
Producer: Neil Tuson *(1947 Production)*
            Morris West *(1949 Production)*

CAST:

Dick Barton	Noel Johnson *(1947 Production)*
	Douglas Kelly *(1949 Production)*
Snowey White	John Mann *(1947 Production)*
	William Lloyd *(1949 Production)*
Jock Anderson	Alex McCrindle *(1947 Production)*
Paragon	Morris Sweden *(1947 Production)*
Announcer	Hamilton Humphreys *(1947 Production)*

STORY:
Dick, Snowey and Jock assist Sir Alexander Morton to catch a gang of audacious smash and grab raiders.

BROADCAST:

Broadcast Station		BBC	ARP
PART 1	*Episode 101*	24/02/47	xx/xx/49
PART 2	*Episode 102*	25/02/47	xx/xx/49
PART 3	*Episode 103*	26/02/47	xx/xx/49
PART 4	*Episode 104*	27/02/47	xx/xx/49
PART 5	*Episode 105*	28/02/47	xx/xx/49
PART 6	*Episode 106*	03/03/47	xx/xx/49
PART 7	*Episode 107*	04/03/47	xx/xx/49
PART 8	*Episode 108*	05/03/47	xx/xx/49
PART 9	*Episode 109*	06/03/47	xx/xx/49
PART 10	*Episode 110*	07/03/47	xx/xx/49
PART 11	*Episode 111*	10/03/47	xx/xx/49
PART 12	*Episode 112*	11/03/47	xx/xx/49
PART 13	*Episode 113*	12/03/47	xx/xx/49
PART 14	*Episode 114*	13/03/47	xx/xx/49
PART 15	*Episode 115*	14/03/47	xx/xx/49
PART 16	*Episode 116*	17/03/47	xx/xx/49
PART 17	*Episode 117*	18/03/47	xx/09/49
PART 18	*Episode 118*	19/03/47	xx/09/49
PART 19	*Episode 119*	20/03/47	xx/09/49
PART 20	*Episode 120*	21/03/47	xx/09/49

DICK BARTON – SPECIAL AGENT: EPISODE GUIDE

7: *Dick Barton and the Tibetan Adventure* (1947)
AKA *Dick Barton and The Bullion Robbery*
20 x 15 minute episodes (approx.)
1947 Production – BBC Radio
1949 Production – ARP (Australasian Radio Productions)
Written by Geoffrey Webb
Producer: Raymond Raikes *(1947 Production)*
               Morris West *(1949 Production)*

CAST:
Dick Barton	Noel Johnson *(1947 Production)*
	Douglas Kelly *(1949 Production)*
Snowey White	John Mann *(1947 Production)*
Jock Anderson	Alex McCrindle *(1947 Production)*
Ra-Mo	Brian Oulton *(1947 Production)*
Announcer	Hamilton Humphreys *(1947 Production)*

STORY:
When some Tibetan gold is stolen, Dick and his friends are sent to recover it and travel to the lair of Foo-dow, the brigand, deep in the foothills of Tibet.

BROADCAST:

Broadcast Station		BBC	ARP
PART 1	*Episode 121*	24/03/47	12/09/49
PART 2	*Episode 122*	25/03/47	13/09/49
PART 3	*Episode 123*	26/03/47	14/09/49
PART 4	*Episode 124*	27/03/47	15/09/49
PART 5	*Episode 125*	28/03/47	19/09/49
PART 6	*Episode 126*	31/03/47	20/09/49
PART 7	*Episode 127*	01/04/47	21/09/49
PART 8	*Episode 128*	02/04/47	22/09/49
PART 9	*Episode 129*	03/04/47	26/09/49
PART 10	*Episode 130*	04/04/47	27/09/49
PART 11	*Episode 131*	07/04/47	28/10/49
PART 12	*Episode 132*	08/04/47	29/10/49
PART 13	*Episode 133*	09/04/47	03/10/49
PART 14	*Episode 134*	10/04/47	04/10/49
PART 15	*Episode 135*	11/04/47	05/10/49
PART 16	*Episode 136*	14/04/47	06/10/49
PART 17	*Episode 137*	15/04/47	10/10/49
PART 18	*Episode 138*	16/04/47	11/10/49
PART 19	*Episode 139*	17/04/47	12/10/49
PART 20	*Episode 140*	18/04/47	13/10/49

SERIAL THRILLERS

NOTES:
An internal BBC memo from programme planner John McMillan dated 22 August 1947, makes a passing reference to a *Dick Barton* serial called *Dick Barton and the Bullion Robbery*. This title doesn't appear on any surviving scripts in the BBC's archives and it isn't entirely clear which *Dick Barton* story is being referred to. However, the date of the memo and the general tone of the title, seem to suggest that McMillan was talking about this serial here. The surviving scripts for this serial have the title *Dick Barton and the Tibetan Adventure*, written on the opening page of each episode.

Adapted into the comic strip, 'Dick Barton and the Tibetan Adventure'. Produced by Frank Mason and Co. Ltd. Released through Land Newspapers Ltd. for Ayres and James Co.

8: *Dick Barton and the Canadian Adventure* (1947)
18 x 15 minute episodes (approx.)
1947 Production – BBC Radio
1949 Production – ARP (Australasian Radio Productions)
Written by Geoffrey Webb
Producer: Raymond Raikes *(1947 Production)*
  Morris West *(1949 Production)*

CAST:
Dick Barton	Noel Johnson *(1947 Production)*
	Douglas Kelly *(1949 Production)*
Snowey White	John Mann *(1947 Production)*
Jock Anderson	Alex McCrindle *(1947 Production)*
Robert Raggart	Michael Hordern *(1947 Production)*
Announcer	Hamilton Humphreys *(1947 Production)*

STORY:
Dick, Snowey and Jock go to Toronto on the trail of a haul of priceless diamonds, which have been stolen from a railway baggage car.

BROADCAST:
Broadcast Station		BBC	ARP
PART 1	*Episode 141*	19/04/47	xx/10/49
PART 2	*Episode 142*	21/04/47	xx/10/49
PART 3	*Episode 143*	23/04/47	xx/10/49
PART 4	*Episode 144*	22/04/47	xx/10/49
PART 5	*Episode 145*	24/04/47	xx/10/49
PART 6	*Episode 146*	25/04/47	xx/10/49
PART 7	*Episode 147*	26/04/47	xx/10/49

DICK BARTON – SPECIAL AGENT: EPISODE GUIDE

PART 8	Episode 148	28/04/47	xx/10/49
PART 9	Episode 149	29/04/47	xx/10/49
PART 10	Episode 150	30/04/47	xx/10/49
PART 11	Episode 151	01/05/47	xx/10/49
PART 12	Episode 152	02/05/47	xx/10/49
PART 13	Episode 153	03/05/47	xx/10/49
PART 14	Episode 154	05/05/47	xx/10/49
PART 15	Episode 155	06/05/47	xx/10/49
PART 16	Episode 156	07/05/47	xx/10/49
PART 17	Episode 157	08/05/47	xx/11/49
PART 18	Episode 158	09/05/47	xx/11/49

NOTES:
According to some contemporary reports, the BBC accidentally broadcast episodes 143 and 144 (Parts 3 and 4) in the wrong order. The episodes were swapped over in the schedule. Episode 144 went out first, followed by episode 143 the week after. Obviously, the continuity of the story would have been disrupted as a result.

9: *Dick Barton and the Affair of the Black Panther* (1947)
19 x 15 minute episodes (approx.)
1947 Production – BBC Radio
1949 Production – ARP (Australasian Radio Productions)
Written by Geoffrey Webb
Producer: Raymond Raikes *(1947 Production)*
             Morris West *(1949 Production)*

CAST:
Dick Barton	Noel Johnson *(1947 Production)*
	Douglas Kelly *(1949 Production)*
Snowey White	John Mann *(1947 Production)*
Jock Anderson	Alex McCrindle *(1947 Production)*
Carl Von Reinitz	Eric Phillips *(1947 Production)*
Announcer	Hamilton Humphreys *(1947 Production)*

STORY:
While looking for treasure in the Pacific Ocean, Dick discovers a secret Nazi organisation on the nearby Black Panther Island.

BROADCAST:
Broadcast Station		BBC	ARP
PART 1	Episode 159	10/05/47	03/11/49

PART 2	*Episode 160*	12/05/47	xx/11/49
PART 3	*Episode 161*	13/05/47	xx/11/49
PART 4	*Episode 162*	14/05/47	xx/11/49
PART 5	*Episode 163*	15/05/47	xx/11/49
PART 6	*Episode 164*	16/05/47	xx/11/49
PART 7	*Episode 165*	17/05/47	xx/11/49
PART 8	*Episode 166*	19/05/47	xx/11/49
PART 9	*Episode 167*	20/05/47	xx/11/49
PART 10	*Episode 168*	21/05/47	xx/11/49
PART 11	*Episode 169*	22/05/47	xx/11/49
PART 12	*Episode 170*	23/05/47	xx/11/49
PART 13	*Episode 171*	24/05/47	xx/11/49
PART 14	*Episode 172*	26/05/47	xx/11/49
PART 15	*Episode 173*	27/05/47	xx/xx/49
PART 16	*Episode 174*	28/05/47	xx/xx/49
PART 17	*Episode 175*	29/05/47	xx/xx/49
PART 18	*Episode 176*	30/05/47	xx/xx/49
PART 19	*Episode 177*	31/05/47	xx/xx/49

NOTES:
Adapted into the comic strip 'Dick Barton and the Affair of the Black Panther'. Produced by Frank Mason and Co. Ltd. Released through Land Newspapers Ltd. for Ayres and James Co.

On 23 May 1947, Bill MacLurg (a member of BBC staff) sent an internal memo about the *Dick Barton* programme, which was then nearing the end of its first series. In this memo, he refers to a recent serial, which he calls *Dick Barton and the Chain Gang*. It is not clear exactly which story he was referring to. No other BBC paperwork ever seems to have mentioned a serial called *Dick Barton and the Chain Gang*. It may well have been a title that MacLurg invented. Although I have had access to scripts and recordings for a number of serials, I have been unable to pinpoint exactly what serial MacLurg was referring to. However, it seems very likely, that it would have been broadcast during the programme's first year.

SERIES TWO

10: *Dick Barton and the Vulture* (1947)
AKA *Dick Barton and the Vulture Strikes Again*
20 x 15 minute episodes (approx.)
1947 Production – BBC Radio
19xx Production – ARP (Australasian Radio Productions)
Written by Edward J Mason

DICK BARTON – SPECIAL AGENT: EPISODE GUIDE

Producer: Neil Tuson *(1947 Production)*
               Morris West *(19xx Production)*

CAST:
Dick Barton	Noel Johnson *(1947 Production)*
	Douglas Kelly *(19xx Production)*
Snowey White	John Mann *(1947 Production)*
Jock Anderson	Alex McCrindle *(1947 Production)*
Tony Patelli	Dino Galvani *(1947 Production)*
Announcer	John Fitchen *(1947 Production)*

STORY:
Barton and his friends are on the trail of Tony Patelli, a criminal mastermind, otherwise known as *The Vulture*. Patelli has stolen a lorry-load of gold bullion, which he is hiding in a quarry. However, Barton's plans to defeat Patelli are foiled when Patelli kidnaps a girl (Mary Blake), and holds her as hostage against Barton's interference.

BROADCAST:

Broadcast Station		BBC	ARP
PART 1	*Episode 178*	29/09/47	unknown
PART 2	*Episode 179*	30/09/47	unknown
PART 3	*Episode 180*	01/10/47	unknown
PART 4	*Episode 181*	02/10/47	unknown
PART 5	*Episode 182*	03/10/47	unknown
PART 6	*Episode 183*	06/10/47	unknown
PART 7	*Episode 184*	07/10/47	unknown
PART 8	*Episode 185*	08/10/47	unknown
PART 9	*Episode 186*	09/10/47	unknown
PART 10	*Episode 187*	10/10/47	unknown
PART 11	*Episode 188*	13/10/47	unknown
PART 12	*Episode 189*	14/10/47	unknown
PART 13	*Episode 190*	15/10/47	unknown
PART 14	*Episode 191*	16/10/47	unknown
PART 15	*Episode 192*	17/10/47	unknown
PART 16	*Episode 193*	20/10/47	unknown
PART 17	*Episode 194*	21/10/47	unknown
PART 18	*Episode 195*	22/10/47	unknown
PART 19	*Episode 196*	23/10/47	unknown
PART 20	*Episode 197*	24/10/47	unknown

NOTES:
Adapted into the short story 'The Vulture Strikes Again' by Edward J Mason

and Geoffrey Webb. Printed in *Dick Barton - Special Agent*, published by Contact in 1950.

11: *Dick Barton and the Production Report* (1947)
20 x 15 minute episodes (approx.)
1947 Production - BBC Radio
19xx Production - ARP (Australasian Radio Productions)
Written by Basil Dawson
Producer: Neil Tuson *(1947 Production)*
                   Morris West *(19xx Production)*

CAST:
Dick Barton	Noel Johnson *(1947 Production)*
	Douglas Kelly *(19xx Production)*
Snowey White	John Mann *(1947 Production)*
Jock Anderson	Alex McCrindle *(1947 Production)*
Kreisler	Alan Pearce *(1947 Production)*
Sir Donald	Gordon Phillott *(1947 Production)*
Winnington	Derek Birch *(1947 Production)*
Colonel Gardiner	George Bishop *(1947 Production)*
RAF Officer	Richard Williams *(1947 Production)*
Betsy Horrock	Courtney Hope *(1947 Production)*
Vilma	Tucker McGuire *(1947 Production)*
Peasant	Ian Sadler *(1947 Production)*
Slim	Basil Jones *(1947 Production)*
Special Branch Man	Stanley Groome *(1947 Production)*
Announcer	John Fitchen *(1947 Production)*

STORY:
Colonel Gardiner calls in Dick Barton to investigate a wave of industrial sabotage.

BROADCAST:
Broadcast Station		BBC	ARP
PART 1	*Episode 198*	27/10/47	unknown
PART 2	*Episode 199*	28/10/47	unknown
PART 3	*Episode 200*	29/10/47	unknown
PART 4	*Episode 201*	30/10/47	unknown
PART 5	*Episode 202*	31/10/47	unknown
PART 6	*Episode 203*	03/11/47	unknown
PART 7	*Episode 204*	04/11/47	unknown
PART 8	*Episode 205*	05/11/47	unknown

DICK BARTON – SPECIAL AGENT: EPISODE GUIDE

PART 9   *Episode 206*   06/11/47   unknown
PART 10   *Episode 207*   07/11/47   unknown
PART 11   *Episode 208*   10/11/47   unknown
PART 12   *Episode 209*   11/11/47   unknown
PART 13   *Episode 210*   12/11/47   unknown
PART 14   *Episode 211*   13/11/47   unknown
PART 15   *Episode 212*   14/11/47   unknown
PART 16   *Episode 213*   17/11/47   unknown
PART 17   *Episode 214*   18/11/47   unknown
PART 18   *Episode 215*   19/11/47   unknown
PART 19   *Episode 216*   20/11/47   unknown
PART 20   *Episode 217*   21/11/47   unknown

12: *Dick Barton and the Bonazio Gang* (1947)
AKA *Dick Barton – Wanted for Murder*
20 x 15 minute episodes (approx.)
1947 Production – BBC Radio
1950 Production – ARP (Australasian Radio Productions)
Written by Geoffrey Webb
Producer: Neil Tuson *(1947 Production)*
              Morris West *(1950 Production)*

CAST:
Dick Barton   Noel Johnson *(1947 Production)*
                       Douglas Kelly *(19xx Production)*
Snowey White   John Mann *(1947 Production)*
Jock Anderson   Alex McCrindle *(1947 Production)*
Bonazio   Ian Sadler *(1947 Production)*
Rocky   John Blythe *(1947 Production)*
Thompson   Jack Shaw *(1947 Production)*
Inspector Burke   Colin Douglas *(1947 Production)*
Smudge   Howieson Cliff *(1947 Production)*
Tate   Malcolm Hayes *(1947 Production)*
Joe   Charles LeFeaux *(1947 Production)*
Rusty   Myrtle Rowe *(1947 Production)*
Dandy   Eric Phillips *(1947 Production)*
Thug   Alan Tilvern *(1947 Production)*
Announcer   John Fitchen *(1947 Production)*

STORY:
Dick is framed for murder by criminal overlord Bonazio (head of the infamous Pellora Gang).

BROADCAST:

Broadcast Station		BBC	ARP
PART 1	Episode 218	24/11/47	unknown
PART 2	Episode 219	25/11/47	unknown
PART 3	Episode 220	26/11/47	unknown
PART 4	Episode 221	27/11/47	unknown
PART 5	Episode 222	28/11/47	unknown
PART 6	Episode 223	01/12/47	unknown
PART 7	Episode 224	02/12/47	unknown
PART 8	Episode 225	03/12/47	unknown
PART 9	Episode 226	04/12/47	unknown
PART 10	Episode 227	05/12/47	unknown
PART 11	Episode 228	08/12/47	unknown
PART 12	Episode 229	09/12/47	unknown
PART 13	Episode 230	10/12/47	unknown
PART 14	Episode 231	11/12/47	unknown
PART 15	Episode 232	12/12/47	unknown
PART 16	Episode 233	15/12/47	unknown
PART 17	Episode 234	16/12/47	unknown
PART 18	Episode 235	17/12/47	unknown
PART 19	Episode 236	18/12/47	unknown
PART 20	Episode 237	19/12/47	unknown

NOTES:
Adapted into the short story 'Dick Barton – Wanted for Murder' by Edward J Mason and Geoffrey Webb. Printed in *Dick Barton – Special Agent*, published by Contact in 1950.

13: *Dick Barton and the Li-Chang Adventure* (1947)

1947 Production – 23 x 15 minute episodes (approx.)
1950 Production – 19 x 15 minute episodes (approx.)
1947 Production – BBC Radio
1950 Production – ARP (Australasian Radio Productions)
Written by Edward J Mason
Producer:	Neil Tuson *(1947 Production)*
		Morris West *(1950 Production)*

CAST:
Dick Barton	Noel Johnson *(1947 Production)*
	Douglas Kelly *(19xx Production)*
Snowey White	John Mann *(1947 Production)*
Jock Anderson	Alex McCrindle *(1947 Production)*

DICK BARTON – SPECIAL AGENT: EPISODE GUIDE

Wu San	Colin Gordon *(1947 Production)*
Max Latour	Noel Morris *(1947 Production)*
Inspector Burke	Colin Douglas *(1947 Production)*
Pat Crowther	June Spencer *(1947 Production)*
Anna	Diana Wong *(1947 Production)*
Betsy Horrock	Courtney Hope *(1947 Production)*
Joe Crowther	John Sharp *(1947 Production)*
Pat	Olive Spencer *(1947 Production)*
Lao	Ian Catford *(1947 Production)*
Atkins	Charles Leno *(1947 Production)*
Postman	Stanley Groome *(1947 Production)*
Announcer	John Fitchen *(1947 Production)*
	Derek Birch *(1947 Production)*
	Ian Catford *(1947 Production)*
	John Morgan *(1950 Production)*

STORY:
Joe Crowther – former Commando and old friend of Dick Barton – has become involved with a gang of Oriental counterfeiters, who are spreading forged currency around the country.

BROADCAST:

Broadcast Station		BBC	ARP
PART 1	*Episode 238*	22/12/47	unknown
PART 2	*Episode 239*	23/12/47	unknown
PART 3	*Episode 240*	24/12/47	unknown
PART 4	*Episode 241*	29/12/47	unknown
PART 5	*Episode 242*	30/12/47	unknown
PART 6	*Episode 243*	31/12/47	unknown
PART 7	*Episode 244*	01/01/48	unknown
PART 8	*Episode 245*	02/01/48	unknown
PART 9	*Episode 246*	05/01/48	unknown
PART 10	*Episode 247*	06/01/48	unknown
PART 11	*Episode 248*	07/01/48	unknown
PART 12	*Episode 249*	08/01/48	unknown
PART 13	*Episode 250*	09/01/48	unknown
PART 14	*Episode 251*	12/01/48	unknown
PART 15	*Episode 252*	13/01/48	unknown
PART 16	*Episode 253*	14/01/48	unknown
PART 17	*Episode 254*	15/01/48	unknown
PART 18	*Episode 255*	16/01/48	unknown
PART 19	*Episode 256*	19/01/48	unknown
PART 20	*Episode 257*	20/01/48	

SERIAL THRILLERS

PART 21 *Episode 258* 21/01/48
PART 22 *Episode 259* 22/01/48
PART 23 *Episode 260* 23/01/48

NOTES:
The second (ARP) production of *Dick Barton and the Li-Chang Adventure* was abridged from twenty-three episodes, to nineteen episodes.

14: *Dick Barton and the Case of Conrad Ruda* (1948)
20 x 15 minute episodes (approx.)
1948 Production – BBC Radio
19xx Production – ARP (Australasian Radio Productions)
Written by Basil Dawson
Producer: David H Godfrey *(1948 Production)*
                 Morris West *(19xx Production)*

CAST:
Dick Barton	Noel Johnson *(1948 Production)*
	Douglas Kelly *(19xx Production)*
Snowey White	John Mann *(1948 Production)*
Jock Anderson	Alex McCrindle *(1948 Production)*
Cara Liebling	Margaret Diamond *(1948 Production)*
Jessie Pettigrew	Thora Hird *(1948 Production)*
Conrad Ruda	Oliver Burt *(1948 Production)*
Jimmy Morgan	Peter Laughton *(1948 Production)*
Inspector Bostock	Clifford Buckham *(1948 Production)*
Sam	Pete Garstein *(1948 Production)*
Finch	John Sharp *(1948 Production)*
Charlie Chicolini	Anthony Holles *(1948 Production)*
Dr Sean O'Leary	Allan McLelland *(1948 Production)*
Mr Harvey	Neil Arden *(1948 Production)*
Father Callaghan	Macdonald Parke *(1948 Production)*
Mr Hoddle	Wilfrid Fletcher *(1948 Production)*
Jules Bardier	Basil Dawson *(1948 Production)*
Gregory	Richard Hurndall *(1948 Production)*
Announcer	John Fitchen *(1948 Production)*
	John Morgan *(1950 Production)*

STORY:
Dick is called in to help when a Hollywood film star starts receiving death-threats.

DICK BARTON – SPECIAL AGENT: EPISODE GUIDE

BROADCAST:

Broadcast Station		BBC	ARP
PART 1	*Episode 261*	26/01/48	unknown *(Ep.257)*
PART 2	*Episode 262*	27/01/48	unknown *(Ep.258)*
PART 3	*Episode 263*	28/01/48	unknown *(Ep.259)*
PART 4	*Episode 264*	29/01/48	unknown *(Ep.260)*
PART 5	*Episode 265*	30/01/48	unknown *(Ep.261)*
PART 6	*Episode 266*	02/02/48	unknown *(Ep.262)*
PART 7	*Episode 267*	03/02/48	unknown *(Ep.263)*
PART 8	*Episode 268*	04/02/48	unknown *(Ep.264)*
PART 9	*Episode 269*	05/02/48	unknown *(Ep.265)*
PART 10	*Episode 270*	06/02/48	unknown *(Ep.266)*
PART 11	*Episode 271*	09/02/48	unknown *(Ep.267)*
PART 12	*Episode 272*	10/02/48	unknown *(Ep.268)*
PART 13	*Episode 273*	11/02/48	unknown *(Ep.269)*
PART 14	*Episode 274*	12/02/48	unknown *(Ep.270)*
PART 15	*Episode 275*	13/02/48	unknown *(Ep.271)*
PART 16	*Episode 276*	16/02/48	unknown *(Ep.272)*
PART 17	*Episode 277*	17/02/48	unknown *(Ep.273)*
PART 18	*Episode 278*	18/02/48	unknown *(Ep.274)*
PART 19	*Episode 279*	19/02/48	unknown *(Ep.275)*
PART 20	*Episode 280*	20/02/48	unknown *(Ep.276)*

NOTES:
From this serial on, the numbering of the episodes for the second (ARP) productions is different to the original BBC productions.

15: *Dick Barton and the Jewel Thieves* **(1948)**
1948 Production – 20 x 15 minute episodes (approx.)
19xx Production – 26 x 15 minute episodes (approx.)
1948 Production – BBC Radio
19xx Production – ARP (Australasian Radio Productions)
Written by Geoffrey Webb *(1948 Production)*
          Geoffrey Webb and Morris West *(19xx Production)*
Producer: Neil Tuson *(1948 Production)*
              Morris West *(19xx Production)*

CAST:
Dick Barton	Noel Johnson *(1948 Production)*
	Douglas Kelly *(19xx Production)*
Snowey White	John Mann *(1948 Production)*
Inspector Burke	Colin Douglas *(1948 Production)*

SERIAL THRILLERS

Mary Russell	Anne Cullen *(1948 Production)*
Petersen	Arthur Bush *(1948 Production)*
Johnny Dufray	Harold Ayer *(1948 Production)*
	Alan Gifford *(19xx Production)*
Sonia	Maria Barry *(1948 Production)*
Gaston	Vivian Milroy *(1948 Production)*
Lofty	Jack Shaw *(1948 Production)*
Lady Weatherstone	Rosemary Johnson *(1948 Production)*
Edward Harding	Arthur Young *(1948 Production)*
Announcer	John Fitchen *(1948 Production)*

STORY:
Inspector Burke enlists Dick and his friends to help break up a gang of jewel thieves.

BROADCAST:

Broadcast Station		BBC	ARP
PART 1	*Episode 281*	23/02/48	unknown *(Ep.277)*
PART 2	*Episode 282*	24/02/48	unknown *(Ep.278)*
PART 3	*Episode 283*	25/02/48	unknown *(Ep.279)*
PART 4	*Episode 284*	26/02/48	unknown *(Ep.280)*
PART 5	*Episode 285*	27/02/48	unknown *(Ep.281)*
PART 6	*Episode 286*	01/03/48	unknown *(Ep.282)*
PART 7	*Episode 287*	02/03/48	unknown *(Ep.283)*
PART 8	*Episode 288*	03/03/48	unknown *(Ep.284)*
PART 9	*Episode 289*	04/03/48	unknown *(Ep.285)*
PART 10	*Episode 290*	05/03/48	unknown *(Ep.286)*
PART 11	*Episode 291*	08/03/48	unknown *(Ep.287)*
PART 12	*Episode 292*	09/03/48	unknown *(Ep.288)*
PART 13	*Episode 293*	10/03/48	unknown *(Ep.289)*
PART 14	*Episode 294*	11/03/48	unknown *(Ep.290)*
PART 15	*Episode 295*	12/03/48	unknown *(Ep.291)*
PART 16	*Episode 296*	15/03/48	unknown *(Ep.292)*
PART 17	*Episode 297*	16/03/48	unknown *(Ep.293)*
PART 18	*Episode 298*	17/03/48	unknown *(Ep.294)*
PART 19	*Episode 299*	18/03/48	unknown *(Ep.295)*
PART 20	*Episode 300*	19/03/48	unknown *(Ep.296)*
PART 21			unknown *(Ep.297)*
PART 22			unknown *(Ep.298)*
PART 23			unknown *(Ep.299)*
PART 24			unknown *(Ep.300)*
PART 25			unknown *(Ep.301)*
PART 26			unknown *(Ep.302)*

DICK BARTON – SPECIAL AGENT: EPISODE GUIDE

NOTES:

The second (ARP) production of *Dick Barton and the Jewel Thieves* was extended from the original twenty episodes, to twenty-six episodes. The longer edition featured new material written by producer, Morris West.

16: *Dick Barton and the Firefly Adventure* (1948)
1948 Production – 10 x 15 minute episodes (approx.)
19xx Production – 16 x 15 minute episodes (approx.)
1948 Production – BBC Radio
19xx Production – ARP (Australasian Radio Productions)
Written by Edward J Mason *(1948 Production)*
          Edward J Mason and Morris West *(19xx Production)*
Producer: Neil Tuson *(1948 Production)*
             Morris West *(19xx Production)*

CAST:
Dick Barton	Noel Johnson *(1948 Production)*
	Douglas Kelly *(19xx Production)*
Snowey White	John Mann *(1948 Production)*
Ferraro	Jack London *(1948 Production)*
Inspector Burke	Colin Douglas *(1948 Production)*
Mr Airedale	Marten Wyldeck *(1948 Production)*
Denise	Freda Falconer *(1948 Production)*
Nurse	Denise Bryer *(1948 Production)*
Cashier	Ernest Brightmore *(1948 Production)*
Announcer	John Fitchen *(1948 Production)*

STORY:

The American master-criminal Ferraro (The Firefly) has come to Britain, bringing a violent protection racket to the streets of London.

BROADCAST:
Broadcast Station		BBC	ARP
PART 1	Episode 301	22/03/48	unknown *(Ep.303)*
PART 2	Episode 302	23/03/48	unknown *(Ep.304)*
PART 3	Episode 303	24/03/48	unknown *(Ep.305)*
PART 4	Episode 304	25/03/48	unknown *(Ep.306)*
PART 5	Episode 305	26/03/48	unknown *(Ep.307)*
PART 6	Episode 306	29/03/48	unknown *(Ep.308)*
PART 7	Episode 307	30/03/48	unknown *(Ep.309)*
PART 8	Episode 308	31/03/48	unknown *(Ep.310)*
PART 9	Episode 309	01/04/48	unknown *(Ep.311)*

PART 10 Episode 310 02/04/48 unknown *(Ep.312)*
PART 11   unknown *(Ep.313)*
PART 12   unknown *(Ep.314)*
PART 13   unknown *(Ep.315)*
PART 14   unknown *(Ep.316)*
PART 15   unknown *(Ep.317)*
PART 16   unknown *(Ep.318)*

NOTES:
The second (ARP) production of *Dick Barton and the Firefly Adventure* was extended from the original ten episodes, to sixteen episodes. The longer edition featured new material written by producer, Morris West.

SERIES THREE

17: *Dick Barton and the J B Case* (1948)
AKA *Dick Barton and the J B Story*
1948 Production – 20 x 15 minute episodes (approx.)
19xx Production – 22 x 15 minute episodes (approx.)
1948 Production – BBC Radio
19xx Production – ARP (Australasian Radio Productions)
Written by Edward J Mason *(1948 Production)*
          Edward J Mason and Morris West *(19xx Production)*

Producer: Neil Tuson *(1948 Production)*
               Morris West *(19xx Production)*

CAST:
Dick Barton   Noel Johnson *(1948 Production)*
                       Douglas Kelly *(19xx Production)*
Snowey White   John Mann *(1948 Production)*
Jock Anderson   Alex McCrindle *(1948 Production)*
Martin Quayle   Dudley Rolph *(1948 Production)*
John Butler   Denis McCarthy *(1948 Production)*
Flash   Sydney Vivian *(1948 Production)*
Mrs Butler   Marjorie Mars *(1948 Production)*
Freda   Violet Loxley *(1948 Production)*
Andy   Jack Shaw *(1948 Production)*
Jeff   John Calthrop *(1948 Production)*
Inspector Burke   Colin Douglas *(1948 Production)*
Rufus   Henry Hutchinson *(1948 Production)*
Banks   Anthony Cope *(1948 Production)*

DICK BARTON – SPECIAL AGENT: EPISODE GUIDE

Announcer   Hamilton Humphreys *(1948 Production)*

STORY:
Millionaire John Butler (JB), owner of Butler's department stores, offers Dick a job as his personal bodyguard, to safeguard against an attempt on his life.

BROADCAST:

Broadcast Station		BBC	ARP
PART 1	*Episode 311*	20/09/48	unknown *(Ep.319)*
PART 2	*Episode 312*	21/09/48	unknown *(Ep.320)*
PART 3	*Episode 313*	22/09/48	unknown *(Ep.321)*
PART 4	*Episode 314*	23/09/48	unknown *(Ep.322)*
PART 5	*Episode 315*	24/09/48	unknown *(Ep.323)*
PART 6	*Episode 316*	27/09/48	unknown *(Ep.324)*
PART 7	*Episode 317*	28/09/48	unknown *(Ep.325)*
PART 8	*Episode 318*	29/09/48	unknown *(Ep.326)*
PART 9	*Episode 319*	30/09/48	unknown *(Ep.327)*
PART 10	*Episode 320*	01/10/48	unknown *(Ep.328)*
PART 11	*Episode 321*	04/10/48	unknown *(Ep.329)*
PART 12	*Episode 322*	05/10/48	unknown *(Ep.330)*
PART 13	*Episode 323*	06/10/48	unknown *(Ep.331)*
PART 14	*Episode 324*	07/10/48	unknown *(Ep.332)*
PART 15	*Episode 325*	08/10/48	unknown *(Ep.333)*
PART 16	*Episode 326*	11/10/48	unknown *(Ep.334)*
PART 17	*Episode 327*	12/10/48	unknown *(Ep.335)*
PART 18	*Episode 328*	13/10/48	unknown *(Ep.336)*
PART 19	*Episode 329*	14/10/48	unknown *(Ep.337)*
PART 20	*Episode 330*	15/10/48	unknown *(Ep.338)*
PART 21			unknown *(Ep.339)*
PART 22			unknown *(Ep.340)*

NOTES:
The second (ARP) production of *Dick Barton and the J B Case* was extended from the original twenty episodes, to twenty-two episodes. The longer edition featured new material written by producer, Morris West.

18: Serial R (1948)
20 x 15 minute episodes (approx.)
1948 Production – BBC Radio
19xx Production – ARP (Australasian Radio Productions) (Final serial)
Written by Geoffrey Webb
Producer: Neil Tuson *(1948 Production)*

SERIAL THRILLERS

Morris West *(19xx Production)*

CAST:

Dick Barton	Noel Johnson *(1948 Production)*
	Douglas Kelly *(19xx Production)*
Snowey White	John Mann *(1948 Production)*
Jock Anderson	Alex McCrindle *(1948 Production)*
Williams	Lionel Stevens *(1948 Production)*
Roberts	Victor Lucas *(1948 Production)*
Alan	Denis Webb *(1948 Production)*
Betty	John Wyndham *(1948 Production)*
Laura	Daphne Maddox *(1948 Production)*
Barker	Basil Jones *(1948 Production)*
Mills	Adrian Thomas *(1948 Production)*
Announcer	Hamilton Humphreys *(1948 Production)*

STORY:
Alan Kendal's sister and baby son have been kidnapped by the master-criminal, Edgar Roberts. They are now being held to ransom. It's up to Dick and Inspector Burke to track down the kidnappers and diffuse the situation.

BROADCAST:

Broadcast Station		BBC	ARP	
PART 1	*Episode 331*	18/10/48	unknown	*(Ep.341)*
PART 2	*Episode 332*	19/10/48	unknown	*(Ep.342)*
PART 3	*Episode 333*	20/10/48	unknown	*(Ep.343)*
PART 4	*Episode 334*	21/10/48	unknown	*(Ep.344)*
PART 5	*Episode 335*	22/10/48	unknown	*(Ep.345)*
PART 6	*Episode 336*	25/10/48	unknown	*(Ep.346)*
PART 7	*Episode 337*	26/10/48	unknown	*(Ep.347)*
PART 8	*Episode 338*	27/10/48	unknown	*(Ep.348)*
PART 9	*Episode 339*	28/10/48	unknown	*(Ep.349)*
PART 10	*Episode 340*	29/10/48	unknown	*(Ep.350)*
PART 11	*Episode 341*	01/11/48	unknown	*(Ep.351)*
PART 12	*Episode 342*	02/11/48	unknown	*(Ep.352)*
PART 13	*Episode 343*	03/11/48	unknown	*(Ep.353)*
PART 14	*Episode 344*	04/11/48	unknown	*(Ep.354)*
PART 15	*Episode 345*	05/11/48	unknown	*(Ep.355)*
PART 16	*Episode 346*	08/11/48	unknown	*(Ep.356)*
PART 17	*Episode 347*	09/11/48	unknown	*(Ep.357)*
PART 18	*Episode 348*	10/11/48	unknown	*(Ep.358)*
PART 19	*Episode 349*	11/11/48	unknown	*(Ep.359)*
PART 20	*Episode 350*	12/11/48	unknown	*(Ep.360)*

DICK BARTON – SPECIAL AGENT: EPISODE GUIDE

NOTES:
The original scripts for this production refer to the story only by its internal BBC production code. The 'production code' was an alphabetical classification given to all the *Dick Barton* serials. The designation for this story is 'Serial R'. If this serial ever had a full name, it isn't known now.

19: *Dick Barton and the Secret Formula* **(1948)**
20 x 15 minute episodes (approx.)
BBC Radio
Written by John Sharp and George Court
Based on an original idea by John McMillan (uncredited)
Producer: Neil Tuson

CAST:
Dick Barton	Noel Johnson
Snowey White	John Mann
Jock Anderson	Alex McCrindle
Karolli	Rudolf Offenbach
Ventrio	Charles Lloyd Pack
Blitzer	John Blythe
Garaghan	Macdonald Parke
Jack Sheridan	Lloyd Brydon
Kenyon	Gerry Metcalfe
Walker	Joel O'Brien
Shorty	John Blythe
Announcer	Hamilton Humphreys

STORY:
Eminent British scientist, Dr Fenston is murdered and a top-secret formula is stolen. The perpetrators are Ventrio and Blitzer. Ventrio is masquerading as a ventriloquist, with Blitzer (a dwarf) pretending to be his dummy. Dick must travel all the way to New York, in order to stop the formula falling into foreign hands. However, time is running out.

BROADCAST:
PART 1	*Episode 351*	15/11/48	PART 8	*Episode 358*	24/11/48
PART 2	*Episode 352*	16/11/48	PART 9	*Episode 359*	25/11/48
PART 3	*Episode 353*	17/11/48	PART 10	*Episode 360*	26/11/48
PART 4	*Episode 354*	18/11/48	PART 11	*Episode 361*	29/11/48
PART 5	*Episode 355*	19/11/48	PART 12	*Episode 362*	30/11/48
PART 6	*Episode 356*	22/11/48	PART 13	*Episode 363*	01/12/48
PART 7	*Episode 357*	23/11/48	PART 14	*Episode 364*	02/12/48

PART 15   *Episode 365*   03/12/48
PART 16   *Episode 366*   06/12/48
PART 17   *Episode 367*   07/12/48
PART 18   *Episode 368*   08/12/48
PART 19   *Episode 369*   09/12/48
PART 20   *Episode 370*   10/12/48

20: *Dick Barton and the Voice* (1948)
19 x 15 minute episodes (approx.)
BBC Radio
Written by Edward J Mason
Producer: Neil Tuson

CAST:
Dick Barton	Noel Johnson
Snowey White	John Mann
Jock Anderson	Alex McCrindle
Sir Charles Lomas	Noel Morris
Valta	Malcolm Graeme
Miss Galway	Beatrice Kane
Inspector Burke	Colin Douglas
Carl	Gordon Little
Announcer	Hamilton Humphreys

STORY:
A mysterious criminal mastermind known only as 'The Voice' is revealed to be behind the recent theft of some supplies of Radium from a number of London hospitals.

BROADCAST:
PART 1   *Episode 371*   13/12/48
PART 2   *Episode 372*   14/12/48
PART 3   *Episode 373*   15/12/48
PART 4   *Episode 374*   16/12/48
PART 5   *Episode 375*   17/12/48
PART 6   *Episode 376*   20/12/48
PART 7   *Episode 377*   21/12/48
PART 8   *Episode 378*   22/12/48
PART 9   *Episode 379*   23/12/48
PART 10   *Episode 380*   27/12/48
PART 11   *Episode 381*   28/12/48
PART 12   *Episode 382*   29/12/48
PART 13   *Episode 383*   30/12/48
PART 14   *Episode 384*   31/12/48
PART 15   *Episode 385*   03/01/49
PART 16   *Episode 386*   04/01/49
PART 17   *Episode 387*   05/01/49
PART 18   *Episode 388*   06/01/49
PART 19   *Episode 389*   07/01/49

DICK BARTON – SPECIAL AGENT: EPISODE GUIDE

21: *Dick Barton and Jordan's Folly* **(1949)**
20 x 15 minute episodes (approx.)
BBC Radio
Written by Geoffrey Webb
Producer: Neil Tuson *(5 Episodes)*
                        Frank Hauser *(15 Episodes)*

CAST:

Dick Barton	Noel Johnson
Snowey White	John Mann
Jock Anderson	Alex McCrindle
Mark Long	Anthony Hooper
Jim Long	Richard Taylor
Joan	Jill Bennett
Turner	Loris Somerville
Martus	Geoffrey Lumsden
Churchman	William Sherwood
Campbell	Charles Thomas
Announcer	Hamilton Humphreys
	Geoffrey Lumsden
	John Richmond

STORY:
Dick and his friends investigate strange goings-on at St Martins School in Suffolk and look into the mystery of a nearby gothic folly.

BROADCAST:

PART 1	*Episode 390*	10/01/49		PART 11	*Episode 400*	24/01/49
PART 2	*Episode 391*	11/01/49		PART 12	*Episode 401*	25/01/49
PART 3	*Episode 392*	12/01/49		PART 13	*Episode 402*	26/01/49
PART 4	*Episode 393*	13/01/49		PART 14	*Episode 403*	27/01/49
PART 5	*Episode 394*	14/01/49		PART 15	*Episode 404*	28/01/49
PART 6	*Episode 395*	17/01/49		PART 16	*Episode 405*	31/01/49
PART 7	*Episode 396*	18/01/49		PART 17	*Episode 406*	01/02/49
PART 8	*Episode 397*	19/01/49		PART 18	*Episode 407*	02/02/49
PART 9	*Episode 398*	20/01/49		PART 19	*Episode 408*	03/02/49
PART 10	*Episode 399*	21/01/49		PART 20	*Episode 409*	04/02/49

NOTES:
Adapted into the short story 'Jordan's Folly' by Edward J Mason and Geoffrey Webb. Printed in *Dick Barton – Special Agent*, published by Contact in 1950.

SERIAL THRILLERS

22: Serial V (1949)
20 x 15 minute episodes (approx.)
BBC Radio
Written by Geoffrey Webb
Producer: Neil Tuson *(9 Episodes)*
Frank Hauser *(11 Episodes)*

CAST:
Dick Barton	Duncan Carse (First appearance)
Snowey White	John Mann
Jock Anderson	Alex McCrindle
Eduardo	Philip Lennard
Borges	Victor Lucas
Leopoldo	Victor Reitty
Carmen	Olive Gregg
Wanda	Phyllis Silvern
Miguel	Stanley Van Beers
Announcer	John Fitchen

STORY:
Jock is approached by a man called Falinari, who believes that someone is trying to kill him.

BROADCAST:

PART 1	*Episode 410*	07/02/49	PART 11	*Episode 420*	21/02/49
PART 2	*Episode 411*	08/02/49	PART 12	*Episode 421*	22/02/49
PART 3	*Episode 412*	09/02/49	PART 13	*Episode 422*	23/02/49
PART 4	*Episode 413*	10/02/49	PART 14	*Episode 423*	24/02/49
PART 5	*Episode 414*	11/02/49	PART 15	*Episode 424*	25/02/49
PART 6	*Episode 415*	14/02/49	PART 16	*Episode 425*	28/02/49
PART 7	*Episode 416*	15/02/49	PART 17	*Episode 426*	01/03/49
PART 8	*Episode 417*	16/02/49	PART 18	*Episode 427*	02/03/49
PART 9	*Episode 418*	17/02/49	PART 19	*Episode 428*	03/03/49
PART 10	*Episode 419*	18/02/49	PART 20	*Episode 429*	04/03/49

NOTES:
The original scripts for this production refer to the story only by its internal BBC production code. The 'production code' was an alphabetical classification given to all the *Dick Barton* serials. The designation for this story is 'Serial V'. If this serial ever had a full name, it isn't known now.

23: *Dick Barton and the Betts Plan* (1949)
15 x 15 minute episodes (approx.)
BBC Radio
Written by Edward J Mason
Producer: Neil Tuson

CAST:
Dick Barton	Duncan Carse
Snowey White	John Mann
Jock Anderson	Alex McCrindle
Betts	Felix Felton
Inspector Burke	Colin Douglas
Hartmann	Denis McCarthy
Henrietta	Anne Cullen
Metterling	Paul Martin
Mrs Metterling	Marjorie Somerfield
Betsy Horrock	Courtney Hope
Announcer	John Fitchen
'Other Actors'	John Calthrop
	James Raglan

STORY:
German scientist, Hans Metterling has developed a new form of herbicide, with the power to destroy any living vegetation. When Metterling is kidnapped by an organisation of Nazi war criminals, it falls to Dick Barton to save Britain from the threat of botanical devastation.

BROADCAST:
PART 1	*Episode 430*	07/03/49		PART 9	*Episode 438*	17/03/49
PART 2	*Episode 431*	08/03/49		PART 10	*Episode 439*	18/03/49
PART 3	*Episode 432*	09/03/49		PART 11	*Episode 440*	21/03/49
PART 4	*Episode 433*	10/03/49		PART 12	*Episode 441*	22/03/49
PART 5	*Episode 434*	11/03/49		PART 13	*Episode 442*	23/03/49
PART 6	*Episode 435*	14/03/49		PART 14	*Episode 443*	24/03/49
PART 7	*Episode 436*	15/03/49		PART 15	*Episode 444*	25/03/49
PART 8	*Episode 437*	16/03/49				

SERIAL THRILLERS

SERIES FOUR

24: ***Dick Barton and the Vallonian Adventure*** **(1949)**
AKA Dick Barton in Vallonia
20 x 15 minute episodes (approx.)
BBC Radio
Written by Edward J Mason
Producer: David H Godfrey

CAST:

Dick Barton	Duncan Carse
Snowey White	John Mann
Jock Anderson	Alex McCrindle
Colonel Gardiner	Cyril Gardiner
Prince Paul	Oliver Burt
Homer Kraft	Eddy Reed
Stefan	Kenneth Cleveland
Announcer	John Fitchen

STORY:
A man called Josef Karvan (a native of Vallonia) is found murdered on Dick's doorstep, with potentially dire consequences for international diplomacy.

BROADCAST:

PART 1	*Episode 445*	26/09/49	PART 11	*Episode 455*	10/10/49
PART 2	*Episode 446*	27/09/49	PART 12	*Episode 456*	11/10/49
PART 3	*Episode 447*	28/09/49	PART 13	*Episode 457*	12/10/49
PART 4	*Episode 448*	29/09/49	PART 14	*Episode 458*	13/10/49
PART 5	*Episode 449*	30/09/49	PART 15	*Episode 459*	14/10/49
PART 6	*Episode 450*	03/10/49	PART 16	*Episode 460*	17/10/49
PART 7	*Episode 451*	04/10/49	PART 17	*Episode 461*	18/10/49
PART 8	*Episode 452*	05/10/49	PART 18	*Episode 462*	19/10/49
PART 9	*Episode 453*	06/10/49	PART 19	*Episode 463*	20/10/49
PART 10	*Episode 454*	07/10/49	PART 20	*Episode 464*	21/10/49

25: ***Dick Barton and the Colonel's Cavemen*** **(1949)**
20 x 15 minute episodes (approx.)
BBC Radio
Written by Geoffrey Webb
Producer: Charles LeFeaux

DICK BARTON – SPECIAL AGENT: EPISODE GUIDE

CAST:
Dick Barton	Duncan Carse
Snowey White	John Mann
Jock Anderson	Alex McCrindle
The Colonel	Julian Somers
Whiffy Smith	Ronald Sidney
Inspector Burke	James Raglan
Harrison	Lewis Stringer
Eve	Margaret Diamond
Announcer	John Fitchen

STORY:
Dick and his friends set out on the trail of the escaped convict, Whiffy Smith.

BROADCAST:
PART 1	*Episode 465*	24/10/49		PART 11	*Episode 475*	07/11/49
PART 2	*Episode 466*	25/10/49		PART 12	*Episode 476*	08/11/49
PART 3	*Episode 467*	26/10/49		PART 13	*Episode 477*	09/11/49
PART 4	*Episode 468*	27/10/49		PART 14	*Episode 478*	10/11/49
PART 5	*Episode 469*	28/10/49		PART 15	*Episode 479*	11/11/49
PART 6	*Episode 470*	30/10/49		PART 16	*Episode 480*	14/11/49
PART 7	*Episode 471*	01/11/49		PART 17	*Episode 481*	15/11/49
PART 8	*Episode 472*	02/11/49		PART 18	*Episode 482*	16/11/49
PART 9	*Episode 473*	03/11/49		PART 19	*Episode 483*	17/11/49
PART 10	*Episode 474*	04/11/49		PART 20	*Episode 484*	18/11/49

26: *Dick Barton and the Black Rock* **(1949)**
20 x 15 minute episodes (approx.)
BBC Radio
Written by Basil Dawson
Producer: Charles LeFeaux

CAST:
Dick Barton	Duncan Carse
Snowey White	John Mann
Jock Anderson	Alex McCrindle
Simon Close	Martin Case
Krelling	Percy Walsh
Maurice Glynne	W E Holloway
Nora	Peggy Thorpe Bates
Evans	John Boxer
Mrs Evans	Madeline Thomas

SERIAL THRILLERS

Announcer   John Fitchen

STORY:
Dick attempts to discover exactly who is trying to force Maurice Glynne to sell off his estate, and why.

BROADCAST:
PART 1	*Episode 485*	21/11/49	PART 11	*Episode 495*	05/12/49
PART 2	*Episode 486*	22/11/49	PART 12	*Episode 496*	06/12/49
PART 3	*Episode 487*	23/11/49	PART 13	*Episode 497*	07/12/49
PART 4	*Episode 488*	24/11/49	PART 14	*Episode 498*	08/12/49
PART 5	*Episode 489*	25/11/49	PART 15	*Episode 499*	09/12/49
PART 6	*Episode 490*	28/11/49	PART 16	*Episode 500*	12/12/49
PART 7	*Episode 491*	29/11/49	PART 17	*Episode 501*	13/12/49
PART 8	*Episode 492*	30/11/49	PART 18	*Episode 502*	14/12/49
PART 9	*Episode 493*	01/12/49	PART 19	*Episode 503*	15/12/49
PART 10	*Episode 494*	02/12/49	PART 20	*Episode 504*	16/12/49

27: *Dick Barton and the House of Windows* (1949)
18 x 15 minute episodes (approx.)
BBC Radio
Written by B D Chapman *(Bertie Chapman)*
Producer: Archie Campbell

CAST:
Dick Barton	Duncan Carse
Snowey White	John Mann
Jock Anderson	Alex McCrindle
Valpone	Bill Staughton
Lustig	Leonard Sachs
Corinna	Miriam Karlin
General Boosta	Vensley Pithey
Mary Taylor	Patricia Gilbert
Announcer	John Fitchen

STORY:
Whilst investigating a murder, Dick, Snowey and Jock become embroiled in the strange politics of the Cazalan Republic.

BROADCAST:
| PART 1 | *Episode 505* | 19/12/49 | PART 3 | *Episode 507* | 21/12/49 |
| PART 2 | *Episode 506* | 20/12/49 | PART 4 | *Episode 508* | 22/12/49 |

DICK BARTON – SPECIAL AGENT: EPISODE GUIDE

PART 5	*Episode 509*	23/12/49		PART 12	*Episode 516*	05/01/50
PART 6	*Episode 510*	28/12/49		PART 13	*Episode 517*	06/01/50
PART 7	*Episode 511*	29/12/49		PART 14	*Episode 518*	09/01/50
PART 8	*Episode 512*	30/12/49		PART 15	*Episode 519*	10/01/50
PART 9	*Episode 513*	02/01/50		PART 16	*Episode 520*	11/01/50
PART 10	*Episode 514*	03/01/50		PART 17	*Episode 521*	12/01/50
PART 11	*Episode 515*	04/01/50		PART 18	*Episode 522*	13/01/50

28: *The Night of the Twenty-Seventh* (1949)
(See also – 'Paul Temple')
60 minutes (approx.)
BBC Radio
Written by Edward J Mason
Producer: Martyn C Webster

CAST:
Dick Barton	Duncan Carse
Paul Temple	Kim Peacock
Steve	Marjorie Westbury
P.C.49	Brian Reece
Philip Odell	Robert Beatty
Mrs Dale	Ellis Powell
Dr Dale	Douglas Burbridge
The Man In Black	Valentine Dyall
Silas Ephraim	Leon Quartermane
Walter Leesham	Max Adrian
Servant	Malcolm Hayes

STORY:
A bizarre Christmas special from the BBC, in which all of Britain's most famous radio characters (from various different programmes) team up to foil the machinations of the insane Mr Silas Ephraim.

BROADCAST:
SPECIAL   27/12/49

29: Untitled Serial (1950)
20 x 15 minute episodes (approx.)
BBC Radio
Written by Geoffrey Webb
Producer: Cleland Finn

SERIAL THRILLERS

CAST:
Dick Barton	Duncan Carse
Snowey White	John Mann
Jock Anderson	Alex McCrindle
Mundos	Arthur Ridley
Esteban	Bruce Anderson
Marjorie Warner	Mary Ward
Announcer	John Fitchen

STORY:
In Rio de Janeiro, Dick and company prevent Marjorie Warner from committing a murder. But what was her motive?

BROADCAST:
PART 1	*Episode 523*	16/01/50		PART 11	*Episode 533*	30/01/50
PART 2	*Episode 524*	17/01/50		PART 12	*Episode 534*	31/01/50
PART 3	*Episode 525*	18/01/50		PART 13	*Episode 535*	01/02/50
PART 4	*Episode 526*	19/01/50		PART 14	*Episode 536*	02/02/50
PART 5	*Episode 527*	20/01/50		PART 15	*Episode 537*	03/02/50
PART 6	*Episode 528*	23/01/50		PART 16	*Episode 538*	06/02/50
PART 7	*Episode 529*	24/01/50		PART 17	*Episode 539*	07/02/50
PART 8	*Episode 530*	25/01/50		PART 18	*Episode 540*	08/02/50
PART 9	*Episode 531*	26/01/50		PART 19	*Episode 541*	09/02/50
PART 10	*Episode 532*	27/01/50		PART 20	*Episode 542*	10/02/50

NOTES:
The original scripts for this production do not refer to any specific story title; nor does any title appear in any other surviving paperwork. If this serial ever had a full name, it isn't known now.

30: Untitled Serial (1950)
15 x 15 minute episodes (approx.)
BBC Radio
Written by Geoffrey Webb
Producer: Charles LeFeaux

CAST:
Dick Barton	Duncan Carse
Snowey White	John Mann
Jock Anderson	Alex McCrindle
Dutchy	Peter Williams

DICK BARTON – SPECIAL AGENT: EPISODE GUIDE

Ben   Philip Wade
Inspector Burke   James Raglan
Announcer   John Fitchen

STORY:
Dick, Snowey and Jock investigate a Bond Street shop, which they suspect to be at the centre of a spate of recent robberies.

BROADCAST:
PART 1	*Episode 543*	13/02/50	PART 9	*Episode 551*	23/02/50
PART 2	*Episode 544*	14/02/50	PART 10	*Episode 552*	24/02/50
PART 3	*Episode 545*	15/02/50	PART 11	*Episode 553*	27/02/50
PART 4	*Episode 546*	16/02/50	PART 12	*Episode 554*	28/02/50
PART 5	*Episode 547*	17/02/50	PART 13	*Episode 555*	01/03/50
PART 6	*Episode 548*	20/02/50	PART 14	*Episode 556*	02/03/50
PART 7	*Episode 549*	21/02/50	PART 15	*Episode 557*	03/03/50
PART 8	*Episode 550*	22/02/50			

NOTES:
The original scripts for this production do not refer to any specific story title; nor does any title appear in any other surviving paperwork. If this serial ever had a full name, it isn't known now.

31: *Dick Barton and the Big Fight Racket* (1950)
AKA *Dick Barton and the Lucifer Adventure*
15 x 15 minute episodes (approx.)
BBC Radio
Written by Edward J Mason
Producer: David H Godfrey

CAST:
Dick Barton   Duncan Carse
Snowey White   John Mann
Jock Anderson   Alex McCrindle
Carol Kennedy   Jean Rolfe
Silky Boden   Allan McLelland
Mr Angell   Roger Snowdon
Announcer   John Fitchen

STORY:
Dick and his associates team up with reporter Carol Kennedy, who has reason to believe that the boxer Sailor Jones has thrown a fight.

BROADCAST:

PART 1	*Episode 558*	06/03/50		PART 9	*Episode 566*	16/03/50
PART 2	*Episode 559*	07/03/50		PART 10	*Episode 567*	17/03/50
PART 3	*Episode 560*	08/03/50		PART 11	*Episode 568*	20/03/50
PART 4	*Episode 561*	09/03/50		PART 12	*Episode 569*	21/03/50
PART 5	*Episode 562*	10/03/50		PART 13	*Episode 570*	22/03/50
PART 6	*Episode 563*	13/03/50		PART 14	*Episode 571*	23/03/50
PART 7	*Episode 564*	14/03/50		PART 15	*Episode 572*	24/03/50
PART 8	*Episode 565*	15/03/50				

32: *Dick Barton and the Lucky Gordon Affair* (1950)
13 x 15 minute episodes (approx.)
BBC Radio
Written by Edward J Mason
Producer: Charles LeFeaux

CAST:
Dick Barton	Duncan Carse (Last appearance)
Snowey White	John Mann
Jock Anderson	Alex McCrindle
Lucky Gordon	Allan Jeayes
Tony Horrock	Donald Pleasence
Graf	Godfrey Kenton
Vanzetti	Heron Carvic
Inspector Burke	James Raglan
Betsy Horrock	Courtney Hope
Announcer	Andrew Faulds

STORY:
Dick postpones his holiday to help Betsy Horrock find her nephew, Tony.

BROADCAST:

PART 1	*Episode 573*	27/03/50		PART 8	*Episode 580*	05/04/50
PART 2	*Episode 574*	28/03/50		PART 9	*Episode 581*	06/04/50
PART 3	*Episode 575*	29/03/50		PART 10	*Episode 582*	11/03/50
PART 4	*Episode 576*	30/03/50		PART 11	*Episode 583*	12/03/50
PART 5	*Episode 577*	31/03/50		PART 12	*Episode 584*	13/03/50
PART 6	*Episode 578*	03/04/50		PART 13	*Episode 585*	14/04/50
PART 7	*Episode 579*	04/04/50				

DICK BARTON – SPECIAL AGENT: EPISODE GUIDE

SERIES FIVE

33: *Dick Barton and the* **SS Golden Main** *Story* **(1950)**
20 x 15 minute episodes (approx.)
BBC Radio
Written by Edward J Mason
Producer: Charles LeFeaux

CAST:
Dick Barton	Gordon Davies (First appearance)
Snowey White	John Mann
Jock Anderson	Alex McCrindle
Professor Curtis	Keith Pyott
Captain Steel	Philip Cunningham
Carl Hartz	John Gabriel
Inspector Burke	James Raglan
Pat	Sonia Williams
Announcer	John Fitchen

STORY:
Dick and his friends travel down to Cornwall to investigate the mystery of the sunken treasure ship, the S.S. Golden Main.

BROADCAST:
PART 1	*Episode 586*	02/10/50	PART 11	*Episode 596*	16/10/50
PART 2	*Episode 587*	03/10/50	PART 12	*Episode 597*	17/10/50
PART 3	*Episode 588*	04/10/50	PART 13	*Episode 598*	18/10/50
PART 4	*Episode 589*	05/10/50	PART 14	*Episode 599*	19/10/50
PART 5	*Episode 590*	06/10/50	PART 15	*Episode 600*	20/10/50
PART 6	*Episode 591*	09/10/50	PART 16	*Episode 601*	23/10/50
PART 7	*Episode 592*	10/10/50	PART 17	*Episode 602*	24/10/50
PART 8	*Episode 593*	11/10/50	PART 18	*Episode 603*	25/10/50
PART 9	*Episode 594*	12/10/50	PART 19	*Episode 604*	26/10/50
PART 10	*Episode 595*	13/10/50	PART 20	*Episode 605*	27/10/50

34: Untitled Serial (1950)
20 x 15 minute episodes (approx.)
BBC Radio
Written by Geoffrey Webb
Producer: Charles LeFeaux *(15 Episodes)*
              Archie Campbell *(5 Episodes)*

SERIAL THRILLERS

CAST:
Dick Barton	Gordon Davies
Snowey White	John Mann
Jock Anderson	Alex McCrindle
Hegel	Charles Farrell
Lawrence	John Bushelle
Matthews	Godfrey Kenton
Charter	Raf De La Tour
Announcer	John Fitchen

STORY:
On the waterfront in Brisbane, Dick and his friends prevent a murder from taking place.

BROADCAST:
PART 1	*Episode 606*	30/10/50		PART 11	*Episode 616*	13/11/50
PART 2	*Episode 607*	31/10/50		PART 12	*Episode 617*	14/11/50
PART 3	*Episode 608*	01/11/50		PART 13	*Episode 618*	15/11/50
PART 4	*Episode 609*	02/11/50		PART 14	*Episode 619*	16/11/50
PART 5	*Episode 610*	03/11/50		PART 15	*Episode 620*	17/11/50
PART 6	*Episode 611*	06/11/50		PART 16	*Episode 621*	20/11/50
PART 7	*Episode 612*	07/11/50		PART 17	*Episode 622*	21/11/50
PART 8	*Episode 613*	08/11/50		PART 18	*Episode 623*	22/11/50
PART 9	*Episode 614*	09/11/50		PART 19	*Episode 624*	23/11/50
PART 10	*Episode 615*	10/11/50		PART 20	*Episode 625*	24/11/50

NOTES:
The original scripts for this production do not refer to any specific story title; nor does any title appear in any other surviving paperwork. If this serial ever had a full name, it isn't known now.

35: *Dick Barton and the Bridge* (1950)
20 x 15 minute episodes (approx.)
BBC Radio
Written by B D Chapman (*Bertie Chapman*)
Producer: David H Godfrey *(15 Episodes)*
              Ayton Whitaker *(5 Episodes)*

CAST:
Dick Barton	Gordon Davies
Snowey White	John Mann
Jock Anderson	Alex McCrindle

DICK BARTON – SPECIAL AGENT: EPISODE GUIDE

Q   Allan McLelland
Kasslas   Oliver Burt
Announcer   John Fitchen

STORY:
Dick and his companions investigate the sabotage of a bridge that is being built in the Middle East.

BROADCAST:
PART 1	*Episode 626*	27/11/50	PART 11	*Episode 636*	11/12/50
PART 2	*Episode 627*	28/10/50	PART 12	*Episode 637*	12/12/50
PART 3	*Episode 628*	29/11/50	PART 13	*Episode 638*	13/12/50
PART 4	*Episode 629*	30/11/50	PART 14	*Episode 639*	14/12/50
PART 5	*Episode 630*	01/12/50	PART 15	*Episode 640*	15/12/50
PART 6	*Episode 631*	04/12/50	PART 16	*Episode 641*	18/12/50
PART 7	*Episode 632*	05/12/50	PART 17	*Episode 642*	19/12/50
PART 8	*Episode 633*	06/12/50	PART 18	*Episode 643*	20/12/50
PART 9	*Episode 634*	07/12/50	PART 19	*Episode 644*	21/12/50
PART 10	*Episode 635*	08/12/50	PART 20	*Episode 645*	22/12/50

36: Untitled Serial (1950)
18 x 15 minute episodes (approx.)
BBC Radio
Written by Anthony Garwood
Producer: Archie Campbell

CAST:
Dick Barton   Gordon Davies
Snowey White   John Mann
Jock Anderson   Alex McCrindle
Lord Cattering   Arthur Ridley
Announcer   John Fitchen

STORY:
On the Scottish Moors, Dick rescues a journalist called Rawlings, who is being pursued by a gang of crooks.

BROADCAST:
PART 1	*Episode 646*	27/12/50	PART 5	*Episode 650*	02/01/51
PART 2	*Episode 647*	28/12/50	PART 6	*Episode 651*	03/01/51
PART 3	*Episode 648*	29/12/50	PART 7	*Episode 652*	04/01/51
PART 4	*Episode 649*	01/01/51	PART 8	*Episode 653*	05/01/51

PART 9   *Episode 654*   08/01/51
PART 10 *Episode 655*   09/01/51
PART 11 *Episode 656*   10/01/51
PART 12 *Episode 657*   11/01/51
PART 13 *Episode 658*   12/01/51

PART 14 *Episode 659*   15/01/51
PART 15 *Episode 660*   16/01/51
PART 16 *Episode 661*   17/01/51
PART 17 *Episode 662*   18/01/51
PART 18 *Episode 663*   19/01/51

NOTES:
The original scripts for this production do not refer to any specific story title; nor does any title appear in any other surviving paperwork. If this serial ever had a full name, it isn't known now.

37: Untitled Serial (1951)
15 x 15 minute episodes (approx.)
BBC Radio
Written by Geoffrey Webb
Producer: Charles LeFeaux

CAST:
Dick Barton   Gordon Davies
Snowey White   John Mann
Jock Anderson   Alex McCrindle
Labonne   George Hays
Henri   Colin Gordon
Elyse   Janet Butler
Announcer   John Fitchen

STORY:
Returning to France, Dick, Snowey and Jock investigate a bombing at a Paris Concert Hall.

BROADCAST:
PART 1   *Episode 664*   22/01/51
PART 2   *Episode 665*   23/01/51
PART 3   *Episode 666*   24/01/51
PART 4   *Episode 667*   25/01/51
PART 5   *Episode 668*   26/01/51
PART 6   *Episode 669*   29/01/51
PART 7   *Episode 670*   30/01/51
PART 8   *Episode 671*   31/01/51

PART 9   *Episode 672*   01/02/51
PART 10 *Episode 673*   02/02/51
PART 11 *Episode 674*   05/02/51
PART 12 *Episode 675*   06/02/51
PART 13 *Episode 676*   07/02/51
PART 14 *Episode 677*   08/02/51
PART 15 *Episode 678*   09/02/51

NOTES:
The original scripts for this production do not refer to any specific story title;

nor does any title appear in any other surviving paperwork. If this serial ever had a full name, it isn't known now.

38: *Dick Barton and the Green Triangle Gang* **(1951)**
20 x 15 minute episodes (approx.)
BBC Radio
Written by Edward J Mason
Producer: David H Godfrey

CAST:
Dick Barton	Gordon Davies
Snowey White	John Mann
Jock Anderson	Alex McCrindle
Amos Bennion (Benny)	Charles Lamb
Sid	Roger Snowdon
Nipper	David Kean
Inspector Burke	James Raglan
Sugar	Thora Hird
Announcer	John Fitchen

STORY:
Dick Barton and his friends are sent to the circus in search of members of the sinister Green Triangle Gang.

BROADCAST:
PART 1	*Episode 679*	12/02/51		PART 11	*Episode 689*	26/02/51
PART 2	*Episode 680*	13/02/51		PART 12	*Episode 690*	27/02/51
PART 3	*Episode 681*	14/02/51		PART 13	*Episode 691*	28/02/51
PART 4	*Episode 682*	15/02/51		PART 14	*Episode 692*	01/03/51
PART 5	*Episode 683*	16/02/51		PART 15	*Episode 693*	02/03/51
PART 6	*Episode 684*	19/02/51		PART 16	*Episode 694*	03/03/51
PART 7	*Episode 685*	20/02/51		PART 17	*Episode 695*	06/03/51
PART 8	*Episode 686*	21/02/51		PART 18	*Episode 696*	07/03/51
PART 9	*Episode 687*	22/02/51		PART 19	*Episode 697*	08/03/51
PART 10	*Episode 688*	23/02/51		PART 20	*Episode 698*	09/03/51

39: *Dick Barton and the Trail of the Rocket* **(1951)**
1951 Production – 13 x 15 minute episodes (approx.)
2013 Production – 2 x 45 minute episodes (approx.)
1951 Production – BBC Radio
2013 Production – BBC Audiobooks

SERIAL THRILLERS

Written by B D Chapman *(Bertie Chapman)*
             B D Chapman and Charles Norton *(2013 Production)*
Producer: Charles LeFeaux *(1951 Production)*
             Charles Norton *(2013 Production)*
Director: Rob Thrush *(2013 Production)*

CAST:
Dick Barton	Gordon Davies *(1951 Production)*
	Tim Bentinck *(2013 Production*
Snowey White	John Mann *(1951 Production)*
	Terry Molloy *(2013 Production)*
Jock Anderson	Alex McCrindle *(1951 Production)*
	Nick Scovell *(2013 Production)*
Joyce Gray	Alvys Maben *(1951 Production)*
	Lisa Bowerman *(2013 Production)*
Annette Leroux	Cecile Chevreau *(1951 Production)*
	Lisa Bowerman *(2013 Production)*
Inspector Burke	Arnold Diamond *(1951 Production)*
	David Benson *(2013 Production)*
Zettner	Ian Sadler *(1951 Production)*
	Barnaby Edwards *(2013 Production)*
Julius Streicher	Eric Pohlmann *(1951 Production)*
	David Benson *(2013 Production)*
The Dandy	Richard Williams *(1951 Production)*
	David Benson *(2013 Production)*
Dr Leroux	Noel Howlett *(1951 Production)*
	Barnaby Edwards *(2013 Production)*
Sgt. Gallere	Godfrey Kenton *(1951 Production)*
	Barnaby Edwards *(2013 Production)*
Colonel Fonataine	Neil Tuson *(1951 Production)*
Nutty Templeton	Robert Raglan *(1951 Production)*
Lisa Hugo	Mavis Villiers *(1951 Production)*
Max Schumann	Olaf Olsen *(1951 Production)*
Doll	Robert Raglan *(1951 Production)*
Pattison	Robert Sewell *(1951 Production)*
Abu Ramel	Victor Fairley *(1951 Production)*
	David Benson *(2013 Production)*
Lunt	Michael Golden *(1951 Production)*
	Nick Scovell *(2013 Production)*
Arab	John Fitchen *(1951 Production)*
	Terry Molloy *(2013 Production)*
Rapella	Arnold Diamond *(1951 Production)*
The Boatman	Eric Lugg *(1951 Production)*

DICK BARTON – SPECIAL AGENT: EPISODE GUIDE

Announcer   John Fitchen *(1951 Production)*
                   Rob Thrush *(2013 Production)*

STORY:
After foiling a plan to launch a deadly rocket, Dick Barton's freelance adventuring comes to an end, when he receives his Z-Papers and is called up into service.

BROADCAST:
PART 1	*Episode 699*	12/03/51	PART 8	*Episode 706*	21/03/51
PART 2	*Episode 700*	13/03/51	PART 9	*Episode 707*	22/03/51
PART 3	*Episode 701*	14/03/51	PART 10	*Episode 708*	27/03/51
PART 4	*Episode 702*	15/03/51	PART 11	*Episode 709*	28/03/51
PART 5	*Episode 703*	16/03/51	PART 12	*Episode 710*	29/03/51
PART 6	*Episode 704*	19/03/51	PART 13	*Episode 711*	30/03/51
PART 7	*Episode 705*	20/03/51			

NOTES:
The 2013 production of *Dick Barton and the Trail of the Rocket* was abridged from 13x15 minute episodes, to 2x45 minute episodes. Some additional material was written by Charles Norton to make this reduction possible.

The Adventures of Dan Dare – Pilot of the Future

THE GREAT 208:

In the last years of the 1940s, the BBC faced a new threat. The threat was so totally beyond its comprehension nobody knew how to stop it. It came at night. It came across the oceans – through the air. It came into your home and took your children. It came from Luxembourg.

Radio Luxembourg was the only real broadcasting competition the BBC ever had in the late forties and early fifties. As the name suggests, it wasn't technically a British radio station at all. It instead broadcast via a transmitter in Luxembourg. The BBC had a state-assured monopoly on British radio at the time and rival broadcasting was against the law. Radio Luxembourg was a clever way of circumventing the legislation. It was technically classified as a foreign broadcaster. However, it was never really designed for the people of Luxembourg. This was a station for British people with British music and British programmes. Having their transmitter in Luxembourg meant that although the station was officially on foreign soil, it was also (just) close enough for those in Britain to pick up the station on their wireless sets. In effect, it was something of a pirate station – albeit an entirely legal one.

The station had its origins in the creation of the Luxembourg Broadcasting Company (Compagnie Luxembourgeoise de Radiodiffusion) in late 1929. The chief outlet of this organisation was the newly formed Radio Luxembourg, which continued to have a good deal of success with its targeted transmissions to Britain until 1939.

In 1939, war broke out and Luxembourg was soon to be occupied by the Nazis. Radio Luxembourg was similarly placed under German control for the duration. On 1 July 1946, the station was reopened to business as usual – broadcasting popular programmes to Great Britain, in direct competition with the BBC.

Of course, the BBC was a non-profit-making and essentially philanthropic endeavour with a simple remit to inform, educate and entertain and to do so with as little commercial motivation as possible. Radio Luxembourg had no such principles. Radio Luxembourg was a commercial radio station, which would sell airtime to any company who had enough money to pay for the publicity. Its first post-war shows were sponsored by William Hill, the bookmakers.

Radio Luxembourg was the exact antithesis of the BBC and at a time when there was growing pressure for the legalisation of commercial broadcasting in the UK, this young upstart from across the oceans, was of very great concern to the Corporation.

It didn't help matters that Radio Luxembourg was hoovering up an increasingly vast quantity of listeners with their own infectious brand of popularism.

There was little public disapproval of the programming on the new station (bar the odd spot of snobbery). However, for many, the pure free-market capitalism that underpinned it was something of far greater criticism.

The (Labour) government of the day, expressed particular concern – spelling out their reservations in a formal white paper in 1946.

On 16 July 1946, the MP Herbert Morrison (also an ardent devotee of the BBC's *Dick Barton* serials) went so far as to say in the Commons: 'We will do our best not to have commercial broadcasting … We do not like this effort to set up a business in Luxembourg for the purpose of directing broadcasting at this country.'[178]

In 1948, BBC Monitoring began to selectively monitor Radio Luxembourg with help from Radio Services Ltd. The results from 1948 and 1949 revealed the true extent to which the new rival was making inroads into established BBC territory. At 5PM on a Sunday in December 1949, it was discovered, that around three percent of the adult British population was listening to Radio Luxembourg on 208. This was about a million listeners. The Light Programme was still ahead, with an audience share of around twenty-one percent. However, the Luxembourg problem was still too big to be ignored.

Radio Luxembourg's own figures quoted audiences of as high as 4 million. Crucially much of Luxembourg's audience-share was drawn from the 16-34 bracket – an audience which the BBC was clearly doing little to cater for. The BBC's cancellation of *Dick Barton* in 1951 was hardly a good move in the ratings-war either – with the rest of the BBC's output pitching to an increasingly marginal demographic of the 'serious-minded'.

Despite the cynically exploitative nature of Luxembourg, there was little denying that it was providing a much-needed outlet for light entertainment and music, almost totally absent on the BBC, at the time.

People like Val Gielgud did little to redress the balance and throughout the late 1940s the BBC stubbornly stuck to higher more Reithian ideals and ran the risk of losing their monopoly to its commercial rivals altogether. W H Grey, Chairman of Radio Luxembourg Advertising in 1949, put this stubbornness simply down to, 'the prejudice which it is known the BBC Directorate entertain against Radio Luxembourg's sponsored programmes.'[179]

---

[178] From *Hansard – Volume 425 –* The House of Commons (16/07/46)
[179] From *Sound & Vision* by Asa Briggs – Oxford University Press (1979)

THE ADVENTURES OF DAN DARE – PILOT OF THE FUTURE

The killing off of *Dick Barton* in 1951 was a particularly notable case of the BBC's failure to understand its new problem. *Barton* was one of the few instances where the Light Programme had the edge on its chief competitor. *Barton*'s replacement with an 'everyday story of country-folk' was ratings-suicide. It instantly drove off what was left of the 16-34s, straight into the waiting arms of commercial radio. And Luxembourg knew it. They had another radio hero all ready and lined up for the newly disenchanted BBC listeners.

DAN DARE – SPECIAL AGENT:

Radio Luxembourg was quick to identify the popularity of the BBC's daily *Dick Barton* serial (quicker than the BBC themselves perhaps). And even before the last episode had been recorded, they had already started thinking about mounting a similar series of their own.

Serials like *Perry Mason*[180] (sponsored by Tide washing powder) and *The Glyndale Star*[181] (sponsored by Dreft washing powder) were highly popular draws for Luxembourg. However, these shows had always been targeted principally at Luxembourg's large female listenership. The suggestion was now for something a little different and there were plenty of ex-BBC staff available for advice.

The BBC didn't approve of any of its staff going off to work for Radio Luxembourg. However, many still did so (often in secret). One of the many defectors was former BBC Drama Repertory Company member, Desmond Carrington, who explains that, 'if you worked for Luxembourg, you were persona-non-grata at the BBC, in those days.'

Moonlighting for Luxembourg soon became endemic among the BBC's freelancers (and even staff). The reasons often came down to a combination of money and greater creative liberalism. Carrington continues that his Luxembourg 'work overlapped with some of my BBC work and I began to think that I could have more fun or more money on my own, doing those recorded programmes for Luxembourg.'

A notable presence on the Luxembourg payroll was Neil Tuson, *Dick Barton*'s former producer and co-creator. *The Glyndale Star* – a popular serial about the running of a family newspaper – was co-written by half of the *Barton* writing team, Geoffrey Webb. It even starred *Barton* actresses Courtney Hope (formerly *Barton*'s Betsy Horrock) and Anne Cullen (former *Barton* guest star and wife of Neil Tuson). As such, it was hardly surprising that *Dick Barton* was

---

[180] Based on the popular Erle Stanley Gardner detective novels from America, serials like *The Case of the Martyred Mother* would be frequent attractions on the station.
[181] 'The exciting story of the Kent family and their newspaper'.

foremost in the minds of Radio Luxembourg.

At some point in 1951, Luxembourg approached *Barton*'s two founding fathers, Edward J Mason and Geoffrey Webb about working on a daily serial for their station. They both appear to have agreed. Possibly reluctant to blot their copybooks with the BBC however, neither Mason nor Webb would be credited in the programmes.

The new serial was to be an audio adaptation of one of the most popular comic strips of the day – *Dan Dare – Pilot of the Future*.

The *Dan Dare* comic strip was the flagship serialisation featured in the British comic, *Eagle*. Starting on 14 April 1950, *Eagle* had been created by the Rev Marcus Morris, a vicar from the Southport church of St James and the *Dan Dare* strip was largely the work of legendary artist Frank Hampson (and later the equally legendary Frank Bellamy). Telling the story of the titular Dan Dare, a space-pilot in the far-flung future of the late 1990s, it followed Dare on his adventures through the solar system, encountering strange new life forms and alien civilisations. The *Dan Dare* team comprised Dan and his associates (Albert) Digby and Professor Jocelyn (Mabel) Peabody. Their chief foe was the megalomaniac Mekon, the super-intelligent ruler of the alien Treens.

It was at this point that the famous advertising agency J(ames) Walter Thompson (later known as JWT) entered the frame. JWT had only recently been involved in the syndication of the BBC's *Dick Barton* serials to South African radio and were clearly keen to further exploit the marketable potential of the daily adventure serial. With interest in sponsorship from the malted drinks company Horlicks, JWT became involved in the development of Luxembourg's latest plans for a *Dan Dare* serial.

The people at *Eagle*, including Frank Hampson, were contacted and a deal was struck, whereby Radio Luxembourg would have the rights to translate the *Dan Dare* comic strip into radio form. The new series would be based on the original strips. However, after establishing the basic story premise, the radio series would largely invent its own original material for the wireless and would not rely on any of the writers from *Eagle*.

With Mason and Webb's agreement to take part, the next step was casting. Obviously wishing to carry the *Dick Barton* feel even further, there was one very obvious candidate to play the part of Dan – the original *Dick Barton* himself – Noel Johnson.

Johnson had found little work on the radio, since leaving the *Dick Barton* series in 1949. 'It took a long time for me to be accepted as a straight actor again,'[182] Johnson later explained. In 1951, Johnson was on the lookout for work and with Radio Luxembourg were scouting around for a Dick Barton-type for their new serial, Noel Johnson was the only possible candidate. The BBC's current Dick Barton was still (technically) contracted to another *Barton*

---

[182] From *The Wireless Stars* by George Nobbs – Wensum Books (1972)

radio series. The previous actor in the part Duncan Carse, was on a dangerous expedition somewhere near the South Pole. It isn't surprising that Johnson was at the top of Luxembourg's list.

'It all started,' remembered Johnson, 'with my being asked to go along to a studio one evening by J Walter Thompson and do a test recording on tape. There were two or three other actors there and they were looking for a Dan Dare and the upshot of it all was that they said, "Would I play it?"'[183]

Johnson was keen for further work and Luxembourg was known for being a good employer for actors. But, Johnson had his reservations. It had been work on the BBC's *Barton* serials that had seen him typecast in the first place and he was reluctant to put himself in such a position again. He accepted the part on one condition – total anonymity: 'I said ... "What about publicity?" And they misunderstood me and said, "We're afraid that there won't be any publicity." And I said, "that's fine. That suits me." Because, I was going to say that I didn't want any. I would play it anonymously.'[184]

Of course, there were other possible reasons for contributing to Luxembourg anonymously. 'Again, he wouldn't have wanted the BBC to know about that, I'm sure,' says Desmond Carrington.

In line with the vast majority of Radio Luxembourg's output, *Dan Dare* was never actually recorded in Luxembourg itself. Instead, programmes would be recorded in specially hired private recording studios in London. The most commonly used studios were Star Sound Studios (SSS). SSS had two studios in London. One was in mews just off Baker Street and the other was in Hampstead. The SSS company was run by Derek Faraday, who also lived above the Hampstead studio. It was at Faraday's SSS facilities where the new *Dan Dare* series was recorded.

Other cast members were soon quickly attracted to the new show (most remaining anonymous). The Mekon was played by former *Barton* guest, Francis de Wolff, who had still yet to begin his long-standing relationship with the BBC's Drama Repertory Company. Digby was played by John Sharp – a then little known actor who had only recently appeared as a desk sergeant in another cinema adaptation of BBC Radio's *PC 49* (*A Case for PC 49*).

Actor and scriptwriter Geoffrey Bond was brought in to play a character called Vultan. Bond had been a member of the BBC Drama Rep' and was better known as one of the writers of the BBC's gentle radio soap opera, *Mrs Dale's Diary*. Anne Cullen (then Mrs Neil Tuson) completed the regular cast, playing Professor Peabody. However Cullen's appearances were apparently restricted, due to her many other jobs on other Luxembourg dramas, including her regular part in a Western.

Other voices came from former Paul Temple Howard Marion Crawford.

---

[183] From an interview with Noel Johnson for *The Eagle Society* (C.1980s)
[184] From an interview with Noel Johnson for *The Eagle Society* (C.1980s)

According to Derek Faraday, Crawford 'would play every part under the sun and he'd have a wonderful scene with himself, playing three voices.'[185]

The very first serial would be based upon the storyline of the very first comic strip – *Voyage to Venus*. Following the pattern laid down by *Dick Barton*, the serial would be stripped across a series of 15-minute episodes. Approximately eighteen episodes were set aside for this first serial, which was recorded in mid 1951 at Faraday's SSS facilities. The producer was John Glyn-Jones.

'There would be a run-through – fifteen minutes,' recalled Faraday. 'The producer would make a note of certain small parts that might need a little bit of extra rehearsal and that would take, at the most, half an hour. There would be a slight pause for coffee, or it might have been something else, if the pub across the road was open, and we'd come back and do the programme in one take. In the earliest days we were recording on disc. It had to be one take. We couldn't edit it.'[186]

As with *Barton* before it, the signature tune was chosen very carefully. However, unlike *Barton*, no single piece of music was chosen to represent the programme. Instead a number of pieces of library music were used selectively, in conjunction with some specially created sound effects, in order to give the programme its musical identity. As with *Barton*, all the music came from existing stock recordings conducted by Charles Williams with the Queen's Light Orchestra. The programme opened with a snatch of music from the very start of *Radio Location*, written by Clive Richardson, before dissolving into a high-pitched sound-effect of a rocket taking off. Over this would be read the authoritative words – 'Spaceship Away! The makers of Horlicks present: *Dan Dare – Pilot of the Future*.' Then the opening would cut to a section of *Searchlight* by Charles Williams, which would fade into the opening of the show. Every episode would close with a further section of *Radio Location*, with a third piece (*Commandos* by Charles Williams) used for incidental music. The editing together of disparate sections of existing recordings to make a theme tune may seem strange, but it was quite common at the time. Even as late as 1961, the BBC used the technique to make up a theme for their television science fiction drama, *A For Andromeda*.

'We didn't run over time,' explained Faraday, 'because you always would have theme music at the top and tail and the theme music was a god-send. It wasn't put there just to be pretty. It gave you time to fade in and fade out.'[187]

This first serial was transmitted from 2 July to 25 July 1951, running five days a week (as had *Barton*). It had been very much designed to test the water and to see if the new series was worth going any further with. In March 1951,

---

[185] From an interview with Derek Faraday for *The Eagle Society* (1984)
[186] From an interview with Derek Faraday for *The Eagle Society* (1984)
[187] From an interview with Derek Faraday for *The Eagle Society* (1984)

the BBC had axed *Dick Barton* from its schedules, leaving the airwaves free for the new interloper to move in on its audience. With this in mind, by October, the *Dan Dare* project had been judged a sufficient enough success for Radio Luxembourg to commission a full and continuous series, which would start in November – again running five days a week.

THE ADVENTURES OF DAN DARE – PILOT OF THE FUTURE:

Existing documentation is highly unclear over how the new series picked up from the initial run of July 1951. However, it seems that much of the cast and crew from the pilot series made a return.

Again, the surviving evidence doesn't give us a very clear picture, but among the scriptwriters were both Edward J Mason and Geoffrey Webb, with Webb very much in the lead. However, there was also some input from Bertie (B D) Chapman as well, who had also worked on a number of *Barton* scripts and would later script his own BBC radio science fiction series, *Orbiter X* (1951)

'Different writers were used,' Faraday remembered. 'Obviously, one writer couldn't write five programmes a week and then do five programmes for the next week. So, there was a staff of writers and the great thing was to make one writer aware of what the writer before him had said, so there was an element of continuity about the thing.'[188]

Over the next five months, *Dan Dare* would run without break or interruption (even over Christmas). The series soon caught on and became a massive ratings hit for the station. The programme continued to be sponsored by Horlicks, with advertising announcements going out before and after each episode, promoting the hot drink. A later episode from 1956 closed with: '*Dan Dare – Pilot of the Future* was presented by the makers of Horlicks – the warm drink that helps to give you a relaxed sleep, so that you wake revived, alert and refreshed.'[189] Pathé's famous voice of the newsreel, Bob Danvers Walker, traditionally read these announcements and the credits themselves – very much in the style of *Dick Barton*'s John Fitchen[190].

These advertisements were obviously something *Dick Barton* hadn't had to contend with, but they were kept as unobtrusive as possible. 'It wouldn't interfere with the programme,' said Faraday 'We had fifteen minutes undiluted *Dan Dare*. In point of fact, it was fourteen minutes, thirty seconds, because you had thirty seconds undiluted Horlicks at the end. There was

---

[188] From an interview with Derek Faraday for *The Eagle Society* (1984)
[189] *The Lost World on Mars* – Episode 53 (19/03/53)
[190] John Fitchen was another BBC man who ended up doing work for Radio Luxembourg, on the side. He worked as an announcer on several Luxembourg programmes (just as he did for the BBC). Surprisingly he never seems to have worked on *Dan Dare* (as far as we know).

obviously no continuity between the programme and the commercial.'[191]

It seems that by the time of this first full run in November, Faraday had stopped recording the *Dare* programmes on disc and had taken the unusual move of recording them to tape. This was something of a pioneering step for Faraday. Tape recording was certainly a technical move forward in terms of broadcast quality, but was little used by the BBC. Even American radio had not long adopted it.

It may have been something that Faraday was prompted to do by Luxembourg itself, as the station increasingly turned to magnetic tape to source its output. Even certain music programmes were moving over to the new technology. Desmond Carrington recalls: 'I got hold of a tape recorder, before there were any in this country, from America. That would, I suppose, have been about that time ... People didn't have tape recorders – domestic ones anyway. There were some professional ones and Radio Luxembourg had those. They sent their programmes over by plane once a week, I think. And they were broadcast from the Duchy and it picked up on 208 metres in Britain.'

This was certainly the pattern of production on *Dan Dare*. Following the broadcast of each episode, the tapes were routinely returned to Faraday and then wiped for reuse – either in the production of another *Dan Dare* episode, or perhaps on one of the many other programmes Faraday was involved in. Needless to say, there was a very sharp turnaround on material between London and Luxembourg.

'We used to do five a day,' explained Noel Johnson, 'three in the morning and two in the afternoon ... We certainly did a week's output – usually on a Thursday. We worked one day a week, but they were very very accommodating like that with J Walter Thompson. I mean, they weren't paying vast sums of money either, but it was a useful bit of income on the side and consequently, they knew one did other things. So, if anybody really said, "Look, I have been offered a television or a few days filming or something or other. Can we vary the recording?" They'd say, "Well, yes. So, we'll miss a week or do two days the following week or something like that." They were awfully good like that and so it was worth doing it for the mutual convenience of everyone.'[192]

'The actors themselves were very very glad and anxious to get on Luxembourg,' agreed Faraday 'because Luxembourg paid more than the BBC.'[193]

There must have been well over a hundred *Dan Dare* studio recordings over the five years of the programme's production for Luxembourg. As with *Barton* and *Paul Temple* before it, something of a family atmosphere was developed

---

[191] From an interview with Derek Faraday for *The Eagle Society* (1984)
[192] From an interview with Noel Johnson for *The Eagle Society* (C.1980s)
[193] From an interview with Derek Faraday for *The Eagle Society* (1984)

through the regular gatherings. However as Faraday remembered when he was interviewed in 1984, such conviviality could also extend beyond the studio (and across the road to the local pub).

'They had one common failing and some might call it a virtue, in that they were all connoisseurs of Scotch and they kept themselves in training quite well. We would work until eleven o'clock in the morning on coffee and the programmes would improve miraculously after eleven thirty, by which time, we'd made our first visit to the pub.'[194]

208 MAGAZINE:

In keeping with the epic nature of some of the *Dan Dare* comic-strip adventures, most of the Radio Luxembourg serials were very long. Most serials were over thirty episodes long and some were a lot more. *The Lost World on Mars* (January 1953 – April 1953) ran for a colossal sixty-four episodes. Series three, which began on 21 September 1953 kicked off with an even longer story, *Marooned on Mercury,* which was strung out over seventy-six episodes.

Obviously, with such involved and continuing storylines, the serialisations demanded the attention of dedicated listeners and, by all accounts, it got them. In January 1952, the results of a poll revealed *Dan Dare* to be the fourth top-rated programme on Radio Luxembourg. It was just behind *Nightly Requests* and *Twenty Questions* at joint third. *Movie Magazine* took second place, with the incredibly popular *Top Twenty* at number one.

By February, *Dan Dare* had leapt up to number three in the charts, with *Nightly Requests* also up a place at number two. *Time for a Song* was a new entry in *Dare*'s former number four spot and *Top Twenty* held on at the top.

These radio ratings charts were published by *208 Magazine*, Radio Luxembourg's principal publication. Luxembourg itself didn't technically print the magazine, but it was essentially its mouthpiece. No actual production paperwork is known to survive from Radio Luxembourg from this time and *208 Magazine* is the main (and sometimes only) source of information on the *Dan Dare* series. This is slightly unfortunate, because the magazine wasn't always absolutely accurate and there are other drawbacks too.

The biggest problem with *208 Magazine* is it's spectacular lack of impartiality. It is very well recorded that the higher echelons of the BBC had serious objections about Radio Luxembourg and didn't have very much time for the organisation as a whole. However, it shouldn't be forgotten that this was a two-way thing. Many of those working for Radio Luxembourg were ardent believers in the idea of commercial broadcasting. For many, the BBC's (state-funded) monopoly was public enemy number one.

208 Magazine was not just an active vehicle for the promotion of Radio

---

[194] From an interview with Derek Faraday for *The Eagle Society* (1984)

Luxembourg and commercial broadcasting in general, it was also rabidly anti-BBC. Nowhere was any publication so regularly printing such vitriolic attacks against the BBC as *208 Magazine*.

One contributor to the magazine was Richard Langley, whose monthly *Radio Commentary* opinion piece was a particularly notable venting of anti-BBC bile.

Sadly, the magazine's overtly antagonistic stance sometimes got in the way of the actual purpose of the magazine – to provide accurate programme information.

However, despite its lack of impartiality, *208 Magazine* was not over-inflating the series popularity. That was genuine. *Dan Dare* was a real hit for the station and children all over the UK were tuning in. Interestingly, overtones of the early days of *Dick Barton*'s popularity were repeated in *Dan Dare*'s fanmail.

Gloria McCutcheon from Ayrshire in Scotland echoed 1947's *Barton* homework controversy, when she wrote to *208 Magazine* in February 1952 saying: 'As I spend most week-nights studying, I find it most pleasant to leave my "German Unification" or "Cosine Rule" and fly about the heavens with Dan Dare for a little before regretfully returning to earth and the intricacies of "French Irregular Verbs". This programme may seem far-fetched, but it is interesting and exciting. I hate to miss an episode.'[195]

A comment from Langley's February 1952 column also draws some telling parallels with *Barton*, as he commented that the BBC had still made: 'No move to reprieve *Dick Barton* – even with the amazing success of *Dan Dare* on Luxembourg as a beacon of light showing what the kids want.'[196]

'Dan's fans grow day by day,' added Langley in March. 'They number as many thousands as Barton's ever did.'[197]

DAN DARE UNMASKED:

One thing that Noel Johnson had always insisted upon when taking the Dan Dare part was, of course, the preservation of his total anonymity from the listeners. This was, in theory, a fairly easy thing to maintain on the radio and would allow Johnson to continue with other work. Johnson's name was never read out on air and never appeared in print in connection with the series. However, in March 1952, partway through the second season, Luxembourg were to (possibly unwittingly) renege on their half of the deal when Noel Johnson was publicly revealed as the voice of Dan Dare.

As early as January 1952, a letter had appeared in *208 Magazine* asking:

---

[195] From *208 Magazine* (February 1952)
[196] From *208 Magazine* (February 1952)
[197] From *208 Magazine* (March 1952)

THE ADVENTURES OF DAN DARE - PILOT OF THE FUTURE

'Who does play Dan Dare? Every small boy wants to know. Many fathers are certain they know. Are they right?'[198] The question was left unanswered for the time being. However, one person clearly decided that it was a query worth addressing.

It was in Richard Langley's contentious *Radio Commentary* column, where all was eventually revealed, in the March 1952 edition. 'I wonder how many Luxembourg listeners recognise that famous and familiar voice in *Dan Dare?*' Langley began. 'Yes – it is that of Noel Johnson, the original Dick Barton, probably the most experienced radio hero this side of the Atlantic.'[199]

It is not recorded whether or not Langley's comment was an accidental slip, or a planned 'outing', but it was a clear breach of Johnson's agreement.

It seems that Johnson didn't read *208 Magazine*. Few people did. Astonishingly, news of the statement didn't make its way to him either. Johnson seems to have never found out about the indiscretion and Langley was somewhat less specific in his gossip from this point on.

It perhaps wasn't that much of a major announcement anyway, as many listeners had had their suspicions about Johnson for some time. He did, after all, have one of the most recognisable voices in British radio.

JOINING THE CLUB:

By March 1952, *The New Adventures of Dan Dare – Pilot of the Future* (as it was now known[200]) had dropped out of the list of *208 Magazine*'s top rated shows altogether. Although, it did reappear at number six in August. Despite these fluctuations however, *Dare* was still popular and maintained its ratings power enough to be re-commissioned for a third series from September 1953 to May 1954. Then there was a fourth run from September 1954 to May 1955. Significantly, unlike the BBC's *Dick Barton*, *Dan Dare* never even stopped for a religious holiday – running through Christmas and Easter.

With such a non-stop treadmill of new programming being transmitted

---

[198] From *208 Magazine* (January 1952)
[199] From *208 Magazine* (March 1952)
[200] To begin with, it seems that Radio Luxembourg's *Dan Dare* serial was simply called *The Adventures of Dan Dare*. However, in early 1952, the series begins to be referred to by the slightly extended title of *The Adventures of Dan Dare – Pilot of the Future*. In February 1952, the title of the programme was extended even further and listings and publicity materials begin to refer to the programme as *The New Adventures of Dan Dare – Pilot of the Future*. This could be considered to be the 'full' title of the Radio Luxembourg serial. However, just to complicate matters, *208 Magazine* sometimes referred to the series simply as *Dan Dare* and the broadcasts themselves were usually announced as *Dan Dare – Pilot of the Future*. In truth, it seems that there was never a definitive consensus on what to call the series, although the appellation *Dan Dare* was always used.

every weekday over such a sustained period of time, the pressure on Faraday at SSS must have been immense. However, *Dan Dare* was proving its worth, and Luxembourg were easily able to justify their expenditure on *Dare* due to the vast amounts of advertising revenue that the show brought in.

The show's sponsor, Horlicks were especially pleased by the upturn in publicity. And the drinks' company soon began to tie into the series even further, with a succession of branded *Dan Dare* novelties produced for listeners of the show.

It was fairly early in the serial's history that Horlicks launched its 'Horlicks Spacemen's Club' as a way of adding to the listening experience (and selling more jars of Horlicks).

An advert in the March 1952 edition of *208 Magazine* puts it: 'Every member of the Horlicks Spacemen's Club wears Dan Dare's authentic cap badge – which is only available to members of the club. And only members of the club are eligible to receive the many other offers made every evening Monday to Friday, in *The Adventures of Dan Dare, Pilot of the Future* from Radio Luxembourg.'[201]

It was, of course, all another well-thought out piece of marketing from the ad-men at J Walter Thompson. The key to the concept was in how you applied to the club. You not only had to be a listener of *Dan Dare*. You also had to drink your Horlicks. You would 'write your name and address ... on the back of a label from a bottle of Horlicks and send it with a sixpenny postal order to Dan Dare, 40 Berkeley Square, London, W1.'[202]

The message was firmly hammered home with repeated advertising spots on Radio Luxembourg, clearly targeted at the show's mainly juvenile audience.

'Are you one of the thousands who are wearing Dan Dare's authentic colour cap-badge?' asked one announcement from March 1956. 'You're not? Then kindly join the Horlicks' Spaceman's Club, so that you'll be able to avail yourself of the many offers made in this programme for members only.'[203]

Despite the bluntly profit-driven nature of the club's motivation, it did provide a comparatively good deal for its large membership. Special products made available to members included an 'authentic *Dan Dare* spaceship,'[204] as advertised in the October 1952 edition of *208 Magazine*. To tie in with the Coronation, readers of the May 1953 edition were advised to use their membership to 'see the Coronation with the *Dan Dare* periscope.'[205] In January 1955, members could also send off for a Horlicks Space Cup.

---

[201] From *208 Magazine* (March 1952)
[202] From *208 Magazine* (March 1952)
[203] Radio Luxembourg announcement (21/03/56)
[204] From *208 Magazine* (October 1952)
[205] From *208 Magazine* (May 1953)

THE ADVENTURES OF DAN DARE – PILOT OF THE FUTURE

However, probably the best of the Horlicks tie-ins was *The Horlicks Spaceman's Book* from April 1954. With contributions from *Dan Dare* (and *Dick Barton*) scriptwriters Edward J Mason, Geoffrey Webb and Bertie (B D) Chapman, it was a brief but well put together book telling us much about the *Dan Dare* back-story. Many decades on, it is an extremely valuable guide to the radio series. Although it doesn't give us anything as specific as an episode list, it does recount a number of Dan's adventures. In total, it goes through eight rough plot outlines, including some mention of a serial featuring flying saucers, which may well have developed out of Mason and Webb's ideas from the *Dick Barton* comic strip. To historians of radio serials in general it's a mine of information.

The tie-in scheme boosted both Radio Luxembourg's listening figures and Horlicks' drinking figures. It was a very clever idea, simultaneously building 'brand loyalty' for two very different companies at the same time. However, toward the end of *Dan Dare*'s association with Radio Luxembourg, it tailed off somewhat and finally perished in the mid-fifties, when Horlicks moved to television advertising. Television was eventually judged to offer what Luxembourg could not – a bigger audience and much better transmission quality.

FADING OUT:

There was one persistent problem throughout much of Radio Luxembourg's life on air. It was an area where the BBC always had the edge on it. Put simply, the radio reception for Luxembourg was dreadful.

It was a constant battle. Not only did listeners struggle to tune in to Radio Luxembourg's weak radio signal to begin with, but even once they'd found it, there was no guarantee that it would remain stable for very long.

The plain fact was that Luxembourg was just too far away from the UK for anything other than the weakest of radio signals to cross the Channel. By the time you picked up Luxembourg on your wireless in Dover, the signal had already travelled around 250 miles to reach you. If you lived in Scotland that was nearer a thousand miles. Added to this were climatic conditions. Everything from rain to low cloud-cover might affect the strength of the signal. Other stray radio signals also played their part in making the life of a Radio Luxembourg listener very difficult.

Programmes would fade in an out of interference without warning. Strange noises would creep in from nowhere and lengthy sections would suddenly become very quiet for no adequately explainable reason. Were it not for Radio Luxembourg's unique brand of popularism, it is highly unlikely anybody would ever have tuned in at all.

'The thing is, Luxembourg had to be big and punchy and loud to get through all the fing static,' says former BBC Transcriptions engineer Ted

Kendall. 'It was plagued with whistles and things … [It was] propagation conditions – there's nothing you can do about that.'

The appalling sound quality also cast doubts over the honesty of a certain edition of *208 Magazine* from November 1951.

In the November 1951 edition, an anonymous listener was credited on the letters' page with the following question for his favourite radio station: 'Why,' he asks, 'when practically every sponsored programme is recorded on the latest form of magnetic tape, does the BBC still use the outdated and more expensive acetate disc method?'[206] This may seem like a reasonable question. However, the more you think about it, the less likely it is that this letter was from a genuine Luxembourg listener at all.

Firstly, it's 1951 and the average man in the street has never even seen a tape recorder, let alone knows what sort of sound it might produce. Then secondly, even if this listener did know what a tape sounded like, it is highly unlikely that any Luxembourg listener would have ever had a clear enough radio reception to pick up on dynamic range. No average listener would have had the slightest clue how the recordings were made. In fact, many still believed that all the radio presenters and actors lived in Luxembourg itself.

It may be casting an unfair accusation, but it is far more likely that this particular letter was created by someone with a direct connection to Radio Luxembourg – as a surreptitious boast of an otherwise poor standard of radio broadcasting.

Of course, there were other problems too, in the area of human error, but these are shared by many broadcasters even today. Luxembourg's Pete Murray, recalled just such a traumatic memory in 1984: 'It was Seven Thirty and it was time for *Dan Dare* to go on,' he remembered. 'I hit the gong. "This is Radio Luxembourg on 208 metres on the medium wave band and now we invite you to listen to *Dan Dare*." And we had rather a dopey technician on – notably dopey – always half-asleep. And suddenly we heard Felix King and his piano and orchestra, playing on behalf of some other product, like Sliverkrin. And I said, he's put the wrong programme on. Then, someone else, who was in the studio with me, said, "You realise the red light was on" … The only reaction I ever got from any listener was from a nun in Dublin, who wrote to me and said that she was listening to the programme and she'd had hysterics and I was obviously human – which I thought was rather good, from a nun anyway. Later on, I met people who were obviously listening to the programme and one fellow, who was in the RAF at the time, said they all rushed out of their house screaming with laughter. I actually got no complaints, but I was practically suicidal, because I was quite sure that it was the end of my career.'[207]

---

[206] From *208 Magazine* (November 1951)
[207] From *Searching The Ether* – LBC (1984)

THE END:

On 2 May 1955, Radio Luxembourg transmitted the final episode of *Dan Dare*'s fourth radio series (episode 40 of *Surprise Assassin*). It was their 764th original episode. It was also the last original episode ever to be made. The following day, Radio Luxembourg picked up the series with a run of repeats.

The first episode to be repeated was *Trapped in Space* (Episode 66) from January 1952. A solid line of repeats then ran through five days a week without interruption until 31 May 1956. The run came to an end with a repeat of the final episode of *Revolt on Mars* (originally from May 1953).

It isn't clear exactly what form these repeats took. They were billed in radio listings as new episodes. However, they quite obviously were not new episodes. Neither Faraday nor Radio Luxembourg seem to have kept any tape recordings of any *Dan Dare* episodes for more than a few weeks after broadcast. So, if Luxembourg re-broadcast a recording of *Revolt on Mars* (a serial from 1953) in mid-1956, where did the recordings come from? One explanation is that these broadcasts came from coarse-groove disc recorded copies, that Luxembourg may have made themselves. Another, explanation is that they simply brought the cast back into the studio to re-record the old scripts.

The only recording definitely known to survive from the repeat run is an off-air recording of episode 378 (*The Lost World on Mars* – Episode 53). If you listen very carefully, it sounds like this recording 'might' have come from a tape, suggesting that these were new recordings of old scripts. However, it is very difficult to tell.

Whatever the explanation, these *Dan Dare* repeats would have saved Luxembourg from having to pay for the writing of any new *Dan Dare* scripts. It was obviously an economy measure. It was also a sign that Radio Luxembourg and its sponsor were losing interest in the *Dare* serials. It was the beginning of the end.

Dan Dare had been a very big hit. However, by 1956, audiences had begun to dip. It was possibly a sign that listeners were growing weary of the incessant static and poor radio reception. Or maybe, it had something to do with the fact that the BBC had begun to fight back with their own space-age drama serial, which started on the Light Programme in 1953 (See next chapter).

Regardless of the cause, the declining ratings were obviously enough of a sign for Horlicks and JWT to reconsider their whole radio strategy.

In the mid-1950s, radio was no longer the same national focal point that it had once been. Television was bigger and better than ever before and then in 1955, much to the delight of people like Norman Collins, the government finally allowed a network of commercial television to be introduced to Britain. ITV launched on 22 September 1955. Many at the BBC were horrified (possibly with good reason) and all the stops were pulled out to fight the new foe (including the broadcast of a new *Quatermass* serial for television and the surprise incineration of a much-loved character in *The Archers*). Little Luxembourg couldn't really compete anymore.

JWT were the first to make a television advertisement for the new ITV and it is likely that they would have been heartily advising their clients at Horlicks that this was also the best way forward for their business. It seems that Horlicks agreed.

Noel Johnson recalled how the final decision was broken to the team: 'Colonel Horlicks came along and thanked us all very much for our efforts and said that we had been responsible for increasing the sale of Horlicks malted milk and this, that and the other. He gave us all a case of Horlicks and said that it was because of television that they were going to use the money, that they had set aside for radio, in television and that was that.'[208]

With the termination of the *Dan Dare* series, much of the cast and crew went their separate ways. Many would still contribute to Luxembourg, but soon even that would start to tail off, as the station started to focus more on music programming and less on drama serials.

POST DARE:

The year following the programme's cancellation, Noel Johnson made a bid to return to the BBC – hoping that his work with Luxembourg had remained secretive enough for nobody at the corporation to have noticed it. It seems he was right.

'Val Gielgud,' he recalled 'never really approved of my playing the *Barton* role and I didn't work for him for many years. Then in 1957 I decided to write to him and I said that by now I hoped I had been 'forgiven' for playing *Dick Barton*. I think I was because he asked me to play the Kenny More part in *The Deep Blue Sea*.'[209]

In the years to come, Johnson's work on radio diminished. Meanwhile however, his work on film and television increased dramatically. He played Henry VIII in a television adaptation of *A Man for All Seasons* in 1957 for the BBC. He appeared in an episode of ITV's *Ivanhoe* in 1958 and assumed a number of parts in the BBC's memorable *Age of Kings* cycle in 1960. He was in the BBC's science fiction hit *A for Andromeda*, alongside Julie Christie in 1961 and returned in its 1962 sequel *The Andromeda Breakthrough*. The sixties remained a busy time for him and he joined the cast of *Coronation Street* in 1964, also spending much time in crime dramas like *Z-Cars, Dixon of Dock Green* and *No Hiding Place*. In 1972, he appeared in Hitchcock's *Frenzy* and is

---

[208] From an interview with Noel Johnson for *The Eagle Society* (C.1980s)
[209] From *The Wireless Stars* by George Nobbs – Wensum Books (1972)

also remembered for parts in two *Doctor Who* stories: *The Underwater Menace* (1967) and *Invasion of the Dinosaurs* (1974). Johnson's list of credits through the 1970s and 1980s is far too large to go through in full, but few major television series didn't make use of his services during the period. He also did a James Bond film. His final credit was a 1997 episode of *A Touch of Frost*.

Without doubt, the most quoted of his later performances came on BBC 2 in 1982, with the standalone play *The Combination*. Set in 1951, Johnson played an officious magistrate who has an occasion to reprimand two ten-year old boys who are brought before him. With deliberate irony, Johnson's magistrate blames the boys' irresponsible behaviour on one thing, saying that, 'If I had to point the finger at any single responsible body, it would be the BBC for churning out *Dick Barton* every solitary night of the week. If anything was guaranteed to warp the spirit of the young, it's that perverted rubbish!'[210]

Johnson died on 1 October 1999, aged 82.

Even before the cancellation of *Dan Dare*, Edward J Mason and Geoffrey Webb's involvement in the series had come to an end. They had ceased to work on the series as scriptwriters around 1955. Of course, all the time *Dan Dare* was around, they had still continued to work for the BBC as the lead writers of *The Archers* and after *Dare* had ended, they remained with the programme. It would, arguably become their life's work. They were among the programme's co-creators and dedicated themselves to it with great vigour.

Webb and Mason's partnership had been behind some of radio's most enduring programmes. *Dick Barton*, *Dan Dare*, *The Archers* and *My Word* all benefited from their involvement. As well as a fruitful joint writing career, theirs was a lasting friendship. It would finally be Geoffrey Webb that would break up the partnership.

In June 1962, Webb was admitted to hospital with a serious illness. He would make a full recovery and even whilst in the hospital, still continued with his writing for *The Archers*. The doctors discharged him in June 1962. A few days later he met his son from school. They were to drive home together. However, Webb never made it.

'I switched on the news on 21 June 1962 and heard that Geoff had died,' remembered *Archers* cast member Norman Painting. 'He had been killed in a head-on crash with a furniture van. He had sold his old Rolls-Royce, which he loved because it was built on the same expansive lines as himself, and bought a brand-new pale-blue Austin Princess.'[211] He was in his new car, when the collision took place. His son Kit survived with minor injuries. Geoffrey Webb was 42 years old. Only a few hours before his death, the

---

[210] *Playhouse: The Combination* – BBC (09/01/82)
[211] From *Forever Ambridge* by Norman Painting – Michael Joseph Ltd. (1975)

3000th episode of *The Archers* (which he had written) had been recorded in the BBC's Birmingham studios.

The death of Webb had a devastating effect on *The Archers'* small pool of writers. New people were brought in to take up the increased workload, but Edward J Mason remained at the show's heart. He continued to write for the programme until his death.

In fact, Mason worked on *The Archers* up until the day he died. Even though he lived in care at a nursing home in Edgbaston, he remained a core part of the writing team, churning out over a hundred scripts a year. He died on 3 February 1971, one of the last remaining members of the show's original creative team.

Anne Cullen, who had played Professor Peabody, also went to work on *The Archers* (playing Carol Tregorran *nee* Grey). She divorced her husband (*Dick Barton* producer) Neil Tuson in 1963 and in December of that year married her *Archers* co-star Monte Crick (the second Dan Archer). Crick died in 1969, but Cullen continued in the series for some years to come.

Radio Luxembourg would continue to broadcast for a very long time. By the mid to late fifties, they were increasingly turning to more music-based programmes, which hit their peak in the 1960s. Alan Dell, Jimmy Savile, Jimmy Young and Alan Freeman all recorded programmes at the station's London studios at 38 Hertford Street around this period. However, the 1960s also saw a change in British radio listening habits. In March 1964, Radio Caroline began commercial broadcasts from a small ship anchored just off the British coast. It was the first of the 'pirate radio stations', which broadcast as close to Britain's shores as the law would allow and thus revolutionised British radio forever.

Finally, in 1967, both the government and the BBC conceded that there was an audience for popular music that was not being properly served under the current broadcasting system. Accordingly, the entire structure of BBC radio was changed. The Light Programme and the Home Service closed down, as did the Third Programme. Radio 1, Radio 2, Radio 3 and Radio 4 were born. Radios 1 and 2 had a devastating effect on both the pirate stations (which were under legal threat anyway) and Radio Luxembourg. Radio 1 and 2 offered the same music with many of the same presenters and with improved sound quality. Added to this, you didn't even have to listen to any adverts.

The new BBC radio all but killed off the off-shore pirates and for a time, Luxembourg was alone as the only commercial broadcaster for Britain. Then, in 1973, the government effectively lifted its ban on inland commercial radio and Radio Luxembourg was left without the purpose for which it had been founded.

In the 1980s, both the BBC and innumerable independent radio stations made Luxembourg's position difficult and on New Year's Day 1992, the station's AM transmitter was powered down for the last time. In theory, the Luxembourg legacy continued through satellite broadcasts and the Internet, but it was effectively over.

What little was left of the company was absorbed into the great RTL Group media empire, which also included the UK TV station, Channel Five.

The *Dan Dare* comic strip would continue in various guises for a number of years, but there would only be one further foray (to date) into the world of British radio. This came in 1990.

To celebrate the fortieth anniversary of *Dan Dare* in April 1990, BBC Radio 4 decided to broadcast its own version of the *Dare* story. This took the form of a new four-part adaptation of the very first *Dan Dare* comic strip serial – *Voyage to Venus*.

Of course, Radio Luxembourg's version of the same material had previously spanned several months' worth of airtime back in 1951. Radio 4's much shorter production was written by Nick McCarty and was recorded between 29 January and 3 February 1990. Mick Ford played Dan, with Donald Gee as Digby. Other members of the cast included Sean Barrett, Richard Pearce, Terence Alexander, John Moffatt, David King, Simon Treves and Shirley Dixon. It was broadcast from 19 April to 10 May 1990 and was directed by Glyn Dearman. The entire production still exists in the BBC Sound Archives, but has not (to date) been commercially released on CD.

DIEGO VALOR:

Although Radio Luxembourg's transmitter range did not extend very far across the European continent, listeners in at least one further territory did get to enjoy the adventures of *Dan Dare* in the 1950s.

As part of a boom in serialised radio drama in Spain at around that time, the *Dan Dare* series was also picked up by the Madrid-based Cadena SER radio service. Although to Spanish audiences, he was not Dan Dare, but Diego Valor – a name presumably expecting to grab local listeners more effectively.

Details on the exact content of each episode (and the degree to which they were reworked for Spanish radio) are rather hazy and few recordings appear to have survived. However, at least some of the Radio Luxembourg scripts appear to have been sent to Spain from 1953. These were translated (and possibly elaborated upon) by a Spanish production team led by Enrique Jarnés Bergua, who changed Dan/Diego into a Spanish astronaut and renamed his faithful friends from Digby, Lafayette and Professor Peabody into Portolés, Laffite and Beatriz Fontana.

The show was broadcast across four seasons between late 1953 and June 1958 (when it transferred briefly to television). By all accounts the series soon became a hugely popular staple on Spanish radio.

Series one went out titled simply *Diego Valor*. Series two was broadcast as *Diego Valor y el Príncipe Diabólico* (*Diego Valor and the Devil Prince*). Series three was *Diego Valor y el Misterio de Júpiter* (*Diego Valor and the Jupiter Mystery*). And series four became *Diego Valor y el Planeta Errante* (*Diego Valor and the Wandering Planet*).

The Spanish series reportedly ran for around 1,200 episodes (each around 15 minutes long). It is unclear how many of these episodes may have been unique to Spain (if any). The show ended in 1958, when Diego moved to television, for a one-off production. There appears also to have been a *Diego Valor* stage show and Spanish *Dan Dare* comics (again under the *Diego Valor* name) were popular around the same time.

MISSING IN ACTION:

Sadly, despite its great cultural impact, astonishingly little survives of Luxembourg's *Dan Dare* radio series.

The BBC has been heavily criticised for its lack of foresight in allowing so many of its radio and television programmes to go un-archived. It is true that substantial chunks of the BBC's radio and television heritage have been lost by a BBC that failed to understand the significance of a broadcasting record. However, the BBC did *have* an archive, no matter how badly maintained it may sometimes have been. The story of commercial radio archiving in Britain is very different.

Organisations like Radio Luxembourg were motivated almost wholly by profit. It was here to make money, if it managed to entertain you somewhere along the way, that's great, but that was not what it was for. The main aim of JWT and the backers of the *Dan Dare* series was to sell jars of malted Horlicks powder. They were very successful at doing this. However, many were uninterested in what happened to the recordings after they had done their job. Radio Luxembourg made little or no attempt to preserve their history for prosperity. Why would they? This wasn't a philanthropic endeavour. That was what the BBC was for. This was a business.

'The programmes that we made were made for other people and they were the property of those other persons,' explained Derek Faraday. 'In actual fact, they'd be the property of Horlicks, in the case of *Dan Dare* … Whoever sponsored the programme was the person who owned them. What happened to the programme after it left the studio on its way to Radio Luxembourg or wherever, I just don't know.'[212]

Following broadcast, master tapes would be erased and re-recorded over the top of. After all, Luxembourg had no plans on repeating them.

'Furthermore, where would they be kept?' asked Faraday. 'Doing

---

[212] From an interview with Derek Faraday for *The Eagle Society* (1984)

upwards of a total of fifty recordings in a week – not necessarily all for Luxembourg, over a period of around about thirty years – means that one would need a great deal of space in order to accommodate them.'[213]

Luxembourg completely failed to have any understanding of the potential importance their programmes could have in years to come. As such, Radio Luxembourg did not keep an archive. Not a single recording of *Dan Dare* was ever officially archived anywhere. And it gets worse.

Not only did Luxembourg fail to keep any recordings, they didn't keep any paperwork either. Not a single original script is known to survive from *Dan Dare*. There are no cast lists; no episode titles, no production files. Practically everything we know about the series comes from contemporary magazines and newspapers and from the memories of those who were there.

Despite its massive popularity, *Dan Dare* remains one of the least recorded radio serials of all time. It is startling, but a series that made such an indelible mark on British culture has left barely a trace upon the pages of history. I can't give you a complete episode guide to *Dan Dare*. I can't tell you what happened in each individual episode and who played which character. I can't tell you, because I simply don't know. There is a very good chance that nobody knows. It seems deeply tragic, but it really was just a different attitude to making radio.

There is something of a happy ending however.

In theory, Radio Luxembourg didn't keep any recordings of *Dan Dare*, nor did they keep any records. Therefore, all these stories should be lost to us forever. However, there is a little light at the end of the tunnel.

In 1955, as we know, Radio Luxembourg started to repeat a number of earlier *Dan Dare* episodes, starting with episode 66 *Trapped in Space*. This series of repeats ran for a very long time. Except, if Luxembourg and SSS had wiped all of their old episodes of *Dare*, then where did these repeats come from? With no surviving paperwork, there is little way of knowing for certain. They could have been new re-recordings, of maybe some form of disc recordings.

One possible answer to this question can be found in an unlikely place – Australia.

On 28 October 1954, an article appeared in the *Adelaide Advertiser*. The article said: 'A new space serial will begin from *The Advertiser* Broadcasting Network today. It will be *Dan Dare, Pilot of the Future*, a radio dramatisation of the popular space pilot featured in *Eagle* magazine.'[214]

It's widely known that *Dan Dare*'s comic strip self was popular in Australia in the 1950s. What this clipping confirms is that some form of radio serial was also broadcast in Australia. The article goes on to say that the new

---

[213] From an interview with Derek Faraday for *The Eagle Society* (1984)
[214] From *The Adelaide Advertiser* (28/10/54)

radio episodes have been 'produced in London'. There can be little doubt that these were episodes of the Radio Luxembourg series that were being broadcast in Australia.

JWT had been involved in this area before and took part in the deal that saw Australian recordings of *Dick Barton* broadcast in South Africa only a few years earlier.

Of course, there is no known official paperwork still in existence, but it seems that episodes of the *Dan Dare* series (probably from episode 66 onwards) were copied onto transcription discs, while the original tapes still existed. The tapes were then wiped and the transcription discs were sold to an Australian broadcasting company, who then broadcast them in Australia.

Dan Dare's Australian broadcasts are a little difficult to pin down, but it seems that the series began on 28 October 1954 on the 5AD network, broadcasting at 5.30 PM every Wednesday, Thursday and Friday. The series was also broadcast in the Queensland area on the 4BK and 4AK networks every 6.15 PM on Mondays and Tuesdays. The series was sponsored by a company going by the name of 'Joysticks'.

Of course, the obvious question is, 'what happened to these Australian disc recordings?'

The most likely answer is that there were probably sent back to Luxembourg, who seem to have then either lost or destroyed them. The National Film and Sound Archive of Australia (NFSA) don't seem to have any recordings and neither does RTL, who now hold the Radio Luxembourg copyright.

To date, only one episode has ever come to light from this set of Australian recordings. In 2010, a private collector made it known that he had a copy of *Under Sentence of Death* from 21 January 1952 (episode 76). I have listened to this episode and the sound quality is very good, although clearly taken from a transcribed coarse-groove disc.

Attempts have been made (with the consent of the owner of the recording) to arrange some sort of broadcast of the disc. Two separate approaches have been made to different parts of the BBC. Although the suggestion was seriously considered, the idea foundered due to concerns over costs and copyright. It is something that may be reviewed in the future.

There is only one other *Dare* recording from the Luxembourg series, but it is barely worth mentioning. The recording comes from the resourceful Pat Hetherington who made her own home-made off-air recording of the 1956 repeat broadcast of The *Lost World on Mars* – episode 53, using an early reel-to-reel tape machine. Unfortunately, the sound quality of this recording is appalling[215], to the extent that it isn't even listenable. There is practically no

---

[215] The chief technical problem with Pat Hetherington's recording is its very narrow frequency range. The minimum frequency range for a telephone call would peak at

THE ADVENTURES OF DAN DARE – PILOT OF THE FUTURE

chance of it ever being restored to any acceptable level of quality. Most of the time, the sound is so indistinct that it is only possible to discern the most nondescript of noises. If it were not for Hetherington's meticulous labelling, it is unlikely that we would even be able to figure out what this recording was meant to be. The tape itself was made by holding a microphone close to a low-powered domestic radio set, which accounts for something of the poor audio fidelity.

So far, no further episodes have come to light. The disc recording of episode 76[216] is the only surviving (audible) recording of Radio Luxembourg's *Dan Dare* series. Its precise origins are shrouded in a certain element of mystery, but it does at least give us the tiniest hope that somewhere out there, more may survive.

UPDATE:
16/06/25: Two further episodes of the *Dan Dare* radio series have now come to light in the hands of private collectors. One is episode 75 of the series (originating from the same source as the surviving episode 76). The other episode comes from the 'Lost World on Mars' serial from 1953, although the episode number is unknown.

---

around 3 kHz (at least), and the Hetherington tape is below that. There is nothing above 2 kHz and for the second half of the recording, the top end peaks even lower. Added to this, there is a great deal of background noise. There's heavy interference and occasional fading of the sound. The recording is also very quiet.

[216] This is the point where dozens of collectors and radio enthusiasts contact me, asking for a copy of this lost *Dan Dare* recording. I would like to make it clear that, although I do have a copy of the *Dan Dare* episode, I am unwilling to distribute it. Not only would it be a breach of copyright (and a criminal offence), but I would also be breaking the trust of the collector (and current owner) who allowed me to have a copy for the purposes of research. I do not own the master recording, just a copy. If this recording is ever exploited for broadcast or commercial release, it will have to be with the full consent and co-operation of the current owner. The recording is his personal property and the copyright is the joint intellectual property of RTL and the 'Dan Dare Corporation Ltd.' I am aware that many people would dearly love to listen to this recording again, but I'm sorry, I'm not the person to ask.

THE ADVENTURES OF DAN DARE – PILOT OF THE FUTURE: PLOT SUMMARIES

Precise story information concerning the *Dan Dare* radio episodes is extremely scarce. Very little is known about the contents and events of each episode. None of the original scripts survive and there is very little related paperwork. What follows are brief plot breakdowns for just a few hundred episodes.

The following information has been assembled from listings magazines, contemporary publications, the memories and notes of contemporary listeners and the only two surviving recorded episodes. Contents and plot details for the other episodes are unknown.

1-18. *Voyage to Venus* **(02/07/51 – 25/07/51)**

> Dan Dare and his friends embark on their first adventure. On their way to land on the planet Venus, the crew encounter a strange electrical barrier circling the planet. Once on the planet's surface, they discover that the barrier is the work of the Treens and their crazed scientific leader – the Mekon. Dan and his friends join forces with the benevolent Therons from the South of the planet and together they put the Mekon to flight.
>
> (*Based on* The Venus Story, *a comic strip by Frank Hampson, published by* Eagle *between 14 April 1950 and 28 September 1951.*)

19. Untitled Serial: Part 1 (01/11/51)

> 'Disguised as Atlantines, Dare and his friends mingle with an angry crowd in an Atlantine village. Goaded by Ur Gait, the Atlantines are planning to rebel against the Treens, who are on the way to the village to recruit more men for the armies.'

20. Untitled Serial: Part 2 (02/11/51)

> 'Dan and Digby set out to rescue Sir Hubert and Professor Jocelyn.

They get to an Atlantine village where Dan is mistaken for Kargaz, the Atlantines' legendary hero and the two men are taken to the house of Ur-Tag, chief of the tribe.'

21. Untitled Serial: Part 3 (05/11/51)

'News comes that the Treens are on their way to conscript all the able-bodied Atlantine slaves for their army. Meanwhile, in the Mekon's Palace, the Professor and Sir Hubert plan their escape with Sondar, their Treen friend.'

22. Untitled Serial: Part 4 (06/11/51)

'While making their plans, the Professor and Sir Hubert hear a hissing sound and a deadly gas fills the cell. Meanwhile, Dan Dare joins the conscripts.'

23. Untitled Serial: Part 5 (07/11/51)

'Dan is befriended by his new Sergeant-Major, the Cohort-Dapon in Chief. As they plan their next move, the first sounds of war are heard.'

24. Untitled Serial: Part 6 (08/11/51)

'While the Sergeant-Major teaches Dan the duties of the Palace guard, the war between the Treens and Therons begins overhead.'

25. Untitled Serial: Part 7 (09/11/51)

'The Mekon summons the prisoners and sentences them to work in the North Pole mines.'

26. Untitled Serial: Part 8 (12/11/51)

'Dan and Digby, smuggled into the Palace as guards, soon find Sir Hubert and the Professor.'

27. Untitled Serial: Part 9 (13/11/51)

'The party takes off in flying chairs and soon lands on Space Station 9.'

28. Untitled Serial: Part 10 (14/11/51)

'The Mekon recovers consciousness and turns the tables on Dan.'

29. Untitled Serial: Part 11 (15/11/51)

'The Treens rush to rescue the drowning Mekon whilst Digby swims to Dan's aid. Donning the gas masks given them by Sondar, they dive deep into the Lagoon to avoid the Treens' guns.'

30. Untitled Serial: Part 12 (16/11/51)

'In the grounded space-ship Z, Professor Peabody endeavours to persuade Sondar to show him (sic) the subterranean route to the Therons, as Dan and Digby are carried into an underwater cavern.'

31. Untitled Serial: Part 13 (19/11/51)

'In an effort to locate Dare and Digby, the Professor and Sondar don diving helmets and go underwater, where the girl is attacked by electro-aqua snakes.'

32. Untitled Serial: Part 14 (20/11/51)

'Professor Peabody who, accompanied by Sondar, is walking underwater in a fruitless search for Dan and Digby, is seen by the Mekon, who sets off underwater in his flexo-glass car.'

33. Untitled Serial: Part 15 (21/11/51)

'Professor Peabody is again captured by the Mekon. She threatens to blow the flexo-glass car to pieces if the Mekon does not put Sondar ashore.'

34. Untitled Serial: Part 16 (22/11/51)

'Sondar locates Dan and Digby, but although they outwit Pendel, the mechanic-in-chief, they are by no means out of the woods.'

35. Untitled Serial: Part 17 (23/11/51)

'Professor Peabody is put ashore by the Mekon and makes a dash for safety. Dan, Digby and Sondar overcome Pendel, and making themselves temporarily invisible, the party hide on one of the thought-controlled space-ships.'

36. Untitled Serial: Part 18 (26/11/51)

'Attacked by the Mekon, the friends don dive masks. On the other side of the Flame Belt, Hank and Pierre have left the friendly Therons to return to "Ranger", still circling around Venus.'

37. Untitled Serial: Part 19 (27/11/51)

'Dan, Digby and Sondar are fired upon by the Mekon from his flexo-glass car and only just succeed in gaining the safety of space-ship Z, where they join Professor Peabody and Sir Hubert.'

38. Untitled Serial: Part 20 (28/11/51)

'The Mekon orders his deadly Telezero rays to be focused on the station, causing untold chaos and destruction. As the last supports of the ship melt, Sondar makes a final desperate effort and in the nick of time, space-ship Z takes off. Meanwhile, Hank and Pierre have been forced once more to return to Theronland and are watching the president's men excavating the underground river.'

39. Untitled Serial: Part 21 (29/11/51)

'The Mekon has forced Sir Hubert and Professor Peabody to record messages and be photographed so that the people on Earth will believe that they are being well treated.'

40. Untitled Serial: Part 22 (30/11/51)

'Despite the destruction of the space station by the Mekon, Dan, Digby, Professor Peabody and Sir Hubert succeed in generating sufficient power and in the nick of time, they take off. Meanwhile, in Theronland, where Hank and Pierre are with the president, reports of the space ship's take-off reaches the war control room. Thinking it is a hostile craft and realising its terrible destructive power, the president orders the ship to be destroyed at all costs. The Mekon gives similar instructions and the Telezero space-ship Z is trapped between the two squadrons of spacecraft.'

41. *The Therons Attack* – Untitled Serial: Part 23 (03/12/51)

'Dan Dare, Digby, Sir Hubert and Professor Peabody try to outwit the Mekon, ruler of the Treens, who is attempting to ruin Dan's efforts to raise food supplies on Venus for the starving Earth.'

42-65. Untitled Serial: Parts 24-47 (04/12/51 – 04/01/52)

In the concluding episodes of this story, Dan, Digby and their friends escape the clutches of the Mekon and make it back to Earth. They later return to Venus and mount a full-scale invasion. With all kinds of technology having been rendered inoperable by the Treen overlords, our heroes are forced to use gliders, bows and arrows to stage their assault. Although the Earth wins through, they do not destroy the Mekon, who lives to menace the crew another day.

66-74. *The Ice Men of Venus:* Parts 1-9 (07/01/52 – 17/01/52)

The Mekon has survived his first encounter with Dare and his team and has now joined forces with the Ice Men of Venus, to help create a new Ice Age on the planet. In the ensuing chaos, supply lines between Venus and Earth are disrupted, with a devastating effect on humankind

75. *Sabotage* – Untitled Serial: Part 10 (18/01/52)

'Establishing magnetic ray machines in the Polar Regions of Venus, the Mekon, with the assistance of the Ice-Men is causing the Poles to expand. As their great shadow moves across the face of the planet, spaceships are grounded; vital food supplies to the Earth are cut and the country is devastated by synthetic storms. Meanwhile, as floodwater rises around the Theron factory, where a ship capable of reaching the Pole is being assembled, Dan and his friends discover that Extron, a Treen scientist, has wrecked the safety valve on a giant boiler. Clad in asbestos suits, the Dare team climb to the top of the red-hot casing, in a desperate effort to release the pressures of gases, before they explode and wreck the vital plant. But the heat becomes intolerable ... '[217]

---

[217] Quotation from the opening announcement of Episode 76: *Under Sentence of Death* (21/01/52) Produced by John Glyn-Jones for Radio Luxembourg.

DAN DARE – PLOT SUMMARIES

76. *Under Sentence of Death* – Untitled Serial: Part 11 (21/01/52)

Dan and his friends hurry to the rescue of President Kalon. They find the president lying unconscious in his quarters. He has been drugged by Extron, who plans to kidnap the president and take him to the Mekon. The team disable Extron and steal a space-ship, in order mount a daring attack on the Mekon's base of operations. However, the Mekon has been alerted to their plans and retaliates with targeted rocket fire.

77-xx. *The Ice Men of Venus*: Parts 12 – xx (22/01/52 – xx/xx/52)

Dan thwarts the Mekon's plans by destroying the Ice Men's cosmic cloud transmitters and the crisis on Earth is averted. Defeated, the Mekon flees Venus and takes his space-craft to Jupiter.

(It is unclear exactly how many episodes made up The Ice Men of Venus *serial. There were at least 15 episodes, and possibly a great many more. The story certainly continued to run into January 1952 and finished at some point prior to the second week of April 1952. Surviving documentation does not record what the storylines were in any of the 150-odd* Dan Dare *episodes broadcast between February and September 1952.)*

236-260. *The Mankton Menace* (01/09/52 – 03/10/52)

Mankton is a form of plant-life, native to the planet Mars. When the plant is introduced to Earth by the discredited Earth scientist (and former World Government Organisation councillor), Perranault, it causes a rapid drop in oxygen levels of the planet's oceans. Fish and other marine life begin to die, as the seas can no longer support them. And with fish stocks dwindling, there is soon another looming food shortage.

291-325. *Invaders from Space* (17/11/52 – 02/01/53)

A series of large and mysterious flying saucers land on the Earth. The strange ships are surrounded by a shimmering silver haze – the synic barrier. The flying saucers are revealed to belong to the Altrons, a race of squat scientifically advanced alien. The Altrons have come to Earth to mine the planet's core, in search of a rare radioactive element, called Evamin. If the Altrons are to succeed in releasing Evamin from beneath the Earth's crust, it could threaten to destroy the planet. Dan leads an attack against the Altrons and their leaders Taran and Vertek.

SERIAL THRILLERS

The attack is a success and the Altron plan is thwarted. The Altrons themselves retreat to the barren asteroid of Albra, to eke out what existence they can. However, they leave behind many of their scientific secrets, including the synic barrier.

326-389. *The Lost World on Mars* **(05/01/53 – 03/04/53)**

The team are on the trail of the discredited Earth scientist, Perranault. They trace him to Zinram, a lost world, hidden among the mountains of Northern Mars. This lost world is the last refuge of the survivors of an epic Martian war that raged many years ago. The region is also home to a fierce race of wild Melon Men – twenty-foot high monsters with huge tentacles and reactor bags for eyes. Perranault's plan is to wipe out the Melon Men and establish a new civilisation in the lost world, with himself at its leader.

(Written by Geoffrey Webb)

430-504. *Marooned on Mercury* **(21/09/53 – 01/01/54)**

A crash landing leaves Dan Dare and his friends marooned in the temperate Blue Zone of Mercury. Once there, the team find a race of super-intelligent Quartz Men. Their leader, Mistag, is secretly working with the Mekon and a team of renegade Treens, in their new 'Battery X' headquarters. In the Quantos Penal Colony, the Mekon is using lobster-like prison guards to manufacture deadly Panthanaton gas. He plans to use the gas to attack Venus. Dan gains the support of the rest of the Quartz Men, and together they destroy Battery X and drive the Mekon off into space.

(Loosely based on Marooned on Mercury, *a comic strip by Frank Hampson and Harold Johns, published by* Eagle *between 27 June 1952 and 20 February 1953.)*

505-539. *Attack on the Space Stations* **(04/01/54 – 19/02/54)**

A tenth planet enters into the solar system, circling the Sun, outside the Earth's orbit. The new planetoid is Vultan – driven out of its own orbit by a series of large cosmic explosions, many centuries ago. Vultan is populated by the peaceful Lexons, who live in massive airtight domes on the planet's surface. The Lexons suffer under the harsh scientific tyranny of the Vultans and their leader Spada (and his overbearing mother).The Vultans attempt to invade the Earth, but

DAN DARE – PLOT SUMMARIES

Dan and his friends foil the plan. The Lexons are liberated and go on to rule Vultan by themselves, under their new leader, Starmet.

540-599. *Sabotage on Venus* (22/02/54 – 14/05/54)

The crew travel to the peaceful planet of Jupiter, in search of a cure for a great cosmic plague, caused by the Mekon, which has been devastating vegetation on Venus. Jupiter is inhabited by the Jovians – an advanced people, led by Pluvis – a benevolent dictator who rules the planet from his grand HQ, based on Spartus Island. Meanwhile, his people live largely underground in great heated cities. Jupiter has also become the home of the ISF Weather Station, used to regulate conditions on Earth. Pluvis. Dan fears that, in the future, the Jovians may become aggressive and the ISF station may be in danger.

600-619. *Mystery on the Moon* (13/09/54 – 08/10/54)

The moon's Cosmet Lunar Stations are under threat from the Mekon and his aide, Robix. The Mekon's plan is to destroy the stations with the help of ex-convicts and a brainwashed scientist called Mackano.

620-654. *The Automatons* (11/10/54 – 26/11/54)

On Mars, in the underground city of Ukonda, a group of warlike Martians have gathered under the leadership of the warlord, Zinka. Zinka is building an army of robotic Automatons, ready to attack Earth. The team's new Robot Space Ship comes under attack by Zinka, who tries to steal its reactor cell, to use in his Automatons. Dan and his friends stop Zinka, who is later defeated when his own robotic creations rebel against him.

655-679. *The Mekon on Mars* (29/11/54 – 31/12/54)

A Theron scientist named Andoras has a plan to develop a new electronic defence system that will stop the Mekon's missiles reaching Earth. He is travelling to Earth to begin work on the constructing the system, when he falls into a coma.

725-764. *Surprise Assassin* (07/03/55 – 02/05/55)

The asteroid Nogra is soon to be destroyed. Dan and his crew are dispatched to rescue Professor Fletcher from the doomed planetoid before it's too late. When they arrive, they discover that Nogra is inhabited by a race called the Thelians, led by a being named Vixo.

xx?-xx?. *The Sirlium Stealers*

Almost certainly a repeat of an earlier serial. The title is not an original one, but rather a descriptive one invented by *Dan Dare* fan, Philip Harbottle, who did much to catalogue the series during its original run. This serial appears to have been repeated during the early months of 1956, possibly starting as early as December 1955. However, Radio Luxembourg schedule listings make no mention of it. In fact, *208 Magazine* says that the early months of 1956 were taken up with a repeat of *The Lost World on Mars*. One avid listener even recorded an episode of *The Lost World on Mars* during this repeat run. So, how can two quite different serials both be repeated seemingly at the same time? Nobody seems to be sure.

A number of old *Dan Dare* serials were repeated between early May 1955 and the end of April 1956. However, there is no proper scheduling information to confirm exactly how this repeat run was constructed. *The Sirilium Stealers* appears to have been one of the stories that was repeated, but we don't know exactly when it was repeated, nor when the original broadcasts went out.

There is similar confusion surrounding the April/May 1956 repeat broadcasts of *Revolt on Mars*. *208 Magazine* says that *Revolt on Mars* was repeated in 40 episodes, concluding on 31 May 1956. However, there is also evidence to suggest that this story wasn't *Revolt on Mars* at all, but actually a story set on the planet Venus.

Quotations in this section are from 208 Magazine: *November 1951 – April 1954 (Published through Radio Luxembourg).*

THE ADVENTURES OF DAN DARE – PILOT OF THE FUTURE PRODUCTION INFORMATION

Radio Luxembourg
764 x 15 minute episodes approx.
Recorded: Star Sound Studios – London
Writers: Edward J Mason
           Geoffrey Webb
           B D (Bertie) Chapman
Producer: John Glyn-Jones
Studio Manager: Derek Faraday

CAST:
Dan Dare	Noel Johnson
Digby	John Sharp
Prof Jocelyn Peabody	Anne Cullen
	Cecile Chevreau
The Mekon	Francis de Wolff
Spada	Geoffrey Bond
Spada's Mother	Marjorie Mars
Announcer	Bob Danvers Walker
'Various Characters'	Howard Marion Crawford

SERIAL THRILLERS

JOURNEY INTO SPACE

TWO MEN IN CEYLON:

Charles Chilton was born in 1917 in Euston. Following a brief career in sheet-metal working, he joined the BBC as a messenger boy at the newly opened Broadcasting House[218], in 1933. As a 'Youth in Training' (YIT), the BBC paid for Chilton's further education at night school. He soon began working in the publications' department on the *Radio Times, World Radio* and *The Listener*. The job brought him into regular contact with Lord Reith.

Following some work in the Gramophone Library, Chilton made his first direct contribution to a programme, when he and his BBC Boys' Band made an appearance on the popular *In Town Tonight* series in the mid 1930s. Chilton's fascination with Jazz music then led him to become the producer of *I Hear America Singing*, presented by his friend Alistair Cooke.

By now, working with the BBC Variety Department, Chilton went on to be a regular voice on the radio, presenting a number of popular music programmes. His head of department, who disliked Chilton's cockney accent, briefly took him off the air. However, he soon returned.

During the war, Chilton served with the RAF. Chilton recalls: 'I was a flying radio instructor. In other words, I took people up into the air and taught them how to communicate with the ground.'

One of Chilton's friends was David Jacobs who was then working with the Air Ministry. 'I had met him in London,' Chilton remembers. 'The Air Ministry used to call me down ... I would narrate radio programmes and write radio programmes for them, which were then recorded and then shipped out for services overseas. It was called the Overseas Recorded Broadcasting Service and David Jacobs was the announcer on this thing. One day I was told that I was going to be posted overseas and I told David and he said, "Don't be silly. They can't send you overseas." "Why not?" "Well, you're too valuable here with all the stuff we do." I said that, "they can send me anywhere they like at anytime." "Bet you ten bob they don't send you. You're too valuable." Well anyway, I was sent and I arrived in India. I went back as an ordinary radio operator for a while and then I was suddenly told

---

[218] BBC Broadcasting House officially opened on 1 May 1932, although some members of staff had been installed there as early as April. The first programmes began to be broadcast from the new facilities on 15 May. By February 1933, plans were already being drawn up for the building of a new extension.

that I was to go to Sri Lanka [then known as Ceylon] to join the new Radio Forces station that was started there, to be a writer and producer. When I got there, I rang the station and said, "Chilton here." They said, "Wait there we'll come and pick you up." So a car arrived and David Jacobs got out and said, "Here's your ten bob. You were right. I was wrong." It was in Rupees.'

'David was there as announcer for the navy radio,' continues Chilton. 'We all shared the same studio ... and everything.' Chilton was eventually discharged from the army in 1946. Jacobs was later joined in Ceylon by a new companion, Desmond Carrington. However, Chilton and Jacobs had built up a good working relationship in Ceylon, which would later pay dividends in years to come.

In the meantime, Chilton would return to the BBC in London. He had recently married a colleague from Bush House[219] and was about to resume a highly productive career with the corporation.

RIDERS OF THE RANGE:

Chilton returned to the BBC in 1946, just as the structure of the BBC was changing, with the formation of the new Light Programme.

The position that Chilton had occupied before the war had been taken over by someone else in his absence and it was no longer available to him. As such, he soon found himself promoted to fully-fledged producer status, in the BBC's Light Entertainment department. Many of the programmes he produced were still largely music based, but his new position allowed him much greater flexibility to pursue his creative ambition on a number of varied productions, including *In Town on Two Pianos* with George Shearing and Arthur Young.

There was even a reunion with David Jacobs. 'I did a programme called *Music: When Soft Voices Die* which I narrated,' says Jacobs. 'It was a programme about poetry and various other things.'

By 1949, Chilton was well established within the department, when he embarked on his biggest project to date – a radio Western.

This new series would combine Chilton's joint loves of the American West and serial drama in a series called *Riders of the Range*.

Chilton would both write and produce the new serial. However, because he was only employed by the BBC as a producer, Chilton's new additional duties as scriptwriter went largely without due recognition. 'I wrote all these

---

[219] Penny Chilton (wife of Charles) worked at Bush House, which was the London home of the BBC's Empire Service – an ancestor of the BBC World Service. Among the many people working on the Empire Service at this time, were George Orwell (Eric Blair) and Norman Collins (future head of the Light Programme) and co-creator of *Dick Barton*.

things, but I didn't get paid,' Chilton explains. 'My job was to produce. If I wanted to write as well, that was up to me. In the end they changed that. They did give me an extra bit on my salary because I was doing the writing, but it wasn't very much, I can tell you.'

Riders of the Range was set in the days of the American frontier. Using appropriate music and historical research, Chilton attempted to evoke the West in serial form.

The central character of the first series was a rancher played by Cal McCord. His daughter Mary was played by Carole Carr with Paul Carpenter as Jeff Arnold. Charles Irwin was Luke (a cowhand) and regular music came from the Four Ramblers and the Sons of the Saddle, led by Jack Fallon and Freddie Phillips. There was also a dog called Rustler.

The first serial began transmission on 13 January 1949 and ran to sixteen episodes. It was a great success and a second twelve part series followed in October, which centred on the real life construction of the Atcheson, Topeka and Santa Fe Railroads.

The twenty-two episodes of series three went even further with its historical content and introduced Billy the Kid as character, played by Alan Keith. The third series began in April 1950 and was followed by a fourth (set in Tombstone) in May 1951, which ran for thirteen episodes. This fourth run dispensed with Cal McCord and introduced (*Paul Temple* semi-regular) Macdonald Parke as a new rancher.

A fifth series started in April 1952 and featured Jesse James. The light mixture of music and serial drama was a winning formula with listeners and clearly catered for a section of the audience that had previously been ignored by the BBC Drama Department. 'The drama department ... would never have written a thing like *Riders of the Range*, which was musical, as well as dramatic,' says Chilton. 'Light Entertainment was far more suited to the kind of things that I was doing.'

Chilton's Western spawned a popular comic strip tie-in with *Eagle* and numerous annuals and additional merchandise spun-off from it.

The series continued to be a favourite with children and on 15 June 1953, a sixth series began broadcasting, following the story of the building of the Union Pacific Railway

However, series six would be the final series of *Riders of the Range*. The show remained popular, but by 1953, there were other things on the horizon for Chilton. He had begun work on a new project, which would take him off in an altogether different direction.

JOURNEY TO THE MOON:

The BBC's decision to axe *Dick Barton* in 1951 did not reflect well in the Light Programme's ratings. *The Archers* would eventually prove its worth.

However, it would be some time before it would manage to beat some of the massive audiences *Barton* had achieved at his peak.

It doesn't seem that Val Gielgud had very much remorse over the programme's cancellation. However, the instant popularity of a *Barton* imitation (*Dan Dare*) on Radio Luxembourg between 1951 and 1956, may have provided some food for thought.

Radio Luxembourg's *Dan Dare* series shared many of the same cast and crew as *Dick Barton*. However, in other respects it was a very different show. Whereas Dick had pursued his adventures from a wholly terrestrial base, Dan had far broader cosmic concerns. *Dan Dare* was science fiction, and in the 1950s, science fiction was more popular than ever.

Never before had the genre so dominated cinemas and bookshelves. Much of this new wave of material came from the United States, with a host of 'B' movie invasion pictures streaming out of Hollywood. It was really only a matter of time before radio and television caught up with the trend. Radio Luxembourg was the first to transfer the concept to the form of the long-running radio serial (following success in the comics). The first serious televisual exploitation was just around the corner, with a new serial from the people at Alexandra Palace.

'Space was in the air, as you might say,' remembers Chilton. 'There were many scripts arriving from various writers who wanted to do a serial or plays about space and the BBC didn't think any of them were any good,' Chilton continues. 'One day I was sent for by my boss Michael Standing. I sat down. He said, "We want you to write some science fiction." I said, "Science fiction – me? Why me?" He said, "Well, you write serials. You're good at that." I said, "Yeah, but I write Westerns. I don't write science fiction." He says, "Anyone that can write a Western must be able to write science fiction." "Well," I said, "it doesn't follow." "Oh yes it does. You go away and think about it."

Chilton was an unusual, but lateral choice to develop the new serial. After all, what had *Dan Dare* been, other than Cowboys and Indians in space?

However, Chilton's previous programmes had never been mere genre-exploitation and just as he had spent time meticulously researching the history of the West for *Riders of the Range*, Chilton was keen to bring the same dedication to his latest venture.

'I joined the British Astronomical Association (BAA),' says Chilton, who then built a small observatory in his garden, with the assistance of Charles Irwin from *Riders of the Range*. '[I] bought a telescope, which I set up in my garden and I used to study the moon and things, while my wife sat in the freezing cold taking notes.'

Among those of Chilton's fellow BAA members that he could call upon for advice was an ever-enthusiastic Patrick Moore and the rocket scientist

Kenneth Gatland. Gatland worked at a government run aerospace research centre in Farnborough and would effectively go on to become Chilton's scientific advisor.

'So, I said, "Alright, I'll try and write a science fiction," which I did, which turned out to be *Journey into Space*.'

The new series was initially planned for a run of twelve episodes.

Elsewhere in the BBC, another science fiction serial was also in production at the same time: a live television serial from the innovative writer/producer team of Nigel Kneale and Rudolf Cartier. This was the groundbreaking *The Quatermass Experiment*, a six-part serial that began broadcasting on 18 July 1953.

The Quatermass Experiment was an astonishing piece of work that helped redefine television drama in Britain, with a scope that far exceeded anything the BBC had previously done with the medium.

However, the drawback of *Quatermass*, as Chilton saw it, was that the action was still entirely based on planet Earth, what he planned to do with his new serial was take things into a territory BBC drama had never really visited before – outer space.

Chilton: '*Quatermass* was on, but that ... was always on the ground. I suppose it was science fiction, but it didn't explore the stars. It didn't go to the moon, or anything like that.'

Journey into Space (as Chilton's new serial was named) would be a largely space-based adventure. Like *Quatermass*, it would have a more thoughtful (even philosophical side). However, unlike *Quatermass*, it would also be an adventure in the truest sense of the word, including cliffhangers.

'I was a great fan of H G Wells,' says Chilton. 'I used to read him when I was a boy and I studied his form. I thought I'd base myself on him mainly. I had no thoughts beyond that, except of doing a good radio programme.'

Once again, Chilton was to act as producer (for which he was paid) and as writer (for which he was not paid).

A number of the cast had worked with Chilton before, while others were brought in afresh. Veteran actor Wilfred Walter was recommended to Chilton to play rocket scientist Sir William Morgan in the first few episodes. American medical officer Doc Matthews was to be played by Guy Kingsley Poynter, with whom Chilton had worked before. David Kossoff (who had also worked with the BBC Repertory Company) was cast as cheery Cockney radio operator Lemmy (Lemuel) Barnet.

From episode three onwards, the cast also included the familiar presence of Chilton's old friend David Jacobs.

'I was never in the Drama Rep',' says Jacobs. 'I was just a freelancer and I played in dozens of features. Voice One here, Voice Two there. I was narrating one long series called *Book of Verse*, which was produced by John Arlott – all those sort of things. It was lovely. I'd go from one thing to another, with great enjoyment ... I enjoyed it so hugely and had to play such an enormous number of parts because Charles Chilton ... knew that I could change my voice, because we'd worked together in Forces Radio.'

The show's principal lead was Captain (Andrew) Jet Morgan. He was played by respected Scottish actor Andrew Faulds (who had also worked with the BBC Repertory Company). 'He was a lovely larger than life character – naughty boy,' says Jacobs. 'Lovely chap with the ladies. He was magical. He had a vast personality – great charisma.'

The first episode of *Journey into Space* was recorded on 10 September 1953, at the BBC's Piccadilly 2 studio. This was not a purpose-built set of studios, but had been converted for recording only a few years before.

The building was, 'next to Simpson's the tailors and clothing shop,' remembers Chilton.

The actual recording space itself was located 'in part of the premises which during the War accommodated the Stage Door Canteen,' explained Val Gielgud in 1957. It was 'not as large as 6A or 8A [at Broadcasting House] ... having been built for quite other purposes. But after gutting ... [it was] reconstructed and treated on the same general principles of studio subdivision, numerous microphone-points and proximity of producer-control.'[220]

'It had a very big ground floor studio,' says Michael Kilgarriff (who worked there in the '60s). 'That was used for band shows. It had an enormous stage, with seating for a hundred people or something like that and below, under the ground floor there was a very big green room, which I suppose was really to furnish the musicians. Behind that, virtually under the road, now that I think of it, was this enormous drama studio.'

'It's not there anymore,' says Jacobs. 'It was, I think, where BAFTA is now.'

The cast and crew had a seventy-five minute session in the studio for the first episode, first rehearsing and then recording. 'We got our scripts when we got there and we had a sort of read-through,' says Jacobs. 'We had to have rehearsals, you see, for the music and the effects. That's what had to be rehearsed.'

'We rehearsed all day until six o'clock,' adds Chilton. 'Then we had a break and recorded until seven on Sundays.'

Incidental music for the production had been composed by Van Phillips, who had previously worked with Chilton on a musical documentary about the American Civil War (*The Blue and the Grey*). Phillips' score was played into the studio sessions from acetate disc recordings. Many of these music cues had descriptive titles like: 'Music for Outer Space', 'A Picture of the

---

[220] From *British Radio Drama: 1922-1956* by Val Gielgud – George G Harrap Ltd (1957)

SERIAL THRILLERS

Universe' and 'Rocket Away'. A later episode also included a snatch of music from a 1952 recording of Hank Snow and the Rainbow Ranch Boys. The opening theme music clearly owed a little to Radio Luxembourg's *Dan Dare* series, with the sound of soaring rocket motor screaming overhead.

Unfortunately, Chilton soon developed something of a reputation for being late to complete his scripts, which had an obvious effect on the recording sessions. 'We didn't even get the end of the script until while we were recording,' says Jacobs. 'Charles was always so late with it all.'

'I would turn up on a Sunday morning, in the studio,' explains Chilton, 'with the script written and stencilled, but not printed, because I hadn't written it in time for it to be printed. So, the cast spent the first hour or two of the day printing the script. And the rumour went round that if you wanted to audition for Chilton, you had to learn how to use a Roneo machine before you applied.'

The situation would, no doubt, have caused terrible headaches for any producer. However, as Chilton was both writing and producing, it was a problem that only he had to deal with. 'Being producer's easy. Being a writer is hard,' he says. 'As I was in charge – fully in charge – both producing it and writing it, if I did get into a mess, having finished it, I could say, "Well, I'm sorry folks, but you'll have to record this bit on Monday," or something like that.'

Despite the eleventh hour scripting, Chilton did manage to complete the first episode's recording on time and by the following week the series was being heavily promoted in the *Radio Times*. In the 12 – 18 September edition, a piece in the *Both Sides of the Microphone* section spoke about Chilton and his latest project. The following week's edition trailed the series again, with a special illustration of a rocket blasting off. The article outlined the series' set-up, saying: 'The year is 1965 and at a proving ground in New Mexico, Sir William Morgan, a leading research scientist, is about to launch an experimental space rocket.'[221]

On 14 September 1953, the BBC Light Programme broadcast the final episode of *Riders of the Range*[222]. The following week at 7.30 PM on 21 September, the first episode of *Journey into Space* took to the air. The serial was billed in the *Radio Times* simply as, *A Tale of the Future,* but by 1955, the serial was being referred to in BBC paperwork as *Journey to the Moon.*

Ratings for the BBC's new serial were healthy. The first episode attracted an estimated 5.1 million listeners. This was appreciably more than the previous week's *Riders of the Range* finale. '*Journey into Space* ... was far far

---

[221] From *Radio Times* (19/09/53 – 25/09/53)
[222] Sadly, the BBC didn't keep any recordings of any of the 90 episodes of *Riders of the Range*. Today, all that survives of the series are the original scripts and the memories of listeners.

more popular than the cowboys I'd been writing before,' says Chilton. However, the reaction index (the way the BBC measured audience appreciation) was below the Light Programme's average – scoring a disappointing 59. Ratings would soon fall to less than four million.

Nevertheless, it was still considered to be a strong start for a new serial and cast and crew were confident. 'Right from the very beginning we knew we were on a winner,' recalls Jacobs.

A BBC audience research report also returned a generally positive response. One listener commented that, 'it was a first class affair ... I expected some *Buck Rogers* trash and had a very pleasant surprise.'[223]

Not that the BBC's report was entirely without criticism, however. Wilfred Walter was singled out as having given a very poor acting performance in his rôle as Sir William Morgan and Chilton had already decided to write Walter out of the series altogether, with a new character introduced in his place. This new character was to be a fiery Australian engineer called Mitch, played by Bruce Beeby[224]. Also soon to be joining the cast would be former *ITMA* regular, Deryck Guyler.

Following the broadcast of episode three, a review in *The Listener* from J C Trewin was still upbeat about the serial's potential, saying: 'The first instalments of two current serials have each opened a gate to the moon.[225] *Journey into Space* (Light) is an instalment ahead ... I daresay the story will soon begin in earnest.'[226]

Others were less sure of Chilton's vision. Jonah Barrington wrote in *The Daily Sketch*: 'After three instalments of *Journey into Space*, his party has travelled no farther than Bombay. May we reasonably expect that in instalment four some attempt will be made to begin space travelling? Otherwise, here's one listener who's going to give up on the serial as a bad job.'[227]

Chilton concedes that he struggled with the early episodes of this first serial, in which the main action was concerned with the preparation for a space flight that had yet to happen. 'For the first week or two ... I didn't even take off the ground and critics began to complain, saying, "Look when are we going to take off?" So, I thought I better take off.'

After four weeks of entirely earth-based action, the atomic rocket motors of the spaceship finally roared into life at the start of episode five, broadcast

---

[223] From *Operation Luna* (CD Sleeve Notes) by Andrew Pixley – BBC Audiobooks (2004)
[224] When Beeby was unavailable towards the end of October, Australian film director Don Sharp took over from him.
[225] Autumn 1953 also saw the BBC Light Programme begin a new radio dramatisation of H G Wells' *First Men in the Moon*. *Journey into Space* was in production at the same time.
[226] From *The Listener* (08/10/53)
[227] From *The Daily Sketch* (06/10/53)

on 19 October.

With this new injection of adventure, the series soon rose dramatically in the ratings. 'It was a phenomenal success,' says Chilton. 'It was a great surprise – very satisfying.'

By episode five even Jonah Barrington had revised his opinion, reporting in *The Daily Sketch* that, 'the whole thing came alive … Here's one listener who has seldom been so excited, so absorbed, or so completely neglectful of his TV set.'[228]

The show's more prominent profile was soon reflected in the minor public outcry from some of the show's younger listeners, when the schedulers moved the series to 8PM on a Tuesday. In response to this, the show's final two episodes later got a 6PM repeat slot on subsequent Saturdays.

Riding high on the juvenile success, Chilton would make an appearance at the Westminster *Schoolboys' Own Exhibition* in January 1954, with accompanying coverage in the *Radio Times*.

Journey to the Moon was soon extended from a planned 12 episodes to a final 18, with final instalment broadcast on 19 January 1954. By now, an average of 8 million people were following the serial on a weekly basis. This was twice that of *Riders of the Range*. The reaction index had also improved – now sitting at a comfortable 77.

Following the serial's final episode, a listener research report quoted one listener as proclaiming, 'the sooner Jet and Co. return to the air, the better.'[229] The BBC clearly took heed of the advice. Before the year had ended, a sequel would enter into production.

THE RED PLANET:

Chilton's second *Journey into Space* serial began to be planned even as the first finished broadcasting. *The Red Planet* (as the new serial was named) was to be bigger than the original, both in scope and duration. As the title suggested, the plot concerned itself with an expedition to Mars. There was a new spaceship (The *Discovery*), but the old cast of characters was essentially the same. Faulds, Kossoff and Kingsley Poynter all returned, as did Bruce Beeby, who had left partway through the first series.

This time, the story stretched across twenty episodes – an extension on the original. However, there was another innovation too.

As, Chilton was already fairly certain that there would later be a third serial, he structured *The Red Planet* to be left open-ended. The first *Journey*

---

[228] From *Auntie's Charlie* by Charles Chilton – Fantom Publishing (2011)
[229] From *Operation Luna* (CD Sleeve Notes) by Andrew Pixley – BBC Audiobooks (2004)

into Space serial had been an essentially standalone story. However, this second offering would end on a cliffhanger, which would then be picked up in a third (as yet unwritten) serial, in the future. It was a bold strategy, which relied upon Chilton's confidence that the series would be a big enough success for him to have the chance to follow through his wider story plans.

The team returned to the BBC's Piccadilly studios, for the recording of the first of the new episodes on the evening of the 15 August 1954. The first four episodes were then recorded over the coming weeks until 5 September. Then on 6 September, the first episode was broadcast on the BBC Light Programme, back at 7.30 PM on Mondays.

The new serial had been trailed in the *Radio Times*, with a special photo-session with the cast, for which a genuine experimental space suit had been loaned to the BBC.

Meanwhile, as the serial began in earnest, the studio recording continued. Music for the production was again by Van Phillips, but it seems that this time, a small orchestra may have been used, rather than just pre-recorded discs.

'We had the musicians in the studio – in the Piccadilly studio,' remembers David Jacobs. 'It wasn't a big orchestra. It was only about six pieces, but it was a big studio.'

Although the new series was arguably even better received than its predecessor, Chilton still struggled to keep apace with the weekly recording schedule, as he worked on his scripts right up to the last minute, before they were rushed to the actors.

'If I wasn't doing it at the last minute, it wasn't any good,' explains Chilton. 'I did discover that inspiration comes *while* you're working, not before.'

Penny Chilton (Charles' wife) remembers: 'One time, when he was working, because it was always a nightmare for the week, trying to get the thing finished, I said, "Well, couldn't you get one week ahead?" And he said, "Oh, well I'll try." So he started on Monday and wrote and wrote all the week, until it came to Friday, then he tore it up. He couldn't do it.'

Naturally, this made life in the studio difficult, but as Chilton was also acting as producer, he was usually able to reschedule his studio time accordingly.

A number of studio sessions came to a close before the cast had finished recording all of their scripted material. This would have been a massive problem just a few years ago, but as *Journey into Space* was recorded on the BBC's latest 15 inch per second tape recorders, it was no longer always necessary to record everything 'as live'. This was something Chilton used to his advantage.

Material from episode 13, featuring the actress Miriam Karlin was scheduled to be recorded on 21 November, but time ran out that day and so the scenes were recorded on 28 November, along with most of episode 14. However, episode 14 also overran and so all of John Cazabon's material was deferred until 5 December. Madi Hedd[230], who appeared in episodes 15 and 16, recorded all of her material together on the same day on 12 December, during the studio session for episode 16.

This kind of shuffling of actors' schedules was unusual at the time, but would soon become common practice in radio recording in years to come. At the time, it was the only way of getting the programmes ready for transmission in time.

'We were doing the programmes on a Sunday and it would be going out next week in the same time,' says David Jacobs. 'It was done at the time, within days of each transmission.'

Despite the occasionally fraught studio days, the production seems to have been a happy one.

'They were always easy to work with,' continues Jacobs. 'Nobody was difficult at all. We didn't go in for difficult people in those days. We were all a team and we got on very well.'

'It got a bit too happy, actually,' remembers Chilton. 'I mean, the cast used to play tricks on each other ... I remember once, Andrew Faulds was at the microphone doing a serious bit and he was squirming ... because David Jacobs was pouring a jug of water down his trousers, while he was on the air doing the drama. That was the sort of cast I had. Andrew retaliated. He got his own back on David ... We used to have lip-mics, which went straight up [to the mouth] and you could then distort the voice and make a Martian out of it. David Jacobs played ... a Martian voice one day and so he put the microphone straight up to his mouth and started – not knowing that inside it had all been lathered with mustard. Tears were coming down his face, while he was trying to behave as though everything was normal.'

On January 2 1955, the programme made broadcasting history, when the series scored a 17% audience share. This was not particularly remarkable in itself. However, it was significant, because at the same time, the audience share for Britain's only television channel was just 16%. This was the last time that a British television programme would be outscored by a radio programme.

The Red Planet was very well received by the listening public. The BBC audience research reports commented that: 'This is obviously very much a family occasion in many homes, the entire household following the adventures of Jet Morgan and Co. with great interest ... Most listeners made it clear that *The Red Planet* had been an important event in their lives

---

[230] Actress Madi Hedd was married to Bruce Beeby.

over the past weeks.'[231]

The final episode of *The Red Planet* was broadcast on 17 January. The series ended on a cliffhanger, which was to set up the action for what was intended to follow – a third serial later in the year.

'I knew that they wanted another series, so I prepared for it,' says Chilton. 'I made people, I hope, want to hear the next series to see what actually happened in the end. Left a bit of a cliffhanger and then three months later, started up again.'

MERCHANDISE:

The impact of *Journey into Space* was so immediate that the BBC had begun to be approached over various marketing opportunities even before the second episode of the first serial had aired. On 11 September 1953, the BBC had been contacted by Waltham Enterprises over their plans for a toy space-helmet to tie in with the programme. On 23 October, Amalgamated Press had approached the BBC over a possible *Journey into Space* comic strip (as there had been for *Riders of the Range*). On 29 December, Alan Wingate inquired about the possibility of book deal – something Routlege and Kegan Paul Ltd, also pursued. Numerous similar book offers followed from a number of publishing houses. And three separate studios were fighting for the cinematic rights. There was even talk of a *Journey into Space* musical.

Ultimately, only one of these many proposed ventures would be followed up with any immediacy. This was a deal that Chilton had signed with Herbert Jenkins Ltd., which saw Chilton write a novelisation of his first serial, which was printed in hardback in November 1954. Paperback editions followed in 1958 (Pan Books) and 1963 (Digit).

Notably, the novelised version of 'the story that enthralled millions,' jettisoned most of the plot that had originally made up the first four episodes. The novel instead opened with a scene inside the rocket, just after it had completed its first orbit around the Moon.

The novelisation of *The Red Planet* followed in January 1956 (again from Herbert Jenkins Ltd.), with paperbacks from Pan and Digit in 1960 and 1963 respectively.

With the broadcast of *The Red Planet*, requests from commercial companies wishing to tie-in with the series resumed with renewed vigour. The BBC rejected many of these requests. However, some were more seriously pursued. One such deal, was an arrangement with Lyon's Coffee, which saw Jet Morgan used in one of their long-running advertising campaigns. January 1955 also saw Chilton in negotiations over the prospect of *Journey into Space* toys.

---

[231] From *Operation Luna* (CD Sleeve Notes) by Andrew Pixley – BBC Audiobooks (2004)

SERIAL THRILLERS

JOURNEY TO THE CINEMA:

The prospect of a *Journey into Space* cinema feature was mooted very early on during the series' production and was taken very seriously by the BBC. Other BBC radio hits such as *PC 49*, *Dick Barton*, *Paul Temple*, *Dr Morelle* and *Life With the Lyons* had all been adapted for the cinema by numerous British studios. And crucially, Hammer Films had recently had a tremendous success with their version of BBC television's *The Quatermass Experiment* in 1955.

By 1954, 20th Century Fox, Paramount Pictures and Havelock Allan had all made inquiries with the BBC over the possibility of producing a *Journey into Space* picture. It doesn't seem that any of these offers were taken very far, either by the companies concerned or the BBC. However, on 4 January 1955, things began to move more positively, when Norman Spencer approached the BBC on behalf of the celebrated film director David Lean. Spencer requested a recording of one of the episodes for Lean to listen to.

The BBC was clearly very interested in Lean and Spencer's proposal. However, only days later, on 7 January, the BBC was to be given another offer from T H Sachs of Rembrandt Films. Rembrandt's offer was possibly less prestigious than Lean's, but it was also more definite, with a firm proposal to make both a UK cinema feature and a twelve/thirteen episode mini-series on US television.

On 12 January, Michael Standing (Chilton's superior in the Variety department) indicated that he would prefer to wait on a more concrete offer from the illustrious Lean, rather than go for the Rembrandt proposal. The Light Programme's H Rooney Pelletier suggested that any such film could be released in mid-1956, by which time he predicted that the radio series would have run its course.

Standing's patience bore fruit and on 26 January, Dennis Van Thal offered a deal where the BBC would give London Films a three month option on the filmic exploitation of both serials, with David Lean attached as director.

On 28 January, the BBC agreed to the proposal and the film was set on the road toward pre-production. The next month, on 29 February, Van Thal (on behalf of London Films) made a formal offer of £2,500 for the motion picture rights to *Journey into Space*.

However, the BBC seem to have been reluctant to sign straightaway and, on 11 March, made its own approaches to ABPC, Pinewood (who had already expressed interest) and Ealing Studios. J Arthur Rank at Pinewood rejected the idea, as did ABPC. However, Michael Balcon at Ealing asked to consider the offer more carefully and requested to view copies of the radio scripts in April 1955.

By this point, Lean had stepped away from the offer with London Films. However, the company was still interested in the idea, alongside the veteran director Alexander Korda.

On 23 September, Hammer Films made another offer for the rights, via their studio-head Anthony Hinds. The company were very pleased indeed with the whirlwind success of *The Quatermass Xperiment*.[232] Following the film's release they had tried to persuade *Quatermass'* writer Nigel Kneale to allow the use of his character in another entirely new production. However, Kneale had refused. With *Journey into Space*, they tried the same thing again and proposed to buy only the rights to the characters of the BBC series. The actual script for the film itself would be entirely new and would be written by Chilton. Unfortunately, Chilton was already under contract to the BBC and so the offer was formally declined on 18 November.

By November, even more film companies had joined the queue of interested parties, with both George Maynard Productions and Rayant Pictures contacting the BBC. On 16 January 1956, J Arthur Rank had also begun to reconsider the project and wrote to the BBC.

However, with the BBC refusing to make an official deal with any one party, it seems that the entire notion of a *Journey into Space* film eventually faded away. Possibly, if the BBC had signed earlier with London Films, then the outcome may have been different, but after over a year of deliberation, all there was to show for the enterprise was a mounting stack of letters and paperwork. *Journey into Space* never made it to any cinema screens anywhere.

THE WORLD IN PERIL:

Chilton had left things very much up in the air with his cliffhanger ending to *The Red Planet*. Earth was under threat of imminent invasion from an extraterrestrial foe and Jet and his friends were millions of miles away, seemingly helpless to stop it.

A sequel, which would tie up loose ends, was never in any serious doubt. Chilton's third serial would be called *The World in Peril* and opened with Jet and his crew, making their way back to Earth.

The previous two productions in the cycle had both been recorded at the BBC's Piccadilly Studios. However, for the latest serial, the series was to relocate to the Aeolian Hall Studios on Bond Street (where Chilton's office

---

[232] The BBC's six-part television serial *The Quatermass Experiment* was released under three separate titles. Originally, Hammer screened the picture as *The Quatermass Xperiment*. However, in American cinemas it was called *The Creeping Unknown*. It wasn't until much later that the film was re-released as *The Quatermass Experiment*.

was based). It was here that cast and crew convened for the recording of the first episode on the afternoon of 7 September 1955.

However, there were other changes too. Most notable was the recasting of core supporting character, Lemmy. David Kossoff had originally played Lemmy in both of the two previous productions, but new work commitments conflicted with the latest serial.

'I was quite happy with the first Lemmy, David Kossoff, but he went off to make a film called *The Kid for Two Farthings* (sic). So, I had to get somebody else. So, I found Alfie Bass who was very good.'

Alfie Bass was an outside artist (ie not in the BBC Repertory Company). He would later go on to a highly successful television career in programmes like *The Army Game* and its two sequels *Bootsie and Snudge* and *Foreign Affairs*. At the time he was cast as Lemmy, he had just recently appeared in the BBC television drama *The Bespoke Overcoat*. He was currently appearing in *The Punch Bowl* revue show at the Duke of York's Theatre.

David Kossoff invented the voice of Lemmy,' remembers Jacobs 'but then ... Alfie Bass took over and we welcomed him and he played Lemmy. I don't know how many people cared. We didn't, in the studio.'

Bruce Beeby had also played Mitch for the last time as well. In *The World in Peril*, Don Sharp played Mitch.

The first episode of the new adventure was broadcast on the Light Programme at 7.30 PM on 26 September – later episodes following in the same timeslot. There was also a repeat every Sunday at 6.30 PM.

Critics and audiences alike continued to respond well to the series. A BBC audience research report on 17 October quoted a fitter's wife as saying: 'Our family has waited a long time for the programme to come back ... and if this is as good as the last series it will be fine with us.'[233]

The new serial drew in an estimated 14% share of the potential British audience. Although, this was not as high as it had been in the past, it was still a very strong showing.

In September 1955, the arrival of commercial television had redrawn the broadcasting landscape of Great Britain and there was now a lot more competition for ratings. Not only were there two television channels, but there was Radio Luxembourg as well. All this had an effect on the listenership of *Journey into Space*, as it did all radio programmes.

Nevertheless, the latest serial pulled in healthy figures, in comparison with its rivals and the series continued to entertain its followers with some success, and with little in the way of production problems.[234]

---

[233] From *The World in Peril* (CD Sleeve Notes) by Andrew Pixley – BBC Audiobooks (2004)
[234] One small problem arose on 9 January, during the broadcast of episode 16, when technical problems disrupted the transmission.

The World in Peril came to a close with the transmission of its final episode on 6 February 1956. It had gone done very well and another audience research report on 29 February, commented that many listeners were hopeful that Chilton had 'left the door open for further adventures at some future date.'[235] Listeners clearly had an appetite for further serials with Jet Morgan and his crew and there was an obvious expectation of more to come. However, fans would have a long wait. *The World in Peril* would be the last full *Journey into Space* serial to come from Charles Chilton.

David Jacobs doesn't seem to have been told why the series was to end at this point. 'I've no idea at all,' he says. 'I suppose they just said that they'd had enough ... Perhaps Charles Chilton ran out of ideas. I don't know. Perhaps he'd done as much as he wanted to ... Who knows what goes on in programme-planners' minds?'

'I didn't want to write anymore,' explains Chilton. 'It was too hard. They did ask me to carry on, but I said, "No, I don't want to do it."'

On 17 July, this was effectively confirmed, when Chilton's boss Michael Standing relinquished the BBC's rights back to Chilton. This was (and still is) a highly unusual move for the BBC.

THE COMIC STRIP:

There would only be one further (entirely original) set of *Journey into Space* adventures, before the end of the decade. This came in the form of a comic strip (following in the footsteps of *Dick Barton* and *Paul Temple*).

The BBC had been approached by the *Junior Express* comic over the possibility of a *Journey into Space* comic strip on 14 February 1956. The BBC quickly agreed to the deal and confirmed this a few days later on 27 February. The only proviso to the arrangement was that there was to be no conflict between the strip and the BBC's own radio serial. However, with the transmission of the final episode of *The World in Peril*, the programme was no longer on the air anyway and work was soon put under way on the proposed strip.

Following on from his experience with the strip of *Riders of the Range*, Chilton would write many of the early episodes. The first serial was *Planet of Fear*, which picked up from the end of *The World in Peril*. It began in issue 84 on 28 April 1956. Later serials included *Shadow Over Britain* and *World Next Door*. The series was originally illustrated by Milanese artists Ferdinando (Nando) Tacconi and later Terence Patrick. The strip also spawned a number of special annuals, with art by Tacconi and Bruce Cornwall.

Chilton was especially impressed with Tacconi. 'Nando was most

---

[235] From *The World in Peril* (CD Sleeve Notes) by Andrew Pixley – BBC Audiobooks (2004)

painstaking and determined to be accurate,' he said.[236]

Charles Chilton's son David remembered the series particularly well. 'I was always looking at those as a kid,' he says. 'That had an effect on me. They had to have an Italian drawing all the illustrations, because they couldn't find any English artists, because no English artist could draw something real, they could only do very abstract things, whereas in Italy, they have hundreds of commercial artists.'

Tacconi's comic strip career was cut tragically short by blindness, but he remained friends with the Chilton family for the rest of his life, sometimes visiting them in England. He died in April 2006.

The serialisations drew to a close on 5 October 1957. Although moderately successful, it was never as well known as its radio originator, nor did it catch on in the same way. In retrospect, the strip was never going to win the whole-hearted affection of the country's youth. After all, mid-fifties Britain already had a popular space-age comic strip in *Eagle*: *Dan Dare – Pilot of the Future*.

A TRIP TO THE MOON:

Although there would be no further full *Journey into Space* serials after *The World in Peril*, there would still be a number of opportunities for studio reunions in the years that followed.

The first of these came in October 1957, with another full-cast *Journey into Space* drama for BBC Radio. Although, this time it would not be an entirely original presentation.

In mid-1957, Geoffrey S Hall, a BBC producer, was working on a special five-part educational series for school children called *Our Own and Other Worlds*. The third episode was to be a programme about lunar exploration called *A Trip to the Moon*.

Hall approached Chilton in October, asking if he would be prepared to produce something for the slot. With his work on *Journey into Space*, he was an obvious candidate and seems to have been recommended to Hall by a Dr J G Porter.

Chilton's script for *A Trip to the Moon* wasn't an original piece of work. Instead, he just adapted the script from the very first *Journey into Space* serial of 1953. The new script picked up the narrative a few episodes in from where the original serial had begun and contained edited scenes from a number of early episodes.

By 1957, the original tape recordings from 1953 had been disposed of. Therefore, all of the recycled material for *A Trip to the Moon* was re-recorded from scratch, using some of the original cast.

---

[236] From *Auntie's Charlie* by Charles Chilton – Fantom Publishing (2011)

The play was recorded in Studio 8A at Broadcasting House on the afternoon of 27 October. Andrew Faulds, Guy Kingsley Poynter and David Jacobs all returned from the original team. However, there was yet another change to the casting of Mitch – who was now played by David Williams. Williams was, of course, another Australian actor.

David Williams was the third person to play the character of Mitch. 'The reason I had those three characters,' says Chilton, 'is that they were all Australians and I had an Australian character. So, it wasn't difficult, if I got a real Australian, they all sound much the same I suppose. They were able to take over quite well.'

A Trip to the Moon was transmitted over the BBC Home Service at 11.20 AM (during the school-day) on 19 November.

The new programme had never been intended to be much more than a short educational episode for schools and received little publicity. However, the new recording perhaps had some further effect, because before the show was even transmitted, a much more elaborate recording along similar lines was already in the studio.

OPERATION LUNA:

Shortly after they were broadcast, both *The Red Planet* and *The World in Peril* were selected by BBC Transcription Services for overseas distribution. The original master recordings of both serials were copied onto sixteen-inch coarse groove discs and were then offered for sale to overseas radio networks. Once a contract was signed between the BBC and an overseas station, copies of the serials were then shipped over on disc.

Journey into Space was just one among several BBC programmes then in international circulation – including *Paul Temple*.

Sadly, the BBC hadn't kept any master recordings for the very first *Journey into Space* serial – *Journey to the Moon*. As such, it was not in the Transcription Services' catalogue.

In Autumn 1957, the BBC Transcription Services decided that they would plug the hole in the trilogy and re-record the first serial from scratch, so that they would then be able to offer all three serials for foreign sale.

It was not an especially unusual move. Episodes of both *The Goon Show* and *Hancock's Half-Hour* were also re-recorded in the same way at around the same time.

The new production was intended to be an almost exact replica of the original – with the same cast and crew and the same script. Charles Chilton was, of course, assigned as producer.

However, Chilton hadn't been entirely happy with some of his early episodes on *Journey to the Moon*. He felt that he was still finding his way with the unfamiliar format – not really hitting his stride until after he had written the first four or five episodes. 'I think I took off on the fifth episode,' he says.

As such, Chilton took the drastic decision to completely cut the first four episodes altogether. The new Transcription's production would begin at the start of episode five, largely ignoring what had gone before and going straight through from there. Episode five would become the new episode one. Episode six was the new episode two and so on. The scripts for episodes twelve and thirteen were also heavily edited. The remaining material from these two episodes would be then brought together as part of the new episode eight. This brought the serial down from eighteen episodes to just thirteen, which also cut down on recording time.

The new production retained much of the cast from *The World in Peril* and *A Trip to the Moon*. Andrew Faulds was still Jet Morgan. Guy Kingsley Poynter was Doc and David Williams returned as Mitch, with David Jacobs providing voices for a number of other characters.

The series also saw Alfie Bass return to the part of Lemmy – something that caused some minor disagreement with original Lemmy, David Kossoff. Kossoff had left the cast of *Journey into Space* some time before, to work on the film *A Kid for Two Farthings*. However, with the new serial about to enter the studio, Chilton remembers being approached by Kossoff again.

'When *Kid for Two Farthings* was finished,' he says, 'Kossoff came back and said, "Alright, I'll continue playing." And I said, "No, you can't. The chap that's doing it, is doing it very well." I wouldn't change it. I kept Alfie Bass on.'

The new recording also had a new title – *Operation Luna*, which derived from the name of the crew's spaceship. Studio sessions began on 10 November 1957, with two hour-long recordings following over successive Sundays in a variety of different BBC studios.[237]

The recordings soon went into circulation through the BBC Transcription Services, where they were offered for sale on the latest micro-groove disc format, alongside the other two serials. The trilogy was complete. The new transcriptions were also broadcast on the Light Programme between 26 March and 18 June 1958.

BACK TO EARTH:

Operation Luna proved to be the very last time that Faulds and company would be reunited around the microphone to journey into space. There would be no further serials, although a novelisation of *The World in*

---

[237] The first four episodes were all recorded in Studio 8A at Broadcasting House. Piccadilly 2 was used for the recording of episodes 5 and 6. Then it was back to Broadcasting House for the recording of episodes 7 and 8 (in Studio 6A). Episode 9 to 12 returned to Piccadilly 2 and the final episode (episode 13) was recorded in the Paris Theatre.

Peril was printed in 1960.

Charles Chilton would continue his highly successful career as a producer with the BBC. He went onto produce *The Goon Show* (which he had earlier been instrumental in setting up) and also headed the production of *Take it from Here*, as well as being behind a great number of well-remembered documentaries and features on the history of popular music and culture. Arguably his greatest success came with his work on *Oh! What a Lovely War*, the critically lauded wartime musical, which began life on radio before moving to the stage under the stewardship of Joan Littlewood. The play later made it to the cinema in 1969 through the direction of Sir Richard Attenborough.

In the seventies, Chilton reached the BBC's (then compulsory) retirement age of 60 and was forced to leave the staff. He continued to return in various freelance capacities. Just before his retirement, he was awarded the MBE in 1976.

His many programming contributions to the BBC, are too numerous to recount, but love of both the BBC and programme production in general stayed with him. At the time of writing, his last contribution to a BBC programme was in 2009.

Andrew Faulds' career, following his work as Jet Morgan, was highly varied. In 1966 he became MP for the Smethwick (later Warley East) constituency as a Labour candidate and served passionately on a platform of racial tolerance, against the likes of Enoch Powell and Peter Griffiths. His political ferocity made some of his colleagues wary of him, however. He famously described a Tory opposite as 'an honourable shit' in 1988 and it is possible that such outspoken behaviour cost him political advancement. However, he remained a well-known presence in the House, until his retirement in 1997.

He continued to act in a number of films up to the 1970s. However, for many, his most remembered part was in the much-loved 1963 escapist fantasy *Jason and the Argonauts*. He died on may 31 2000.

David Jacobs continued largely as a presenter for the BBC, Radio Luxembourg and Capital Radio. His BBC shows have included *Housewives Choice, Pick of the Pops* and *Midday Spin*. On television, he was among the first presenters of *Top of the Pops*, but is much better known for his chairmanship of the fondly remembered *Juke Box Jury* from 1959 to 1967.

In 1984 he received the Sony Gold Award for his outstanding contribution to radio broadcasting and in 1996 was awarded a CBE. At the time of writing, he has a weekly programme on BBC Radio 2. Old Ceylon comrade Desmond Carrington is also on Radio 2.

SERIAL THRILLERS

TELEVISION:

Although *Journey into Space* had always remained a resolutely radio-only affair, the calls for a television version were inevitable.

Television was growing in strength and influence throughout the 1950s and by the 1960s, it had largely won through in the battle for ratings. *Journey into Space* was the last programme to ever beat television in terms of audience figures and its celebrated status as the BBC's best loved science fiction series made it ripe for some sort of television spin-off.

One of the earliest suggestions for a TV version of the series came in January 1955, when Rembrandt Films had spoken to the BBC about the possibility of 13 part TV series for American television. At the time, the BBC's Head of Television Drama Michael Barry felt that the series wouldn't work well on TV and the offer was dismissed. However, the idea would resurface after the series had finished its radio run.

On 23 March 1959, British Lion also approached the BBC about a filmed TV series for the American market. By this time, television was a lot better established at the BBC and the idea was taken more seriously. On 6 May, the BBC tentatively agreed to the idea in principal, on the condition that the finished product was of sufficient quality and that the BBC retained the UK broadcast rights. Oddly, the idea seems to have died at this point.

By the 1960s, the television landscape had changed dramatically. Both the BBC and ITV had a number of science-fiction based shows in production. The BBC had their *Andromeda* series, *Out of the Unknown* and *Doctor Who*. ITV had their *Pathfinders* series, *The Avengers* and innumerable American imports. It was against this background that the idea of *Journey into Space* TV show would resurface.

On 9 April 1965, Michael Fenton from the independent Free Lance Productions Ltd. came to the BBC about the possibility of a series in Canada.

The idea was apparently rejected on the grounds that the BBC themselves were considering to use the show as a replacement for their *Doctor Who* series, which was then in its second year.[238] However, this idea was also dropped, with *Doctor Who* continuing for a very long time to come.

Of course, these were only some of the many TV proposals to been brought forward over what was seen by many to be a logical progression for the series. *Hancock's Half-Hour*, *Paul Temple* and *Dick Barton* all made it to the small screen with varying degrees of success. However, it was something Chilton opposed with *Journey into Space*. 'I always resisted it,'

---

[238] However, there is no evidence of this being the case contained within the existing paperwork for *Doctor Who*.

he says, 'because it was very very difficult to do a science fiction the way I was doing it. Going to the moon on television in those days – I mean, the scenery, where are you going to get all the scenes from and so forth? So, I resisted doing science fiction on TV.'

THE RETURN FROM MARS:

Ultimately, there never would be any kind of transfer to television for *Journey into Space*. However, that didn't mean the series was entirely over. And in 1981, after over two decades away from the radio, the series did (briefly) make an overdue return.

As early as October 1979, Charles Chilton had returned to the field of science fiction, when he was approached to write the script for a new Radio 2 series, called *Space Force*. However, around the same time, he also began work on a return for the characters of Jet and friends in a special reunion episode of *Journey into Space*.

1981 was planned to be a special year for science fiction on BBC Radio 4. New dramatisations of Arthur C Clarke's *A Fall of Moondust* and John Wyndham's *The Chrysalids* were both planned and a new *Journey into Space* was to be another of the attractions.

Entitled *The Return From Mars*, Chilton's new 90-minute drama would carry on from the end of *The World in Peril* (although there were some continuity errors).

Chilton would, for the first time, not be acting as producer. He had now left the BBC's payroll and was a freelancer. However, the script would come from him. He delivered his final copy on 26 January 1981, although he'd been formally commissioned over a year earlier on 9 January 1980.

The new episode was conceived very much as a continuation of the saga. However, it would not see any return from the original cast. Even Jet Morgan was recast.

John Pullen was the new Jet, with Anthony Hall as Lemmy and Ed Bishop as Doc. Nigel Graham was Mitch and Elizabeth Proud was new character Cassia. The new producer was Glyn Dearman.

Unlike the comparatively hurried 'as live' recordings of the original three serials, the new play was granted the luxury of four days recording between 14 and 17 February 1981, in Studio 10 at Broadcasting House.

The play was broadcast on BBC Radio 4 at 8.30 PM on 7 March, with a repeat a few days later at 3.02 PM on 9 March. In an interesting twist of coincidence, Radio 4 also produced a new radio adaptation of Wells' *The First Men in the Moon* as part of that season's new science fiction dramas. A new radio dramatisation of *The First Men in the Moon* had also been in production when the very first *Journey into Space* drama was aired, back in 1953.

SERIAL THRILLERS

Unfortunately, the response to the new play was not overwhelmingly strong. 'I don't think they really got the characters quite right in that,' says Charles Chilton's son David. 'It never quite got off the ground, that one.'

The play did lead to some benefit for Charles Chilton, as he was soon after commissioned to write a full run of his *Space Force* series (essentially *Journey into Space* by another name). However, the *Journey into Space* experiment was not repeated – at least not for a very long time.

ARCHIVE:

Against all the laws of probability, *Journey into Space* occupies something of a unique place in the history of the British radio adventure serial. Unlike *Paul Temple*, *Dick Barton* and *Dan Dare*, we are incredibly fortunate in that very nearly all of it still survives for us to listen to.

Of the three (original) serial productions that were recorded in the 1950s, the BBC archives has something in some form to represent them all. This is *highly* unusual for any radio series from this period. Few series survive so (comparatively) intact.

However, it wasn't always thought that the series *had* survived.

Certainly when Radio 4 produced *The Return from Mars*, it was largely assumed that *Journey into Space* was just another in a long line of lost radio dramas. The main BBC sound archive didn't have any complete episodes in its collection and one of the reasons why there are so many continuity errors in *The Return from Mars*, is that Charles Chilton didn't have any recordings of earlier serials to refer back to when he was writing it.

This changed in 1986, thanks to a man called Ted Kendall – a BBC engineer working with the BBC Sound Archive. At the time, there were two separate (and entirely independent) archives of sound recordings within the BBC. There was the main BBC Sound Archive and then there was the BBC Transcription Services Archive. The Transcriptions' store was full of recordings that had been made for international distribution, whereas the Sound Archive was more a historical depository. Ted Kendall knew that the chances were that there was probably a good deal of otherwise 'lost' radio programming stored by Transcriptions that the main Sound Archive didn't know about and with an active interest in the area, he was given the job of finding out the full extent of this.

'Sound archives wanted to know what Transcriptions was still holding,' explains Kendall. 'I got attached to sound archives for six months to trawl through the Transcription archive storage at North Acton on an industrial estate and basically to go through and document what was there. This was all on sixteen-inch disc and micro-groove disc and tape. Pretty much everything from 1954 ... There were one or two things earlier than that, but very very few.'

It was fairly well documented that both *The Red Planet* and *The World in Peril* had been copied by Transcription Services back in the mid-fifties and that they had also made a special re-recording of *Operation Luna*. It was clear that the material must have been held by Transcription Services at some point, only leaving the question of what had happened to it. Before long, Kendall found out.

'In due course, I stumbled across the archive copies of *The Red Planet* and *The World in Peril* in North Acton,' he says, 'and very swiftly got safety copies made of those, because everybody in the world, it seemed, had been looking for these things, except in the one place that they were to be found and I happened to be there. It took a while to sort out *Operation Luna*. The stuff that was held in North Acton was nominally the archive, and there was also in Transcriptions ... several shelves of what was known as "library copies". The basic difference being that the archive copies were only for use by engineers to retrieve the programme and library copies were to be used by anybody with an interest in the department to play the material. No archive copies of *Operation Luna* survived. It was just the one set of library discs that had been pretty well played. So, within a fairly short space of time, we actually had the three stories back.'

Transcription Services had never had any copies of the original 1953 recording of *Journey to the Moon* and consequently, this serial still remains lost (bar a short surviving extract). However, as *Operation Luna* covers most of the same plot with much of the same cast, we are not missing as much we perhaps might have been. 'We probably haven't lost much, to be honest,' confirms Kendall.

Following on the success of a series of *Paul Temple* repeats in the late 1980s, a repeat run of the rediscovered material was quickly under consideration.

'Given the internal politics of the BBC,' says Kendall, 'if I dug something up, Transcriptions always used to make a bit of hoo-ha about it, because it raised the profile of the unit. So, it became fairly well known, fairly early on, that these things had actually been recovered. And it was Andy Aliffe [at BBC Radio 2] who picked up the ball on that one, or had it thrown to him. I prepared the masters for transmission on Radio 2. I did all the technical work and then they were sent to Andy to be hacked about to fit the slot ... for length, basically. The original shows were all sort of 29'45" or something like that, but the Radio 2 slot was twenty-seven minutes or twenty-eight, I can't remember. Anyway, it was less than half an hour, so some material had to be nipped out.'

With due fanfare, *Operation Luna* was re-broadcast on BBC Radio 2 in a Friday evening slot at 10PM from 19 May to 11 August 1989. A (slightly cut) release of the material followed on cassette from BBC Audio.

The following year, Radio 2 repeated *The Red Planet*. This time they split the repeats into two separate runs of ten episodes. The first run had a 7PM slot on a Friday and ran from 27th July to 28th September. The serial then concluded with a second run from 28th December 1990 to 1st March 1991 – in the same slot. As before, BBC Audio released an edited version on cassette in 1991 – across six tapes.

The World in Peril arrived on Radio 2 in 1991. Again the serial was split into two sections. The first ten episodes ran from 21 June to 23 August, with the final ten episodes running from 13 September to 15 November. The six-cassette commercial release from BBC Audio followed in 1994.

Although those first four original episodes remain lost, much of what is left gives a very good flavour of the series and still enables us to appreciate it from beginning to end – a very rare thing indeed for radio of this period.

All three serials have been released multiple times, since those early edited cassette releases. They were released uncut on cassette in the late 1990s and then were digitally restored for a series of CD and download releases in 2004 – again from BBC Audio. Sound restoration was by Kendall.

FATHER AND SON:

Although there had been a few short documentaries on the history of the programme – *Journey into Space ... Again* (1999) and *Another Journey into Space* (2000) – for many years *The Return from Mars* was the last *Journey into Space* story. This changed, quite unexpectedly in 2008.

The whole endeavour came about through David Chilton (the son of Charles Chilton). David remembered his father's work on the series from when he was a child and later joined the BBC himself. David went on to become a member of the famous BBC Radiophonic Workshop, before going freelance and getting involved in various music based projects as both producer and sound-designer/composer.

In 2008, he decided that the time could be right for a revival of his father's most memorable radio creation and he approached his father and a fellow producer about the possibility. It was an unusual suggestion – particularly since most of the original cast were now dead.

'It was partly because the people who were in the original cast were getting fewer and fewer,' he says. 'They died off and so there was only really David Jacobs left. Partly, it was to do something, while there was still somebody alive from the original series.'

Of prime concern was who would play the new Jet Morgan. 'Andrew Faulds who was Jet Morgan, had died a few years before,' continues David Chilton. With David Jacobs the only principal member of the original cast who was still alive – the decision was taken that he would be the new Jet Morgan.

Jacobs was now in his eighties and so the increased age of the character was accordingly built into the script for the new production.

'They got me to play Jet Morgan – aged eighty, or something or other,' remembers Jacobs. 'Nowadays, I only do my music programme, but I'm always happy to do something else for a change. It's lovely.'

Although most of the cast was new, the script, of course, came from Charles Chilton himself, who returned to radio writing after a very long time away. 'It came back very easily,' he says, 'and my bank manager was very pleased.'

The new script was called *Frozen in Time* and told the story of the aged Jet Morgan returning home in an antiquated spaceship. Ill equipped and very tired, the crew are pressed into service again in a new adventure in the year 2013.

David Jacobs was particularly pleased to be back. 'He was very happy to take part in it,' says David Chilton.' He was more than pleased. Of course, he remembered how they did the original. It was very different. We do it in a very different way now. He used to record it with a live orchestra – very different to how it's done now.'

'It wasn't very different,' counters Jacobs 'It was like going back in time. It was lovely.'

The new *Journey into Space* was produced as an independent radio production on behalf of the BBC – rather than *by* the BBC itself. As such, the production wasn't recorded at the BBC in any of its own studios. Instead, recording took place at the studios of Essential Music on Great Chapel Street in Soho – under the direction of Essential's Nicholas Russell-Pavier. 'Of course, we did everything in post-production,' says David Chilton. 'We just recorded the words and wove everything else round it.'

Alongside the returning David Jacobs, the rest of the entirely new cast included: Chris Moran (Lemmy), Michael Beckley (Mitch) and Alan Marriott (Doc).

Frozen in Time was broadcast as a standalone play on BBC Radio 4 on 12 April 2008. A CD release soon followed.

It was the last *Journey into Space* to be written by Charles Chilton and (to date) his last radio script for the BBC.

Reaction to the drama had been mixed, but was still deemed to have been sufficiently successful for a sequel to be quickly considered.

Both Nicholas Russell-Pavier and David Chilton were to be behind this next *Journey into Space* production. However, this time, they decided to be even bolder in their treatment of the series.

This new play would be the first *Journey into Space* not to be written by Charles Chilton (although he was involved in the production). It was also decided to cast an entirely new (and younger) actor as Jet Morgan. Much of the series' continuity was also quietly put to one side as a consequence.

The new play was to be called *The Host* and entered into production in

2009. The sixty-minute one-off drama was designed to entirely reboot the series.

'In the first one we sort of played around with harking back,' says David Chilton. 'In the second one we just made it completely modern ... The BBC was thinking and may be still thinking that they wanted it to sort of be a sort of series that could maybe still come back. You know, maybe once a year or once every two years – something like that. And they were quite keen that, rather like the *Star Trek* film updated the *Star Trek* characters, they wanted it to sort of be a revitalised version of the original. So, that meant not too many throwbacks to the original and so they were keen to get a young cast.'

David Jacobs would still have a part to play in the new drama, but no longer as Jet Morgan. Instead, he would be given a supporting rôle – just as he had in the 1950s.

'We kept David in, but as a different character,' continues Chilton. 'This time he played the alien character. He's a good actor and he can play lots of parts.'

The writer charged with taking over from Charles Chilton was experienced radio scribe Julian Simpson. 'We had some consultancy with my dad about characters and so forth,' says Chilton, 'but Julian wrote the script. I'd worked with him before on other plays that he'd done for the radio.'

The new Jet Morgan (the fourth in the part) was to be leading film and TV actor Toby Stephens, who hadn't even been born when the original trilogy finished.

'I always saw him as a sort of Jet Morgan type,' says David Chilton. 'It's actually one of the hardest things, to find our leading actors. It's easier to find character actors, than it is to find a leading actor – someone who actually convinces you that he's a hero-type. I think that it's a different type of acting, in a way. He's got that quality of sort of always being himself when he's acting. I think that's something that's sometimes quite good for a hero.'

Only David Jacobs and Alan Marriott returned from the cast of the previous year's *Frozen in Time*. Chris Pavlo was the new Lemmy and Mitch was played by Jot Davies. However, there was still one familiar voice. Charles Chilton himself stepped back in front of the microphone as announcer for the programme.

The Host was arguably a little better received than its immediate predecessor and was broadcast on 27 June 2009 on BBC Radio Four, with a subsequent CD release from BBC Audio.

'There wasn't really much explanation as to why you were suddenly with these younger updated characters,' says David Chilton. 'You just sort of completely accept it and that's kind of worked quite well. In some ways, I reckon that the second one was better than the first one.'

JOURNEY INTO SPACE

There have (so far) been no further *Journey into Space* productions following the broadcast of *The Host*. However, both David Chilton and David Jacobs remain enthusiastic about the series and (at the time of writing) another *Journey into Space* drama is something that is being actively entertained. At the moment, the concept remains in the hands of the BBC commissioning editors.

'I suppose that we'd like to do another one,' says David Chilton. 'You have to get them commissioned by the BBC, which is the problem ... If we can think of another twist they'll probably do another one. That's the nice thing about it. We sort of conceived it as maybe having guest writers – different writers writing different series. So, if we did another one, we'd most likely have another writer to do another one ... I'd quite like (noted radio writer) Mike Walker to write one ... It always surprises me that they don't do more things like that on the radio, because it is so cheap. It doesn't matter if you want to destroy the world or have an atom bomb or any scenario you can imagine. You can do it and it doesn't cost you anything ... You can do some quite radical things and you can do them very quickly.'

JOURNEY INTO SPACE: EPISODE GUIDE

1: *Operation Luna* **(1953)**
AKA *Journey to the Moon*
AKA *A Tale of the Future*
1953 Production – 18 x 30 minute episodes (approx.)
1958 Production – 13 x 30 minute episodes (approx.)
BBC Radio
Written by Charles Chilton
Producer: Charles Chilton

CAST:
Jet Morgan	Andrew Faulds *(1953 and 1958 Productions)*
Sir William Morgan	Wilfred Walter *(1953 Production)*
Mackenzie	Robert Perceval *(1953 Production)*
Lemmy	David Kossoff *(1953 Production)*
	Alfie Bass *(1958 Production)*
Mitch	Bruce Beeby *(1953 Production)*
	Don Sharp *(1953 Production)*
	David Williams *(1958 Production)*
Doc	Guy Kingsley Poynter *(1953 and 1958 Productions)*
The Time Traveller	Deryck Guyler *(1953 and 1958 Productions)*
Earth Control	John Cazabon *(1958 Production)*
London Correspondent	Alan Keith *(1958 Production)*
Uncle Hector	Duncan McIntyre *(1953 and 1958 Productions)*
'Other Actors'	Mark Baker *(1953 Production)*
	Errol McKinnon *(1953 Production)*
	Jessica Dunning *(1953 Production)*
	David Jacobs *(1953 and 1958 Productions)*
	Wyndham Milligan *(1953 Production)*

STORY:
In the year 1965, a seemingly impossible diary tells the story of the first manned journey to the moon. The purpose of the expedition was to explore the barren surface of Earth's closest neighbour. However, for Captain Jet Morgan, and the crew of the rocket ship Luna, it will take them much further than anyone could ever have predicted. It will be a journey through both space and time.

JOURNEY INTO SPACE: EPISODE GUIDE

BROADCAST:
EPISODE 1	21/09/53	
EPISODE 2	28/09/53	
EPISODE 3	05/10/53	
EPISODE 4	12/10/53	
EPISODE 5	19/10/53	26/03/58 (*Episode 1*)
EPISODE 6	26/10/53	02/04/58 (*Episode 2*)
EPISODE 7	02/11/53	09/04/58 (*Episode 3*)
EPISODE 8	09/11/53	16/04/58 (*Episode 4*)
EPISODE 9	16/11/53	23/04/58 (*Episode 5*)
EPISODE 10	23/11/53	30/04/58 (*Episode 6*)
EPISODE 11	30/11/53	07/05/58 (*Episode 7*)
EPISODE 12	07/12/53	14/05/58 (*Episode 8A*)[239]
EPISODE 13	14/12/53	14/05/58 (*Episode 8B*)[240]
EPISODE 14	21/12/53	21/05/58 (*Episode 9*)
EPISODE 15	29/12/53	28/05/58 (*Episode 10*)
EPISODE 16	05/01/54	04/06/58 (*Episode 11*)
EPISODE 17	12/01/54	11/06/58 (*Episode 12*)
EPISODE 18	19/01/54	18/06/58 (*Episode 13*)

NOTES:
In 1958 the serial was re-recorded by the BBC. This 'second production' was condensed and ran to only thirteen episodes. The material that had made up the first four episodes of the original production was cut from the second production. As such, the second production opened with episode five (retitled, episode one).

Novelised as *Journey into Space* by Charles Chilton. Published by Herbert Jenkins Ltd. in 1954.

2: *The Red Planet* (1954)
20 x 30 minute episodes (approx.)
BBC Radio
Written by Charles Chilton
Producer: Charles Chilton

CAST:

---

[239] Much of the material that had originally made up episodes twelve and thirteen in the original 1953 production, didn't appear in the second production. The scripts were heavily edited, with a number of scenes deleted altogether. The remaining material was edited together to form a new 'double-episode' omnibus. This episode was retitled to become episode 8.
[240] IBID

SERIAL THRILLERS

Jet Morgan	Andrew Faulds
Lemmy	David Kossoff
Mitch	Bruce Beeby
Doc	Guy Kingsley Poynter
Whitaker	Anthony Marriott
Mrs Barnet	Miriam Karlin
Frank Rogers *(and others)*	David Jacobs
Bill Webster *(and others)*	John Cazabon
Martha Bodie	Madi Hedd
Sam	Don Sharp
'Other parts'	Deryck Guyler

STORY:
A number of years after their mysterious lunar adventure, Jet and his team set out on a journey to explore Mars, 'the Red Planet'. Following a perilous voyage, the crew discovers that the planet is not quite as lifeless as they had assumed, and they embark upon their most dangerous mission yet. On the surface of the planet Mars something is watching and waiting – ready to attack the Earth.

BROADCAST:

EPISODE 1	06/09/54	EPISODE 11	15/11/54
EPISODE 2	13/09/54	EPISODE 12	22/11/54
EPISODE 3	20/09/54	EPISODE 13	29/11/54
EPISODE 4	27/09/54	EPISODE 14	06/12/54
EPISODE 5	04/10/54	EPISODE 15	13/12/54
EPISODE 6	11/10/54	EPISODE 16	20/12/54
EPISODE 7	18/10/54	EPISODE 17	27/12/54
EPISODE 8	25/10/54	EPISODE 18	03/01/55
EPISODE 9	01/11/54	EPISODE 19	10/01/55
EPISODE 10	08/11/54	EPISODE 20	17/01/55

NOTES:
Novelised as *The Red Planet* by Charles Chilton. Published by Herbert Jenkins Ltd. in 1956.

3: *The World in Peril* (1955)
20 x 30 minute episodes (approx.)
BBC Radio
Written by Charles Chilton
Producer: Charles Chilton
CAST:

JOURNEY INTO SPACE: EPISODE GUIDE

Jet Morgan	Andrew Faulds
Lemmy	Alfie Bass
Mitch	Don Sharp
Doc	Guy Kingsley Poynter
Frank Rogers (and others)	David Jacobs
Jenkins	John Cazabon
Jack Evans	Alan Tilvern
Mr Moore	Fred Yule
Paddy Flynn	Pat Campbell

STORY:
Earth is under the threat of an invasion from space and only Jet and his friends can stop it. However, with enemies all around, they can trust no one, and the alien menace approaches ever closer.

BROADCAST:

EPISODE 1	26/09/55	EPISODE 11	05/12/55
EPISODE 2	03/10/55	EPISODE 12	12/12/55
EPISODE 3	10/10/55	EPISODE 13	19/12/55
EPISODE 4	17/10/55	EPISODE 14	26/12/55
EPISODE 5	24/10/55	EPISODE 15	02/01/56
EPISODE 6	31/10/55	EPISODE 16	09/01/56
EPISODE 7	07/11/55	EPISODE 17	16/01/56
EPISODE 8	14/11/55	EPISODE 18	23/01/56
EPISODE 9	21/11/55	EPISODE 19	30/01/56
EPISODE 10	28/11/55	EPISODE 20	06/02/56

NOTES
Novelised as *The World in Peril* by Charles Chilton. Published by Herbert Jenkins Ltd. in 1960.

4: *The Return from Mars* (1981)
90 minutes episodes (approx.)
BBC Radio
Written by Charles Chilton
Producer: Glyn Dearman

CAST:

Jet Morgan	John Pullen
Lemmy	Anthony Hall
Mitch	Nigel Graham
Doc	Ed Bishop

SERIAL THRILLERS

Cassia	Elizabeth Proud
Nichols	Patrick Barr
Countdown voice	David Bradshawe
Talian	Graham Faulkner
Controller	Stephen Garlick
Junior officer	John McAndrew
Sotteer	Sion Probert
Harry	Christopher Scott
Supervisor	John Webb
Announcer	Peter Donaldson

STORY:
After more then three decades lost in space, the crew of the space ship Discover finally returns to Earth, led by their Captain – Jet Morgan.

BROADCAST:
SPECIAL   07/03/81

5: *Frozen in Time* (2008)
60 minutes episodes (approx.)
BBC Radio
Written by Charles Chilton
Producers: Nicholas Russell-Pavier and David Chilton

CAST:

Jet Morgan	David Jacobs
Lemmy	Chris Moran
Mitch	Michael Beckley
Doc	Alan Marriott
Astrid	Emma Fielding
Jensen	Stephen Hogan
Radio Operator	Kate Harbour

STORY:
A malfunction has left the crew of the Ares sleeping in suspended animation, piloted through the depths of space by the ageing Captain Jet Morgan. Now in the year 2013, the crew finally reawakens. They are low on fuel and hopelessly ill equipped. However, when the ship receives a SOS call from Mars, the old friends are called into service once more.

BROADCAST:
SPECIAL   12/04/08

6: *The Host* (2009)
60 minutes episodes (approx.)
BBC Radio
Written by Julian Simpson
Producer: Nicholas Russell-Pavier

CAST:
Jet Morgan	Toby Stephens
Lemmy	Chris Pavlo
Mitch	Jot Davies
Doc	Alan Marriott
The Host	David Jacobs
Edie	Jana Carpenter
J J Andreev	Basher Savage
Announcer	Charles Chilton

STORY:
In answer to an intergalactic distress call, Jet Morgan and his crew board a seemingly desolate space freighter. On board, they discover a semi-sentient entity living inside the ship's computer. It is the 'Host' and it could threaten the very future of mankind itself.

BROADCAST:
SPECIAL   27/06/09

APPENDIX A: PAUL TEMPLE ARCHIVE HOLDINGS

CBC = Canadian Broadcasting Corporation
ABC = Australian Broadcasting Commission
Abr. = Abridged

ALL RECORDINGS ARE HELD BY THE BBC
(Except for a CBC recording of *Send for Paul Temple*, which is stored by CBC in Vancouver, and *Paul Temple and the Vandyke Affair*, which is stored by the British Library)

1: Send for Paul Temple
Episodes: 8
1st Recording: April 8th 1938
2nd Recording: April xx 1939 ABC
3rd Recording: May 31st 1940 CBC
4th Recording: October 13th 1941 (Abr.)
Archive Holdings: Episode 6 of 1st Recording: & Complete 3rd Recording

2: Paul Temple and the Front Page Men
Episodes: 8
1st Recording: November 2nd 1938
2nd Recording: xx xx 1942 (Abr.)
Archive Holdings: Episode 8 of 1st Recording

3: News of Paul Temple
Episodes: 6
1st Recording: November 13th 1939
2nd Recording: July 5th 1944 (Abr.)
Archive Holdings: NONE

4: Paul Temple Intervenes
Episodes: 8
1st Recording: October 30th 1942
Archive Holdings: Complete 1st Recording

APPENDIX A: PAUL TEMPLE ARCHIVE HOLDINGS

5: Send for Paul Temple Again
Episodes: 8
1st Recording: September 13th 1945
Archive Holdings: NONE

6: A Case For Paul Temple
Episodes: 8
1st Recording: February 7th 1946
2nd Recording: August 24th 2011
Archive Holdings: Complete 2nd Recording

7: Paul Temple and the Gregory Affair
Episodes: 10
1st Recording: October 17th 1946
2nd Recording: July 3rd 2013
Archive Holdings: Complete 2nd Recording

8: Paul Temple and Steve
Episodes: 8
1st Recording: March 30th 1947
2nd Recording: June 11th 2010
Archive Holdings: Complete 2nd Recording

9: Mr And Mrs Paul Temple
Episodes: 1
1st Recording: November 23rd 1947
Archive Holdings: NONE

10: Paul Temple and the Sullivan Mystery
Episodes: 8
1st Recording: December 1st 1947
2nd Recording: May 27th 2006
Archive Holdings: Complete 2nd Recording

11: Paul Temple and the Curzon Case
Episodes: 8
1st Recording: December 7th 1948
Archive Holdings: NONE

12: Paul Temple and the Madison Mystery
Episodes: 8
1st Recording: October 12th 1949
2nd Recording: June 20th 1955
3rd Recording: May 16th 2008
Archive Holdings: Complete 3rd Recording

13: The Night of the Twenty-Seventh
Episodes: 1
1st Recording: December 27th 1949
Archive Holdings: NONE

14: Paul Temple and the Vandyke Affair
Episodes: 8
1st Recording: October 31st 1950
2nd Recording: January 1st 1959
Archive Holdings: Complete 1st Recording & Complete 2nd Recording

15: Paul Temple and the Jonathan Mystery
Episodes: 8
1st Recording: May 10th 1951
2nd Recording: October 14th 1963
Archive Holdings: Extract from 1st Recording[241] & Complete 2nd Recording

16: Paul Temple and Steve Again
Episodes: 1
1st Recording: April 8th 1953
Archive Holdings: NONE

17: Paul Temple and the Gilbert Case
Episodes: 8
1st Recording: March 29th 1954
2nd Recording: November 22nd 1959
Archive Holdings: Complete 1st Recording & Complete 2nd Recording

18: Paul Temple and the Lawrence Affair
Episodes: 8
1st Recording: April 11th 1956
Archive Holdings: Complete 1st Recording

---

[241] 2' 11" Extract from Episode 8 (28/06/51)

APPENDIX A: PAUL TEMPLE ARCHIVE HOLDINGS

19: Paul Temple and the Spencer Affair
Episodes: 8
1st Recording: November 13th 1957
Archive Holdings: Complete 1st Recording

20: Paul Temple and the Conrad Case
Episodes: 8
1st Recording: March 2nd 1959
Archive Holdings: Complete 1st Recording

21: Paul Temple and the Margo Mystery
Episodes: 8
1st Recording: January 1st 1961
Archive Holdings: Complete 1st Recording

22: Paul Temple and the Geneva Mystery
Episodes: 6
1st Recording: April 11th 1965
Archive Holdings: Complete 1st Recording

23: Paul Temple and the Alex Affair
Episodes: 8
1st Recording: February 26th 1968
Archive Holdings: Complete 1st Recording

APPENDIX B
PAUL TEMPLE SERIALS ISSUED FOR INTERNATIONAL SYNDICATION (1946-1970)

Original BBC Transcription Service Paperwork from the 1940s and 1950s is very rare. What follows is a list of all confirmed *Paul Temple* recordings distributed for international sale by the BBC Transcription Service from 1946 onwards. Earlier serials may also have been copied by the service[242], but no documented evidence exists to confirm this. The following are the only absolutely 'confirmed' *Paul Temple* serials to have been sold abroad. The Transcription Services own catalogue reference is listed where known.

Paul Temple and the Gregory Affair
Episodes: 10
First Broadcast: October 17th 1946
BBC Cat. Number: Unknown
Archive Holdings: MISSING

Paul Temple and Steve
Episodes: 8
First Broadcast: March 30th 1947
BBC Cat. Number: Unknown
Archive Holdings: MISSING

Paul Temple and the Sullivan Mystery
Episodes: 8
First Broadcast: December 1st 1947
BBC Cat. Number: Unknown
Archive Holdings: MISSING

---

[242] There is some evidence to suggest that the 1942 serial *Paul Temple Intervenes* may possibly have been distributed at some point prior to 1946, but there is no documented record of this.

APPENDIX B: PAUL TEMPLE SYNDICATION

Paul Temple and the Curzon Case
Episodes: 8
First Broadcast: December 7th 1948
BBC Cat. Number: Unknown
Archive Holdings: MISSING

Paul Temple and the Madison Mystery
Episodes: 8
First Broadcast: October 12th 1949
BBC Cat. Number: Unknown
Archive Holdings: MISSING

Paul Temple and the Vandyke Affair
Episodes: 8
First Broadcast: October 31st 1950
BBC Cat. Number: Unknown
Archive Holdings: Held by the British Library

Paul Temple and the Jonathan Mystery
Episodes: 8
First Broadcast: May 10th 1951
BBC Cat. Number: Unknown
Archive Holdings: MISSING

Paul Temple and the Gilbert Case
Episodes: 8
First Broadcast: March 29th 1954
BBC Cat. Number: CN1114001
Archive Holdings: Held by BBC Sound Archives

Paul Temple and the Lawrence Affair
Episodes: 8
First Broadcast: April 11th 1956
BBC Cat. Number: CN1240001
Archive Holdings: Held by BBC Sound Archives

Paul Temple and the Spencer Affair
Episodes: 8
First Broadcast: November 13th 1957
BBC Cat. Number: CN1055001
Archive Holdings: Held by BBC Sound Archives

Paul Temple and the Vandyke Affair *(2nd Production)*
Episodes: 8
First Broadcast: January 1st 1959
BBC Cat. Number: CN0731001
Archive Holdings: Held by BBC Sound Archives

Paul Temple and the Conrad Case
Episodes: 8
First Broadcast: March 2nd 1959
BBC Cat. Number: CN0803001
Archive Holdings: Held by BBC Sound Archives

Paul Temple and the Margo Mystery
Episodes: 8
First Broadcast: January 1st 1961
BBC Cat. Number: CN1000001
Archive Holdings: Held by BBC Sound Archives

Paul Temple and the Jonathan Mystery *(2nd Production)*
Episodes: 8
First Broadcast: October 14th 1963
BBC Cat. Number: CN0081001
Archive Holdings: Held by BBC Sound Archives

Paul Temple and the Geneva Mystery
Episodes: 6
First Broadcast: April 11th 1965
BBC Cat. Number: CN0377001
Archive Holdings: Held by BBC Sound Archives

Paul Temple and the Alex Affair
Episodes: 8
First Broadcast: February 26th 1968
BBC Cat. Number: CN0889001
Archive Holdings: Held by BBC Sound Archives

APPENDIX C
DICK BARTON
ARCHIVE HOLDINGS

Recordings: BBC Archives, NFSA (National Film and Sound Archives) Australia and Private Collections

1: 1.1 Dick Barton and the Secret Weapon
Archive Holdings: Complete 10-Part BBC Recording (1972) + Complete 20-Part Australian Recording

2: 1.2 Dick Barton and the Paris Adventure
Archive Holdings: Complete 20-Part Australian Recording

3: 1.3 Dick Barton and the Cabatolin Diamonds
Archive Holdings: Complete 20-Part Australian Recording

4: 1.4 Dick Barton in South America
Archive Holdings: Episodes 1-12 of 20-Part Australian Recording

5: 1.5 Dick Barton and the Smugglers
Archive Holdings: Episode 20 of BBC Recording + Episodes 3-20 of 20-Part Australian Recording

6: 1.6 Dick Barton and the Smash and Grab Raiders
Archive Holdings: Complete 20-Part Australian Recording

7: 1.7 Dick Barton and the Tibetan Adventure
Archive Holdings: Complete 20-Part Australian Recording

8: 1.8 Dick Barton and the Canadian Adventure
Archive Holdings: Episodes 1-4 + 7-18 of 18-Part Australian Recording

9: 1.9 Dick Barton and the Affair of The Black Panther
Archive Holdings: Complete 19-Part Australian Recording

10: 2.1 Dick Barton and the Vulture
Archive Holdings: Complete 20-Part Australian Recording

11: 2.2 Dick Barton and the Production Report
Archive Holdings: Episodes 1-19 of 20-Part Australian Recording

12: 2.3 Dick Barton and the Bonazio Gang
Archive Holdings: Extract from Episode 20 of BBC Recording + Episodes 2-20 of 20-Part Australian Recording

13: 2.4 Dick Barton and the Li-Chang Adventure
Archive Holdings: Complete Abridged 19-Part Australian Recording

14: 2.5 Dick Barton and the Case of Conrad Ruda
Archive Holdings: Complete 20-Part Australian Recording

15: 2.6 Dick Barton and the Jewel Thieves
Archive Holdings: Complete Extended 25-Part Australian Recording

16: 2.7 Dick Barton and the Firefly Adventure
Archive Holdings: Complete Extended 16-Part Australian Recording

17: 3.1 Dick Barton and the J B Case
Archive Holdings: Complete Extended 22-Part Australian Recording

18: 3.2 *Untitled Serial*
Archive Holdings: 01' 35" Extract from Episode 11 (BBC) + Episodes 1-18 of 20-Part Australian Recording

19: 3.3 Dick Barton and the Secret Formula
Archive Holdings: Missing

20: 3.4 Dick Barton and the Voice
Archive Holdings: 03' 20" Extract from Episode 14 of BBC Recording

21: 3.5 Dick Barton and Jordan's Folly
Archive Holdings: Missing

22: 3.6 *Untitled Serial*
Archive Holdings: Missing

23: 3.7 Dick Barton and the Betts Plan
Archive Holdings: Episode 13 of BBC Recording + 01' 48" Extract from Episode 15 of BBC Recording

APPENDIX C: DICK BARTON ARCHIVE HOLDINGS

24: 4.1 Dick Barton and the Vallonian Adventure
Archive Holdings: Missing

25: 4.2 Dick Barton and the Colonel's Cavemen
Archive Holdings: Missing

26: 4.3 Dick Barton and the Black Rock
Archive Holdings: Missing

27: 4.4 Dick Barton and the House of Windows
Archive Holdings: Missing

UNNUMBERED
The Night of The 27th (Christmas Special)
Archive Holdings: Missing

28: 4.5 *Untitled Serial*
Archive Holdings: Missing

29: 4.6 *Untitled Serial*
Archive Holdings: Missing

30: 4.7 Dick Barton and the Big Fight Racket
Archive Holdings: Missing

31: 4.8 Dick Barton and the Lucky Gordon Affair
Archive Holdings: Missing

32: 5.1 Dick Barton and the SS Golden Main Story
Archive Holdings: Missing

33: 5.2 *Untitle Serial*
Archive Holdings: Missing

34: 5.3 Dick Barton and the Bridge
Archive Holdings: Missing

35: 5.4 *Untitled Serial*
Archive Holdings: Missing

36: 5.5 *Untitled Serial*
Archive Holdings: Missing

SERIAL THRILLERS

37: 5.6 Dick Barton and the Green Triangle Gang
Archive Holdings: Missing

38: 5.7 Dick Barton and the Trail of The Rocket
Archive Holdings: Episode 13 of BBC Recording (+ 2013 Remake)

APPENDIX D
DICK BARTON:
THE ARP RECORDINGS

The following is a list of the internationally distributed re-recordings of *Dick Barton – Special Agent*, produced by Australasian Radio Productions (ARP) in association with the BBC, between 1948 and 1950. These international recordings were distributed as transcriptions for broadcast in New Zealand, Australia and South Africa.

The first transmission dates for Australia are listed where possible. However, information is complicated by the regional broadcasting structure in Australia, which makes it difficult to pin-point the first national broadcast for each episode. A small amount of maths based on a calendar from 1949, enables us to deduce when certain episodes must have aired. At some stage, some Australian networks stopped broadcasting four episodes a week and started to change the scheduling to around five episodes a week. At this point it becomes almost impossible to follow exactly when each episode was broadcast. There's just too little information to go on. Without more paperwork, this is all that can be confirmed.

1: Dick Barton and the Secret Weapon
EPISODES: 20
SERIES COUNT: 1-20
AUSTRALIAN BROADCASTS: 07/02/49 - 10/03/49

2: Dick Barton and the Paris Adventure
EPISODES: 20
SERIES COUNT: 21-40
AUSTRALIAN BROADCASTS: 14/03/49 - 14/04/49

3: Dick Barton and the Case of the Synthetic Diamond Smugglers[243]
EPISODES: 20
SERIES COUNT: 41-60
AUSTRALIAN BROADCASTS: 18/04/49 - 19/05/49

---

[243] *Dick Barton and the Case of the Synthetic Diamond Smugglers* is a re-titled recording of *Dick Barton and the Cabatolin Diamonds*(1946)

4: Dick Barton and the Godstone of Maribana[244]
EPISODES: 20
SERIES COUNT: 61-80
AUSTRALIAN BROADCASTS: 23/05/49 - 23/06/49

5: Dick Barton and the Smugglers
EPISODES: 20
SERIES COUNT: 81-100
AUSTRALIAN BROADCASTS: 27/06/49 - xx/07/49

6: Dick Barton and the Smash and Grab Raiders
EPISODES: 20
SERIES COUNT: 101-120
AUSTRALIAN BROADCASTS: xx/xx/49 - xx/09/49

7: Dick Barton and the Tibetan Adventure
EPISODES: 20
SERIES COUNT: 121-140
AUSTRALIAN BROADCASTS: 12/09/49 - 13/10/49

8: Dick Barton and the Canadian Adventure
EPISODES: 18
SERIES COUNT: 141-158
AUSTRALIAN BROADCASTS: xx/10/49 - xx/11/49

9: Dick Barton and the Affair of The Black Panther
EPISODES: 19
SERIES COUNT: 159-177
AUSTRALIAN BROADCASTS: 03/11/49 - xx/xx/49

10: Dick Barton and the Vulture
EPISODES: 20
SERIES COUNT: 178-197
AUSTRALIAN BROADCASTS: unknown - unknown

11: Dick Barton and the Production Report
EPISODES: 20
SERIES COUNT: 198-217
AUSTRALIAN BROADCASTS: unknown - unknown

---

[244] *Dick Barton and the Godstone of Maribana* is a re-titled recording of *Dick Barton in South America* (1946/7).

APPENDIX D: DICK BARTON: THE ARP RECORDINGS

12: Dick Barton and the Bonazio Gang
EPISODES: 20
SERIES COUNT: 218-237
AUSTRALIAN BROADCASTS: unknown - unknown

13: Dick Barton and the Li-Chang Adventure
EPISODES: 19[245]
SERIES COUNT: 238-256
AUSTRALIAN BROADCASTS: unknown - unknown

14: Dick Barton and the Curse of the Conrad Ruda
EPISODES: 20
SERIES COUNT: 257-276
AUSTRALIAN BROADCASTS: unknown - unknown

15: Dick Barton and the Jewel Thieves
EPISODES: 26[246]
SERIES COUNT: 277-302
AUSTRALIAN BROADCASTS: unknown - unknown

16: Dick Barton and the Firefly Adventure
EPISODES: 16[247]
SERIES COUNT: 303-318
AUSTRALIAN BROADCASTS: unknown - unknown

17: Dick Barton and the J B Case
EPISODES: 22[248]
SERIES COUNT: 319-340
AUSTRALIAN BROADCASTS: unknown - unknown

18: Untitled Serial
EPISODES: 20
SERIES COUNT: 341-360
AUSTRALIAN BROADCASTS: unknown - unknown

---

[245] The BBC's original 1947 production of *Dick Barton and the Li-Chang Adventure* was 23 episodes long. The scripts were abridged to form ARP's 19 part recording

[246] The BBC's original 1948 production of *Dick Barton and the Jewel Thieves* was 20 episodes long. The scripts were extended to form ARP's 26 part recording

[247] The BBC's original 1948 production of *Dick Barton and the Firefly Adventure* was 10 episodes long. The scripts were extended to form ARP's 16 part recording

[248] The BBC's original 1948 production of *Dick Barton and the J B Case* was 20 episodes long. The scripts were extended to form ARP's 22 part recording

APPENDIX E
DAN DARE –
PILOT OF THE FUTURE
EPISODE LIST

No original scripts survive for any of Radio Luxembourg's *Dan Dare* radio episodes. However, broadcast master recordings survive for two episodes and a poor-quality home recording survives of a third. In addition, detailed story synopses exist for a number of later episodes – based on notes made at the time of transmission by *Dan Dare* fan, Philip Harbottle. What follows is a complete list of all of the original episodes (as opposed to repeats) broadcast by Radio Luxembourg. Episodes for which an original recording survives, are marked out in bold/italics.

SERIES ONE

Episode 1	02/07/51	Voyage to Venus - Episode 1
Episode 2	03/07/51	Voyage to Venus - Episode 2
Episode 3	04/07/51	Voyage to Venus - Episode 3
Episode 4	05/07/51	Voyage to Venus - Episode 4
Episode 5	06/07/51	Voyage to Venus - Episode 5
Episode 6	09/07/51	Voyage to Venus - Episode 6
Episode 7	10/07/51	Voyage to Venus - Episode 7
Episode 8	11/07/51	Voyage to Venus - Episode 8
Episode 9	12/07/51	Voyage to Venus - Episode 9
Episode 10	13/07/51	Voyage to Venus - Episode 10
Episode 11	16/07/51	Voyage to Venus - Episode 11
Episode 12	17/07/51	Voyage to Venus - Episode 12
Episode 13	18/07/51	Voyage to Venus - Episode 13
Episode 14	19/07/51	Voyage to Venus - Episode 14
Episode 15	20/07/51	Voyage to Venus - Episode 15
Episode 16	23/07/51	Voyage to Venus - Episode 16
Episode 17	24/07/51	Voyage to Venus - Episode 17
Episode 18	25/07/51	Voyage to Venus - Episode 18

SERIES TWO

Episode 19	01/11/51	Serial B - Episode 1
Episode 20	02/11/51	Serial B - Episode 2
Episode 21	05/11/51	Serial B - Episode 3
Episode 22	06/11/51	Serial B - Episode 4
Episode 23	07/11/51	Serial B - Episode 5

APPENDIX E: DICK BARTON EPISODE LIST

Episode 24	08/11/51	Serial B - Episode 6
Episode 25	09/11/51	Serial B - Episode 7
Episode 26	12/11/51	Serial B - Episode 8
Episode 27	13/11/51	Serial B - Episode 9
Episode 28	14/11/51	Serial B - Episode 10
Episode 29	15/11/51	Serial B - Episode 11
Episode 30	16/11/51	Serial B - Episode 12
Episode 31	19/11/51	Serial B - Episode 13
Episode 32	20/11/51	Serial B - Episode 14
Episode 33	21/11/51	Serial B - Episode 15
Episode 34	22/11/51	Serial B - Episode 16
Episode 35	23/11/51	Serial B - Episode 17
Episode 36	26/11/51	Serial B - Episode 18
Episode 37	27/11/51	Serial B - Episode 19
Episode 38	28/11/51	Serial B - Episode 20
Episode 39	29/11/51	Serial B - Episode 21
Episode 40	30/11/51	Serial B - Episode 22
Episode 41	03/12/51	Serial B - Episode 23: The Therons Attack
Episode 42	04/12/51	Serial B - Episode 24: Fighting For Life
Episode 43	05/12/51	Serial B - Episode 25: Floating in Space
Episode 44	06/12/51	Serial B - Episode 26: The Marshall's Treachery
Episode 45	07/12/51	Serial B - Episode 27: The Glass Bubble
Episode 46	10/12/51	Serial B - Episode 28: Spaceship On Fire
Episode 47	11/12/51	Serial B - Episode 29: Certain Death
Episode 48	12/12/51	Serial B - Episode 30: The Mystery Plane
Episode 49	13/12/51	Serial B - Episode 31: The Traitors Escape
Episode 50	14/12/51	Serial B - Episode 32: Dapon Goes Back
Episode 51	17/12/51	Serial B - Episode 33: Command Cruiser Cracks Up
Episode 52	18/12/51	Serial B - Episode 34: Trapped by the Traitors
Episode 53	19/12/51	Serial B - Episode 35: The Underground Passage
Episode 54	20/12/51	Serial B - Episode 36: Dan to the Rescue
Episode 55	21/12/51	Serial B - Episode 37: Back to Earth
Episode 56	24/12/51	Serial B - Episode 38: The Plans of the Mekon
Episode 57	25/12/51	Serial B - Episode 39: Take-off from Venus
Episode 58	26/12/51	Serial B - Episode 40: Colonel Dare Dead?
Episode 59	27/12/51	Serial B - Episode 41: Aunt Anastasia and the Secret
Episode 60	28/12/51	Serial B - Episode 42: Welcome home Dan!
Episode 61	31/12/51	Serial B - Episode 43: The New Plan
Episode 62	01/01/52	Serial B - Episode 44: Off to Venus
Episode 63	02/01/52	Serial B - Episode 45: The Battle
Episode 64	03/01/52	Serial B - Episode 46: The Atlantynes (sic) Revolt
Episode 65	04/01/52	Serial B - Episode 47: Out of Control
Episode 66	07/01/52	The Ice Men of Venus - Episode 1: Trapped in Space
Episode 67	08/01/52	The Ice Men of Venus - Episode 2: The Moon Brothers
Episode 68	09/01/52	The Ice Men of Venus - Episode 3: The Floating Platform
Episode 69	10/01/52	The Ice Men of Venus - Episode 4: The Cosmic Whirlpool
Episode 70	11/01/52	The Ice Men of Venus - Episode 5: The Ice Men!
Episode 71	14/01/52	The Ice Men of Venus - Episode 6: Return of the Mekon

Episode 72	15/01/52	The Ice Men of Venus - Episode 7: Escape from the Ice Men
Episode 73	16/01/52	The Ice Men of Venus - Episode 8: Battle Against Death
Episode 74	17/01/52	The Ice Men of Venus - Episode 9: The Traitor's Trap
Episode 75	*18/01/52*	*The Ice Men of Venus - Episode 10: Sabotage*
Episode 76	*21/01/52*	*The Ice Men of Venus - Episode 11: Under Sentence of Death*
Episode 77	22/01/52	The Ice Men of Venus - Episode 12: The End of the Road
Episode 78	23/01/52	The Ice Men of Venus - Episode 13: No Way Out
Episode 79	24/01/52	The Ice Men of Venus - Episode 14: The Fury of the Mekon
Episode 80	25/01/52	The Ice Men of Venus - Episode 15: Race to Destruction
Episode 81	28/10/52	TITLE UNKNOWN
Episode 82	29/01/52	TITLE UNKNOWN
Episode 83	30/01/52	TITLE UNKNOWN
Episode 84	31/01/52	TITLE UNKNOWN
Episode 85	01/02/52	TITLE UNKNOWN
Episode 86	04/02/52	TITLE UNKNOWN
Episode 87	05/02/52	TITLE UNKNOWN
Episode 88	06/02/52	TITLE UNKNOWN
Episode 89	07/02/52	TITLE UNKNOWN
Episode 90	08/02/52	TITLE UNKNOWN
Episode 91	11/02/52	TITLE UNKNOWN
Episode 92	12/02/52	TITLE UNKNOWN
Episode 93	13/02/52	TITLE UNKNOWN
Episode 94	14/02/52	TITLE UNKNOWN
Episode 95	15/02/52	TITLE UNKNOWN
Episode 96	18/02/52	TITLE UNKNOWN
Episode 97	19/02/52	TITLE UNKNOWN
Episode 98	20/02/52	TITLE UNKNOWN
Episode 99	21/02/52	TITLE UNKNOWN
Episode 100	22/02/52	TITLE UNKNOWN
Episode 101	25/02/52	TITLE UNKNOWN
Episode 102	26/02/52	TITLE UNKNOWN
Episode 103	27/02/52	TITLE UNKNOWN
Episode 104	28/02/52	TITLE UNKNOWN
Episode 105	29/02/52	TITLE UNKNOWN
Episode 106	03/03/52	TITLE UNKNOWN
Episode 107	04/03/52	TITLE UNKNOWN
Episode 108	05/03/52	TITLE UNKNOWN
Episode 109	06/03/52	TITLE UNKNOWN
Episode 110	07/03/52	TITLE UNKNOWN
Episode 111	10/03/52	TITLE UNKNOWN
Episode 112	11/03/52	TITLE UNKNOWN
Episode 113	12/03/52	TITLE UNKNOWN
Episode 114	13/03/52	TITLE UNKNOWN
Episode 115	14/03/52	TITLE UNKNOWN
Episode 116	17/03/52	TITLE UNKNOWN
Episode 117	18/03/52	TITLE UNKNOWN
Episode 118	19/03/52	TITLE UNKNOWN
Episode 119	20/03/52	TITLE UNKNOWN

APPENDIX E: DICK BARTON EPISODE LIST

Episode 120 21/03/52 TITLE UNKNOWN
Episode 121 24/03/52 TITLE UNKNOWN
Episode 122 25/03/52 TITLE UNKNOWN
Episode 123 26/03/52 TITLE UNKNOWN
Episode 124 27/03/52 TITLE UNKNOWN
Episode 125 28/03/52 TITLE UNKNOWN
Episode 126 31/03/52 TITLE UNKNOWN
Episode 127 01/04/52 TITLE UNKNOWN
Episode 128 02/04/52 TITLE UNKNOWN
Episode 129 03/04/52 TITLE UNKNOWN
Episode 130 04/04/52 Unknown Serial - Concluding Episode
Episode 131 07/04/52 Unknown Serial - Episode 1
Episode 132 08/04/52 Unknown Serial - Episode 2
Episode 133 09/04/52 TITLE UNKNOWN
Episode 134 10/04/52 TITLE UNKNOWN
Episode 135 11/04/52 TITLE UNKNOWN
Episode 136 14/04/52 TITLE UNKNOWN
Episode 137 15/04/52 TITLE UNKNOWN
Episode 138 16/04/52 TITLE UNKNOWN
Episode 139 17/04/52 TITLE UNKNOWN
Episode 140 18/04/52 TITLE UNKNOWN
Episode 141 21/04/52 TITLE UNKNOWN
Episode 142 22/04/52 TITLE UNKNOWN
Episode 143 23/04/52 TITLE UNKNOWN
Episode 144 24/04/52 TITLE UNKNOWN
Episode 145 25/04/52 TITLE UNKNOWN
Episode 146 28/04/52 TITLE UNKNOWN
Episode 147 29/04/52 TITLE UNKNOWN
Episode 148 30/04/52 TITLE UNKNOWN
Episode 149 01/05/52 TITLE UNKNOWN
Episode 150 02/05/52 TITLE UNKNOWN
Episode 151 05/05/52 TITLE UNKNOWN
Episode 152 06/05/52 TITLE UNKNOWN
Episode 153 07/05/52 TITLE UNKNOWN
Episode 154 08/05/52 TITLE UNKNOWN
Episode 155 09/05/52 TITLE UNKNOWN
Episode 156 12/05/52 TITLE UNKNOWN
Episode 157 13/05/52 TITLE UNKNOWN
Episode 158 14/05/52 TITLE UNKNOWN
Episode 159 15/05/52 TITLE UNKNOWN
Episode 160 16/05/52 TITLE UNKNOWN
Episode 161 19/05/52 TITLE UNKNOWN
Episode 162 20/05/52 TITLE UNKNOWN
Episode 163 21/05/52 TITLE UNKNOWN
Episode 164 22/05/52 TITLE UNKNOWN
Episode 165 23/05/52 TITLE UNKNOWN
Episode 166 26/05/52 TITLE UNKNOWN
Episode 167 27/05/52 TITLE UNKNOWN

Episode 168	28/05/52	TITLE UNKNOWN
Episode 169	29/05/52	TITLE UNKNOWN
Episode 170	30/05/52	TITLE UNKNOWN
Episode 171	02/06/52	TITLE UNKNOWN
Episode 172	03/06/52	TITLE UNKNOWN
Episode 173	04/06/52	TITLE UNKNOWN
Episode 174	05/06/52	TITLE UNKNOWN
Episode 175	06/06/52	TITLE UNKNOWN
Episode 176	09/06/52	TITLE UNKNOWN
Episode 177	10/06/52	TITLE UNKNOWN
Episode 178	11/06/52	TITLE UNKNOWN
Episode 179	12/06/52	TITLE UNKNOWN
Episode 180	13/06/52	TITLE UNKNOWN
Episode 181	16/06/52	TITLE UNKNOWN
Episode 182	17/06/52	TITLE UNKNOWN
Episode 183	18/06/52	TITLE UNKNOWN
Episode 184	19/06/52	TITLE UNKNOWN
Episode 185	20/06/52	TITLE UNKNOWN
Episode 186	23/06/52	TITLE UNKNOWN
Episode 187	24/06/52	TITLE UNKNOWN
Episode 188	25/06/52	TITLE UNKNOWN
Episode 189	26/06/52	TITLE UNKNOWN
Episode 190	27/06/52	TITLE UNKNOWN
Episode 191	30/06/52	TITLE UNKNOWN
Episode 192	01/07/52	TITLE UNKNOWN
Episode 193	02/07/52	TITLE UNKNOWN
Episode 194	03/07/52	TITLE UNKNOWN
Episode 195	04/07/52	TITLE UNKNOWN
Episode 196	07/07/52	TITLE UNKNOWN
Episode 197	08/07/52	TITLE UNKNOWN
Episode 198	09/07/52	TITLE UNKNOWN
Episode 199	10/07/52	TITLE UNKNOWN
Episode 200	11/07/52	TITLE UNKNOWN
Episode 201	14/07/52	TITLE UNKNOWN
Episode 202	15/07/52	TITLE UNKNOWN
Episode 203	16/07/52	TITLE UNKNOWN
Episode 204	17/07/52	TITLE UNKNOWN
Episode 205	18/07/52	TITLE UNKNOWN
Episode 206	21/07/52	TITLE UNKNOWN
Episode 207	22/07/52	TITLE UNKNOWN
Episode 208	23/07/52	TITLE UNKNOWN
Episode 209	24/07/52	TITLE UNKNOWN
Episode 210	25/07/52	TITLE UNKNOWN
Episode 211	28/07/52	TITLE UNKNOWN
Episode 212	29/07/52	TITLE UNKNOWN
Episode 213	30/07/52	TITLE UNKNOWN
Episode 214	31/07/52	TITLE UNKNOWN
Episode 215	01/08/52	TITLE UNKNOWN

APPENDIX E: DICK BARTON EPISODE LIST

Episode 216 04/08/52 TITLE UNKNOWN
Episode 217 05/08/52 TITLE UNKNOWN
Episode 218 06/08/52 TITLE UNKNOWN
Episode 219 07/08/52 TITLE UNKNOWN
Episode 220 08/08/52 TITLE UNKNOWN
Episode 221 11/08/52 TITLE UNKNOWN
Episode 222 12/08/52 TITLE UNKNOWN
Episode 223 13/08/52 TITLE UNKNOWN
Episode 224 14/08/52 TITLE UNKNOWN
Episode 225 15/08/52 TITLE UNKNOWN
Episode 226 18/08/52 TITLE UNKNOWN
Episode 227 19/08/52 TITLE UNKNOWN
Episode 228 20/08/52 TITLE UNKNOWN
Episode 229 21/08/52 TITLE UNKNOWN
Episode 230 22/08/52 TITLE UNKNOWN
Episode 231 25/08/52 TITLE UNKNOWN
Episode 232 26/08/52 TITLE UNKNOWN
Episode 233 27/08/52 TITLE UNKNOWN
Episode 234 28/08/52 TITLE UNKNOWN
Episode 235 29/08/52 Unknown Serial - Concluding Episode
Episode 236 01/09/52 The Mankton Menace - Episode 1
Episode 237 02/09/52 The Mankton Menace - Episode 2
Episode 238 03/09/52 The Mankton Menace - Episode 3
Episode 239 04/09/52 The Mankton Menace - Episode 4
Episode 240 05/09/52 The Mankton Menace - Episode 5
Episode 241 08/09/52 The Mankton Menace - Episode 6
Episode 242 09/09/52 The Mankton Menace - Episode 7
Episode 243 10/09/52 The Mankton Menace - Episode 8
Episode 244 11/09/52 The Mankton Menace - Episode 9
Episode 245 12/09/52 The Mankton Menace - Episode 10
Episode 246 15/09/52 The Mankton Menace - Episode 11
Episode 247 16/09/52 The Mankton Menace - Episode 12
Episode 248 17/09/52 The Mankton Menace - Episode 13
Episode 249 18/09/52 The Mankton Menace - Episode 14
Episode 250 19/09/52 The Mankton Menace - Episode 15
Episode 251 22/09/52 The Mankton Menace - Episode 16
Episode 252 23/09/52 The Mankton Menace - Episode 17
Episode 253 24/09/52 The Mankton Menace - Episode 18
Episode 254 25/09/52 The Mankton Menace - Episode 19
Episode 255 26/09/52 The Mankton Menace - Episode 20
Episode 256 29/09/52 The Mankton Menace - Episode 21
Episode 257 30/09/52 The Mankton Menace - Episode 22
Episode 258 01/10/52 The Mankton Menace - Episode 23
Episode 259 02/10/52 The Mankton Menace - Episode 24
Episode 260 03/10/52 The Mankton Menace - Episode 25
Episode 261 06/10/52 Space Pirates - Episode 1
Episode 262 07/10/52 Space Pirates - Episode 2
Episode 263 08/10/52 Space Pirates - Episode 3

SERIAL THRILLERS

Episode 264　09/10/52　Space Pirates - Episode 4
Episode 265　10/10/52　Space Pirates - Episode 5
Episode 266　13/10/52　Space Pirates - Episode 6
Episode 267　14/10/52　Space Pirates - Episode 7
Episode 268　15/10/52　Space Pirates - Episode 8
Episode 269　16/10/52　Space Pirates - Episode 9
Episode 270　17/10/52　Space Pirates - Episode 10
Episode 271　20/10/52　Space Pirates - Episode 11
Episode 272　21/10/52　Space Pirates - Episode 12
Episode 273　22/10/52　Space Pirates - Episode 13
Episode 274　23/10/52　Space Pirates - Episode 14
Episode 275　24/10/52　Space Pirates - Episode 15
Episode 276　27/10/52　Space Pirates - Episode 16
Episode 277　28/10/52　Space Pirates - Episode 17
Episode 278　29/10/52　Space Pirates - Episode 18
Episode 279　30/10/52　Space Pirates - Episode 19
Episode 280　31/10/52　Space Pirates - Episode 20
Episode 281　03/11/52　Space Pirates - Episode 21
Episode 282　04/11/52　Space Pirates - Episode 22
Episode 283　05/11/52　Space Pirates - Episode 23
Episode 284　06/11/52　Space Pirates - Episode 24
Episode 285　07/11/52　Space Pirates - Episode 25
Episode 286　10/11/52　Space Pirates - Episode 26
Episode 287　11/11/52　Space Pirates - Episode 27
Episode 288　12/11/52　Space Pirates - Episode 28
Episode 289　13/11/52　Space Pirates - Episode 29
Episode 290　14/11/52　Space Pirates - Episode 30
Episode 291　17/11/52　Invaders from Space - Episode 1
Episode 292　18/11/52　Invaders from Space - Episode 2
Episode 293　19/11/52　Invaders from Space - Episode 3
Episode 294　20/11/52　Invaders from Space - Episode 4
Episode 295　21/11/52　Invaders from Space - Episode 5
Episode 296　24/11/52　Invaders from Space - Episode 6
Episode 297　25/11/52　Invaders from Space - Episode 7
Episode 298　26/11/52　Invaders from Space - Episode 8
Episode 299　27/11/52　Invaders from Space - Episode 9
Episode 300　28/11/52　Invaders from Space - Episode 10
Episode 301　01/12/52　Invaders from Space - Episode 11
Episode 302　02/12/52　Invaders from Space - Episode 12
Episode 303　03/12/52　Invaders from Space - Episode 13
Episode 304　04/12/52　Invaders from Space - Episode 14
Episode 305　05/12/52　Invaders from Space - Episode 15
Episode 306　08/12/52　Invaders from Space - Episode 16
Episode 307　09/12/52　Invaders from Space - Episode 17
Episode 308　10/12/52　Invaders from Space - Episode 18
Episode 309　11/12/52　Invaders from Space - Episode 19
Episode 310　12/12/52　Invaders from Space - Episode 20
Episode 311　15/12/52　Invaders from Space - Episode 21

APPENDIX E: DICK BARTON EPISODE LIST

Episode 312	16/12/52	Invaders from Space - Episode 22
Episode 313	17/12/52	Invaders from Space - Episode 23
Episode 314	18/12/52	Invaders from Space - Episode 24
Episode 315	19/12/52	Invaders from Space - Episode 25
Episode 316	22/12/52	Invaders from Space - Episode 26
Episode 317	23/12/52	Invaders from Space - Episode 27
Episode 318	24/12/52	Invaders from Space - Episode 28
Episode 319	25/12/52	Invaders from Space - Episode 29
Episode 320	26/12/52	Invaders from Space - Episode 30
Episode 321	29/12/52	Invaders from Space - Episode 31
Episode 322	30/12/52	Invaders from Space - Episode 32
Episode 323	31/12/52	Invaders from Space - Episode 33
Episode 324	01/01/53	Invaders from Space - Episode 34
Episode 325	02/01/53	Invaders from Space - Episode 35
Episode 326	05/01/53	The Lost World on Mars - Episode 1
Episode 327	06/01/53	The Lost World on Mars - Episode 2
Episode 328	07/01/53	The Lost World on Mars - Episode 3
Episode 329	08/01/53	The Lost World on Mars - Episode 4
Episode 330	09/01/53	The Lost World on Mars - Episode 5
Episode 331	12/01/53	The Lost World on Mars - Episode 6
Episode 332	13/01/53	The Lost World on Mars - Episode 7
Episode 333	14/01/53	The Lost World on Mars - Episode 8
Episode 334	15/01/53	The Lost World on Mars - Episode 9
Episode 335	16/01/53	The Lost World on Mars - Episode 10
Episode 336	19/01/53	The Lost World on Mars - Episode 11
Episode 337	20/01/53	The Lost World on Mars - Episode 12
Episode 338	21/01/53	The Lost World on Mars - Episode 13
Episode 339	22/01/53	The Lost World on Mars - Episode 14
Episode 340	23/01/53	The Lost World on Mars - Episode 15
Episode 341	26/01/53	The Lost World on Mars - Episode 16
Episode 342	27/01/53	The Lost World on Mars - Episode 17
Episode 343	28/01/53	The Lost World on Mars - Episode 18
Episode 344	29/01/53	The Lost World on Mars - Episode 19
Episode 345	30/01/53	The Lost World on Mars - Episode 20
Episode 346	02/02/53	The Lost World on Mars - Episode 21
Episode 347	03/02/53	The Lost World on Mars - Episode 22
Episode 348	04/02/53	The Lost World on Mars - Episode 23
Episode 349	05/02/53	The Lost World on Mars - Episode 24
Episode 350	06/02/53	The Lost World on Mars - Episode 25
Episode 351	09/02/53	The Lost World on Mars - Episode 26
Episode 352	10/02/53	The Lost World on Mars - Episode 27
Episode 353	11/02/53	The Lost World on Mars - Episode 28
Episode 354	12/02/53	The Lost World on Mars - Episode 29
Episode 355	13/02/53	The Lost World on Mars - Episode 30
Episode 356	16/02/53	The Lost World on Mars - Episode 31
Episode 357	17/02/53	The Lost World on Mars - Episode 32
Episode 358	18/02/53	The Lost World on Mars - Episode 33
Episode 359	19/02/53	The Lost World on Mars - Episode 34

Episode 360	20/02/53	The Lost World on Mars - Episode 35
Episode 361	23/02/53	The Lost World on Mars - Episode 36
Episode 362	24/02/53	The Lost World on Mars - Episode 37
Episode 363	25/02/53	The Lost World on Mars - Episode 38
Episode 364	26/02/53	The Lost World on Mars - Episode 39
Episode 365	27/02/53	The Lost World on Mars - Episode 40
Episode 365	02/03/53	The Lost World on Mars - Episode 40 *(Repeat)*
Episode 366	03/03/53	The Lost World on Mars - Episode 41
Episode 367	04/03/53	The Lost World on Mars - Episode 42
Episode 368	05/03/53	The Lost World on Mars - Episode 43
Episode 369	06/03/53	The Lost World on Mars - Episode 44
Episode 370	09/03/53	The Lost World on Mars - Episode 45
Episode 371	10/03/53	The Lost World on Mars - Episode 46
Episode 372	11/03/53	The Lost World on Mars - Episode 47
Episode 373	12/03/53	The Lost World on Mars - Episode 48
Episode 374	13/03/53	The Lost World on Mars - Episode 49
Episode 375	16/03/53	The Lost World on Mars - Episode 50
Episode 376	17/03/53	The Lost World on Mars - Episode 51
Episode 377	18/03/53	The Lost World on Mars - Episode 52
Episode 378	***19/03/53***	***The Lost World on Mars - Episode 53***
Episode 379	20/03/53	The Lost World on Mars - Episode 54
Episode 380	23/03/53	The Lost World on Mars - Episode 55
Episode 381	24/03/53	The Lost World on Mars - Episode 56
Episode 382	25/03/53	The Lost World on Mars - Episode 57
Episode 383	26/03/53	The Lost World on Mars - Episode 58
Episode 384	27/03/53	The Lost World on Mars - Episode 59
Episode 385	30/03/53	The Lost World on Mars - Episode 60
Episode 386	31/03/53	The Lost World on Mars - Episode 61
Episode 387	01/04/53	The Lost World on Mars - Episode 62
Episode 388	02/04/53	The Lost World on Mars - Episode 63
Episode 389	03/04/53	The Lost World on Mars - Episode 64
Episode 390	06/04/53	Revolt on Mars - Episode 1
Episode 391	07/04/53	Revolt on Mars - Episode 2
Episode 392	08/04/53	Revolt on Mars - Episode 3
Episode 393	09/04/53	Revolt on Mars - Episode 4
Episode 394	10/04/53	Revolt on Mars - Episode 5
Episode 395	13/04/53	Revolt on Mars - Episode 6
Episode 396	14/04/53	Revolt on Mars - Episode 7
Episode 397	15/04/53	Revolt on Mars - Episode 8
Episode 398	16/04/53	Revolt on Mars - Episode 9
Episode 399	17/04/53	Revolt on Mars - Episode 10
Episode 400	20/04/53	Revolt on Mars - Episode 11
Episode 401	21/04/53	Revolt on Mars - Episode 12
Episode 402	22/04/53	Revolt on Mars - Episode 13
Episode 403	23/04/53	Revolt on Mars - Episode 14
Episode 404	24/04/53	Revolt on Mars - Episode 15
Episode 405	27/04/53	Revolt on Mars - Episode 16
Episode 406	28/04/53	Revolt on Mars - Episode 17

APPENDIX E: DICK BARTON EPISODE LIST

Episode 407 29/04/53 Revolt on Mars - Episode 18
Episode 408 30/04/53 Revolt on Mars - Episode 19
Episode 409 01/05/53 Revolt on Mars - Episode 20
Episode 410 04/05/53 Revolt on Mars - Episode 21
Episode 411 05/05/53 Revolt on Mars - Episode 22
Episode 412 06/05/53 Revolt on Mars - Episode 23
Episode 413 07/05/53 Revolt on Mars - Episode 24
Episode 414 08/05/53 Revolt on Mars - Episode 25
Episode 415 11/05/53 Revolt on Mars - Episode 26
Episode 416 12/05/53 Revolt on Mars - Episode 27
Episode 417 13/05/53 Revolt on Mars - Episode 28
Episode 418 14/05/53 Revolt on Mars - Episode 29
Episode 419 15/05/53 Revolt on Mars - Episode 30
Episode 420 18/05/53 Revolt on Mars - Episode 31
Episode 421 19/05/53 Revolt on Mars - Episode 32
Episode 422 20/05/53 Revolt on Mars - Episode 33
Episode 423 21/05/53 Revolt on Mars - Episode 34
Episode 424 22/05/53 Revolt on Mars - Episode 35
Episode 425 25/05/53 Revolt on Mars - Episode 36
Episode 426 26/05/53 Revolt on Mars - Episode 37
Episode 427 27/05/53 Revolt on Mars - Episode 38
Episode 428 28/05/53 Revolt on Mars - Episode 39
Episode 429 29/05/53 Revolt on Mars - Episode 40

SERIES THREE
Episode 430 21/09/53 Marooned On Mercury - Episode 1
Episode 431 22/09/53 Marooned On Mercury - Episode 2
Episode 432 23/09/53 Marooned On Mercury - Episode 3
Episode 433 24/09/53 Marooned On Mercury - Episode 4
Episode 434 25/09/53 Marooned On Mercury - Episode 5
Episode 435 28/09/53 Marooned On Mercury - Episode 6
Episode 436 29/09/53 Marooned On Mercury - Episode 7
Episode 437 30/09/53 Marooned On Mercury - Episode 8
Episode 438 01/10/53 Marooned On Mercury - Episode 9
Episode 439 02/10/53 Marooned On Mercury - Episode 10
Episode 440 05/10/53 Marooned On Mercury - Episode 11
Episode 441 06/10/53 Marooned On Mercury - Episode 12
Episode 442 07/10/53 Marooned On Mercury - Episode 13
Episode 443 08/10/53 Marooned On Mercury - Episode 14
Episode 444 09/10/53 Marooned On Mercury - Episode 15
Episode 445 12/10/53 Marooned On Mercury - Episode 16
Episode 446 13/10/53 Marooned On Mercury - Episode 17
Episode 447 14/10/53 Marooned On Mercury - Episode 18
Episode 448 15/10/53 Marooned On Mercury - Episode 19
Episode 449 16/10/53 Marooned On Mercury - Episode 20
Episode 450 19/10/53 Marooned On Mercury - Episode 21
Episode 451 20/10/53 Marooned On Mercury - Episode 22
Episode 452 21/10/53 Marooned On Mercury - Episode 23

Episode 453	22/10/53	Marooned On Mercury - Episode 24
Episode 454	23/10/53	Marooned On Mercury - Episode 25
Episode 455	26/10/53	Marooned On Mercury - Episode 26
Episode 456	27/10/53	Marooned On Mercury - Episode 27
Episode 457	28/10/53	Marooned On Mercury - Episode 28
Episode 458	29/10/53	Marooned On Mercury - Episode 29
Episode 459	30/10/53	Marooned On Mercury - Episode 30
Episode 460	02/11/53	Marooned On Mercury - Episode 31
Episode 461	03/11/53	Marooned On Mercury - Episode 32
Episode 462	04/11/53	Marooned On Mercury - Episode 33
Episode 463	05/11/53	Marooned On Mercury - Episode 34
Episode 464	06/11/53	Marooned On Mercury - Episode 35
Episode 465	09/11/53	Marooned On Mercury - Episode 36
Episode 466	10/11/53	Marooned On Mercury - Episode 37
Episode 467	11/11/53	Marooned On Mercury - Episode 38
Episode 468	12/11/53	Marooned On Mercury - Episode 39
Episode 469	13/11/53	Marooned On Mercury - Episode 40
Episode 470	16/11/53	Marooned On Mercury - Episode 41
Episode 471	17/11/53	Marooned On Mercury - Episode 42
Episode 472	18/11/53	Marooned On Mercury - Episode 43
Episode 473	19/11/53	Marooned On Mercury - Episode 44
Episode 474	20/11/53	Marooned On Mercury - Episode 45
Episode 475	23/11/53	Marooned On Mercury - Episode 46
Episode 476	24/11/53	Marooned On Mercury - Episode 47
Episode 477	25/11/53	Marooned On Mercury - Episode 48
Episode 478	26/11/53	Marooned On Mercury - Episode 49
Episode 479	27/11/53	Marooned On Mercury - Episode 50
Episode 480	30/11/53	Marooned On Mercury - Episode 51
Episode 481	01/12/53	Marooned On Mercury - Episode 52
Episode 482	02/12/53	Marooned On Mercury - Episode 53
Episode 483	03/12/53	Marooned On Mercury - Episode 54
Episode 484	04/12/53	Marooned On Mercury - Episode 55
Episode 485	07/12/53	Marooned On Mercury - Episode 56
Episode 486	08/12/53	Marooned On Mercury - Episode 57
Episode 487	09/12/53	Marooned On Mercury - Episode 58
Episode 488	10/12/53	Marooned On Mercury - Episode 59
Episode 489	11/12/53	Marooned On Mercury - Episode 60
Episode 490	14/12/53	Marooned On Mercury - Episode 61
Episode 491	15/12/53	Marooned On Mercury - Episode 62
Episode 492	16/12/53	Marooned On Mercury - Episode 63
Episode 493	17/12/53	Marooned On Mercury - Episode 64
Episode 494	18/12/53	Marooned On Mercury - Episode 65
Episode 495	21/12/53	Marooned On Mercury - Episode 66
Episode 496	22/12/53	Marooned On Mercury - Episode 67
Episode 497	23/12/53	Marooned On Mercury - Episode 68
Episode 498	24/12/53	Marooned On Mercury - Episode 69
Episode 499	25/12/53	Marooned On Mercury - Episode 70
Episode 500	28/12/53	Marooned On Mercury - Episode 71

APPENDIX E: DICK BARTON EPISODE LIST

Episode 501 29/12/53 Marooned On Mercury - Episode 72
Episode 502 30/12/53 Marooned On Mercury - Episode 73
Episode 503 31/12/53 Marooned On Mercury - Episode 74
Episode 504 01/01/54 Marooned On Mercury - Episode 75
Episode 505 04/01/54 Attack on the Space Stations - Episode 1
Episode 506 05/01/54 Attack on the Space Stations - Episode 2
Episode 507 06/01/54 Attack on the Space Stations - Episode 3
Episode 508 07/01/54 Attack on the Space Stations - Episode 4
Episode 509 08/01/54 Attack on the Space Stations - Episode 5
Episode 510 11/01/54 Attack on the Space Stations - Episode 6
Episode 511 12/01/54 Attack on the Space Stations - Episode 7
Episode 512 13/01/54 Attack on the Space Stations - Episode 8
Episode 513 14/01/54 Attack on the Space Stations - Episode 9
Episode 514 15/01/54 Attack on the Space Stations - Episode 10
Episode 515 18/01/54 Attack on the Space Stations - Episode 11
Episode 516 19/01/54 Attack on the Space Stations - Episode 12
Episode 517 20/01/54 Attack on the Space Stations - Episode 13
Episode 518 21/01/54 Attack on the Space Stations - Episode 14
Episode 519 22/01/54 Attack on the Space Stations - Episode 15
Episode 520 25/01/54 Attack on the Space Stations - Episode 16
Episode 521 26/01/54 Attack on the Space Stations - Episode 17
Episode 522 27/01/54 Attack on the Space Stations - Episode 18
Episode 523 28/01/54 Attack on the Space Stations - Episode 19
Episode 524 29/01/54 Attack on the Space Stations - Episode 20
Episode 525 01/02/54 Attack on the Space Stations - Episode 21
Episode 526 02/02/54 Attack on the Space Stations - Episode 22
Episode 527 03/02/54 Attack on the Space Stations - Episode 23
Episode 528 04/02/54 Attack on the Space Stations - Episode 24
Episode 529 05/02/54 Attack on the Space Stations - Episode 25
Episode 530 08/02/54 Attack on the Space Stations - Episode 26
Episode 531 09/02/54 Attack on the Space Stations - Episode 27
Episode 532 10/02/54 Attack on the Space Stations - Episode 28
Episode 533 11/02/54 Attack on the Space Stations - Episode 29
Episode 534 12/02/54 Attack on the Space Stations - Episode 30
Episode 535 15/02/54 Attack on the Space Stations - Episode 31
Episode 536 16/02/54 Attack on the Space Stations - Episode 32
Episode 537 17/02/54 Attack on the Space Stations - Episode 33
Episode 538 18/02/54 Attack on the Space Stations - Episode 34
Episode 539 19/02/54 Attack on the Space Stations - Episode 35
Episode 540 22/02/54 Sabotage On Venus - Episode 1
Episode 541 23/02/54 Sabotage On Venus - Episode 2
Episode 542 24/02/54 Sabotage On Venus - Episode 3
Episode 543 25/02/54 Sabotage On Venus - Episode 4
Episode 544 26/02/54 Sabotage On Venus - Episode 5
Episode 545 01/03/54 Sabotage On Venus - Episode 6
Episode 546 02/03/54 Sabotage On Venus - Episode 7
Episode 547 03/03/54 Sabotage On Venus - Episode 8
Episode 548 04/03/54 Sabotage On Venus - Episode 9

Episode 549	05/03/54	Sabotage On Venus - Episode 10
Episode 550	08/03/54	Sabotage On Venus - Episode 11
Episode 551	09/03/54	Sabotage On Venus - Episode 12
Episode 552	10/03/54	Sabotage On Venus - Episode 13
Episode 553	11/03/54	Sabotage On Venus - Episode 14
Episode 554	12/03/54	Sabotage On Venus - Episode 15
Episode 555	15/03/54	Sabotage On Venus - Episode 16
Episode 556	16/03/54	Sabotage On Venus - Episode 17
Episode 557	17/03/54	Sabotage On Venus - Episode 18
Episode 558	18/03/54	Sabotage On Venus - Episode 19
Episode 559	19/03/54	Sabotage On Venus - Episode 20
Episode 560	22/03/54	Sabotage On Venus - Episode 21
Episode 561	23/03/54	Sabotage On Venus - Episode 22
Episode 562	24/03/54	Sabotage On Venus - Episode 23
Episode 563	25/03/54	Sabotage On Venus - Episode 24
Episode 564	26/03/54	Sabotage On Venus - Episode 25
Episode 565	29/03/54	Sabotage On Venus - Episode 26
Episode 566	30/03/54	Sabotage On Venus - Episode 27
Episode 567	31/03/54	Sabotage On Venus - Episode 28
Episode 568	01/04/54	Sabotage On Venus - Episode 29
Episode 569	02/04/54	Sabotage On Venus - Episode 30
Episode 570	05/04/54	Sabotage On Venus - Episode 31
Episode 571	06/04/54	Sabotage On Venus - Episode 32
Episode 572	07/04/54	Sabotage On Venus - Episode 33
Episode 573	08/04/54	Sabotage On Venus - Episode 34
Episode 574	09/04/54	Sabotage On Venus - Episode 35
Episode 575	12/04/54	Sabotage On Venus - Episode 36
Episode 576	13/04/54	Sabotage On Venus - Episode 37
Episode 577	14/04/54	Sabotage On Venus - Episode 38
Episode 578	15/04/54	Sabotage On Venus - Episode 39
Episode 579	16/04/54	Sabotage On Venus - Episode 40
Episode 580	19/04/54	Sabotage On Venus - Episode 41
Episode 581	20/04/54	Sabotage On Venus - Episode 42
Episode 582	21/04/54	Sabotage On Venus - Episode 43
Episode 583	22/04/54	Sabotage On Venus - Episode 44
Episode 584	23/04/54	Sabotage On Venus - Episode 45
Episode 585	26/04/54	Sabotage On Venus - Episode 46
Episode 586	27/04/54	Sabotage On Venus - Episode 47
Episode 587	28/04/54	Sabotage On Venus - Episode 48
Episode 588	29/04/54	Sabotage On Venus - Episode 49
Episode 589	30/04/54	Sabotage On Venus - Episode 50
Episode 590	03/05/54	Sabotage On Venus - Episode 51
Episode 591	04/05/54	Sabotage On Venus - Episode 52
Episode 592	05/05/54	Sabotage On Venus - Episode 53
Episode 593	06/05/54	Sabotage On Venus - Episode 54
Episode 594	07/05/54	Sabotage On Venus - Episode 55
Episode 595	08/05/54	Sabotage On Venus - Episode 56
Episode 596	11/05/54	Sabotage On Venus - Episode 57

APPENDIX E: DICK BARTON EPISODE LIST

Episode 597 12/05/54 Sabotage On Venus - Episode 58
Episode 598 13/05/54 Sabotage On Venus - Episode 59
Episode 599 14/05/54 Sabotage On Venus - Episode 60

SERIES FOUR
Episode 600 13/09/54 Mystery on the Moon - Episode 1
Episode 601 14/09/54 Mystery on the Moon - Episode 2
Episode 602 15/09/54 Mystery on the Moon - Episode 3
Episode 603 16/09/54 Mystery on the Moon - Episode 4
Episode 604 17/09/54 Mystery on the Moon - Episode 5
Episode 605 20/09/54 Mystery on the Moon - Episode 6
Episode 606 21/09/54 Mystery on the Moon - Episode 7
Episode 607 22/09/54 Mystery on the Moon - Episode 8
Episode 608 23/09/54 Mystery on the Moon - Episode 9
Episode 609 24/09/54 Mystery on the Moon - Episode 10
Episode 610 27/09/54 Mystery on the Moon - Episode 11
Episode 611 28/09/54 Mystery on the Moon - Episode 12
Episode 612 29/09/54 Mystery on the Moon - Episode 13
Episode 613 30/09/54 Mystery on the Moon - Episode 14
Episode 614 01/10/54 Mystery on the Moon - Episode 15
Episode 615 04/10/54 Mystery on the Moon - Episode 16
Episode 616 05/10/54 Mystery on the Moon - Episode 17
Episode 617 06/10/54 Mystery on the Moon - Episode 18
Episode 618 07/10/54 Mystery on the Moon - Episode 19
Episode 619 08/10/54 Mystery on the Moon - Episode 20
Episode 620 11/10/54 The Automatons - Episode 1
Episode 621 12/10/54 The Automatons - Episode 2
Episode 622 13/10/54 The Automatons - Episode 3
Episode 623 14/10/54 The Automatons - Episode 4
Episode 624 15/10/54 The Automatons - Episode 5
Episode 625 18/10/54 The Automatons - Episode 6
Episode 626 19/10/54 The Automatons - Episode 7
Episode 627 20/10/54 The Automatons - Episode 8
Episode 628 21/10/54 The Automatons - Episode 9
Episode 629 22/10/54 The Automatons - Episode 10
Episode 630 25/10/54 The Automatons - Episode 11
Episode 631 26/10/54 The Automatons - Episode 12
Episode 632 27/10/54 The Automatons - Episode 13
Episode 633 28/10/54 The Automatons - Episode 14
Episode 634 29/10/54 The Automatons - Episode 15
Episode 635 01/11/54 The Automatons - Episode 16
Episode 636 02/11/54 The Automatons - Episode 17
Episode 637 03/11/54 The Automatons - Episode 18
Episode 638 04/11/54 The Automatons - Episode 19
Episode 639 05/11/54 The Automatons - Episode 20
Episode 640 08/11/54 The Automatons - Episode 21
Episode 641 09/11/54 The Automatons - Episode 22
Episode 642 10/11/54 The Automatons - Episode 23

SERIAL THRILLERS

Episode 643	11/11/54	The Automatons - Episode 24
Episode 644	12/11/54	The Automatons - Episode 25
Episode 645	15/11/54	The Automatons - Episode 26
Episode 646	16/11/54	The Automatons - Episode 27
Episode 647	17/11/54	The Automatons - Episode 28
Episode 648	18/11/54	The Automatons - Episode 29
Episode 649	19/11/54	The Automatons - Episode 30
Episode 650	22/11/54	The Automatons - Episode 31
Episode 651	23/11/54	The Automatons - Episode 32
Episode 652	24/11/54	The Automatons - Episode 33
Episode 653	25/11/54	The Automatons - Episode 34
Episode 654	26/11/54	The Automatons - Episode 35
Episode 655	29/11/54	The Mekon on Mars - Episode 1
Episode 656	30/11/54	The Mekon on Mars - Episode 2
Episode 657	01/12/54	The Mekon on Mars - Episode 3
Episode 658	02/12/54	The Mekon on Mars - Episode 4
Episode 659	03/12/54	The Mekon on Mars - Episode 5
Episode 660	06/12/54	The Mekon on Mars - Episode 6
Episode 661	07/12/54	The Mekon on Mars - Episode 7
Episode 662	08/12/54	The Mekon on Mars - Episode 8
Episode 663	09/12/54	The Mekon on Mars - Episode 9
Episode 664	10/12/54	The Mekon on Mars - Episode 10
Episode 665	13/12/54	The Mekon on Mars - Episode 11
Episode 666	14/12/54	The Mekon on Mars - Episode 12
Episode 667	15/12/54	The Mekon on Mars - Episode 13
Episode 668	16/12/54	The Mekon on Mars - Episode 14
Episode 669	17/12/54	The Mekon on Mars - Episode 15
Episode 670	20/12/54	The Mekon on Mars - Episode 16
Episode 671	21/12/54	The Mekon on Mars - Episode 17
Episode 672	22/12/54	The Mekon on Mars - Episode 18
Episode 673	23/12/54	The Mekon on Mars - Episode 19
Episode 674	24/12/54	The Mekon on Mars - Episode 20
Episode 675	27/12/54	The Mekon on Mars - Episode 21
Episode 676	28/12/54	The Mekon on Mars - Episode 22
Episode 677	29/12/54	The Mekon on Mars - Episode 23
Episode 678	30/12/54	The Mekon on Mars - Episode 24
Episode 679	31/12/54	The Mekon on Mars - Episode 25
Episode 680	03/01/55	Bartley Greenwood - Episode 1
Episode 681	04/01/55	Bartley Greenwood - Episode 2
Episode 682	05/01/55	Bartley Greenwood - Episode 3
Episode 683	06/01/55	Bartley Greenwood - Episode 4
Episode 684	07/01/55	Bartley Greenwood - Episode 5
Episode 685	10/01/55	Bartley Greenwood - Episode 6
Episode 686	11/01/55	Bartley Greenwood - Episode 7
Episode 687	12/01/55	Bartley Greenwood - Episode 8
Episode 688	13/01/55	Bartley Greenwood - Episode 9
Episode 689	14/01/55	Bartley Greenwood - Episode 10
Episode 690	17/01/55	Bartley Greenwood - Episode 11

APPENDIX E: DICK BARTON EPISODE LIST

Episode 691	18/01/55	Bartley Greenwood - Episode 12
Episode 692	19/01/55	Bartley Greenwood - Episode 13
Episode 693	20/01/55	Bartley Greenwood - Episode 14
Episode 694	21/01/55	Bartley Greenwood - Episode 15
Episode 695	24/01/55	Bartley Greenwood - Episode 16
Episode 696	25/01/55	Bartley Greenwood - Episode 17
Episode 697	26/01/55	Bartley Greenwood - Episode 18
Episode 698	27/01/55	Bartley Greenwood - Episode 19
Episode 699	28/01/55	Bartley Greenwood - Episode 20
Episode 700	31/01/55	Bartley Greenwood - Episode 21
Episode 701	01/02/55	Bartley Greenwood - Episode 22
Episode 702	02/02/55	Bartley Greenwood - Episode 23
Episode 703	03/02/55	Bartley Greenwood - Episode 24
Episode 704	04/02/55	Bartley Greenwood - Episode 25
Episode 705	07/02/55	Bartley Greenwood - Episode 26
Episode 706	08/02/55	Bartley Greenwood - Episode 27
Episode 707	09/02/55	Bartley Greenwood - Episode 28
Episode 708	10/02/55	Bartley Greenwood - Episode 29
Episode 709	11/02/55	Bartley Greenwood - Episode 30
Episode 710	14/02/55	Bartley Greenwood - Episode 31
Episode 711	15/02/55	Bartley Greenwood - Episode 32
Episode 712	16/02/55	Bartley Greenwood - Episode 33
Episode 713	17/02/55	Bartley Greenwood - Episode 34
Episode 714	18/02/55	Bartley Greenwood - Episode 35
Episode 715	21/02/55	Bartley Greenwood - Episode 36
Episode 716	22/02/55	Bartley Greenwood - Episode 37
Episode 717	23/02/55	Bartley Greenwood - Episode 38
Episode 718	24/02/55	Bartley Greenwood - Episode 39
Episode 719	25/02/55	Bartley Greenwood - Episode 40
Episode 720	28/02/55	Bartley Greenwood - Episode 41
Episode 721	01/03/55	Bartley Greenwood - Episode 42
Episode 722	02/03/55	Bartley Greenwood - Episode 43
Episode 723	03/03/55	Bartley Greenwood - Episode 44
Episode 724	04/03/55	Bartley Greenwood - Episode 45
Episode 725	07/03/55	Surprise Assassin - Episode 1
Episode 726	08/03/55	Surprise Assassin - Episode 2
Episode 727	09/03/55	Surprise Assassin - Episode 3
Episode 728	10/03/55	Surprise Assassin - Episode 4
Episode 729	11/03/55	Surprise Assassin - Episode 5
Episode 730	14/03/55	Surprise Assassin - Episode 6
Episode 731	15/03/55	Surprise Assassin - Episode 7
Episode 732	16/03/55	Surprise Assassin - Episode 8
Episode 733	17/03/55	Surprise Assassin - Episode 9
Episode 734	18/03/55	Surprise Assassin - Episode 10
Episode 735	21/03/55	Surprise Assassin - Episode 11
Episode 736	22/03/55	Surprise Assassin - Episode 12
Episode 737	23/03/55	Surprise Assassin - Episode 13
Episode 738	24/03/55	Surprise Assassin - Episode 14

Episode 739 25/03/55 Surprise Assassin - Episode 15
Episode 740 28/03/55 Surprise Assassin - Episode 16
Episode 741 29/03/55 Surprise Assassin - Episode 17
Episode 742 30/03/55 Surprise Assassin - Episode 18
Episode 743 31/03/55 Surprise Assassin - Episode 19
Episode 744 04/04/55 Surprise Assassin - Episode 20
Episode 745 05/04/55 Surprise Assassin - Episode 21
Episode 746 06/04/55 Surprise Assassin - Episode 22
Episode 747 07/04/55 Surprise Assassin - Episode 23
Episode 748 08/04/55 Surprise Assassin - Episode 24
Episode 749 11/04/55 Surprise Assassin - Episode 25
Episode 750 12/04/55 Surprise Assassin - Episode 26
Episode 751 13/04/55 Surprise Assassin - Episode 27
Episode 752 14/04/55 Surprise Assassin - Episode 28
Episode 753 15/04/55 Surprise Assassin - Episode 29
Episode 754 18/04/55 Surprise Assassin - Episode 30
Episode 755 19/04/55 Surprise Assassin - Episode 31
Episode 756 20/04/55 Surprise Assassin - Episode 32
Episode 757 21/04/55 Surprise Assassin - Episode 33
Episode 758 22/04/55 Surprise Assassin - Episode 34
Episode 759 25/04/55 Surprise Assassin - Episode 35
Episode 760 26/04/55 Surprise Assassin - Episode 36
Episode 761 27/04/55 Surprise Assassin - Episode 37
Episode 762 28/04/55 Surprise Assassin - Episode 38
Episode 763 29/04/55 Surprise Assassin - Episode 39
Episode 764 02/05/55 Surprise Assassin - Episode 40

Radio Luxembourg began a series of *Dan Dare* repeats, starting on 03/05/55 (See Appendix F)

APPENDIX F
DAN DARE (1955-1956)
REPEAT BROADCASTS

On 3rd May 1955, Radio Luxembourg began broadcasting a series of *Dan Dare* repeats. There is very little surviving paperwork concerning these broadcasts. Evidence suggests that these transmissions were either repeats from the original tapes, or new re-recordings based on the original scripts. It is fairly clear how many repeats there were, but it is not known exactly what form they took and very few other details can be confirmed. What follows is a list of known information concerning the repeat run, which concluded Radio Luxembourg's association with the series. The following episode titles and designations (where known) are reprinted here exactly as they appear in the programme listings pages of *208 Magazine*. There is some evidence to suggest that the listings pages of *208 Magazine* are not entirely accurate. However, it is the only official source we have for the running order of these repeats.

DATE	EPISODE TITLE
03/05/55	Trapped in Space
04/05/55	The Moon Brothers
05/05/55	The Floating Platform
06/05/55	The Cosmic Whirlpool
09/05/55	The Ice Men!
10/05/55	Return of the Mekon
11/05/55	Escape from the Ice Men
12/05/55	Battle Against Death
13/05/55	The Traitor's Trap
16/05/55	Sabotage
17/05/55	Under Sentence of Death
18/05/55	The End of the Road
19/05/55	No Way Out
20/05/55	The Fury of the Mekon
23/05/55	Race to Destruction
24/05/55	Episode 16
25/05/55	Episode 17
26/05/55	Episode 18
27/05/55	Episode 19
30/05/55	Episode 20
31/05/55	Episode 21
01/06/55	Episode 22

SERIAL THRILLERS

02/06/55	Episode 23
03/06/55	Episode 24
06/06/55	Episode 25
07/06/55	Episode 26
08/06/55	Episode 27
09/06/55	Episode 28
10/06/55	Episode 29
13/06/55	Episode 30
14/06/55	Episode 31
15/06/55	Episode 32
16/06/55	Episode 33
17/06/55	Episode 34
20/06/55	Episode 35
21/06/55	Episode 36
22/06/55	Episode 37
23/06/55	Episode 38
24/06/55	Episode 39
27/06/55	Episode 40
28/06/55	Episode 41
29/06/55	Episode 42
30/06/55	Episode 43
01/07/55	Episode 44
04/07/55	Episode 45
05/07/55	Episode 46
06/07/55	Episode 47
07/07/55	Episode 48
08/07/55	Episode 49
11/07/55	Episode 50
12/07/55	Episode 51
13/07/55	Episode 52
14/07/55	Episode 53
15/07/55	Episode 54
18/07/55	Episode 55
19/07/55	Episode 56
20/07/55	Episode 57
21/07/55	Episode 58
22/07/55	Episode 59
25/07/55	Episode 60
26/07/55	Episode 61
27/07/55	Episode 62
28/07/55	Episode 63
29/07/55	Episode 64
01/08/55	Episode 65
02/08/55	Episode 66
03/08/55	Episode 67
04/08/55	Episode 68
05/08/55	Episode 69
08/08/55	Episode 70

APPENDIX F: DAN DARE REPEAT BROADCASTS

09/08/55	Episode 71
10/08/55	Episode 72
11/08/55	Episode 73
12/08/55	Episode 74
15/08/55	Episode 75
16/08/55	Episode 76
17/08/55	Episode 77
18/08/55	Episode 78
19/08/55	Episode 79
22/08/55	Episode 80
23/08/55	Unknown Episode
24/08/55	Unknown Episode
25/08/55	Unknown Episode
26/08/55	Unknown Episode
29/08/55	Unknown Episode
30/08/55	Unknown Episode
31/08/55	Unknown Episode
01/09/55	Unknown Episode
02/09/55	Unknown Episode
05/09/55	Unknown Episode
06/09/55	Unknown Episode
07/09/55	Unknown Episode
08/09/55	Unknown Episode
09/09/55	Unknown Episode
12/09/55	Unknown Episode
13/09/55	Unknown Episode
14/09/55	Unknown Episode
15/09/55	Unknown Episode
16/09/55	Unknown Episode
19/09/55	Unknown Episode
20/09/55	Unknown Episode
21/09/55	Unknown Episode
22/09/55	Unknown Episode
23/09/55	Unknown Episode
26/09/55	Unknown Episode
27/09/55	Unknown Episode
28/09/55	Unknown Episode
29/09/55	Unknown Episode
30/09/55	Unknown Episode
03/10/55	Unknown Episode
04/10/55	Unknown Episode
05/10/55	Unknown Episode
06/10/55	Unknown Episode
07/10/55	Unknown Episode
10/10/55	Unknown Episode
11/10/55	Unknown Episode
12/10/55	Unknown Episode
13/10/55	Unknown Episode

SERIAL THRILLERS

14/10/55	Unknown Episode
17/10/55	Unknown Episode
18/10/55	Unknown Episode
19/10/55	Unknown Episode
20/10/55	Unknown Episode
21/10/55	Unknown Episode
24/10/55	Unknown Episode
25/10/55	Unknown Episode
26/10/55	Unknown Episode
27/10/55	Unknown Episode
28/10/55	Unknown Episode
31/10/55	Unknown Episode
01/11/55	Unknown Episode
02/11/55	Unknown Episode
03/11/55	Unknown Episode
04/11/55	Unknown Episode
07/11/55	Unknown Episode
08/11/55	Unknown Episode
09/11/55	Unknown Episode
10/11/55	Unknown Episode
11/11/55	Unknown Episode
14/11/55	Unknown Episode
15/11/55	Unknown Episode
16/11/55	Unknown Episode
17/11/55	Unknown Episode
18/11/55	Unknown Episode
21/11/55	Unknown Episode
22/11/55	Unknown Episode
23/11/55	Unknown Episode
24/11/55	Unknown Episode
25/11/55	Unknown Episode
28/11/55	Unknown Episode
29/11/55	Unknown Episode
30/11/55	Unknown Episode
01/12/55	Unknown Episode
02/12/55	Unknown Episode
05/12/55	Unknown Episode
06/12/55	Unknown Episode
07/12/55	Unknown Episode
08/12/55	Unknown Episode
09/12/55	Unknown Episode
12/12/55	Unknown Episode
15/12/55	Unknown Episode
16/12/55	Unknown Episode
17/12/55	Unknown Episode
18/12/55	Unknown Episode
19/12/55	Unknown Episode
22/12/55	Unknown Episode

APPENDIX F: DAN DARE REPEAT BROADCASTS

23/12/55　Unknown Episode
24/12/55　Unknown Episode
02/01/56　Unknown Episode
03/01/56　Unknown Episode
04/01/56　Unknown Episode
05/01/56　Unknown Episode
06/01/56　Unknown Episode
09/01/56　The Lost World on Mars - Episode 1
10/01/56　The Lost World on Mars - Episode 2
11/01/56　The Lost World on Mars - Episode 3
12/01/56　The Lost World on Mars - Episode 4
13/01/56　The Lost World on Mars - Episode 5
16/01/56　The Lost World on Mars - Episode 6
17/01/56　The Lost World on Mars - Episode 7
18/01/56　The Lost World on Mars - Episode 8
19/01/56　The Lost World on Mars - Episode 9
20/01/56　The Lost World on Mars - Episode 10
23/01/56　The Lost World on Mars - Episode 11
24/01/56　The Lost World on Mars - Episode 12
25/01/56　The Lost World on Mars - Episode 13
26/01/56　The Lost World on Mars - Episode 14
27/01/56　The Lost World on Mars - Episode 15
30/01/56　The Lost World on Mars - Episode 16
31/01/56　The Lost World on Mars - Episode 17
01/02/56　The Lost World on Mars - Episode 18
02/02/56　The Lost World on Mars - Episode 19
03/02/56　The Lost World on Mars - Episode 20
06/02/56　The Lost World on Mars - Episode 21
07/02/56　The Lost World on Mars - Episode 22
08/02/56　The Lost World on Mars - Episode 23
09/02/56　The Lost World on Mars - Episode 24
10/02/56　The Lost World on Mars - Episode 25
13/02/56　The Lost World on Mars - Episode 26
14/02/56　The Lost World on Mars - Episode 27
15/02/56　The Lost World on Mars - Episode 28
16/02/56　The Lost World on Mars - Episode 29
17/02/56　The Lost World on Mars - Episode 30
20/02/56　The Lost World on Mars - Episode 31
21/02/56　The Lost World on Mars - Episode 32
22/02/56　The Lost World on Mars - Episode 33
23/02/56　The Lost World on Mars - Episode 34
24/02/56　The Lost World on Mars - Episode 35
27/02/56　The Lost World on Mars - Episode 36
28/02/56　The Lost World on Mars - Episode 37
29/02/56　The Lost World on Mars - Episode 38
01/03/56　The Lost World on Mars - Episode 39
02/03/56　The Lost World on Mars - Episode 40
05/03/56　The Lost World on Mars - Episode 41

06/03/56	The Lost World on Mars - Episode 42
07/03/56	The Lost World on Mars - Episode 43
08/03/56	The Lost World on Mars - Episode 44
09/03/56	The Lost World on Mars - Episode 45
12/03/56	The Lost World on Mars - Episode 46
13/03/56	The Lost World on Mars - Episode 47
14/03/56	The Lost World on Mars - Episode 48
15/03/56	The Lost World on Mars - Episode 49
16/03/56	The Lost World on Mars - Episode 50
19/03/56	The Lost World on Mars - Episode 51
20/03/56	The Lost World on Mars - Episode 52
21/03/56	The Lost World on Mars - Episode 53
22/03/56	The Lost World on Mars - Episode 54
23/03/56	The Lost World on Mars - Episode 55
26/03/56	The Lost World on Mars - Episode 56
27/03/56	The Lost World on Mars - Episode 57
28/03/56	The Lost World on Mars - Episode 58
29/03/56	The Lost World on Mars - Episode 59
30/03/56	The Lost World on Mars - Episode 60
02/04/56	The Lost World on Mars - Episode 61
03/04/56	The Lost World on Mars - Episode 62
04/04/56	The Lost World on Mars - Episode 63
05/04/56	The Lost World on Mars - Episode 64
06/04/56	Revolt on Mars - Episode 1
09/04/56	Revolt on Mars - Episode 2
10/04/56	Revolt on Mars - Episode 3
11/04/56	Revolt on Mars - Episode 4
12/04/56	Revolt on Mars - Episode 5
13/04/56	Revolt on Mars - Episode 6
16/04/56	Revolt on Mars - Episode 7
17/04/56	Revolt on Mars - Episode 8
18/04/56	Revolt on Mars - Episode 9
19/04/56	Revolt on Mars - Episode 10
20/04/56	Revolt on Mars - Episode 11
23/04/56	Revolt on Mars - Episode 12
24/04/56	Revolt on Mars - Episode 13
25/04/56	Revolt on Mars - Episode 14
26/04/56	Revolt on Mars - Episode 15
27/04/56	Revolt on Mars - Episode 16
30/04/56	Revolt on Mars - Episode 17
01/05/56	Revolt on Mars - Episode 18
02/05/56	Revolt on Mars - Episode 19
03/05/56	Revolt on Mars - Episode 20
04/05/56	Revolt on Mars - Episode 21
07/05/56	Revolt on Mars - Episode 22
08/05/56	Revolt on Mars - Episode 23
09/05/56	Revolt on Mars - Episode 24
10/05/56	Revolt on Mars - Episode 25

APPENDIX F: DAN DARE REPEAT BROADCASTS

11/05/56	Revolt on Mars - Episode 26
14/05/56	Revolt on Mars - Episode 27
15/05/56	Revolt on Mars - Episode 28
16/05/56	Revolt on Mars - Episode 29
17/05/56	Revolt on Mars - Episode 30
18/05/56	Revolt on Mars - Episode 31
21/05/56	Revolt on Mars - Episode 32
22/05/56	Revolt on Mars - Episode 33
23/05/56	Revolt on Mars - Episode 34
24/05/56	Revolt on Mars - Episode 35
25/05/56	Revolt on Mars - Episode 36
28/05/56	Revolt on Mars - Episode 37
29/05/56	Revolt on Mars - Episode 38
30/05/56	Revolt on Mars - Episode 39
31/05/56	Revolt on Mars - Episode 40[249]

---

[249] *208 Magazine* lists this as the final *Dan Dare* episode to be broadcast on Radio Luxembourg. Contemporary accounts don't agree, however. There is some substantial evidence to suggest that the episodes repeated in April/May 1956 were actually from another serial altogether. It's not clear what that serial was, but reports indicate that it was a storyline set on the planet Venus. A detailed synopsis of this story exists, but does not provide any insight into the title of the story, when it was originally broadcast or who wrote it. The likelihood is that it may have been first transmitted in 1952.

APPENDIX G
RIDERS OF THE RANGE
EPISODE GUIDE

Riders of the Range was set in the days of the old American frontier. Using period music and detailed historical research, writer/producer Charles Chilton attempted to evoke the West in serial form. Produced by the Light Entertainment Department, the series was very popular with children, later finding its way into the pages of *Eagle*, as a regular strip (in December 1950). The strip would actually outlast the radio serial, eventually winding up in 1962. Following the conclusion of the *Riders of the Range* radio series, Chilton would move on to create *Journey into Space*.

Series One: 'The Chisholm Trail' (1949)
16 x 30 minute episodes (approx.)
BBC Light Programme
Written by Charles Chilton
Producer: Charles Chilton

CAST:

Jeff Arnold	Paul Carpenter
Luke	Charles Irwin
Rancher	Cal McCord
Mary	Carole Carr
Bob	Bob Mallin
J C Macdonald	Macdonald Parke
Rustler	Himself
Other Actors	Jack Fallon
	Alan Keith

STORY:
The story of a cattle drive from the 6T6 ranch in Texas to Wichita in Kansas.

BROADCAST (LIVE):		EPISODE 6	17/02/49
EPISODE 1	13/01/49	EPISODE 7	24/02/49
EPISODE 2	20/01/49	EPISODE 8	03/03/49
EPISODE 3	27/01/49	EPISODE 9	10/03/49
EPISODE 4	03/02/49	EPISODE 10	17/03/49
EPISODE 5	10/02/49	EPISODE 11	24/03/49

APPENDIX G: RIDERS OF THE RANGE EPISODE GUIDE

EPISODE 12	31/03/49	EPISODE 15	21/04/49
EPISODE 13	07/04/49	EPISODE 16	28/04/49
EPISODE 14	14/04/49		

Series Two (1949)
12 x 30 minute episodes (approx.)
BBC Light Programme
Written by Charles Chilton
Producer: Charles Chilton

CAST:
Jeff Arnold	Paul Carpenter
Luke	Charles Irwin
Rancher	Cal McCord
Mary	Carole Carr
Bob	Bob Mallin
J C Macdonald	Macdonald Parke
Rustler	Himself
Other Actors	Alan Keith
	Brenda O'Dowda
	Jimmy Bolan
	Dermot Buckley
	Willie O'Toole
	Reed De Rouen

STORY:
The story of the building of the Atcheson, Topeka and Santa Fe Railroad.

BROADCAST (LIVE):
EPISODE 1	02/10/49	EPISODE 7	13/11/49
EPISODE 2	09/10/49	EPISODE 8	20/11/49
EPISODE 3	16/10/49	EPISODE 9	27/11/49
EPISODE 4	23/10/49	EPISODE 10	04/12/49
EPISODE 5	30/10/49	EPISODE 11	11/12/49
EPISODE 6	06/11/49	EPISODE 12	18/12/49

Series Three (1950)
14 x 30 minute episodes (approx.)
BBC Home Service
Written by Charles Chilton
Producer: Charles Chilton

SERIAL THRILLERS

CAST:

Jeff Arnold	Paul Carpenter
Luke	Charles Irwin
Bob	Bob Mallin
Mary	Carole Carr
J C Macdonald	Macdonald Parke
Rustler	Himself
Other Actors	Alan Keith
	Freddie Phillips

STORY:
'A musical drama of the west.' (*Radio Times* 02/04/1950)

BROADCAST:

EPISODE 1	03/04/50	'Rustler Joins the Outfit'
EPISODE 2	04/04/50	'A Brush with Indians'
EPISODE 3	05/04/50	'Jeff and Luke are Captured'
EPISODE 4	06/04/50	'The 6T6 to the Rescue'
EPISODE 5	10/04/50	'The Trail to Mexico'
EPISODE 6	11/04/50	'The Chisholm Trail'
EPISODE 7	12/04/50	'Slim's Last Ride'
EPISODE 8	13/04/50	'Little Joe Joins the Outfit'
EPISODE 9	14/04/50	'Blackie Gets his Bell'
EPISODE 10	17/04/50	'Indian Territory'
EPISODE 11	18/04/50	'An Attack by Apaches'
EPISODE 12	19/04/50	'Stampede'
EPISODE 13	20/04/50	'The Cherry Kid Again'
EPISODE 14	21/04/50	'The End of the Trail'

Series Four (1950)
22 x 30 minute episodes (approx.) + 1 Christmas Special
BBC Light Programme (*Also repeated each week on the BBC Home Service*)
Written by Charles Chilton
Producer: Charles Chilton

CAST:

Rancher	Cal McCord
Jeff Arnold	Paul Carpenter
Luke	Charles Irwin
Bob	Bob Mallin
Mary	Carole Carr
J C Macdonald	Macdonald Parke

APPENDIX G: RIDERS OF THE RANGE EPISODE GUIDE

Billy the Kid	Alan Keith
Rustler	Himself
Other Actors	Freddie Phillips
	Barbara Trevor
	Reed De Rouen
	David Kossoff
	Sybil Baker
	Guy Kingsley Poynter
	Lucille Lisle

STORY:
The ranchers of the 6T6 outfit encounter Billy the Kid.

BROADCAST (PRE-RECORDED):

EPISODE 1	21/04/50	EPISODE 14	22/07/50
EPISODE 2	28/04/50	EPISODE 15	28/07/50
EPISODE 3	05/05/50	EPISODE 16	04/08/50
EPISODE 4	12/05/50	EPISODE 17	11/08/50
EPISODE 5	19/05/50	EPISODE 18	18/08/50
EPISODE 6	26/05/50	EPISODE 19	25/08/50
EPISODE 7	02/06/50	EPISODE 20	01/09/50
EPISODE 8	09/06/50	EPISODE 21	08/09/50
EPISODE 9	16/06/50	EPISODE 22	15/09/50
EPISODE 10	23/06/50		
EPISODE 11	30/06/50	CHRISTMAS SPECIAL	
EPISODE 12	07/07/50	25/12/50	
EPISODE 13	15/07/50		

NOTES:
This is the fourth series to be listed in the radio section of the *Radio Times*. However, the *Radio Times* refers to it as series three and Charles Chilton remembered it as such in his 2011 autobiography. Is that because this series three was merely the third series to appear on the Light Programme, rather than third series overall? Or is it because the previous Home Service series from earlier in 1950 was some just kind of re-packaged repeats run? Sadly, with no recordings surviving, it is difficult to be sure.

Series Five (1951)
13 x 30 minute episodes (approx.)
BBC Light Programme *(Also repeated each week on the BBC Home Service)*
Written by Charles Chilton
Producer: Charles Chilton

SERIAL THRILLERS

CAST:
Jeff Arnold	Paul Carpenter
Luke	Charles Irwin
J C Macdonald	Macdonald Parke
Mary	Carole Carr
Bob	Bob Mallin
Rustler	Himself
Other Actors	Alan Keith
	Guy Kingsley Poynter
	Reed De Rouen

STORY:
Set in Tombstone.

BROADCAST (PRE-RECORDED):
EPISODE 1	22/05/51		EPISODE 8	10/07/51
EPISODE 2	29/05/51		EPISODE 9	17/07/51
EPISODE 3	05/06/51		EPISODE 10	24/07/51
EPISODE 4	12/06/51		EPISODE 11	31/07/51
EPISODE 5	19/06/51		EPISODE 12	07/08/51
EPISODE 6	26/06/51		EPISODE 13	14/08/51
EPISODE 7	03/07/51			

Series Six (1952)
13 x 30 minute episodes (approx.)
BBC Light Programme *(Also repeated each week on the BBC Home Service)*
Written by Charles Chilton
Producer: Charles Chilton

CAST:
Jeff Arnold	Paul Carpenter
Luke	Charles Irwin
J C Macdonald	Macdonald Parke
Mary	Carole Carr
Bob	Bob Mallin
Rustler	Romulus
Other Actors	Alan Keith
	Guy Kingsley Poynter
	Reed De Rouen
	Betsey Lewis

APPENDIX G: RIDERS OF THE RANGE EPISODE GUIDE

STORY:
Featuring Jesse James
BROADCAST (PRE-RECORDED):

EPISODE 1	06/04/52	EPISODE 8	25/05/52
EPISODE 2	13/04/52	EPISODE 9	01/06/52
EPISODE 3	20/04/52	EPISODE 10	08/06/52
EPISODE 4	27/04/52	EPISODE 11	15/06/52
EPISODE 5	04/05/52	EPISODE 12	22/06/52
EPISODE 6	11/05/52	EPISODE 13	29/06/52
EPISODE 7	18/05/52		

Series Seven – 'The Union Pacific' (1953)
14 x 30 minute episodes (approx.)
BBC Light Programme *(Also repeated each week on the BBC Home Service)*
Written by Charles Chilton
Producer: Charles Chilton

CAST:

Jeff Arnold	Paul Carpenter
Luke	Charles Irwin
J C Macdonald	Macdonald Parke
Mary	Carole Carr
Bob	Bob Mallin
Rustler	Himself
Other Actors	Alan Keith
	Guy Kingsley Poynter
	Reed De Rouen

STORY:
The story of the building of the Union Pacific Railroad.

BROADCAST (PRE-RECORDED):

EPISODE 1	15/06/53	EPISODE 8	03/08/53
EPISODE 2	22/06/53	EPISODE 9	10/08/53
EPISODE 3	29/06/53	EPISODE 10	17/08/53
EPISODE 4	06/07/53	EPISODE 11	24/08/53
EPISODE 5	13/07/53	EPISODE 12	31/08/53
EPISODE 6	20/07/53	EPISODE 13	07/09/53
EPISODE 7	27/07/53	EPISODE 14	14/09/53

APPENDIX H: BBC DRAMA REPERTORY COMPANY

Staff Members (1939 – 1956):

Members who joined in 1939:

Laidman Browne
Audrey Cameron
Joan Carr
D A Clarke-Smith
Cathleen Cordell
Barbara Couper
Philip Cunningham
Patric Curwen
Valentine Dyall
Wallace Evennett
Stafford Hilliard
Carleton Hobs
Thea Holme
Angela Kirke
Henry Longhurst
Gordon McLeod
Charles Mason
David Miller
Cyril Nash
Edgar Norfolk
Mary O'Farrell
Macdonald Parke
Leslie Perrins
Bryan Powley
John B Rowe
Ivan Samson
Norman Shelley
Ewart Scott
Harold Scott
Susan Taylor
William Trent
Cecil Trouncer
Ralph Truman

Philip Wade
Gladys Young

Members who joined in 1940:

Ivor Barnard
Vivienne Chatterton
Malcolm Graeme
Alan Wheatley

Members who joined 1945 – 1955:

Jack Allen
Eric Anderson
Roland Andrea
Sybil Arundale
Frank Atkinson
Nell Ballantyne
Ivor Barnard
Jane Barrett
Marcus Barron
Thomas St John Barry
Betty Baskcomb
Richard Bebb
Carl Bernard
Derek Birch
Alan Blair
Derek Blomfield
Gabrielle Blunt
Geoffrey Bond
Maurice Braddell
Hester Paton Brown
Laidman Browne
(rejoins)

Denise Bryer
John Bryning
Janet Burnell
Arthur Bush
Sebastian Cabot
Beryl Calder
Audrey Cameron
(rejoins)
Catherine Campbell
Joan Carol
Desmond Carrington
Heron Carvic
Gerald Case
Dermot Cathie
John Cazabon
Vivienne Chatterton
(rejoins)
Andrew Churchman
Norman Claridge
Peter Claughton
Eric Clavering
Frank Cochrane
Ann Cordington
Gerald Cooper
Peter Cozens
Edward Craven
Peter Cresswell
Howieson Culff
Philip Cunningham
(rejoins)
Hugh David
Hilda Davies
Rupert Davies
Roger Delgado
George Dillon
Graham Doody

APPENDIX H: BBC DRAMA REPERTORY COMPANY MEMBERS

Alastair Duncan
Brenda Dunrich
Valentine Dyall
(rejoins)
Olga Edwardes
Roy Emerton
David Enders
Sarah Erskine
Victor Fairley
Freda Falconer
Glen Farmer
Andrew Faulds
Catherine Fleming
Edward Forsyth
William Fox
Cyril Gardiner
Neville Gates
Richard George
Malcolm Graeme
(rejoins)
Donald Gray
Dulcie Gray
Garard Green
Rosamond Mary Greenwood
Olive Gregg
Monica Grey
Stanley Hugh Groome
Deryck Guyler
Betty Hardy
Derek Hart
Joan Hart
Brian Hayes
Malcolm Hayes
Grizelda Hervey
Patricia Hilliard
Carleton Hobbs
(rejoins)
Anthony Holles
Peter Howell
Richard Hurndall
Harry Hutchinson
Anthony Jacobs

Allan Jeayes
Edward Jewesbury
Noel Johnson
Basil P Jones
Mary Jones
Anthony Kearey
Edward Kelsey
Godfrey Kenton
David Kossoff
Margaret Lang
Stanley Lathbury
John Laurie
Arthur Lawrence
Charles LeFeaux
Sarah Leigh
Charles Leno
Curigwen Lewis
Edward Lexy
Lucille Lisle
Jack Livesey
William Lloyd
Preston Lockwood
Elizabeth London
Bessie Love
Jenny Lovelace
Eric Lugg
Geoffrey Lumsden
Doris Lytton
James McKechnie
Duncan McIntyre
John McLaren
Diana Maddox
Hugh Manning
Nan Marriott-Watson
Robert Marsden
Alexander Marsh
Trevor Martin
Joan Matheson
Annabel Maule
Charles Maunsell
Audrey Mendes
Colin Wyndham
Maxwell Milligan

Ella Milne
Norman Mitchell
Sulwell Morgan
Janet Morrison
Charles Mortimer
John Murphy
Nancy Nevinson
Peter Noble
Edgar Norfolk *(rejoins)*
Mary O'Farrell *(rejoins)*
Michael O'Halloran
George Owen
Nicholas Parsons
Frank Partington
Micheline Patton
Laurence Payne
David Peel
Leslie Perrins *(rejoins)*
Bryan Powley *(rejoins)*
Muriel Pratt
Tony Quinn
John Rae
Cecil Ramage
Bernard Rebel
Eddy Reed
Alan Reid
Robert G Rendel
Aubrey Richards
Susan Richards
Robert Rietti
Milton Rosmer
Harry Ross
John Ruddock
Ian Sadler
Catherine Salkeld
Ivan Samson *(rejoins)*
Joan Sanderson
Alexander Sarner
George Schjelderup
Harold Scott *(rejoins)*
Joan Clement Scott
Ernest Sefton
Josephine Shand

SERIAL THRILLERS

Cyril Shaps
Joy Shelton
Lydia Sherwood
Ronald Sidney
Ronald Simpson
Dorothy Smith
Roger Snowdon
Abraham Sofaer
Gladys Spencer
Lionel Stevens
John Stone
David Stringer
Lewis Stringer
Elinore Jane Stuart
Dorothy Summers
Sydney Tafler
Eileen Thorndike
Vanessa Thornton
Frank Charles Tickle
Raf de la Torre
William Trent *(rejoins)*
Patrick Troughton
Cecil Trouncer *(rejoins)*
John Turnbull
Rita Veil

Amy Veness
Margaret Vines
Philip Wade *(rejoins)*
Aline Waites
Margaret Ward
Richard Waring
Marjorie Westbury
Alan Wheatley *(rejoins)*
Colin White
Mary Williams
Mary Wimbush
Virginia Winter
James Woodburn
Arthur Young
Gladys Young *(rejoins)*

Members who joined in 1955:

Beth Boyd
Cecile Chevreau
Belle Chrystall
Gordon Davies
Hamilton Dyce
John Gabriel
Denis Goacher

George Hagan
Brian Haines
Charles Hodgson
Geoffrey Hodgson
Dorothy Holmes-Gore
Annette Kelly
Simon Lack
Rolf Lefebvre
Martin Lewis
Marjorie Mars
Brewster Mason
Geoffrey Matthews
Alan McClelland
George Merritt
Olaf Pooley
Molly Rankin
Arthur Ridley
Mairhi Russell
Jeffrey Segal
James Thomason
Leonard Trolley
Michael Turner
Richard Williams
Manning Wilson

BIBLIOGRAPHY

PRINT:

The following list includes most of the principal texts used in the compilation of the book. However, the list is not entirely comprehensive and excludes some more general background researches.

- *208 Magazine* (November 1951)
- *208 Magazine* (January 1952)
- *208 Magazine* (February 1952)
- *208 Magazine* (March 1952)
- *208 Magazine* (October 1952)
- *208 Magazine* (May 1953)
- *The ABC Weekly* (05/02/49)
- *The Adelaide Advertiser* (28/10/54)
- Asa Briggs – *Sound & Vision* – Published by Oxford University Press (1979)
- Steve Chibnall and Brian McFarlane – *The British 'B' Film* – Published by Palgrave Macmillan (2009)
- Charles Chilton – *Journey into Space* – Published by Pan Books (1958)
- Charles Chilton – *Auntie's Charlie* – Published by Fantom Publishing (2011)
- *The Daily Telegraph* (31 July 2008)
- *The Daily Worker* (19/10/46)
- Bernard Donoughue and G W Jones – *Herbert Morrison: Portrait of a Politician* Weidenfield and Nicolson – Published by (1973)
- Paul Donovan – *The Radio Companion* – Published by Grafton Books (1992)
- Allen Eyles – *The House of Hammer* – Published by Lorrimer (1973)
- Jeff Evans – *The Penguin TV Companion (3 ed.)* – Published by Penguin Books (2006)
- Felix Felton – *The Radio Play: It's Technique and Possibilities* – Published by Sylvan Press (1949)
- Andy Foster and Steve Furst – *Radio Comedy: 1938-1958* – Published by Virgin Publishing Ltd. (1996)
- Val Gielgud – *British Radio Drama: 1922-1956* – Published by George G Harrap and Co. Ltd. (1957)
- Burton Graham – *Television: A 'Do You Remember' Book* – Published by Marshall Cavendish (1974)
- *The Guardian* (30/06/07)
- *Hansard – Volume 425* – Published by the House of Commons (16/07/46)
- Mark Hines – *The Story of Broadcasting House: Home of the BBC* – Published by Merrell Publishers (2008)
- *The Hobart Mercury* (02/05/50)
- *The Independent* (19/12/98)
- Wayne Kinsey – *Hammer Films: The Bray Studios Years* – Published by Reynolds and Hearn (2002)

SERIAL THRILLERS

- Wayne Kinsey – *Hammer Films: The Unsung Heroes* – Published by Tomahawk Press (2010)
- David Kynaston – *Austerity Britain: 1945-51* – Published by Bloomsbury Publishing (2007)
- Doris Lessing – *Walking in the Shade* – Published by Flamingo Books (1998)
- *The Listener* (13/02/47)
- *The Listener* (08/10/53)
- *The Listener* (08/04/54)
- *The Listener* (02/02/61)
- *The Listener* (15/02/90)
- *The New Zealand Listener* (20/08/54)
- George Nobbs – *The Wireless Stars* – Published by Wensum Books (1972)
- Denis Norden – *Clips from a Life* – Published by Harper Collins (2008)
- Norman Painting – *Forever Ambridge* – Published by Michael Joseph Ltd. (1975)
- Gale Pedrick (ed.) *The World Radio and Television Annual* – Published by Sampson Low (1947)
- Michael R Pitts – *Famous Movie Detectives – Volume III* – Published by Scarecrow Press (2004)
- Andrew Pixley – *Operation Luna* (CD Sleeve Notes) – Published by BBC Audiobooks (2004)
- Andrew Pixley – *The Red Planet* (CD Sleeve Notes) – Published by BBC Audiobooks (2004)
- Andrew Pixley – *The World in Peril* (CD Sleeve Notes) – Published by BBC Audiobooks (2004)
- David Pringle (ed.) – *The Ultimate Encyclopedia of Science Fiction* – Published by Carlton Books (1996)
- *Radio Review* (25/05/51)
- *The Radio Times* (19 – 25 September 1953)
- *The Radio Times* (10 – 17 April 1965)
- *The Radio Times* (20 – 27 April 1968)
- Dave Rogers – *The ITV Encyclopedia of Adventure* – Published by Boxtree (1988)
- Jimmy Sangster – *Inside Hammer* – Published by Reynolds and Hearn Ltd. (2001)
- *Six Serial Plays* – A Catalogue issued by the BBC Transcription Service (Circa: 1947-1949)
- *The Sunday Herald* (27/08/50)
- *Sydney Morning Herald* (20/07/50)
- *The Times* (17/12/46)
- *The Times* (19/12/46)
- *The Times* (21/12/46)
- *The Times* (23/12/46)
- *The Times* (01/01/47)
- *The Times* (03/01/47)
- *The Times* (17/08/57)
- *The Times* (15/09/72)
- *To-Day's Cinema* (05/03/48)
- *To-Day's Cinema* (11/03/49)
- E S Turner – *Boys Will Be Boys* – Published by Hollen Street Press (1975)
- Tise Vahimagi – *British Television: An Illustrated Guide (2 ed.)* – Published by

BIBLIOGRAPHY

  Oxford University Press (1996)
- *Cambridge University's 'Varsity'* (02/03/10)
- Peter Lewis (ed.) – *Radio Drama* – Published by Longman (1981)
- Patricia Warren – *British Film Studios: An Illustrated History* – Published by Batsford (1995)
- Geoffrey Webb and Edward J Mason – *The Horlicks Spaceman's Handbook* – Published by Horlicks (1954)
- Geoffrey Webb and Edward J Mason – *The Inside Story of Dick Barton* – Published by Contact Books (1950)
- Roger Wilmut and Jimmy Grafton – *The Goon Show Companion* – Published by Robson Books Ltd. (1976)
- R Wood – *Radio Drama at the Crossroads* – Published by De Montfort University Press (2008)

BROADCASTS AND RECORDINGS:

Some of the following recordings are no longer known to exist. Programmes marked with an asterisk are currently missing. Any quotations sourced from these 'lost' programmes have been taken from production scripts and transcripts.

- *Being Paul Temple* – Produced by Acorn Media DVD (2009)
- *Brief Lives* – Broadcast on BBC Radio 5 (30/08/98)
- *Dick Barton and All That* – Broadcast on BBC Radio 4 (31/10/82)
- *Dick Barton and the Betts Plan* – Episode 15 – Broadcast on the BBC Light Programme (25/03/49)
- *Dick Barton and the Secret Weapon* – Episode 1 – Broadcast on the BBC Light Programme (07/10/46)
- *Dick Barton and the Trail of the Rocket* – Episode 13 – Broadcast on the BBC Light Programme (03/03/51)
- *Dick Barton – A Very Special Agent* – Broadcast on BBC Radio 4 (15/07/10)
- *Dick Barton: Still a Special Agent* – Broadcast on BBC Radio 4 (14/02/90)
- Derek Faraday interview for *The Eagle Society* (1984)
- Noel Johnson Interview for *The Eagle Society* (C.1980s)
- *The Lost World on Mars* – Episode 53 – Broadcast on Radio Luxembourg (19/03/53)
- *The Night of the Twenty-Seventh* – Broadcast on the BBC Light Programme (27/12/49)
- *Paul Temple and the Front Page Men* – Episode 8: The Front Page Men – Broadcast on the BBC Midland Service (21/12/38)
- *Peter Coke and the Paul Temple Affair* – Broadcast on BBC 7 (13/12/05)
- *Radio announcement* – Broadcast on Radio Luxembourg (21/03/56)
- *The Radio Detectives – Send for Paul Temple* – Broadcast on BBC Radio Four (20/05/98)
- *Searching The Ether* – Broadcast on LBC (1984)
- *Playhouse: The Combination* – Broadcast on BBC2 (09/01/82)

SERIAL THRILLERS

WEBSITES:

The following websites were accessed in late 2010 and early 2011. I cannot make any guarantee that these websites will continue to be existence in years to come.

- *The Paul Temple File:* (www.oocities.com/gregorym101/Temple1.html)
- *Paul Vlaanderen En Het Mysterie:* (www.paulvlaanderen.nl/)
- *Radio Listings:* (www.radiolistings.co.uk/index.html)
- *Thrilling Detective Website:* (www.thrillingdetective.com/radio.html)

INTERVIEWS:

Between September and December 2010, a number of those involved in the history of British radio were kind enough to give me some of their time to be interviewed for this book. Quotations from these interviews have been used throughout.

- Desmond Carrington (16/09/10)
- Michael Kilgarriff (26/09/10)
- David Chilton (13/10/10)
- Ted Kendall (14/10/10)
- David Jacobs (25/10/10)
- Patrick Rayner (18/11/10)
- Charles and Penny Chilton (02/12/10)

INDEX

208 Magazine	189-192, 194, 212, 279, 285, 295
2LO	15
A for Andromeda	186, 196
ABC (Australian Broadcasting Commission)	17, 50, 52-53, 107, 248, 295
According to the Evidence	101
Adventures of Robin Hood, The	101
Aeolian Hall	227
Age of Kings, An	196
Alexander, Terence	199
Alexandra Theatre, Birmingham	20
Alibi for a Judge	101
Aliffe, Andy	237
All Creatures Great and Small	123
Anderson, Jock	90, 124, 137, 139-140, 142-147, 149-152, 154, 158, 160-168, 170-178
Appointment With Fear	123
Archers, The	11, 46, 120-123, 127, 135, 196-198, 216
Argyle, John	23, 25, 53
Army Game, The	228
Automatons, The	211, 275-276
Avengers, The	234
AVRO (Holland)	16, 52, 54-55, 57-59, 61-63, 65-66, 68, 71-73, 75-80, 82
Baddeley, John	38, 80
Bailey, Bill	36
Barry, Michael	234
Basely, Godfrey	120
Bass, Alfie	228, 232, 242, 245
BBC 7 / BBC Radio 7 / BBC Radio 4 Extra	42, 133, 297
BBC Audio / BBC Audiobooks	42-45, 127, 130-131, 133-135, 177, 221-222, 225, 228-229, 237-238, 240, 296
BBC Bristol	17-18, 88
BBC Broadcasting House	18, 27, 87, 91, 105, 106, 115, 125, 129, 214, 219, 231-232, 235
BBC Drama Repertory Company	10, 19-21, 23-24, 26, 32-33, 35, 85, 91, 113, 123, 125, 183, 185, 218-219, 228
BBC Grafton Studios	31, 112
BBC Home Service	17, 19, 21, 26, 35 ,38-39, 120, 130, 198, 231, 287-288
BBC Light Programme	21-24, 26, 28-29, 31, 33-39, 83-85, 91, 94, 105, 108, 112-113, 127, 182-183, 195, 198, 215-216, 220-221, 223, 226, 228, 232, 286-291, 297
BBC Maida Vale Studios	121

BBC Midland Service   13, 15-16, 18, 21, 26, 43, 86, 89, 120, 297
BBC Overseas Services   17, 24, 83-84, 106
BBC Piccadilly Studio   219, 223, 227, 232
BBC Radio 2   39, 124, 126, 177, 198, 233, 235, 237-238
BBC Radio 4   39, 41, 45-47, 86, 88-89, 100, 109-111, 116, 120-122, 125-127, 133, 198-199, 235-236, 239, 297
BBC Radiophonic Workshop   119, 238
BBC Scotland   44
BBC Transcription Service / BBC Radio International   23-24, 29, 32, 42-43, 105-106, 130, 135, 193, 231-232, 236-237, 252, 296
BBC Written Archives   45, 47, 131
Beattie, James   32-33, 66, 70-71, 73-76, 79
Beau Geste   24
Beckley, Michael   239, 246
Beeby, Bruce   221-222, 224, 228, 242, 244
Bellamy, Frank   184
Bentine, Michael   112
Bentley, John   25, 29
Bergua, Enrique Jarnés   199
Bernard, Carl   19-20, 50, 56, 292
Bickerton, Roger   134
Birch, Derek   91, 125, 138, 150, 153, 292
Birmingham University   13
Bishop, Ed   235, 246
Bishop, George   101, 130
Blake, Sexton   83
Blake's Seven   46
Bligh of the Bounty   29
Blythe, John   111, 151, 161
Bond, Geoffrey   67, 185, 213, 292
Bond, Julian   128
Boosey and Hawkes   25
Braden, Bernard   17, 43, 50
Bramley Lodge   26
Briscoe, Desmond   119
British Astronomical Association (BAA)   217
British Library, The   43, 134, 248, 253
Broken Horseshoe, The   37
Bromley, Alan   41
Bruce, Brenda   109
Bryant, Peter   41
Burke, Inspector   102, 108, 114, 119, 151, 153, 155-158, 160, 162, 165, 167, 171-173, 177-178
Burke, John   115
Bush, Arthur   108, 138, 143, 156, 292
Butcher's Film Services   23, 25, 29
Cadburys   107-108, 135
Cadfael   44

INDEX

Calling Paul Temple	21, 25, 58
Calthrop, John	108, 158, 165
Campbell, Archie	10, 119, 168, 173, 175
Carleton, Moira	107, 138
Carpenter, Paul	216, 286-288, 290-291
Carr, Carole	216, 286-288, 290-292
Carreras, Enrique	102
Carreras, James	102
Carrington, Desmond	21, 26-27, 33, 42, 48, 66, 120, 183, 185, 188, 215, 233, 292, 298
Carse, Duncan	28, 69, 110-112, 114, 117-119, 127, 130, 164-172, 185
Carvic, Heron	125, 137, 172, 292
Case for Paul Temple, A	22-23, 47, 58, 249
CBC (Canadian Broadcasting Company)	17, 32, 43, 50, 52, 248
Ceylon	23, 26, 214-215, 233
Chamberlain, Neville	17
Chapman, B D (Bertie)	114, 119, 121, 168, 174, 178, 187, 193, 213
Chappell Music	25
Charlie	23-26, 29, 32-33, 38, 40, 46, 60 ,62 ,64-66 ,70-71 ,73-76, 79-80, 97
Children's hospitals	112, 115
Children's Hour	111, 120
Chilton, Charles	19, 129, 214-225, 229-236, 238-247, 286-291, 295
Chilton, David	230, 236, 238-241, 246, 298
Chilton, Penny	215, 223, 298
Christie, Agatha	31
Coke, Peter	25, 30-35, 37-40, 42-43, 46, 66, 69, 71, 74-77, 79-81, 297
Colley, Ronnie and Arthur	97, 144
Collins, Norman	83-84, 86, 89, 92, 94-96, 98, 102, 113-114, 195, 215
Combination, The	197, 304
Communist Party	90, 123
Connor, Cyril	106
Cooke, Alistair	214
Coronation Scot	25, 47
Cosmo, James	128
Coules, Bert	44
Court, George (and Sharp, John)	111, 161
Cowley, Clifford	107, 138
Crawford, Howard Marion	22, 59, 185-186, 213
Creasey, John	29, 107
Crick, Monte	198
Cullen, Anne	101, 112, 156, 165, 183 ,185,198,213
Curran, Vincent	20, 51, 56
Curtain Up	28
Dainton, Patricia	29
Dan Dare – Pilot of the Future, The Adventures of	136, 181,183-197, 199-205, 207-213, 217, 220, 230, 236, 262, 278-279

Daring Dexters, The	101
Dark Road, The	102
Davies, Gordon	75, 118, 121, 123, 173-178, 294
Davies, Jot	240, 247
Davies, Richard	107, 138
Dawson, Basil	101, 114, 150, 154, 167
De Wolff, Francis	125, 137, 185, 213
Death in High Heels	102
Delgado, Roger	6, 72, 292
Deltgen, René	27
Denham, Maurice	17, 54
Dermott, Lorna	91, 95-96,137, 139-140, 142-143
Desert Island Discs	117
Desperate People, The	38
Devil's Galop, The	91, 127
Dial Close	104
Diamond, Arnold	119, 178
Dick Barton – Rules of Conduct	98
Dick Barton – Special Agent	28, 49, 83, 87, 91-92, 96, 101, 106, 112, 116-117, 122, 124, 137, 139, 141, 150, 152, 163, 259
Dick Barton – Special Agent (feature film)	103-105
Dick Barton and Jordan's Folly	111, 163, 256
Dick Barton and Kramer	90, 92, 137
Dick Barton and the Affair of the Black Panther	147-148, 255, 260
Dick Barton and the Betts Plan	111-112, 130-131, 165, 256, 297
Dick Barton and the Big Fight Racket	171, 257
Dick Barton and the Black Rock	114, 167, 257
Dick Barton and the Bonazio Gang	114, 130-131, 151, 256, 261
Dick Barton and the Bridge	174, 257
Dick Barton and the Cabatolin Diamonds	92, 95, 106, 140-141, 255, 259
Dick Barton and the Canadian Adventure	98, 146, 255, 260
Dick Barton and the Case of Conrad Ruda	113, 154, 256
Dick Barton and the Chain Gang	148
Dick Barton and the Colonel's Cavemen	166, 257
Dick Barton and the Firefly Adventure	102, 157-158, 256, 261
Dick Barton and the Flying Saucer Mystery	123
Dick Barton and the Green Triangle Gang	121, 177, 258
Dick Barton and the House of Windows	114, 168, 257
Dick Barton and the J B Case	108, 158-159, 256, 261
Dick Barton and the Jewel Thieves	155, 157, 256, 261
Dick Barton and the Li-Chang Adventure	152, 154, 256, 261
Dick Barton and the Lucifer Adventure	171
Dick Barton and the Lucky Gordon Affair	114, 172, 257
Dick Barton and the Paris Adventure	92, 106, 111, 139, 259
Dick Barton and the Production Report	101, 150, 256, 260
Dick Barton and the Secret Formula	111, 161, 256
Dick Barton and the Secret Weapon	91-92, 106, 124, 137, 138-139, 255, 259, 297
Dick Barton and the Smash and Grab Raiders	96-97, 144, 255, 260

INDEX

Dick Barton and the Smugglers 95, 105, 130-131, 153, 255, 260
Dick Barton and the SS Golden Main Story 119, 173, 257
Dick Barton and the Tibetan Adventure 98, 145-146, 255, 260
Dick Barton and the Trail of the Rocket 119, 121-125, 127, 130-131, 177, 179, 258, 297
Dick Barton and the Vallonian Adventure 114, 166, 257
Dick Barton and the Voice 111, 131, 162, 256
Dick Barton and the Vulture 101, 148, 255, 260
Dick Barton at Bay 104
Dick Barton in South America 95, 141, 255, 260
Dick Barton Strikes Back 103
Dickson, Noel 106-108
Diego Valor 199-200
Digby 78, 184-185, 199, 204-208, 213
Doctor Who 40-41, 46, 117, 197, 234
Douglas, Colin 101, 103, 108, 112, 114, 151, 153, 155, 157-158, 162, 165
Dr Morelle 226
Drinkwater, Ros 40
Durbridge, Francis 13-17, 19-24, 29-31, 33, 36-41, 44, 48, 50, 52-54, 56-58, 60-61, 63, 65-66, 68-69, 71, 74-77, 79-82, 84
Durbridge, Stephen 48
Dyall, Valentine 28-29, 69, 169, 292-293
Eagle 184, 201, 204, 210, 216, 230, 286
East of Algiers 36, 65
Eden, Anthony 15
Ellis, Vivian 25, 40
Eves, Granville 101
Evesham 15, 18, 26
Exton, Clive 38, 128
Faraday, Derek 185-189, 192, 195, 200-201, 213, 297
Faulds, Andrew 67, 172, 219, 222, 224, 231-233, 238, 242, 244-245, 293
Felton, Felix 111, 165, 295
Fitchen, John 108, 112, 149-151, 153-154, 156-157, 164-168, 170-171, 173-179, 187
Forbes, Sir Graham 14-15, 21, 23, 35-38, 40, 46, 51, 53-54, 56, 58-61, 63, 65-66, 69, 71, 73-77, 79, 81
Ford, Mick 199
Forsyte Saga, The 26
Francis, Dick 17, 54-55
Frank Mason and Co. Ltd. 105-106, 108, 139-140, 142, 146, 148
Frenkel, Theo 17
Frozen in Time 239-240, 246
Gallagher, Jock 127
Gantrel, John 128
Gardiner, Colonel 89-91, 96, 101, 114, 128, 137-138, 150, 166, 293
Garwood, Anthony 119, 175
Gatland, Kenneth 218

303

Gee, Donald	199
Ghost Squad	101
Gielgud, Val	10, 14, 16, 18-19, 26-27, 89, 95, 109, 116-117, 121, 123-124, 182, 196, 217, 219, 295
Glasgow Clarion Players	90
Glyndale Star, The	183
Glyn-Jones, John	186, 208, 213
Glynne, Renée	105
Godfrey, David H	113-114, 119-120, 154, 166, 171, 174, 177
Goon Show, The	231, 233, 297
Goulding, Alfred	103
Graham, Nigel	80, 235, 245
Grainer, Ron	40
Grayson, Godfrey	104
Grey, W H	182
Guyler, Deryck	10, 221, 242, 244, 293
Hall, Anthony	71, 80, 235, 245
Hall, Geoffrey S	230
Hammer Films	102-105, 108, 128, 226-227, 295-296
Hampson, Frank	184, 204, 210
Hancock's Half Hour	231, 234
Hassard, Peggy	32, 43, 50, 67, 74
Hatton, Charles	16-17, 21, 38, 54, 56, 58
Heaton, Anthony	128
Hedd, Madi	224, 244
Herge	97
Hermann, Eduard	27, 60-61, 66, 68, 71-72, 75-82
Hervey, Grizelda	10, 25-26, 33, 50, 54, 58, 65, 67, 70-71, 74, 293
Hetherington, Pat	122, 132-134, 202-203
Hinds, Anthony	102, 104, 227
Hinds, William	102
Hodgson, Bernadette	15, 17, 20-21, 50, 53-54, 56
Holme, Thea	19, 50, 292
Holmes, Sherlock	14, 20, 44, 125
Hope, Courtney	50, 95, 97, 140, 150, 153, 165, 172, 183
Hope-Wallace, Philip	95
Hordern, Michael	98, 146
Horlicks	184, 186-187, 192-193, 195-196, 200, 297
Horrock, Betsy	97, 128, 140, 150, 153, 165, 172, 183
Host, The	239-241, 247
Hulme, Anthony	23, 25
Hunter, Jean	91, 96, 128, 137, 139-140, 142-143
Hurndall, Richard	69, 125, 137, 154, 293
Irwin, Charles	216-217, 286-288, 290-291
It's That Man Again (ITMA)	20, 221
Jacobs, David	214-215, 218, 223-224, 229, 231-233, 238-242, 244-247, 298
Johnson, Gareth	122

INDEX

Johnson, Noel	85, 88-89, 94, 97, 100, 103, 108-111, 122-124, 137, 139-141, 143-147, 149-152, 154-155, 157-158, 160-163, 184-185, 188, 190-191, 196, 213, 293, 297
Jones, Basil	39, 55, 58, 64, 81, 108, 150, 160
Journey into Space	214-215, 217-223, 225-239, 241-247, 286, 295
Journey to the Moon	216, 220, 222, 231, 237, 242
Karlin, Miriam	168, 223, 244
Kelloggs'	110
Kelly, Douglas	107, 137, 139-141, 143-147, 149-152, 154-155, 157-158, 160
Kemp, Venetia	118
Kendall, Ted	42-44, 194, 236-238, 298
Kennedy, Carol	171
Kennedy, Patricia	107, 137
Kilgarriff, Michael	19-20, 125-126, 138, 219, 298
King Monmouth	30
Kirby, Olive	101
Kleijn, Kommer	17, 52, 54-55, 57-58, 60-63, 65-66, 68, 71-73, 75-77
Kneale, Nigel	37, 218, 227
Korda, Alexander	227
Korsakov, Nicolai Rimsky	25
Kossoff, David	64, 218, 222, 228, 232, 242, 244, 289, 293
Lack, Simon	33, 67, 69 ,71 ,74-76 ,79-81, 294
Langley, Richard	190-191
Lean, David	226
Lee, Christopher	29
LeFeaux, Charles	72, 113, 119, 125, 151, 166-167, 170, 172-173, 176, 178, 293
Lessing, Doris	90-91, 296
Lisle, Lucille	21, 54, 289, 293
Listener, The	32, 37, 95, 127, 214, 221, 296
Lloyd Pack, Charles	111, 161
Lloyd, William	80, 107, 137, 139-140, 142-144, 161, 293
Logan, Crawford	46-47, 59-61, 63, 66
London Belongs to Me	83
London Evening News	36
Lost World on Mars, The	187, 189, 195, 202, 210, 212, 269-270, 283-284
Mackenzie-Williams, Fiona	135
MacLurg, Bill	95, 148
Man Called Harry Brent, A	38
Man in Black, The	28-29, 69, 169
Mann, John	88, 95, 101, 107-108, 111-112, 114, 119, 124, 133, 137, 139-141, 143-147, 149-152, 154-155, 157-158, 160-168, 170-178
Manning, Hugh	25-26, 65, 67, 76, 78-79, 293
Marley, Sir Richard	128
Marooned on Mercury	189, 210, 271-273
Marriott, Alan	239-240, 246-247
Marylebone Studios	102

Mason, Brewster	33, 75-76, 294
Mason, Edward J	28, 33, 68, 75-76, 87, 90, 92-93, 95, 100-101, 108, 111-112, 114, 119-121, 123-125, 127-128, 136-137, 139, 141, 148-149, 152, 157, 158, 162-163, 165-166, 169, 171-173, 177, 183-184, 187, 193, 197-198, 213, 297
Mason, Perry	183
Matthews, Francis	40
McCarthy, Denis	108, 137, 158, 165
McCord, Cal	216, 286-288
McCrindle, Alex	90-92, 95, 101, 107-108, 111-112, 114, 119, 123-124, 133, 137, 139-140, 142-147, 149-152, 154, 158, 160-168, 170-178
McIntyre, Duncan	26, 55 ,60 ,65 ,71, 74, 242, 293
McMillan, John	84-85, 87-88, 96, 111, 113, 146, 161
McNamara, John	36
Mekon, The	184-185, 204-211, 213, 263-264, 276, 279
Melissa	38
Monchaux, Cecily	116
Moore, Sir Patrick	217
Moran, Chris	239, 246
Morgan, Jet	219, 224-225, 229, 232-233, 235, 239-240, 242, 244-247
Morgan, John	70, 107, 138, 153, 154
Morris, Denis	89
Morris, Rev Marcus	184
Morrison, Herbert	112-113, 182, 295
Morse, Barry	21-22, 24, 57
Morton, Hugh	15, 17, 20-21, 50, 53-54, 101
Movie Magazine	189
Mr and Mrs Paul Temple	24, 63, 249
Mrs Dale's Diary	11, 28, 83, 107, 185
Much Binding in the Marsh	17
Mudditt, Lester	15, 17, 20-22, 24-26, 29, 32-36, 51, 53-54, 56, 58-61, 63, 65-66, 69, 71, 73-76
Muggeridge, Douglas	124
Murray, Pete	194
Music by Melachrino	86, 88
My Friend Charles	37, 40
My Word	197
National Film and Sound Archive of Australia (NFSA)	131, 134-135, 202, 255-256
Nettleford Studios	23, 29
New Zealand Listener, The	32, 296
News of Paul Temple	16-17, 21, 29, 32, 35, 48, 54, 56, 248
Night of the Twenty-Seventh, The	27-28, 68-69, 114, 121, 169, 250, 297
Nightly Requests	189
Norden, Denis	87, 296
Novello, Ivor	30
Oh! What a Lovely War	233
Operation Diplomat	37

INDEX

Operation Luna	221-222, 225, 231-232, 237, 242, 296
Other Man, The	37
Painting, Norman	87, 120, 122, 127, 197, 296
Parke, Macdonald	26, 66, 154, 161, 216, 286-288, 290-292
Parker, Olive Louisa	34-35
Partington, Frank	23, 29, 38, 59-60, 64, 71-72, 76, 293
Paul Temple and Light Fingers	82
Paul Temple and Steve	15, 24-25, 43, 47, 61, 249, 252
Paul Temple and Steve Again	30, 32, 73, 250
Paul Temple and the Alex Affair	39-40, 81, 251, 254
Paul Temple and the Conrad Case	36, 41-42, 77, 251, 254
Paul Temple and the Curzon Case	25, 43, 47-48, 65, 249, 253
Paul Temple and the Front Page Men	15-17, 43, 48, 53-54, 248, 297
Paul Temple and the Geneva Mystery	38, 41, 80-81, 251, 254
Paul Temple and the Gilbert Case	31-32, 36, 74, 250, 253
Paul Temple and the Gregory Affair	22-24, 27, 43, 47-48, 60, 249, 252
Paul Temple and the Harkdale Robbery	41
Paul Temple and the Jonathan Mystery	29, 38, 43, 71, 250, 253-254
Paul Temple and the Kelby Affair	41
Paul Temple and the Lawrence Affair	33, 75, 250, 253
Paul Temple and the Madison Mystery	26-27, 29, 33, 41, 43, 46, 66, 250, 253
Paul Temple and the Margo Mystery	37, 41, 79-80, 251, 254
Paul Temple and the Spencer Affair	34-35, 76, 251, 253
Paul Temple and the Sullivan Mystery	24-25, 36, 43, 45, 63, 249, 252
Paul Temple and the Vandyke Affair	28, 31, 35-36, 43, 69, 248, 250, 253-254
Paul Temple Intervenes	20-21, 29, 44, 56-57, 248, 252
Paul Temple Returns	29, 44, 57
Paul Temple's Triumph	29, 56
Pavlo, Chris	240, 247
PC 49	23, 28, 69, 185, 226
Peabody, Prof Jocelyn	184-185, 198-199, 206-208, 213
Peach, Robert	107, 137
Peacock, Kim	22, 24-26, 29-31, 35, 38, 43, 47, 60-61, 63, 65-66, 69, 71, 73, 169
Pedrick, Gale	20, 101, 128-129, 296
Phillips, Eric	147, 151
Phillips, Freddie	216, 288-289
Phillips, Van	219, 223
Pick, David	128
Pleasence, Donald	114, 172
Plomley, Roy	117
Portrait of Alison	37
Poynter, Guy Kingsley	218, 222, 231-232, 242, 244-245, 289-291
Pride and Prejudice	29
Priestley, J B	16
Promotion	13
Proud, Elizabeth	235, 246
Quatermass	196, 218, 227

Quatermass Experiment, The	218, 226-227
RADA	30
Radio Caroline	198
Radio Forfeits	95
Radio Luxembourg (208)	33, 84, 112, 116, 123, 125, 171-175, 187-196, 198-203, 208, 212-213, 217, 220, 228, 233, 262, 278-279, 285, 295, 297
Raglan, James	108, 114, 119, 165, 167, 171-173, 177
Raglan, Robert	178
Raikes, Raymond	10, 98, 101, 125-126, 137, 145-147
Rayner, Patrick	44-48, 58, 60-61, 63, 66, 298
Red Planet, The	222, 224-225, 227, 231, 237, 243-244, 296
Reece, Brian	28, 69, 169
Reith, Lord	83, 116-117, 182, 214
Return from Mars, The	235-236, 238, 245
Revolt on Mars	195, 212, 270-271, 284-285
Richardson, Clive	186
Riders of the Range	215-217, 220, 222, 225, 229, 286-287, 289, 291
Ridley, Arthur	33, 54, 60, 64, 67, 75, 170, 175, 294
Robinsons, The	83
Rogers, Maclean	25, 29, 56-58
Rohmer, Sax	16
Roy, Ernest G	29
Royal College of Music	21
Russell-Pavier, Nicholas	239, 246-247
Rutherford, Douglas	33, 36, 65
Sadler, Ian	33, 64, 67, 150-151, 178, 293
Saint, The	123
Sangster, Jimmy	103-105, 296
Scarf, The	37
Scheherazade	25
Schmitz, Johan	17
Scoffield, Jon	128
Scottish National Players	14
Send for Paul Temple	13-17, 19-21, 32, 39, 43, 48, 50, 52-53, 57-58, 81, 248-249, 297
Send for Paul Temple (feature film)	23, 25, 53
Send for Paul Temple (stage play)	20, 53
Send for Paul Temple Again	21-22, 25, 39, 57-58, 81, 249
Shakleton, Ernest	117
Sharp, Don	221, 228, 242, 244-245
Sharp, John	153-154, 185, 213
Sharp, John (and Court, George)	111, 161
Shaw, Jack	108, 151, 156, 158
Sheffield, Patience	27
Shelley, Norman	10, 17, 55, 292
Shelton, Joy	23, 25, 294
Sheridan, Dinah	25, 29
Sherwin, Derrick	41

INDEX

Shryane, Tony	120
Simpson, Julian	240, 247
Sindall, Alfred	36
Snowdon, Roger	121, 171, 177, 294
Southern Television	127
Space Force	235-236
Spencer Affair, The	34-35, 76, 251, 253
Spencer, Frank	105
Standing, Michael	217, 226, 229
Stannard, Don	103-105
Star Sound Studios	185, 213
Star Wars	123
Steele, Tommy	126
Stephens, Toby	240, 247
Stevenson, Gerda	46, 59-61, 63, 66
Story of Robin Hood, The	107
Streeton, W L	106
Surprise Assassin	195, 211, 277-278
Sykes, Prudence	104
Tacconi, Nando	229
Taggart	123
Take it From Here	100, 233
Teckman Biography, The	37
Temple, Paul	13-17, 19-86, 97, 101, 105, 114, 133, 135, 169, 185, 188, 216, 226, 229, 231, 234, 236-237, 248-254, 297-298
Temple, Steve (Louise)	14-15, 17, 19, 21, 23-26, 28-30, 32-33, 40, 46-47, 50, 53-54, 56-57, 59-66, 68-71, 73-81, 169, 249-250, 252
Thatcher, Billy	25, 65
There is No Escape	102
Thewes, John	16, 52
Thomas, Barry	38
Thomas, Gareth	46, 59-61, 63, 66
Thomason, James	37-38, 71, 76-81, 294
Thompson, J Walter (JWT)	108, 184-185, 188, 192
Thomson, Aidan	24
Tilvern, Alan	95, 138-140, 151, 245
Time of Day, A	37
Toff, The	29
Touch of Frost, A	197
Trapped in Space	195, 201, 263, 279
Trewin, J C	32, 221
Trip to the Moon, A	230-232
Tuson, Neil	86, 89, 91, 95-96, 98, 100-101, 105, 108, 112-114, 116, 124, 137, 139-141, 143-144, 149-152, 155, 157-159, 161-165, 178, 183, 185, 198
Twentieth Century Fox	115
Twenty Questions	189
Tyler Mystery, The	33
Under Sentence of Death	202, 208-209, 264, 279

Underwood, Nick	46, 59-60, 62, 64, 67
Van Ees, Jan	17, 73, 75-80
Van Putten, Dick	17, 78-79, 81-82
Vic Samson: Special Investigator	84
Viccars, James	101
Viking Studios	104
Vlaanderen, Paul	16, 52, 54-55, 57-63, 65-66, 68, 71-72, 75-82, 298
Vogel, Tony	128
Voyage to Venus	186, 199, 204, 262
Walker, Bob Danvers	187, 213
Walker, Mike	241
Wallace, Edgar	14
Walter, Wilfred	218, 221, 242
WDR (West Germany)	27, 60-61, 66, 68, 71-72, 75-81
Webb, Geoffrey	87, 92, 97, 119-120, 123, 136, 140, 143, 145-147, 150-152, 155, 159, 163-164, 166, 169-170, 173, 176, 183-184, 187, 193, 197, 210, 213, 297
Webb, Maurice	112
Webster, Martyn C	13-17, 19-22, 24, 26-31, 33, 36-39, 50, 53-54, 56-58, 60-61, 63, 65-66, 68-69, 71, 73-77, 79-81, 83-88, 169
Wednesday Matinee	121
Wells, H G	218, 221, 235
West, Inspector	107
West, Morris L	107-108, 137, 139-141, 143-147, 149-152, 154-155, 157-160
Westbury, Marjorie	10, 20-26, 29, 32-38, 56-57, 59-61, 63, 65-66, 69, 71, 73-77, 79-81, 169, 294
Whitaker, Ayton	119, 174
White, Snowey	88, 90, 124, 137-141, 143-147, 149-152, 154-155, 157-158, 160-168, 170-178
Whose Baby?	101
Williams, Cedric	104
Williams, Charles	91, 186
Williams, David	231-232, 242
Williams, Richard	21, 32, 35-36, 54, 62, 64, 67, 69, 75, 77, 101, 150, 178, 294
Wodehouse, P G	16
Wogan, Terry	122
Woman's Hour	95
Worker's Playtime	14
World in Peril, The	227-232, 235, 237-238, 244-245, 296
World of Tim Frazer, The	37-38, 40
World War Two	9-10, 17-21, 26-27, 30, 32, 43, 45, 55, 57, 83-85, 87, 90, 95, 102, 110-111, 113, 118-119, 136, 142, 165, 181-182, 214-215, 219, 233
Zampi, Mario	103

ABOUT THE AUTHOR

Charles Norton was born in Leicester and since 2008, has mostly worked as a writer, director and producer for the BBC. Between 2016 and 2020, he produced and directed a number of *Doctor Who* animated dramas for BBC Studios and BBC America, including 'The Macra Terror', for which he won a Royal Television Society Award. In 2023 he directed and produced the five-part series, *Dad's Army - The Missing Episodes* for BBC Studios and UKTV. He has also produced numerous DVD and Blu Ray projects for BBC Studios, (*Quatermass and the Pit*, *The Morecambe and Wise Show*, *The Likely Lads* etc.) and has worked on a number of documentaries for the BBC's *Inside Out* series, as well as BBC Two and BBC Four.

Charles Norton was also a producer on a variety of titles for BBC Audiobooks between 2008 and 2015, including *Dick Barton - Special Agent*, *Paul Temple*, *Sexton Blake* and *Hancock's Half Hour*. *Serial Thrillers* is one of two books written by him, currently available from Telos Publishing. The other is *Now on the Big Screen* (2013). He has also written for *The Guardian*, *The Times*, *BBC History Magazine*, *SFX Magazine*, *History Today*, *TV Zone*, *Starburst* and *Doctor Who Magazine*.

His first novel *1913* is due to be published by Northodox Press in 2026.

www.ingramcontent.com/pod-product-compliance
Lightning Source LLC
Chambersburg PA
CBHW060816190426
43197CB00038B/1764